W9-BPO-780

Paul Heinberg, Ph.D. State University of Iowa, is Assistant Professor of Speech and Dramatic Art at that institution, and directs scientific research in speech, radio, television, cinema, and theater. He supervises the voice training of all undergraduate and graduate departmental majors. Dr. Heinberg previously taught at Texas Women's University and Oklahoma State University.

VOICE TRAINING

For

Speaking and Reading Aloud

PAUL HEINBERG
University of Iowa

THE RONALD PRESS COMPANY · NEW YORK

2V

Library of Congress Catalog Card Number: 64-16614
PRINTED IN THE UNITED STATES OF AMERICA

Preface

This text provides students of speech and dramatics with an understanding of what is presently known scientifically about the speech process. It supplies this information as a foundation for efficient and effective improvement in speaking ability. It is a text for persons whose present speaking ability is normal. The focus is almost exclusively on oral delivery rather than upon content or physical delivery.

Speech improvement involves the learning of certain skills. The first step toward such improvement is to resolve each general skill into its constituent behaviors or basic skills. In this text, each of Chapters 5 through 10 considers a different skill involved in the process of oral delivery. The second step is to master the concepts required for an understanding of one basic skill before engaging in reinforced performance on that skill. Reinforcement in this sense means that the student is immediately notified about his success or failure on each trial before another trial ensues and, if failure occurs, the student is enabled and directed to perceive the specific nature of his failure. The third step is to integrate each new, basic skill with all previously mastered skills rather than to present each separately and then try to integrate all of the skills at once. This text adheres to this principle by attempting to combine each new skill with all skills previously acquired. Thus, it is organized so that one learns to produce various voice qualities, to combine these voice qualities with various amounts of pitch variety, to utilize these skills in producing various intonations, to combine voice qualities, pitch varieties, and intonations with various speaking rates. Then pronunciation and diction are superimposed upon these previously learned skills.

Better oral delivery can be taught tutorially, using remedial procedures tailored to reduce the extent of each individual's particular and most detrimental vocal deficiencies, or it can be taught as a body of knowledge which presents characteristics of outstanding vocal behavior and provides guides for approaching nearer to these ideals. The latter approach does not require individual instruction; it can be taught to many simultaneously. This book employs that approach. It assumes that each student can acquire greater mastery in every speaking skill, and that when he works on a skill in which he is already proficient, such work is by no means wasted; no matter how proficient, one can always improve.

The assistance of a small army of scientific researchers whose contributions have made possible a work of this nature is gratefully acknowledged. Such a statement can express only a modicum of the author's feeling of indebtedness to them. Their names will not be found in footnotes because the statements herein are seldom based upon a single study, but the bibliography at the end of the text lists the major sources upon which the material in each chapter is based.

PAUL HEINBERG

Iowa City, Iowa
April, 1964

Contents

VOICE TRAINING

For

Speaking and Reading Aloud

1

Speech Training and Personality

Although considerable research effort has been expended in trying to discover relationships between speech behavior and personality, results have generally been negatory.

Good and poor speakers have been compared on their personality traits and, when any differences are found, they are that good speakers as a group are more dominant and better adjusted socially. However, the instruments used to measure personality traits are the type in which testees state how they would behave in various social situations, and those situations which yield dominance and social adjustment scores tend to involve oral behavior. About all we might conclude from this, then, is that what we mean by saying that a person is a good speaker may also be what we mean to some extent by saying that he is well adjusted and tends to be a social leader rather than a follower of others.

The speaking ability of persons near the extremes on various personality traits have been compared, but as yet, we find the proportion of good speakers at either extreme no higher than would occur by chance for any trait except the aforementioned.

We have obtained the correlation (degree of "running togetherness") of personality scores and speech ratings, and a few slight relationships have been revealed, the most frequent again being with dominance and social adjustment.

We have experimented to see if changes in personality occur as a result of speech training, but we have not yet detected a change if, indeed, any occurs. We have found that persons who improve least in speech tend to be similar in personality, but this probably means that persons weak in their desire for self-improvement or attainment of any goals tend to be more alike than those who strongly desire these ends.

We have found that speech and personality relationships are generally closer in males than in females. Perhaps this means that males generally attach greater importance to their ability to communicate than do females.

If by "personality" we mean the behavior or behavioral tendencies of persons in certain ways, we should conclude that, if any relationships exist, they are so slight that behavioral traits and speaking ability must have no direct effect on one another.

However, "personality" may mean something other than behavior or behavioral tendencies, and at least one of the other meanings of the term bears several close relationships to speech. Let us define three kinds of personality: the *self-characterized personality*, the *perceived personality* and the *behavioral personality*.

The self-characterized personality is the way we would describe ourselves: how shy we think we are, how thoughtful, kind, argumentative, and the like. The perceived personality is the way others would describe us, whose only acquaintance with us is listening to us or viewing us when our speech content is not our own, as when we read material written by another. The behavioral personality is how others, especially experts, would characterize us on the basis of considerable study of our behavior, evaluations of our statements about how we would act in various specific situations, or both.

Research has shown numerous remarkable relationships between speaking ability and perceived personality. For example, we have examined such traits as confidence, emotional stability, intelligence, neuroticism, introversion, leadership ability, sales ability, persuasiveness, sincerity, body type, extent of fatigue, and many other factors. In no case can listeners predict better than by chance the relative extent of any trait, ability, or condition of speakers as behavioral tests indicate them to be; but they tend to agree overwhelmingly on a particular degree or extent of each trait, ability, or condition for a given speaker. For example, when persons were instructed to lie or to tell the truth so that, say, Mr. X lied and Mr. Y told the truth, the audience would be right only about 50 per cent of the time in saying that any person was lying or telling the truth but, in most cases, for any one individual, almost all of them either believed that he was lying or that he was telling the truth. Hence, the perceived personality is closely related to the manner of speaking. Perhaps most of our initial judgments of individuals are based on their speech.

If that is true, when we undergo speech training our perceived personality is probably altered. Research provides ample justification of this claim.

Perhaps the few low behavioral and self-characterized personality correlations with speech may be explained thus. A person who undergoes speech training changes the ways others perceive him, and thus changes their reactions to him. To the extent that their different reactions to him produce a re-evaluation of himself or changes in his behavior, speech training can reasonably be said to have an effect on the self-characterized or behavioral personality.

This text, then, can be said to be a guide for effecting desired changes in your perceived personality. As each area of possible progress is introduced, research will be brought to bear on how each type of speaking tends to relate to perceived personality. Insofar as you deem a perceived characteristic desirable, you should make the changes in your delivery to effect this. For example, a certain way of speaking will tend to make others think you are more confident. If you desire to be perceived as more confident, you should adopt that mode of speech. If you do not desire this, the author would maintain that you are entitled to your own opinion and would not encourage you to make the change.

Now let us consider the opposite case. Suppose you consider yourself to be lacking in confidence. Should you adopt a mode of speaking that makes you seem more confident to others than you think you are? Isn't this dissembling, and isn't dissembling immoral?

To face this question dispassionately, let us take a hypothetical case of a female with a breathy voice quality. Breathiness connotes shyness, so that she tends to be perceived by others as being shy because of her breathiness. Thus, shyness is a characteristic of her perceived personality. If she acts in ways classified as manifesting shyness, as, for example, abnormally avoiding opportunities to state her ideas, a characteristic of her behavioral personality would be shyness. If she would describe herself as being shy, shyness is a trait of her self-characterized personality. Now, when we say that a voice quality is suited to a speaker's personality, we are implying that, where the behavioral and self-characterized personalities are consistent with the perceived personality, the voice quality should not be changed. The validity of this argument depends upon the truth of three assumptions about our breathy speaker: (1) She would still behave shyly and think of herself as being shy if she ceased speaking breathily, (2) she desires to continue thinking of herself as being shy, and (3) she desires to continue being treated as if she were shy. The first assumption is probably untrue although no body of experimental proof exists to prove or to refute it. It seems only reasonable to assume that the way persons react toward us can affect the way we think of ourselves and the way we act. If the perceived personality is altered, the self-characterized and behavioral personalities may be altered, so the first assumption is by no means necessarily true. And, if we assume that she considers shyness to any extent an unfavorable characteristic in herself or in others, the other assumptions are also untenable. Only if she prefers being shy and being treated as if she were shy are these assumptions valid.

But the question of morality yet remains. That is, is it morally wrong to enable a person to manifest an estimable personality whose behavior and self-concepts are disestimable? To use an extreme example, should one enable a potential Hitler to adopt a more personable mien so that he can more effectively perpetrate his malevolence? If we assume that a more favorable perceived personality would not effect desirable changes in one's behavioral personality, the answer is obviously that we should not provide such training for him. However, this implies a belief in inherent evil. Is a Hitler born evil or made so? It is more likely that one becomes malevolent by being demeaned. We run the risk, then, of making an evil person more effective rather than less evil. The same risk is involved in the use of plastic surgery on felons. The only guide we have is our estimate of each one's incorrigibility. We should deny such a service to those we believe to be incorrigible. Speech training, then, should not be denied to those whose disestimable perceived personalities are compatible with their behavior unless their disestimable behavior is considered to be incapable of change. However, is any young person truly incorrigible? An older person who may be incorrigible would probably not be able to undergo much speech retraining anyway. For these reasons, the restricting of speech training to those of favorable character is, to the author, an unjust limitation.

To summarize, one is morally justified in speaking so as to be perceived differently from the way he perceives himself, provided that his ends are ethically justified, because he may come to accept the responsibilities placed on him due to his being more favorably received. And our manner of speaking affects drastically how favorably we are received. The following chapters are your guide for determining your own vocal characteristics and the kinds of behavior toward you that others would tend to have were you to change in various ways. The manner in which you do or do not reshape your perceived personality is then solely your concern.

2

Phonetics

Need for a Phonetic System

Phonetics is a language for communicating information about vocal sounds in written form. Each written symbol refers to a specific type of vocal sound. If English were a phonetic language, all words and syllables that are pronounced alike would be spelled alike, and every letter would have a certain sound.

Obviously, a phonetic system can be extremely useful in learning pronunciation. In the process of learning such a system, moreover, one acquires greater skill in listening to speech and greater understanding of acoustic and physiological relationships. Phonetic nuances become apparent; pronunciations which previously seemed identical become recognizably different. Because of these benefits, phonetics is an excellent area in which to begin working for speech improvement.

The International Phonetic Alphabet (I.P.A.)

Any recognized system of representing sounds is useful, but the International Phonetic Alphabet* is superior to diacritic systems found in dictionaries because it uses only one symbol to

* See Table 2–1.

represent a given sound and, since the symbols are simpler, it may be written more rapidly. A diacritic system has the advantage of enabling one to read dictionary pronunciations, but learning another phonetic system is quite easy once any one system is mastered.

Learning the I.P.A.

The overall principle to follow in learning to read or write any language is to strive for *habitual* responses. This means working for correctness first and then working for such speed that no thought processes intervene. Learning to read and to write phonetics should be considered as more closely related to learning to type or to ride a bicycle than to learning history or bridge. Even a good typist cannot, without some thought, describe where the letter *e* is on the keyboard, but he can hit it unfailingly hundreds of times per hour. Conversely, one could memorize the keyboard and not be able to type at even a remotely satisfactory speed. It cannot be said that more work is required to learn something habitually than to learn it intellectually, since the one skill requires hours of practice and the other hours of concentration. But anything learned intellectually tends to be forgotten with disuse. Since phonetics is a tool potentially for lifelong use, it should be learned so as not to be forgotten—habitually. Habitual learning of phonetics is aided by:

1. Avoiding Unnecessary Associations. For example, never use a key word to help you to remember a sound because an association may be formed between the symbol and the key word rather than directly between the symbol and the sound. Avoid paying attention to spelling. Thus, transcribe oral dictation rather than printed matter, and practice on nonsense and foreign words as well as English words.

2. Maximum Use of Audio-Visual Drill Materials. For example, purchase a set of unruled file cards and write each symbol on a separate card.[1] As soon as a few symbols can be flashed and said correctly, they should be flashed with greater rapidity on each successive run-through, and shuffled after each

[1] Cards with printed symbols and instructions for use may be purchased at university bookstores and from commercial sources.

run-through. Practice until each symbol can be flashed as rapidly as possible and can be said without feeling—not thinking—that an error has been made. As soon as a vowel has been learned, use that vowel, with the consonants already learned, to form consonant-vowel (CV), vowel-consonant (VC), CVC, CCVC, CCVCC, and CCCVCC syllables. Then form words of two syllables, and practice accenting them differently. Reading and writing exercises are provided at the close of this chapter. If the classifications of sounds are to be learned, flash cards may also be used for this. After each sound can be said correctly and rapidly, say the sound and then say one of its classifications.[2]

Transcribing Phonetics

When practicing transcription, a good procedure to follow is to have someone dictate words to you, saying each word three times with about an eight-second pause between repetitions. You should try to write as much of the word as possible as rapidly as possible immediately after the first pronunciation. Then listen to the second pronunciation only for those sounds omitted, and insert them. Then pronounce to yourself what you have written, reading it as objectively as possible, and compare your pronunciation of the transcription with the third pronunciation. Be careful to read your transcription as a single word, not syllable by syllable, and to voice all voiced sounds.

Types of Transcription Errors

Your phonetic transcriptions should be analyzed for the types of errors they contain, thus enabling you to alter your learning so that similar errors do not recur. Six common types of errors may be noted:

1. Phonemic Confusion. If you consistently confuse two phonemes,[3] you need, first, clarification sufficient for you to

[2] A commercial device, the *Auvitor,* invented by the author, teaches phonetics in the manner described—by completely automated means.

[3] A phoneme is a family of sounds which comprises all of those various productions recognized as insufficiently different from one another to be symbolized differently. Each phonetic symbol represents a phoneme since no person can repeat a sound identically, especially when it occurs in different syllables, and obviously no two persons produce any sound identically.

perceive the differences between them when you are saying the two correctly and, second, drill on the troublesome sounds in isolation and in context.

2. Spelling Consciousness. If your transcriptions contain alphabetical letters and letter combinations that occur in English, such as *x*, *c*, *q*, *y*, *wh*, *ds*, or *gs*, you are obviously conscious of spelling. Reading what you have written and what you should have written and practicing on nonsense and foreign words should help you to overcome this problem. For example, if you write [whɪtʃ] for [hwɪtʃ], learn to pronounce [wh] in that and other words and even deliberately write a few words containing [hw] as [wh] and pronounce them as written.

3. Silent Repetition. If your transcriptions contain phonetic symbols different from those pronounced, this probably indicates that you have been repeating the dictated words to yourself. Avoid lip movement during dictation except when pronouncing what you have written. That is, pronounce silently what you have transcribed but not what you are trying to transcribe. And when pronouncing softly to yourself do so *in toto* and not slowly, syllable by syllable.

4. Subjective Editing. If your transcription contains only errors you find difficulty in recognizing except upon careful analysis but which you would admit are silly errors when pronounced, your problem is insufficient objectivity in proofreading. Learn to write more rapidly and thereby save more time for proofreading; learn to read more carefully by practicing on the sentences provided in reading exercises at the end of this chapter.

5. Incomplete Transcription. If your transcriptions contain frequent omissions—if, that is, symbols are left out although space was provided for them, or final corrections of symbols were not attempted due to what seemed to be insufficient time—this indicates that (1) you have been trying to learn the sounds consciously and intellectually rather than habitually, or (2) you have learned individual sounds but not common groups of sounds habitually, or (3) you have been testing various sounds by trial and error in these positions. In any case, more practice with flash cards is indicated, especially using the cards grouped as syllables and using faster rates of presentation.

6. Accent Errors. This frequently accompanies the types of errors mentioned under "silent repetition," and is due to repeating syllable by syllable. If this is your problem, listen to the pitch, duration, and intensity of the various syllables of each dictated word and transcribe the accent mark before anything else.

Consonants

Consonants may be defined only generally at best. One could say that a consonant is a sound which may be preceded in context by the vowel schwa [ə]. Obviously, there are exceptions to this, e.g., *pst*, but any other definition may have even more exceptions.[4] The matter of definition is really not too important for our present, utilitarian purposes. It could even be argued that we do not speak in phonemes but in syllables, but it is nevertheless quite useful for certain purposes to act as if we speak in phonemes. In like manner, let us act as if consonants exist as independent units, and by classifying certain sounds as consonants we have in effect defined them. Thus, we can say that a consonant is any sound whose phonemic quality is determined by the following four characteristics: (1) voicing, (2) place of production, (3) duration, and (4) manner of production. A vowel, however, is determined only by the second of these. During the subsequent discussion, frequent reference should be made to Table 2–1.

Voicing refers to whether a consonant is voiced or voiceless. A voiced sound is one which, except during whispering, should be uttered with the vocal folds vibrating for the entire duration of its production. A voiced sound which does not have such vibration throughout is termed an *unvoiced* sound, and is represented by a small circle beneath the voiced symbol, e.g., [tʃɑrlz̥]. A voiceless sound should not have any vocal-fold vibration during any portion of its production. When a voiceless sound is *voiced*, a small *v* is placed beneath the voiceless symbol, e.g., ['lɪt̬l]. Obviously, both voicing and unvoicing are generally considered to be types of mispronunciations.

[4] For those interested in attempts at such definitions, cf. C. M. Wise, *Applied Phonetics*, Prentice-Hall, Inc. (Englewood Cliffs, N.J.), 1957.

TABLE 2–1
Classification of Consonant and Vowel Sounds

CONSONANTS

Manner of Production	Place of Production					
	Bilabial	Labio-dental	Alveolar	Palatal	Velar	Glottal
Plosive	b, p		d, t		g, k	ʔ
Fricative		v, f	z, s, ʒ, ʃ ð, θ			h
Nasal	m		n		ŋ	
Lateral			l, r			
Glide	w			j		

VOWELS

Height of Tongue	Anteroposterior Positioning of Tongue		
	Front	Central	Back
Very high	i		u
High	ɪ		ʊ
Mid-high	e		o
Middle	ɛ	ɝ ɚ	
Mid-low	æ	ɜ ə	ɔ
Low	a	ʌ	ɒ
Very low			ɑ

The place of production refers to the part of the mouth or throat which is particularly instrumental in effecting that phoneme. A bilabial sound is made with the two lips together initially [b, p, w] or throughout the production [m]. An alveolar sound is made with the tongue tip placed on or near the alveolar ridge (just above and behind the upper gum ridge), initially for [d, t] or throughout for [z, s, ʒ, ʃ, n, l, r]. The two sounds [ð] and [θ] may be produced alveolarly as indicated in Table 2–1, or interdentally, with the tongue tip placed between the teeth, or postdentally, with the tip just behind the teeth. A labiodental sound is made with the lower lip against the upper teeth [v, f]. A palatal sound is one in which the back part of the tongue approaches or touches the velum (soft palate) initially [g, k] or throughout [ŋ]. The glottal sound [h] is made by air rushing through the space between the open folds (glottis). A glottal attack [ʔ] is made by closing the folds, building up a great amount of air pressure below the folds, and parting the folds suddenly.

Consonants (except for glides) are generally classifiable, in terms of their duration, as either stops or continuants. A stop is a sound which can vary extremely little in duration because it involves a sudden release of built-up pressure. A continuant is a sound which can vary considerably in duration. The duration of a continuant is generally related to the rate of speaking and to the relative importance of the syllable and word in which it occurs. A continuant preceded by a stop tends to become a stop because, in that context, the tongue is positioned for the stop and the release of the tongue from that position occurs on the continuant sound. Thus, [s] is usually a continuant, but in a word such as *bets* we terminate the *bet-* portion by assuming the tongue position of [t] and by releasing on [s] as a stopped sound, so that we might represent this as [bɛ ts], the final [ts] representing one kind of stopped [s]. Thus, [ps], [ts], and [ks] could be considered three types of stopped [s]. A sound which changes its duration in this manner is termed an *affricate*. The most common affricates in English are [dʒ] and [tʃ], as in *judge* and *church* respectively.

A consonant has one of five different manners of production. Plosives are produced by obstructing the airstream with the lips [b, p], tongue [d, t, g, k], or the folds [ʔ], thus creating a differential in air pressure on the two sides of the obstruction, followed by sudden removal of the obstruction. This release usually produces an explosion, but an implosion would result when speaking during inhalation. In either case, the release is not essential for phonemic identification in a postvocalic position, since the manner in which the preceding vowel is stopped serves to identify the particular plosive, as in *kip*, *kit*, and *kick*, said without any final release. Fricatives involve a constriction rather than an obstruction of the cavity. This constriction may be produced with the lip and teeth [v, f], with the tongue [ð, θ, z, s, ʒ, ʃ], or with the folds slightly apart [h]. Nasals are produced by completely obstructing the mouth cavity bilabially [m], alveolarly [n], or velarly [ŋ], while directing voiced sound into the nasal cavity. Laterals [l, r] are made by the tongue touching the palate so that sound passes around one or both sides of the tongue. Some phoneticians classify [r] as a retroflex sound to indicate that the tongue tip does not completely touch the palate as on [l], hence sound also passes above the tongue. Glides are consonants that have a place of initiation from which the articulator (the lips on [w]; the tongue on [j]) moves, and it is this movement during phonation which serves to identify them. Hence, if we recorded only a small portion of a glide and extended its duration, it would probably not be correctly perceived.

Obviously, these are not all of the consonant sounds which can be produced, but they are the only ones which occur in English when properly articulated. One exercise which may assist you to achieve proper articulation of these sounds is to refer to Table 2–1 and try to pronounce those voiced and voiceless sounds for which only blank spaces are shown. Thus, the bilabial fricative is produced by infants when they blow through their lips, and we produce a velar fricative when we gargle. Some sounds corresponding to blanks in Table 2–1 cannot, of course, be produced, e.g., the glottal nasal, the bilabial, labiodental, or glottal lateral, and the glottal glide; others, such as the velar lateral, are extremely difficult to produce.

Another device that may assist you in learning proper articulation of phonetic symbols is the set of flash cards previously discussed. Place one symbol on each card and, in addition, write each common consonant combination on a separate card. Common combinations used to initiate syllables are [hw, θr, ʃr, st, str, sw], any plosive preceding [r], and the affricates [dʒ] and [tʃ]. Common final syllabic combinations are [ŋk, lk, sts], any voiced plosive preceding [z], any voiceless plosive preceding [s], and the aforementioned affricates.

In learning each consonant, try to feel where your lips and tongue are, and compare their positions to those indicated in the table. Use a mirror when in doubt. Place your fingers on your larynx to be sure that your voiced sounds are not unvoiced. Place your palm in front of your mouth to be sure that you feel practically no air when you produce any voiced sound other than a plosive.

As a guide in first attempts, almost all of the consonants should be pronounced as they occur in one-syllable words in which they serve as terminating consonants, e.g., as in ru*b*, cu*p*, be*d*, be*t*. A few consonants [h, w, j, r] should be said as they occur initially in syllables, e.g., as in *h*it, w*h*ite, *w*it, *y*et, *r*ed.

Be sure that on [l] and [r] you do not have your tongue tip so far back in your mouth that the sound seems "swallowed." The most troublesome consonant is [r] because, unless learned as it occurs initially in syllables, it will be confused with the r-colored vowels to be learned subsequently. Be very sure that your tongue tip touches the alveolar ridge *before* phonation begins. Thus, if you were to pronounce the word *red*, it should not come out sounding like *er-red*.

Vowels

A vowel is a sound whose characteristic quality is determined entirely by place of production, specifically by the location and amount of the constriction between palate and tongue. Considerable differences in manner, duration, or voicing may occur without seriously impairing vowel identifiability. Vowels are therefore classified, as shown in Table 2–1, so as to indicate the place and degree of linguopalatal constriction. Two criteria suffice: location and elevation. Front, central, and back vowels are those whose maximum constriction occurs in the alveolar, palatal, and velar regions of the mouth, respectively. Such words as "very high," "high," "mid-high," "middle," "mid-low," "low," and "very low" are used to indicate degrees of tongue elevation.

Some common diphthongs are [aɪ] as in *ai*sle, [aʊ] as in *ow*l, and [ɔɪ] as in *oi*l, and any vowel followed by schwa [ə] or r-colored schwa [ɚ], as in *hair* [hæə, hɛə, hæɚ, hɛɚ] or *hear* [hɪə, hɪɚ].

In learning any phonetic symbol for a vowel it is especially important to avoid association with a key word. However, the same consonantal frame may be employed with several vowels to facilitate discrimination. Thus, reading down the front vowels (Table 2–1) with the frame [s—t] yields the following sequence: *seat, sit, sate, set, sat,* and an affected pronunciation of *sat.* Reading up the back vowels with [k—d] yields *cod, cawed* (relaxed tongue and lips), *cawed* (tense with lips less open), *code, could,* and *cooed.*

The vowels most frequently confused in the process of learning phonetics are [a] with [æ], and [ɒ] with [ɔ]. The vowel [a] is used by many good speakers only on words in which the letter *a* is followed by [f], [s], or [θ], e.g., as in h*a*lf, *a*fter, l*a*ugh, l*a*st, p*a*ss, *a*sk, p*a*th, m*a*th, and wr*a*th. It is occasionally heard on words in which the vowel sound is followed by [n], as in *au*nt, d*a*nce, ch*a*nts, and comm*a*nd. The vowel [ɒ] is used by many good speakers when the letter *o* is followed by these same consonant sounds, e.g., as in s*o*ft, *o*ff, l*o*ss, c*o*st, cl*o*th, and br*o*th. However, they tend to use [ɔ] on *aw*ful, perhaps merely to contrast it with *o*ffal. The [ɒ] may also be heard, occasionally, when followed by [ŋ] as in l*o*ng and s*o*ng. Since the higher the back vowel the less is the lip opening, a mirror should prove helpful in enabling you to differentiate between [ɒ] and [ɔ]. Notice that on [ɒ] the tongue and lips are more relaxed and that the lip opening is greater than on [ɔ].

The central vowels [ʌ] and [ɝ] can be readily differentiated, using the frame [k—d] to yield *cud* and *curd,* respectively. The one without r-coloring, [ɜ], is found in some Eastern dialects and in cultured British speech on all words in which we would tend to use [ɝ], as in *bird* and *word.* However, when [ɝ] is followed by [r] or a vowel, we all tend to change [ɝ] to [ɜ]. For example, we may pronounce *were* as [wɝ] but *worry* as [wɜrɪ] and, stressing the word *her* in both cases, we might say *her nose* as ['hɝ noz] but *her eyes* as ['hɜ raɪz]. Other words in which [ɜ] would be used thus are *courage, nourish,* and *hurry.* When [ɝ] is followed by [r] or a vowel and not changed to [ɜ], a pause must intervene, as in ['kɝ ɪdʒ, 'nɝ ɪʃ, 'hɝ ɪ, 'hɝ aɪz]. The two sounds of [ɝ] and [ɜ] can be confused with other vowels if you are overly conscious of spelling due to the many different spellings which represent these sounds, e.g., h*er*, s*ir*, *err*, w*or*d, t*ur*n, *ear*n, j*our*ney, g*uer*don, G*oe*the, m*yrrh*, C*olo*nel.

Schwa [ə] and r-colored schwa [ɚ] are best learned by indirection rather than by direction. That is, any sound which is not clearly perceived as any other vowel when it occupies a vocalic position (i.e., adjacent to a consonant or consonantal combination) is very likely [ə] or [ɚ]. Since neither sound can occur in a stressed syllable as the only vowel in that syllable, it follows that schwa cannot be pronounced correctly when said in isolation. Hence, any word which can be repeated slowly, syllable by syllable, and still pronounced correctly cannot contain any syllable in which a schwa is the only vowel. Therefore, learn to read phonetic material by stressing an adjacent syllable containing some other vowel and then quickly adding the syllable containing the schwa. Thus, on *the boy* [ðə 'bɔɪ], do not say slowly [ðʌ 'bɔɪ] but try to get to the word *boy* as quickly as possible. When to use [ɚ] and when to use [ər] follow the same pattern as for [ɝ] and [ɜr] discussed previously. Thus, we might say *mother* as ['mʌðɚ] but *mother is* as ['mʌðə rɪz]. And neither [ɝ] nor [ɚ] would be followed by a vowel unless the vowel were preceded by a pause, so that *camera, opera,* and *machinery* would be said and written as ['kæmərə, 'ɑpərə, mə'ʃinərɪ].

The phonetic system employed in this text is the standard International Phonetic Alphabet, with two exceptions. One is that two methods of transcription are recognized, a so-called broad form and a narrow form. In the narrow form of transcription [eɪ] and oʊ] are recognized as diphthongs, so that differentiation is made between, for example, [weɪ] and [ke'ɑtɪk] and between [goʊ] and [o'beɪ]. The broad form used in this book employs [e] for both the unstressed, brief [e] and the diphthongized [eɪ] and, similarly, [o] is used for both [o] and [oʊ]. The reason the broad form is employed is that the diphthongizing of either [e] or [o] is not considered to be a pronunciation error per se and that this matter is better considered under the aspect of rate. Phoneticians, however, are frequently interested in such durational characteristics, for example in distinguishing between two dialects or speech regions. The second modification is that the colon [:] will be employed only to indicate that, when a word ends in a continuant consonant that is the same as that which initiates the following word, and only one, uninterrupted production of that continuant occurs, the preceding consonant is not doubled, e.g., [kænzəs:ɪtɪ, ɪn:ʌθɪŋ, ɪf:rɛndz, wɪð:ɪs]. If the accent occurs there, it will be placed before the colon. Some phoneticians use the colon to indicate any prolongation which replaces an omitted sound, so that an omitted [r] in *heart* would be written [hɑ:t]. This usage will not be employed here because, again, this text is not concerned with speech differences among regions and dialects but with what is good speech regardless of such differences.

Other I.P.A. symbols which will be employed and have not been discussed previously are the following: [ ], ', ᴴ and ˌ. Brackets are used to indicate that the material within them is written in phonetics. Thus, *l* refers to the letter of the alphabet pronounced [ɛl], but [l] refers to the voiced, lateral, alveolar continuant. A short vertical bar (above the line) is used to indicate primary syllabic stress on the syllable following the stress mark, e.g., [pɚ'hæps], or in an idea, e.g., [tәde әz 'tɪuzdɪ]. For simplicity, the stress mark will be placed before the consonant or consonant combination which can be used to initiate the syllable, e.g., as in [dɪ'son] rather than [dɪs'on]. However, this is done primarily to indicate that, when this rule is violated as in [dɪs'on], attention should be called to the pause that must precede any initiation of a syllable with a vowel. Obviously, if no consonant exists with which to initiate a syllable, the stress mark will be placed before the vowel, e.g., as in [pɪkjulɪ'ærətɪ, wɪ 'itʃ gevə dɑlɚ]. In such situations the pause preceding that syllable is still required, but the pause is not a matter of choice and is, therefore, unimportant. In like manner, a "word" will be written in phonetics such that, wherever possible, it is intiated with a consonant, even if the consonant must be "borrowed" from the end of the preceding word. The reason for this will be discussed in the chapter on pronunciation. Thus, *Give it a try* will appear as [gɪ vɪ tə traɪ] or more simply as [gɪvɪtə traɪ]. The capital ᴴ is used following an initial consonant which is over-aspirated, i.e., said with an excessive emission of air during the final portion of that sound, e.g., as in [pᴴʊʃ, tᴴek, ʃᴴʌv, dʒᴴen]. A short vertical bar placed beneath [l], [n], or [m] when preceded by a plosive, [z], or [s] indicates that the syllable containing [l̩], [n̩], or [m̩] contains no vowel. Thus, ['bɑtl̩, 'bʌtn̩, 'kæzm̩] would syllabify as ['bɑt l, 'bʌt n, 'kæzm] and would sound different from ['bɑtəl, 'bʌtən, 'kæzəm], which would syllabify as ['bɑ təl, 'bʌ tən, 'kæzəm]. Other examples are ['sɪzl̩] and ['hesn̩]. The glottal stop [ʔ] is used to indicate excessive discharge of air prior to uttering a vowel, as in the loud command, *Eat!* [ʔit].

Learning Phonetics

The following exercises are designed to enable you to learn to transcribe and to read phonetics with a minimum of classroom instruction. A reading exercise is designed for you to read aloud without additional assistance. A transcription exercise is designed for you to work with another student so that you dictate some of the words for him to write and he dictates some to you. When working in pairs, remember to check each word carefully before going to the next. The crossword puzzles are included to provide practice on sounds which you have previously learned to read and to transcribe. All reading exercises except the first should be preceded by a use of flash cards on all of the sounds involved in that exercise; only Consonant Reading Exercise I should be followed rather than preceded by the use of such cards.

CONSONANT READING EXERCISE I

Read the list in numerical order as rapidly as possible except when a new sound is introduced. If you are forced to read slowly at any other time, do not forge ahead in the hope that your difficulty will clear up eventually but back up five or ten items and pronounce them again. Brackets have been omitted to facilitate reading.

1. i(as in *e*, *ea*t, n*ie*ce, Gr*ee*ce, p*eo*ple, s*ea*t, k*ey*, q*uay*, mach*i*ne, Ph*oe*be, C*ae*sar)
2. b(as in ru*b*, ho*bb*le)
3. bi
4. ib
5. bib
6. 'bibi(' means to accent following syllable by making it higher pitched, and/or louder and/or longer in duration than the other syllables)
7. i'bi
8. bi'bib
9. bibi'bi
10. p(as in cu*p*, su*pp*er)
11. pi
12. bip
13. pib
14. 'pibi
15. 'ipi
16. i'pib
17. 'bipib
18. d(as in le*d*, ru*dd*er)
19. di
20. did
21. dip
22. bid
23. 'dipib
24. bi'dip
25. t(as in ca*t*, wi*tt*y)
26. ti
27. tip
28. bit
29. pit
30. dit
31. tid
32. ipt(release on [t], not on [p])
33. tipt
34. pipt
35. bipt
36. 'tipi
37. 'ti'bi (accent equally)
38. g(as in le*g*, bi*gg*er)
39. gi
40. ig
41. gip
42. pig
43. digd(release on [d], not [g])
44. 'digi
45. git
46. 'tigip
47. pi'gid
48. bi'gigd
49. k(as in si*ck*, soa*k*, mas*que*, bis*c*uit, hi*cc*ough)
50. ki
51. kip
52. pik
53. tik
54. ikt
55. pikt
56. ki'dig
57. bik
58. 'pibikt
59. pi'bikt
60. piki'dibd
61. ɪ(as in *i*t, pr*e*tty, br*ee*ches, s*ie*ve, w*o*men, b*u*sy, b*ui*ld, h*y*mn)
62. ɪd
63. bɪd
64. dɪp

65. dɪk
66. pɪk
67. kɪd
68. tɪp
69. pɪt
70. 'pɪtɪ
71. dɪt
72. 'dɪtɪ
73. bid
74. bɪ'di
75. 'pɪtɪd
76. pɪ'tid
77. 'kiki
78. 'kikɪ
79. 'kɪkɪ
80. 'pitɪd
81. pɪ'tidɪ
82. tɪpt
83. pipt
84. dɪpt
85. v(as in o*f*, Ste*ph*en, sal*v*e, sa*v*e)
86. vi
87. iv
88. vɪk
89. ɪ'vɪkt
90. gɪv
91. 'bɪvit
92. ɪvd
93. pivd
94. f(as in i*f*, sa*f*e, lau*gh*, pu*ff*, tele*ph*one)
95. fi
96. ɪf
97. fɪt
98. dɪf
99. gɪft
100. fɪg
101. 'fɪtɪd
102. fit
103. dɪ'fit
104. dɪ'fitɪd
105. dɪ'pɪktɪd
106. 'bifɪ
107. z(as in La Pa*z*, i*s*, love*s*, bu*zz*, free*ze*, *x*ylophone)
108. ɪz
109. zɪp
110. iz
111. idz([z] is stopped by release of [d])
112. fiz
113. fidz
114. bidz
115. bɪdz
116. didz
117. gɪvz
118. pɪgz
119. kiz
120. 'tipiz
121. 'tizɪz
122. 'fɪzɪz
123. fɪ'zik
124. 'fɪzɪk
125. 'bɪzɪ
126. 'dɪzɪ
127. dɪ'ziz
128. dɪ'zizɪz
129. s(as in ye*s*, nie*c*e, *c*ell, *sc*ene, *sch*ism, ki*ss*)
130. sɪs
131. sɪp
132. sipt
133. spidz
134. dɪsk
135. fɪst
136. fist
137. 'kɪsɪz

138. spidz
139. tɪps
140. spɪt
141. kɪst
142. ts(release on [s] as a stop)
143. fɪts
144. fits
145. sɪfts
146. gɪfts
147. dɪsk
148. dɪsks
149. fɪsts
150. fists
151. sɪsts
152. fɪks
153. fɪkst
154. sɪ'sid
155. sɪ'sidɪd
156. gis
157. dɪ'sist
158. spiks
159. sizd
160. sist
161. ʒ(as in rou*g*e, a*z*ure, vi*s*ion, absci*ss*ion)
162. iʒ
163. ɪʒ
164. piʒ
165. pɪʒ
166. dʒ(as in re*g*ister, *judge*, sol*di*er)
167. idʒ
168. dʒi
169. dʒɪp
170. dʒɪpt
171. fɪdʒ
172. 'fɪdʒɪt
173. 'fɪʒɪt
174. spɪʒ
175. sidʒ
176. 'sidʒɪz
177. dʒiz
178. 'idʒɪpt
179. 'vɪzɪdʒ
180. ʃ(as in *sh*arp, ma*ch*ine, i*ss*ue, *ch*andelier, con*sc*ience, spe*c*ial)
181. ɪʃ
182. fɪʃ
183. ʃɪp
184. ʃɪpt
185. ʃif
186. ʃɪft
187. fɪʃt
188. ʃiʒ
189. tʃ(as in mu*ch*, wa*tch*, na*t*ure, ques*ti*on, ri*ghte*ous)
190. ɪtʃ
191. tʃɪp
192. tʃɪpt
193. pitʃ
194. tʃiz
195. tʃif
196. 'bitʃɪz
197. 'pitʃɪz
198. 'spitʃɪz
199. 'spiʃiz
200. ɪtʃt
201. 'dɪtʃɪz
202. ð(as in *th*is, ei*th*er, smoo*th*, brea*the*, *y*e)
203. ði
204. ðɪs
205. ið
206. sið
207. dʒɪð
208. 'dʒiðɪgd

209. ðiz
210. stið
211. ʃið
212. ʃip
213. 'ʃipɪʃ
214. 'tʃipɪʃ
215. θ(as in *th*in, e*th*er, too*th*)
216. iθ
217. θɪk
218. θiks
219. dʒiθ
220. ʃiθ
221. 'θisɪs
222. fɪf
223. fɪfθ
224. sɪks
225. sɪksθ
226. ʃiðd
227. við
228. vɪθ
229. spiθ
230. spið
231. spiðd
232. spiθt
233. h(as in *h*e, be*h*aves, *wh*o)
234. hi
235. hid
236. 'hidɪd
237. hɪ'dɪd
238. hɪtʃ
239. hɪst
240. 'hitɪd
241. hɪp
242. 'hɪpɪ
243. 'hɪpɪɪst
244. hivd
245. hiθ
246. hɪ'sidɪdɪt
247. m(as in su*m*, su*mm*er)
248. mi
249. tɪm
250. θɪm
251. dɪm
252. dɪmd
253. dimd
254. simd
255. simz
256. θimz
257. bimd
258. 'mɪstɪk
259. mɪ'stik
260. 'mɪstʃɪf
261. n(as in i*n*, *gn*at, *kn*it, *pn*eumatic, i*nn*)
262. ɪn
263. nɪp
264. pɪn
265. nit
266. 'nisɪz
267. 'sinɪk
268. 'mɪnɪt
269. ɪndʒ
270. sɪndʒ
271. 'fɪtnɪs
272. sin
273. sɪns
274. sɪnts
275. sɪntʃ
276. 'tʃɪmnɪ
277. 'tʃɪmnɪz
278. dɪ'mind
279. 'nidɪd
280. 'nɪtɪd
281. 'bɪskɪt
282. nɪkt
283. 'mɪnɪts
284. 'dʒinɪ
285. 'θɪnɪst

286. 'θɪnnɪs
287. ŋ(as in thi*ng*, i*n*k)
288. ɪŋ
289. kɪŋ
290. kɪŋk
291. sɪŋk
292. 'sɪŋɪŋ
293. 'sɪŋkɪŋ
294. mɪŋk
295. 'pɪŋkɪʃ
296. 'pɪŋkt
297. θɪŋk
298. 'nidɪŋ
299. kɪn
300. kɪng
301. kɪŋ
302. kɪŋk
303. 'ivnɪŋ
304. 'ɪnstɪŋkt
305. 'ɪmɪdʒɪz
306. tʃɪŋks
307. sfɪŋks
308. l(as in channe*l*, se*ll*)
309. li
310. il(avoid saying ee-uhl)
311. sil
312. hilz
313. tʃɪl
314. lɪm
315. lɪmp
316. lɪmpt
317. 'lɪsn̩(ˌ indicates non-vocalic syllable)
318. 'lɪsnɪŋ
319. 'bitl̩
320. 'bitl̩z
321. 'sɪlɪ
322. 'sɪŋl̩
323. 'sɪŋgl̩
324. 'tɪŋl̩
325. 'tɪŋgl̩
326. ɪm'plɪsɪtlɪ
327. 'tɪpɪkl̩
328. lɪŋkt
329. 'blɪŋkɪŋ
330. 'slɪŋkɪŋ
331. 'ɪŋglɪʃ
332. 'tʃɪlɪɪst
333. 'stɪlɪst
334. plidz
335. 'vɪlɪdʒɪz
336. ɪn'vigl̩
337. 'ɪntʃɪz
338. r(as in *r*un, *rh*etoric, so*rr*y, but not as in err)
339. ri
340. rid
341. ritʃ
342. ritʃt
343. rɪp
344. rɪpt
345. 'rɪpl̩
346. krim
347. skrim
348. drim
349. pɪrs(avoid saying *pi uhrs.*)
350. riθ
351. grif
352. 'strɪkn̩
353. 'grifstrɪkn̩
354. 'rɪdʒɪd
355. 'frɪdʒɪd
356. 'sikrɪts
357. w(as in *w*e, pers*u*ade, q*u*it, c*h*oir, mem*o*ir, *o*ne)

358. wi
359. hwi
360. wɪt
361. hwɪt
362. wɪtʃ
363. hwɪtʃ
364. wɪf
365. hwɪf
366. swɪm
367. wɪʃ
368. dɪ'stɪŋgwɪʃ
369. 'wɪtɪɪst
370. 'hwidḷ
371. j(as in hallelu*j*ah, *y*ou, *u*se, on*i*on, f*e*ud, vignette)
372. ji
373. 'jɪdɪʃ
374. jidʒ
375. jið
376. jild
377. 'jildɪd
378. 'jildɪŋ
379. jists
380. 'fij
381. rɪ'mɪs
382. lidʒ
383. sɪksθ
384. bɪ'kwiðd
385. 'idʒɪs
386. sɪ'rɪndʒ
387. 'skɪtɪʃnɪs
388. hɪr'wɪð
389. 'nidɪɪst
390. 'skrɪbḷ
391. 'sidʒɪz
392. 'tritɪs
393. ʃrɪmp
394. 'skwimɪʃ
395. 'hilɪks
396. dɪ'sivd
397. skritʃt
398. 'spɪnɪtʃ
399. ɪnbɪ'twin
400. 'hwitṇ

Consonant Reading Exercise II

hɪ drɪŋks hɪz mɪlk 'itʃ 'ivnɪŋ. 'ʃi θɪŋks hɪzɪmɪdʒɪz plizɪŋ. ðɪsɪz ðɪ ɪmprɪnt hɪ 'minz. 'ɪl spikɪŋ bridzɪl 'filɪŋ. wɪ brɪŋ 'itʃ θɪŋ ɪn hwɪtʃ wɪ θɪŋkḷ 'plizɪm. itʃ trɪp hɪ 'kip sɪnsɪstɪŋ ðɪsɪz hɪz 'drim. hɪz spitʃɪz dɪ'sivɪŋlɪ rɪtṇ ɪnɪŋk. 'ðɪs brɪdʒ bimɪz θɪk; ðɪsɪz 'θɪn. ðiz 'min krɪtɪks brɪŋ wɪkɪd dɪ'fits. hɪ titʃɪ'zɪŋglɪʃ. ðɪs prɪtɪ lɪlɪ ɪz 'tʃip. ɪn 'hwɪtʃ vɪlɪdʒ dɪdɪ si ɪz nis? ðɪs wik kwin wɪl 'fri ðiz findz. ʃɪ switṇ dɪz pɪkḷd pitʃɪz. hɪ fɪkstɪt wɪð 'jistɪn 'mɪlk. wɪl ðɪs prɪnt 'ʃrɪŋk? kwɪk briðɪŋ ɪ'zizɪ. dɪdɪ wɪʃwɪ 'dɪdɪt? hɪ ɪzɪn'did. hɪzɪ'lɪsɪt did wɪl sɪmplɪ simɪn'sɪpɪd. ɪt simz hɪ filz ðɪ ɪn'krisɪŋ hit sɪns hɪ ɪz sɪtɪŋ biniθ ðɪs 'tri. hɪ rɪ'zɪstɪd dɪsplizɪŋ ðɪ ivl wɪtʃ. hɪ hwɪsḷd bɪ'wɪtʃɪŋlɪ. ðɪs wɪʃɪŋ rɪŋ wɪlɪn'did brɪŋ rɪtʃɪz. sɪns ðɪsɪz 'fɪnɪʃt, rɪpitɪŋ ɪt 'kwɪklɪ wɪl brɪŋ ɪn'krist skɪlɪn ridɪŋ.

Consonant Transcription Exercise

1. tiðd
2. 'rɪgl̩
3. 'hwɪskɪ
4. 'dʒɪŋgl̩
5. 'hɪmnɪst
6. 'finɪks
7. sɪndʒd
8. 'riθɪŋk
9. 'lɪkwɪdz
10. 'ʃɪmɪ
11. bɪ'niθ
12. 'ʃɪftɪ
13. 'mɪlkwid
14. lɪmf
15. 'dipɪst
16. 'mɪdʒɪts
17. prɪnts
18. 'stɪltɪd
19. 'mitɪɪst
20. rikt
21. hwɪmz
22. briðd
23. 'nidl̩z
24. 'θɪkɪt
25. 'ʃɪŋgl̩
26. rɪ'strɪktɪv
27. ɪm'pitʃt
28. ɪmbɪ'sɪlɪk
29. ɪndɪ'skritlɪ
30. rɪ'vɪzɪtɪŋ
31. ɪn'frɪndʒɪŋ
32. ɪn'hɪbɪtɪd
33. 'wɪtɪsɪzm̩
34. 'bɪskɪts
35. dɪ'plitɪŋ
36. 'rɪŋkl̩d
37. 'swidɪʃ
38. 'rɪðmɪkl̩
39. 'θisiz
40. dɪ'krisɪŋlɪ
41. sɪkstɪ'θri
42. fɪftɪ'sɪks
43. ɪmɪ'dʒɪstɪk
44. 'hwilɪŋ
45. sɪntʃt
46. 'pɪksɪ
47. jists
48. 'pɪknɪkɪŋ
49. bɪ'wɪtʃɪz
50. grist
51. skimd
52. rɪ'list
53. prɪ'sidɪd
54. dɪs'plizɪz
55. fɪfθ
56. ɪm'pɪndʒd
57. 'fɪftin
58. 'lɪntʃɪz
59. rɪ'dimd
60. mɪs'gɪvɪŋz
61. sɪ'rɪndʒ
62. ɪn'trigɪŋ
63. glɪmps
64. twɪtʃt
65. 'stɪtʃɪz
66. 'dɪzɪɪst
67. 'skwimɪʃ
68. 'rizn̩
69. rɪ'trivd
70. fɪltʃt
71. 'θrɪftɪlɪ
72. 'wikɪst
73. 'prɪtɪɪŋ
74. 'lɪsn̩
75. hiθs
76. skrɪpts
77. 'hilɪks
78. 'dɪstrɪkt
79. ʃrɪft
80. 'slizɪ
81. 'grivɪŋ
82. brɪŋks
83. 'drɪftɪd
84. 'fɪzɪkl̩
85. hɪ'nidzɪt
86. dɪdɪ 'si ɪt
87. wɪ bɪ'livdɪm
88. 'ki pis
89. 'kip pis
90. 'hwɪtʃɪmɪdʒ
91. dɪd 'hi klinɪt
92. hɪ 'ɪz plizd
93. dɪdɪ si 'ðɪs
94. bɪl 'fɪnɪʃtɪt
95. skwizɪt 'kwɪklɪ
96. dɪdɪt 'fɪtɪm
97. dɪdɪt 'fɪt tɪm
98. ðiz 'bɪg gis
99. dɪdɪ 'itɪt
100. ɪt ɪnkrisɪz 'spidɪlɪ

Reading Exercise for Front Vowels Including [ɑ]

1. mɪks
2. 'ʃɪmɪ
3. mɪsts
4. θivz
5. slɪk
6. nit
7. 'rigl̩
8. pɪŋks
9. tiðz
10. 'ʃɪŋgl̩
11. ðiz
12. skwikt
13. 'kwɪkɪst
14. briðd
15. kript
16. prɪnts
17. 'θɪsl̩
18. rikt
19. dʒɪn
20. bɪ'lifs
21. sɪsts
22. 'gridɪɪst
23. 'rɪtʃlɪ
24. 'widɪd
25. prɪ'sidz
26. 'dipɪst
27. rɪ'vild
28. 'dʒɪgl̩
29. sprɪnts
30. 'mɪdʒɪts
31. 'nidl̩z
32. 'stɪltɪd
33. ʃɪfts
34. 'wikn̩d
35. tiðd
36. 'fɪdl̩z
37. θibz
38. rɪnst
39. ʃiðz
40. hwɪst
41. 'stipl̩d
42. krist
43. kwɪts
44. 'lɪkwɪdz
45. 'minɪst
46. lɪmf
47. 'θɪkɪt
48. 'finɪks
49. 'dʒɪfɪ
50. bɪ'lif
51. dʒɪŋks
52. sɪkstɪ'θri
53. rɪ'strɪktɪv
54. frɪndʒd
55. 'riθɪŋk
56. 'hɪmnɪst
57. bɪ'niθ
58. ɪm'pitʃt
59. 'mɪlkwid
60. ɪndɪ'skritlɪ
61. dɪ'spɪrɪtɪd
62. rɪ'vɪzɪtɪŋ
63. 'hwɪskɪ
64. ɪmbɪ'sɪlɪk
65. 'dʒɪŋgl̩
66. ɪn'hɪbɪtɪd
67. ɪm'pɪndʒd
68. ðɪsɪ'zɪt
69. 'rɪtʃlɪ
70. dɪdɪ'siɪt
71. 'likɪdʒ
72. 'pɪtɪɪŋ
73. fɪftɪ'sɪks
74. ɪ'kwɪpt
75. ɪ'midɪɪt
76. filɪ'sɪfɪk
77. ɪn'frɪndʒɪŋ
78. 'dɪksɪ
79. 'wɪkɪdɪst
80. dɪd'hisiɪt
81. bɪ'dɪzn̩
82. sɪ'mɪtɪk
83. 'pɪlɪdʒ
84. 'slizɪ
85. 'ligl̩
86. 'θivɪŋ
87. hwɪft
88. 'ʃrɪvl̩d
89. 'jistɪ
90. 'dʒɪmɪɪŋ
91. sɪlf
92. bɪ'twɪkst
93. 'kwɪk 'friz
94. 'θɪmbl̩
95. 'rɪdl̩z
96. nɪmf
97. 'rɪðm̩
98. 'vɪtl̩z
99. 'kwizɪ
100. 'prɪzm̩
101. e(as in f*e*te, *a*te, b*ai*t, l*ay*, v*ei*l, camp*aig*n, *eigh*t champ*ag*ne, ob*ey*)
102. pe

103. se
104. es
105. pes
106. pest
107. ek
108. ʃek
109. etʃ
110. edʒ
111. beʒ
112. kedʒ
113. 'lɪkwɪd
114. hwe
115. krim
116. ðed
117. dɪtʃ
118. feθ
119. 'klinlɪ
120. reθ
121. krik
122. hest
123. tʃen
124. 'mɪŋgl̩d
125. klem
126. jild
127. dʒel
128. 'ɪnkris
129. ɪn'krist
130. 'bekn̩
131. tʃɪŋks
132. 'rezn̩
133. 'tʃiflɪ
134. tʃendʒ
135. ɪndɪ'skritlɪ
136. 'ledl̩
137. sɪksθ
138. ledðz
139. 'θɪnɪst
140. dʒɪŋks
141. ɪ'midɪɪt
142. 'fetl̩
143. hwɪmz
144. 'ʃɪŋgl̩
145. beðz
146. 'ʃildɪŋ
147. 'rɪgl̩
148. kweks
149. 'jildɪd
150. dʒeld
151. ʃrɪŋk
152. 'klinɪst
153. plest
154. 'rɪdʒɪd
155. blemd
156. 'hesn̩d
157. 'ʃɪftɪ
158. rendʒd
159. 'prɪtɪɪst
160. 'deɪs
161. e'lit
162. 'ekɪŋ
163. 'edɪd
164. 'weɪŋ
165. 'fimel
166. 'streɪŋ
167. 'hetɪd
168. 'sedʒlɪ
169. 'emlɪs
170. 'krezɪ
171. ɛ(as in *e*tch, h*ei*fer, br*ea*d, fr*ie*nd, s*ai*th, l*eo*pard)
172. ɛd
173. ɛks
174. ɛl
175. ɛm
176. hɛm
177. hɪm
178. sɛd
179. pɛks
180. jɛs
181. ðɛn
182. sɛθ
183. dʒɛm
184. sɛlz
185. strendʒ
186. flem
187. flɛm
188. tʃendʒ
189. lɛŋθ
190. brɛdθ
191. 'sleɪŋ
192. ɛtʃt
193. 'pleket
194. dɪ'ked
195. nɛlt
196. swɛl
197. 'greɪŋ
198. 'rɛsl̩
199. 'nevɪz
200. jɛlpt
201. brɛθs
202. 'hɛvɪ
203. 'pɛsl̩
204. tɛnθ
205. grɪ'mes
206. 'edʒɪz
207. 'ɛdʒɪz
208. dɪ'teld
209. brɛθs
210. ʃɛlvz
211. 'lemnɪs

212. sprɛd
213. tʃɛkt
214. 'gretɪs
215. 'mɛdl̩z
216. hwɛns
217. sɛns
218. sɛnts
219. frɛntʃ
220. hwɛlpt
221. dɪ'femd
222. twɛlfθ
223. 'mɛθen
224. 'gretɪst
225. 'θrɛtn̩d
226. ɛk'sɛpt
227. 'findrɪʃ
228. ðɛm'sɛlvz
229. 'rendʒɪz
230. 'plɛntɪ
231. 'jɛlɪŋ
232. prɪ'tɛns
233. dɪ'keɪŋ
234. 'klɛnlɪ
235. hɪ'breɪk
236. 'twɛntɪ
237. sɪ'mɛnt
238. 'wetɪɪst
239. 'dʒɛrɪ
240. 'tʃɛrɪz
241. 'dɛked
242. 'ʃeplɪɪst
243. prɪ'velɪŋ
244. 'lɛtɪs
245. 'wɛnzdɪ
246. ɪ'lɛkt
247. 'dʒɛsɪ
248. ɪk'sklemd
249. dɪ'fɛktɪv
250. 'ɛksɪtɪŋ
251. 'ebl̩
252. 'kebl̩
253. 'sebl̩
254. rɪ'zɛmbl̩
255. vɪn'jɛt
256. dɪ'sɛntɪd
257. dɪ'strɛst
258. ɛg'zɪstɪd
259. rɪ'dʒɛktɛd
260. prɪ'ɛmptɪv
261. ɛk'strimlɪ
262. æ(as in *a*pt, pl*ai*d, gu*a*rantee)
263. æt
264. kæt
265. pæd
266. skæb
267. ræʃ
268. dæʃt
269. ðæt
270. tʃæts
271. jæks
272. græbd
273. ʃæŋks
274. fræns
275. 'dʒækl̩
276. jæmz
277. grænts
278. smæʃt
279. 'kætl̩
280. jæŋks
281. dʒæmd
282. spæŋkt
283. 'bætl̩d
284. 'ʃæsɪ
285. 'stræŋgl̩d
286. 'bægɪ
287. 'ævɪd
288. 'skræmbl̩
289. 'kætɪ
290. skrætʃt
291. 'pælɪs
292. 'lætɪs
293. 'spæŋgl̩d
294. ʃæm'pen
295. θæŋkt
296. 'sædɪst
297. 'sedɪst
298. 'blækn̩d
299. 'nɪknæk
300. 'dæpl̩d
301. 'rænsɪd
302. 'bænɪʃ
303. 'spænɪʃ
304. kræŋkt
305. pɪ'ænɪst
306. 'kærɪdʒ
307. 'æŋgrɪ
308. 'æŋgwɪʃ
309. 'mæŋgl̩d
310. 'tæŋgl̩d
311. 'grævɪd
312. fɪ'næns
313. 'pænfɪʃ
314. 'kæbɪdʒ
315. 'flæksɪd
316. 'hæpɪɪst
317. 'pælɪsɪz
318. 'ɛkskwɪzɪt
319. rɪ'sɛst
320. 'ɪŋkstænd
321. 'kræbmit
322. stæm'pid
323. 'blæŋkɪt

324. 'ræmpedʒ
325. ɪ'læstɪk
326. 'rɛptɪl
327. æθ'lɛtɪk
328. 'fæmɪʃt
329. a (lower tongue position than [æ] when [f], [s], [θ], or [n] follows, as in *laugh*, *pass*, *bath* and *dance*)
330. paθ
331. pæθ
332. haf
333. hæf
334. laf
335. laft
336. 'lafɪŋ
337. pas
338. pæs
339. past
340. 'pasɪv
341. raθ
342. maθ
343. tʃaf
344. graf
345. baθ
346. aft
347. haft
348. haθ
349. task
350. graft
351. staft
352. klaspt
353. blasts
354. masts
355. maskt
356. krafts
357. flasks
358. 'fasn̩
359. 'grasɪ
360. 'ɪmpas
361. 'lafɪŋlɪ
362. 'paθwez
363. 'grafɪk
364. rɪ'past
365. 'hændɪkraft
366. ɑ (as in w*a*n, *o*x, serge*a*nt, p*al*m, h*ah*, sq*ua*d, kn*ow*ledge, h*ea*rth, pato*is*)
367. ɑd
368. pɑd
369. pɑt
370. hɑt
371. ʃɑt
372. tʃɑp
373. kɑp
374. 'kɑpɪ
375. nɑt
376. sɑk
377. rɑk
378. rɑkt
379. ɑr
380. pɑr
381. spɑr
382. spɑrk
383. spɑrkt
384. ɑrt
385. ɑrtʃ
386. ɑrm
387. ɑrmd
388. hɑrmd
389. ɑrk
390. dʒɑrd
391. pɑm
392. kɑm
393. wɑtʃ
394. jɑts
395. nɑbz
396. 'kɑtn̩
397. dʒɑb
398. 'tɑdl̩
399. ɑmz
400. kwɑmz
401. swɑpt
402. skɑtʃ
403. skwɑʃ
404. skɑts
405. snɑbz
406. skwɑbz
407. 'ɑrmɪ
408. 'ʃɑdɪ
409. 'nɑtɪ
410. pɑrtʃt
411. 'ɑnɪst
412. 'nɑvɪs
413. 'sɑkɪt
414. 'kepɑk
415. 'dʒɑlɪ
416. 'dʒɑkɪ
417. gɪ'tɑr
418. 'nɑtɪd
419. 'hɑgɪʃ
420. 'tɑgl̩
421. 'ʃɑkɪŋ
422. blɑ'ze
423. 'ɑksɪn

424. 'fɑrɛd
425. 'ɑnɪks
426. 'rɑkɪts
427. me'nɑʒ
428. 'hɑrɪdlɪ
429. 'ɑrtʃɪz
430. 'nɑlɪdʒ
431. 'hɑrdlɪ
432. 'lɑrʒɛs
433. 'bɑksɪz
434. 'tɑpɪks
435. 'ʃɑrplɪ
436. 'kɑmɪts
437. 'blɑrnɪ
438. 'dʒɑkɪ
439. 'kwɑrɪz
440. 'nɑknid
441. 'mɑdɪst
442. 'klɑtɪd
443. 'tʃɑrmɪŋlɪ
444. 'sɑnɪts
445. brɑŋks
446. 'bæŋkɑk
447. lie'zɑn
448. 'nɑlɪdʒ
449. 'kævɪɑr
450. stɑ'ked
451. 'mɪʃ'mɑʃ
452. 'prɑsɛs
453. 'nɑt'jɛt
454. 'ɑkstel
455. 'fɑnɪks
456. 'ɛnɪbɑdɪ
457. 'kɑndwɪt
458. dɪs'tʃɑrdʒd
459. 'bɑksrɛntʃ
460. 'kɑnkwɛsts
461. 'stɑkmɑrkɪt
462. ɑb'stɛtrɪks
463. 'kɑŋgrɪget
464. 'sɑlɪpsɪzm̩
465. 'lafɪŋstɑk
466. 'metrɪɑrkɪ
467. 'dɛmɪtɑs
468. 'mɑlɪkɑdl̩
469. 'kɑnkrit
470. nɪ'mɑnɪk
471. ɑn'trækt
472. 'slɪpʃɑd
473. 'mɑrtʃɪz
474. 'kɑnsɛpts
475. 'ʃɑdɪist
476. 'jɑrdɪdʒ
477. 'ɛvrɪbɑdɪ
478. mɪ'rɑʒɪz
479. 'swithɑrt
480. æg'nɑestɪk
481. 'kɑndwɪts
482. 'krɑnɪklɪ
483. ɑf'θælmɪk
484. 'rɪst'wɑtʃ
485. 'skeðɪŋ
486. 'rɛspɪt
487. 'semnɪs
488. 'kɑntrækt
489. ɪn'vɛstɪd
490. 'letɪst
491. ɛk'sidɪd
492. 'ɑbsɪkwɪz
493. 'letɛks
494. 'tɑmpsn̩
495. 'rebɪiz
496. 'dʒɑgl̩
497. 'hɑgzhɛd
498. fiɑn'se
499. ɑn'sɑmbl̩
500. 'grifstrɪkn̩

Reading Exercise for Front Vowels Including [ɑ]

1. hɪ kwɪklɪ tʃɛndʒdɪz 'wez.
2. mɛnɪ mɛn sɛlɛvrɪθɪŋ ðe hævɪn sikɪŋ 'nɑlɪdʒ.
3. gret brɪtn̩ me sik ðiz mɛnɪn 'fræns.
4. æktɪv jæŋkɪ tredɪŋ me bɪ ɪl mænɪdʒd hwɛn 'nɑt wɛl 'plænd.
5. ðe ɛkstʃendʒd 'lætʃkiz 'wɛnzdɪ 'ivnɪŋ.
6. sɪ'mɛnt bɪkem 'kɑnkrit hwɛnɪ ædɪd wɛt 'sænd.
7. ɛnɪbɑdɪ me wɛl bɪliv ðætɪzɛksɪt simd 'snɑbɪʃ.
8. bɪlɑsktɪm hwɑt ðɪ ɪmɪdʒ 'wɑz hwɪtʃ ðe plest bɪniθɪt.
9. jɛlɪŋ 'mædlɪ, ðe ritʃt itʃ krɪ'vɑs.

10. hɪ lafɪŋlɪ rɪplest 'hɪz kændɪ ɪn ðɪ ɛmptɪ 'bɑks.
11. 'sɪkstin mɛn wɛntæŋgrɪlɪ 'ɪn.
12. ðe dɪvɪdɪt wɪð 'stiv.
13. vɛrɪ 'strendʒ 'ɑbdʒɪkts me bɪ 'sin.
14. ɪfɪts 'mɛtl̩, ɪtl̩ 'sɪŋk.
15. hɪ plestɪt ɑr'tɪstɪklɪ bɪtwin 'pisɪz.
16. hwɪt∫ paθ lidz ɪn 'ɑnɪst wez?
17. ɑnɪksɪz 'blæk, 'ɪzn̩tɪt?
18. ðɪ 'æŋgrɪɪst pipl̩ sim 'kɑm.
19. 'twɛlv dez past ɪn hwɪt∫ wɪ dɪdn̩t 'si ɪm.
20. ɑr ðiz wɑt∫ɪz ðæt hɪ 'fɪkst 'rɛdɪ jɛt?
21. nɑt 'e 'nɛgets 'nɑt nɑt e.
22. 'hɪz læŋgwɪdʒ ɪz strendʒɪn 'wɛstidʒɪpt.
23. hɪ wɪl bɪ twɛntɪ'θri 'wɛnzdɪ.
24. ðe 'ɑr skɑts, nɑt skɑt∫.
25. 'nɑlɪdʒ jildz 'sɛlf nɑlɪdʒ, 'ænd sɛlf nɑlɪdʒɪz 'strɛŋθ.

Transcription Exercise for Front Vowels Including [ɑ]

1. klaspt
2. bɪ'jɑnd
3. 'kwɑtren
4. 'zɪgzæg
5. 'hwɑtnɑt
6. 'θɪmbl̩
7. spɪ'sɪfɪk
8. 'wɑt∫ɪz
9. dɪs'grest
10. 'ɑrɛsvipi
11. rɪ'tend
12. prɪ'zɛnts
13. 't∫ipn̩d
14. 'bɛlɪek
15. 'dʒæzmɪn
16. 'lezɪnɪs
17. me'nɑʒ
18. ɛlɪ'fæntɪn
19. 'hafwe
20. 'fɑnɪks
21. ɪ'rest
22. 'vɪzɪdʒ
23. 'kræŋk∫aft
24. 'kɑpɪkæt
25. 'ɛks 'red
26. rɪ'zɑlvd
27. 'gastlɪ
28. 'ɛmptɪ
29. 'mɑrdʒɪn
30. æg'nɑstɪk
31. rɛnt∫t
32. 'θrɑtl̩
33. 'mɑdʒɑŋ
34. 'jɑrdstɪk
35. 'rɛdɪɪŋ
36. 'strængl̩
37. 'dʒɑlɪ
38. 'fetɪd
39. 'ɪmpas
40. 'dʒɑkɪ
41. 'pælɪs
42. θrɪld
43. 'æŋkl̩
44. skwɑ∫
45. gɪ'tɑr
46. 'kæzm̩
47. 'pɑmɪst
48. 'edɪd
49. jɛs
50. 'ɛksɪt
51. 'wedʒɪz
52. 'næ∫ɪŋ
53. 'æŋgwɪ∫
54. ∫æm'pen
55. 'jæŋkɪ
56. 'skeðɪŋ
57. 'bɑksɪz
58. 'kæfɪɪn
59. 'rebɪiz
60. brɛdθ

Crossword Puzzle for Front Vowels Including [ɑ]

ACROSS

1. 'plizɪŋ
5. west
10. sɛt
11. 'spik ɑv; 'kændɪ
13. hel
14. snekɪ' fɪʃ
15. 'bæŋks hæv ðɪs
16. nɑt' frɛʃ
17. trel
19. nɑts
20. ɪts 'plæntɪd ɪn
21. plen
23. 'vɛksɪŋ θɪŋ (slæŋ)
25. ɑb'ten
26. stet
29. hɛld 'tizɪŋlɪ
31. se ðɪs ɪn'stɛd; nɑt 'lidɪd
32. 'ɛnɪθɪŋ
34. 'bɛst gredz
35. '____ tas

DOWN

1. 'drɛsɪz me hæv ðiz
2. 'rad ɪn 'relz
3. 'bes, bæd 'sɛlf
4. ɪt 'ɪz, hwɛn 'nɑt strɛst
5. wɪ 'it ðɪs
6. 'ɛnɪθɪŋ
7. ɪt 'stɪŋks
8. kip 'fri ɑv
9. hwɛn hɪ gɛts 'ɛfs
12. 'rɛspɪt
15. 'dʒæk____
16. hɪt 'hɑrd (slæŋ)
18. hɛlpt
19. itn̩ 'delɪ
21. se lɪrɪks ɪn 'ki
22. kasts glænsɪz æt 'fimelz
24. 'ʃi hæz ti vi 'fem
26. haf (prifɪks)
27. 'hɛlpɪŋ
28. ɪl

Transcription Exercise (*Concluded*)

61. vɪn'jɛt
62. rɪ'past
63. 'nɑlɪdʒ
64. 'kɑntræst
65. ɑn'trækt
66. 'sɑkɪt
67. 'fimel
68. rɪ'ske
69. 'swithɑrt
70. sɛθ
71. lɪm'fætɪk
72. 'kwɑrɪ
73. 'deɪs
74. ɑn'sɑmbl̩
75. 'flæksɪd
76. grɪ'mesɪz
77. nɪ'mɑnɪk
78. ɑb'stɛtrɪks
79. 'bekn̩
80. 'ɑbsɪkwɪz
81. rekt
82. 'antre
83. 'pɑrtrɪdʒ
84. 'kepɑk
85. 'jɑrdɪdʒ
86. inɪg'mætɪk
87. 'kwɑdræŋgl̩
88. 'tɑksɪk
89. 'ɑlɪvz
90. 'bɑks rɛntʃ
91. 'semnɪs
92. 'ɑkstel
93. 'kɑŋgrɪget
94. ɪ'midɪɪt
95. mɪ'rɑʒɪz
96. 'klasmet
97. 'dʒægwɑr
98. ʒɑn'dɑrm
99. 'midɪet
100. 'tiɛnti

Note: Write answers in phonetics.

1	2	3		4		5	6		7	8	9
10				11	12				13		
14			15					16			
17		18					19				
20				21		22					
	23		24			25				26	27
28		29			30				31		
32	33				34			35			
36							37				

36. rɪ'tenɪŋ
37. 'stɛpɪŋ

30. 'hæpɪ
31. lɪtḷ, ____, list
33. 'brɪtɪʃ drɪŋk
35. pɑrt ɑv itʃ 'wik

Correct answers to puzzle are on page 328.

Reading Exercise for All Sounds Except Schwa

1. θrɪld
2. bɪ'kwið
3. 'strendʒlɪ
4. 'mɪlkwid
5. rɪ'dʒɛkt
6. 'mitɪɪst
7. 'kelɪf
8. 'rævɪdʒ
9. blas'fim
10. 'kɑlɪdʒɪz
11. æn'dʒɛlɪkḷ
12. sɪm'fɑnɪk
13. 'hɑdʒpɑdʒ
14. ɒ (used on many words spelled with *o* when followed by [f], [s], [θ], or [ŋ], as in *soft, toss, cloth,* and *long*)
15. ɒf
16. tɒs
17. tɒst
18. bɒs

19. bɒst
20. lɒs
21. lɒst
22. kɒst
23. kɒsts
24. klɒθ
25. frɒθ
26. 'ɒfɪs
27. kɒf
28. kɒft
29. 'kɒfɪ
30. trɒθ
31. sɒŋ
32. sɒŋz
33. θɒŋz
34. mɒθ
35. mɒðz
36. lɒft
37. sɒft
38. 'sɒftlɪ
39. rɒŋ
40. lɒŋ
41. strɒŋ
42. 'strɒŋbɑks
43. 'lɒsɪz
44. 'bɒsɪz
45. 'kastɒf
46. 'dɪfθɒŋ
47. 'ɒfɪsɪz
48. 'kɒstlɪ
49. 'hɛdʒhag
50. 'lɒŋhænd
51. 'sɒftʃɛld
52. lɒŋ'wɪndɪdlɪ
53. ɔ(higher tongue position and less lip opening than [ɒ], as in *a*ll, *o*rb, extr*ao*rdinary, Ge*o*rge, br*oa*d)
54. sɔ
55. sɔt
56. sɒft
57. ɔr
58. nɔr
59. ɔl
60. kɔl
61. bɔl
62. ɔt
63. kɔt
64. rɔt
65. fɔt
66. frɔt
67. dɪ'strɔt
68. θɔd
69. tɔl
70. sɔd
71. dwɔrf
72. 'jɔnɪŋ
73. skwɔl
74. skwɔkt
75. 'gɔkɪ
76. 'lɔdɪd
77. dɪ'frɔdɪd
78. 'kɔzwe
79. klɔz
80. 'kɔzl̩
81. 'ɔrɪndʒ
82. ɔr'den
83. dɔnd
84. 'hɔntɪd
85. 'ɔnɪŋ
86. mɪl'wɔkɪ
87. 'lændɔ
88. 'mɔkɪʃ
89. 'ɔtɑpsɪ
90. 'nɔtɪkl̩
91. hwɔrf
92. dwɔrft
93. 'ɔrbɪt
94. 'lɔrdʃɪp
95. dɪ'stɔrtɪd
96. mɪsɪn'fɔrm
97. dɪ'fɔrmd
98. ɛn'θrɔld
99. ɔ'θɛntɪk
100. 'ɔtograf
101. tɑr'pɔlɪn
102. o(as in *o*ld, *oh*, l*oa*m, f*oe*, gr*ow*, s*ew*, b*eau*, d*ough*)
103. do
104. od
105. dʒo
106. dʒok
107. sop
108. spok
109. ðoz
110. mond
111. gropt
112. strokt
113. ʃol
114. loʒ
115. rotʃ
116. brotʃ
117. mo'ros
118. 'gloɪŋ
119. dɪ'sonɪŋ

120. dʒo'kos
121. o'ke
122. 'moɪŋ
123. o'bis
124. 'fɑlod
125. 'mobɪl
126. pro'tɛst
127. 'kloðɪŋ
128. 'tʃɛlo
129. 'roɪŋ
130. so'te
131. do'men
132. dɪs'kors
133. 'hol'hwit
134. 'sovɪɪt
135. 'ɑngoɪŋ
136. vɪ'rego
137. 'mɪsḷto
138. 'swɑlod
139. 'poɪtrɪ
140. 'nobɑdɪ
141. pro'tɛstɪd
142. 'ɔtokræt
143. 'fonograf
144. æb'domɪn
145. 'tʃɒkolɪt
146. ʊ(as in p*u*sh, t*oo*k, w*ou*ld)
147. tʊk
148. ʃʊk
149. kʊk
150. kʊkt
151. rʊk
152. brʊk
153. nʊk
154. lʊk
155. lʊkt
156. hʊd
157. wʊd
158. ʃʊd
159. gʊd
160. wʊl
161. wʊlf
162. wʊlvz
163. pʊʃ
164. pʊʃt
165. 'wʊdn̩
166. hʊkt
167. pʊr
168. ʃʊr
169. jʊr
170. jʊrz
171. 'kʊdn̩t
172. 'bʊkɪʃ
173. 'hʊkɪ
174. 'bʊʃɪz
175. 'fʊtɪŋ
176. 'pʊlɪ
177. 'fʊlnɪs
178. 'bʊlɪ
179. 'gʊdɪz
180. 'pʊʃ'pʊl
181. 'bʊlɪt
182. 'krʊkɪd
183. 'tʊrɪst
184. 'ditʊr
185. 'liʒʊr
186. 'mɛʒʊr
187. 'æʒʊr
188. 'siʒʊr
189. 'fʊtbɔl
190. hjʊ'men
191. 'wʊstɪd
192. 'wofʊl
193. 'fitʃʊr
194. 'netʃʊr
195. 'pɑstʃʊr
196. 'vɛstʃʊr
197. 'pastʃʊr
198. 'vɛntʃʊr
199. 'sɛntʃʊrɪ
200. 'trɛʒʊrɪ
201. bʊr'ʒwɑ
202. 'grændʒʊr
203. 'ɪndʒʊrɪ
204. 'dʒɛstʃʊr
205. 'dɛpjʊtɪ
206. 'medn̩hʊd
207. 'ɑŋkor
208. 'læmzwʊl
209. 'opɪɪt
210. jʊr'sɛlf
211. 'hol'mɪlk
212. 'fɔrmjʊli
213. mɪnjʊ'ɛt
214. dɪ'lʊks
215. ɑfθæl'mɑlodʒɪ
216. u(as in f*oo*d, gr*ou*p, cr*ew*, fr*ui*t, can*oe*, rh*eu*matism)
217. ju
218. ʃu
219. fud
220. fjud
221. nus
222. nɪu
223. nju
224. jus
225. uz
226. juz
227. uzd
228. juzd

229. kud
230. kjud
231. kɪud
232. mut
233. mjut
234. mɪut
235. du
236. dɪu
237. dju
238. hu
239. hju
240. huz
241. hjuz
242. skul
243. ruf
244. rut
245. ruts
246. ruʒ
247. klu
248. fju
249. kjut
250. juθ
251. juðz
252. kruzd
253. hum
254. fjum
255. jul
256. mun
257. tɪun
258. tʃuz
259. dʒus
260. uzl
261. nɪ'uz
262. sɪut
263. mɪuzd
264. fjuzd
265. skɪud
266. kjubd
267. 'buɪ
268. pjus
269. dɪuks
270. 'kulɪŋ
271. 'skulɪŋ
272. 'nɛfju
273. 'debju
274. 'kjupɪd
275. 'junɪt
276. 'egju
277. 'bjuro
278. 'jusɪdʒ
279. 'tʃuzɪz
280. 'wɑʃrum
281. pjur
282. 'pjurɪst
283. dɪ'mjur
284. 'mjuzɪk
285. 'djurɪŋ
286. dɪ'fjuzd
287. 'kupɑnz
288. prɪ'sɪum
289. 'kjutɪkl̩
290. ɑb'skjur
291. 'tʃikruʒ
292. 'hupɪŋkɒf
293. 'sjudonɪm
294. fjutʃʊ'rɪstɪk
295. 'ʃumæk
296. 'dɛswɪtɪud
297. jʊ'niklɪ
298. 'fjurər
299. 'jogʊrt
300. tʊ'kɑn
301. popu'ri
302. fɪgjʊ'rin
303. mænjʊ'mɪt
304. njʊ'mætɪk
305. rezjʊ'me
306. 'fɪgjʊrhɛd
307. 'stɪpjʊlet
308. 'kjumjʊlet
309. 'ɛdʒʊket
310. o'bɪtʃʊɛrɪ
311. dɛbjʊ'tɑnt
312. dʒulɪ'ɛn
313. 'kjurɪoz
314. 'djurɛs
315. di'netʃʊrd
316. ʌ(as in *u*p, d*oe*s, fl*oo*d, t*ou*ch)
317. ʌp
318. kʌp
319. kʌt
320. kʌm
321. rʌm
322. θʌm
323. hʌb
324. rʌbd
325. sʌn
326. wʌn
327. wʌns
328. hʌg
329. θʌg
330. rʌg
331. ʃrʌg
332. mʌtʃ
333. mʌntʃ
334. sʌtʃ
335. tʌtʃ
336. hʌtʃ
337. hʌntʃ
338. hʌntʃt
339. lʌntʃ
340. lʌndʒ

341. bʌntʃ
342. spʌndʒ
343. lʌŋ
344. jʌŋ
345. sʌŋ
346. sʌŋk
347. mʌŋk
348. dʒʌŋk
349. 'ʌŋkḷ
350. dʒʌmp
351. mʌnθs
352. 'mʌdḷ
353. 'sʌkḷ
354. 'nʌkḷ
355. 'dʌfḷ
356. 'bʌtṇ
357. 'bʌsḷ
358. 'ʃʌfḷ
359. 'mʌsḷ
360. 'krʌmbḷd
361. mʌltʃt
362. 'sʌŋkṇ
363. 'ʃrʌŋkṇ
364. 'bʌŋgḷd
365. 'dʒʌŋgḷ
366. 'mʌnɪ
367. 'mʌndɪ
368. 'lʌgɪdʒ
369. ʌn'rɪtṇ
370. 'hɪkʌp
371. 'rʌbɪʃ
372. 'fʌŋgo
373. 'prɑdʌkt
374. ʌn'kloðd
375. 'pʌlpwʊd
376. 'mʌnden
377. ʌn'kuθ
378. 'dʌtʃɪsɪz
379. 'kɑrbʌŋkḷ
380. 'pʌŋktʃʊrd
381. 'hʌŋgrɪɪst
382. 'hʌkḷbɛrɪ
383. ɜ(used when a stressed syllable ends in a vowel that is followed by [r] plus a vowel, as in w*o*-rry, s*u*-rry, c*ou*-rage)
384. hɜ
385. 'hɜrɪ
386. 'hɜrɪd
387. wɜ
388. 'wɜrɪ
389. mɜ
390. 'mɜrɪ
391. 'mɜrɪn
392. kɜ
393. 'kɜrɪ
394. 'kɜrɪd
395. 'skɜrɪd
396. 'kɜrɪdʒ
397. 'kɜrɪɪŋ
398. 'wɜrɪɪŋ
399. 'skɜrɪɪŋ
400. 'tɜrɪt
401. 'nɜrɪʃt
402. 'flɜrɪʃ
403. 'flɜrɪʃɪz
404. 'stɜrɪŋ
405. 'spɜrɪŋ
406. 'slɜrɪŋ
407. 'θɜro
408. 'θɜronɪs
409. 'θɜrobrɛd
410. ɝ(as in t*ur*n, h*er*, b*ir*d, w*or*k, l*ear*n, j*our*ney, G*oe*the, m*yrrh*, g*uer*don)
411. hɝ
412. hɝd
413. 'hɜrɪd
414. 'hɝɪd(pause must separate vowels)
415. fɝ
416. fɝn
417. 'fɜrɪ
418. 'fɝnɪʃ
419. wɝ
420. wɜ
421. 'hɜret (*her* eight or *her* rate)
422. 'hɝ et (*her* eight)
423. 'hɝ ret (*her* rate)
424. vɝs
425. ɝkt
426. lɝkt
427. pɝs
428. wɝm
429. sɝdʒ
430. sɝtʃ
431. tʃɝtʃ
432. 'sɝtṇ

433. 'sɜrɪ
434. ʃɝkt
435. ʃɝts
436. 'mɝtl̩
437. 'fɝtl̩
438. 'wɝsn̩
439. 'hɜrɪɪŋ
440. skwɝmz
441. skwɝts
442. ʃo'fɝ
443. hɪz ʃo'fɝ
444. hɪz ʃo'fɜrɪzɪl
445. hɪz ʃo'fɝ dɪdɪt
446. 'sɝlɪ
447. 'ʃɝlɪ
448. 'ʃʊrlɪ
449. 'tɝkɪ
450. 'fɜrɪ
451. 'ɝθlɪ
452. 'lɝnɪd
453. 'pɝ'si
454. 'mɝkɪ
455. 'gɝnzɪ
456. 'ɝtʃɪn
457. 'wɝʃɪp
458. 'pɝfɪkt
459. 'kɝfju
460. 'wɝkrum
461. 'wɝmwʊd
462. θɝtɪ'wʌn
463. 'wɝkbʊk
464. 'æŋgl̩wɝm
465. 'hʊkwɝm
466. aɪ
467. aɪs
468. baɪ
469. aɪl
470. waɪl
471. hwaɪl
472. aɪt
473. taɪt
474. saɪt
475. faɪt
476. haɪt
477. hwaɪt
478. raɪ
479. raɪp
480. traɪ
481. traɪp
482. aɪr
483. faɪr
484. waɪr
485. laɪ
486. laɪv
487. naɪvz
488. waɪf
489. waɪn
490. hwaɪn
491. ðaɪn
492. saɪð
493. raɪð
494. aɪm
495. daɪm
496. maɪmz
497. twaɪs
498. θraɪvd
499. maɪnz
500. maɪndz
501. 'aɪvɪ
502. 'baɪɪŋ
503. 'traɪɪŋ
504. 'haɪɪst
505. 'vaɪsɪz
506. 'aɪskrim
507. 'saɪklon
508. 'slaɪɪst
509. 'raɪtɪst
510. ɔl'maɪtɪ
511. 'raɪsfild
512. daɪ'næmɪk
513. maɪ'æmɪ
514. 'taɪklasp
515. 'pastaɪm
516. 'ʌmpaɪr
517. ɪn'kwaɪrɪ
518. aɪ'æmbɪk
519. 'laɪbrɛrɪ
520. 'faɪæt
521. 'daɪfezd
522. 'ʃɔrt 'laɪvd
523. 'laɪvlɪhʊd
524. 'daɪnosɔr
525. jʊ'naɪt
526. 'pɔrkjʊpaɪn
527. aʊ
528. kaʊ
529. aʊt
530. baʊt
531. paʊt
532. raʊ
533. raʊt
534. naʊ
535. naʊn
536. aʊl
537. kaʊl
538. skaʊl
539. dʒaʊl
540. maʊs
541. haʊs
542. saʊθ
543. maʊθ
544. maʊð
545. draʊθ
546. draʊt

547. aʊns
548. aʊtʃ
549. aʊsts
550. taʊn
551. raʊnd
552. graʊnd
553. braʊnd
554. faʊnd
555. fraʊnz
556. 'aʊtfɪt
557. 'maʊðɪŋ
558. 'aʊtsɛt
559. 'aʊtlaɪnz
560. aʊt'saɪd
561. 'haɪbraʊ
562. 'laɪthaʊs
563. 'hwaɪthaʊs
564. 'aʊtredʒ
565. 'ʊmlaʊt
566. ko'taʊ
567. 'aʊtworn
568. ɔɪ
569. kɔɪ
570. bɔɪ
571. bɔɪz
572. tɔɪ
573. tɔɪz
574. ɔɪl
575. bɔɪl
576. tɔɪl
577. dʒɔɪ
578. dʒɔɪn
579. dʒɔɪnd
580. dʒɔɪst
581. dʒɔɪsts
582. 'ɔnɪŋ
583. 'ɔɪlɪŋ
584. 'dɔnɪŋ
585. 'dɔɪlɪ
586. spɔn
587. spɔɪl
588. sɔɪld
589. dɪ'kɔɪ
590. dɪ'plɔɪ
591. 'tʃɔɪsɪz
592. 'sɔɪbin
593. 'bɔɪskaʊts
594. 'kɑnvɔɪ
595. 'fɔɪe
596. saɪ
597. sɔɪ
598. saʊ
599. baʊ
600. baɪ
601. bɔɪ
602. 'boɪ(transition from [o] to [ɪ] considered discrete enough to be syllabic division; therefore, accent required)
603. raɪ
604. raʊ
605. rɔɪ
606. daɪ
607. 'doɪ
608. aɪl
609. aʊl
610. ɔɪl
611. fɔɪl
612. faɪl
613. faʊl
614. 'buɪ
615. 'fluɪd
616. 'ruɪn
617. 'druɪd
618. 'dʒuɪʃ
619. dʒʊ'deɪk
620. 'deɪs
621. 'keɑs
622. o'esɪs
623. 'taʊɪst
624. 'haʊz
625. 'lɪkwɪdz
626. ɪn'sɪpɪdlɪ
627. bɪ'kwið
628. 'sɪgnɪt
629. prɪ'vedɪd
630. 'sævɪdʒ
631. 'kredl̩z
632. 'ɔspɪsɪz
633. 'graftɪd
634. 'pɑrtrɪdʒɪz
635. rɪ'ske
636. 'jɑrdɑrm
637. 'dʒɛsɪ
638. 'rɪfraf
639. 'sɒftbɔl
640. 'tæksɪkæbz
641. 'pleket
642. 'æŋgrɪɪst
643. kɔr'tɛʒ
644. kwɪk'sɑtɪk
645. 'bɛlɪlaf
646. 'hændrɪtn̩
647. re'ʒim
648. ʃæŋgrɪ'lɑ
649. 'læŋgwɪdʒ
650. 'rædɪʃɪz
651. blɑ'ze

652. blæs'fim
653. 'protɪɪn
654. 'dʒɪgsɔ
655. 'rævɪʃɪŋ
656. 'lafɪŋlɪ
657. 'flæksɪd
658. 'kæfɪɪn
659. 'ɛnɪhwɛr
660. 'glasɪz
661. 'ɑnslɔt
662. 'sɑlɪsɪzm̩
663. lærɪn'gɑlodʒɪ
664. ɑf'θælmɪk
665. ɑksɪ'morɑn
666. 'lɑrdʒɛst
667. 'ɛksɪtɛd
668. 'lɑrdʒɛs
669. 'lɑrdʒɪst
670. ɛlɪ'fæntɪn
671. eʒɪ'ætɪk
672. 'sjudonɪm
673. 'lɪθograf
674. hwɛ'ræz
675. 'sɑfomor
676. 'lɪpruʒ
677. 'kɑntjʊmilɪ
678. ɛks'jud
679. daɪ'æstoli
680. ʌnɪm'prɛst
681. 'lʌkʃʊrɪ
682. 'ɛrʊdaɪt
683. 'dɛzɪgnet
684. 'ɛm'si
685. 'pʌŋktʃʊet
686. mɪ'nʌskjul
687. 'menɪæk
688. nɑr'kɑtɪk
689. 'ɑbvɪet
690. 'gɑrdn̩paθ
691. dɪ'pɑzɪtɪd
692. 'klɑzɪtɛd
693. 'mɑdjul
694. 'mɑdʒʊlet
695. sɛmɪɔto'mætɪk
696. aɪ'æmbɪk
697. 'dʒuvɪnɪl
698. 'mʌzlɪn
699. 'mɑzlɪm
700. mu'laʒ

Reading Exercise for All Sounds Except Schwa

1. 'sɪkstin mɛn hɝdɪm.
2. kɒfɪ 'wɪð krim, pliz.
3. tek 'ðɪs wɪð ju.
4. ðɪ edʒ hwɛn 'bjutɪ ɛbz ɪz 'nɑt wʌn hwɪtʃ 'plizɪz.
5. mek 'ʃʊr jʊ du ðiz θɪŋz ðɪs we 'onlɪ.
6. sɝtʃ fɔrɪt 'ɛvrɪhwɛr.
7. tek twɛntɪ mɪnɪts fɔr itʃ 'ɪmprɑmptju spitʃ.
8. ðozmɛtl̩z pruv 'sɒft hwɛn smæʃt bɪtwin 'tu 'stil 'dʒɔz.
9. 'mɛnɪ lɒst θɪŋz wɪl bɪ rɪtɝnd 'kwɪklɪ.
10. notɪs ðiz strɛndʒ 'tʃɛndʒɪz ɪn pɑstʃʊr.
11. θæŋkɪm 'kwɪklɪ bɪforɪ 'livz.
12. hɪz past simz 'rɪtʃ ɪn tivi 'vjuɪŋ.
13. hɪ tɔks mʌtʃ wɪð 'gosts.
14. 'strɛndʒ ɑbdʒɪkts me bɪ vjud; ðiz wɪl bɪ mɪ'rɑʒɪz.
15. dontʃʊ θɪŋkiz 'rɒŋ?
16. 'lʊk hu kemɪn bɪfor 'ju dɪd.
17. rumætɪk penz me bɪ rɪlivd wɪð 'hit læmps.
18. ʃɪ lʊks 'wɜrɪd, 'sɪk n̩ 'dold.

19. 'tru lʌv pruvz 'bold; 'fɔls lʌv pruvz 'wik.
20. hæv 'kɜrɪdʒ; ðɛn jʊl 'gen jʊr gol.
21. bɪdɪŋ ɪn brɪdʒ ɪz ɑr'tɪstɪklɪ dʌn bɪtwin 'ɛkspɝts.
22. tɝn 'lɛft 'fɝst; ðɛn go 'tu blɑks.
23. wʊdʒʊ pliz rɪtɝnɪz 'sɪutkes?
24. 'rɪðmɪk tasks me rɪstorɪz hɛlθ.
25. du jʊr ʃuz nid 'fɪksɪŋ?

Transcription Exercise for All Sounds Except Schwa

1. θraɪvd
2. 'dʌlsɪt
3. 'haɪɪst
4. 'ɒfʃut
5. ʌn'kloðd
6. 'aʊtredʒ
7. 'jɛlod
8. dʒo'kos
9. 'bɔɪ skaʊts
10. 'kwɪk 'friz
11. 'haɪbraʊ
12. 'hʌkl̩bɛrɪ
13. 'wɝkbʊk
14. 'pegn̩
15. kɔ'lɑʒ
16. 'lʌgɪdʒ
17. 'dʒʌŋgl̩
18. ɛn'dʒɔɪnd
19. 'haftaɪm
20. 'flɜrɪʃɪz
21. 'mætʃʊret
22. 'kɝfju
23. 'poɪtrɪ
24. 'laɪvlɪhʊd
25. ɑb'skjur
26. 'bjugl̩
27. 'æpodʒi
28. 'ædvokɪt
29. 'slɜrɪŋ
30. 'ɔspɪsɪz
31. 'kɑnsol
32. fjutʃʊ'rɪstɪk
33. 'tɜrɪts
34. 'mjutɪd
35. 'rʌsɪt
36. 'ɝnɪstlɪ
37. kɑz'mɛtɪks
38. 'nɑkaʊt
39. 'kʌzn̩
40. 'ʌŋkl̩
41. 'kæmoflɑʒ
42. 'ɑpozɪt
43. 'mʊrɪʃ
44. 'saɪklon
45. 'aʊtworn
46. 'æksɪs
47. kjʊ'bɪstɪk
48. θwɔrts
49. dɪs'kaʊnts
50. pro'dɪus
51. 'netʃʊr
52. 'hɑrmonaɪz
53. 'θɝzdɪ
54. 'hupɪŋ kɒf
55. dɪ'vɝdʒd
56. 'nɔrwe
57. skwɛltʃt
58. 'hwɝlwɪnd
59. 'pɔrkjʊpaɪn
60. 'dʒɔbon
61. 'pʌŋktʃʊrd
62. 'bɔɪkɑt
63. 'rɛgjʊlet
64. 'ɑksaɪd
65. 'ʃrɑpʃɪr
66. 'dʒɝzɪaɪt
67. bʊrʒ'wɑ
68. 'kɜrɪɪŋ
69. 'felæŋks
70. 'vjupɔɪnt
71. 'rɒŋlɪ
72. 'jultaɪd
73. 'stɛrɪotaɪp
74. 'lʊkaʊt
75. jʊ'naɪtɪd 'stets
76. 'kjurɪo
77. 'kɑmjʊnɪst
78. 'æʒʊr
79. skɪud
80. 'mɜrɪn
81. 'juʒʊrɪ
82. ɑksɪ'morɑn
83. 'bjurokræt
84. mjurɪ'ætɪk

85. 'gɝnzɪ
86. 'fɔrmjʊli
87. 'wɝmwʊd
88. 'ʊmlaʊt
89. 'kɑrbʌŋkl̩
90. 'ɔrɪndʒ
91. popu'ri
92. so'te
93. 'ʃumæk
94. 'bʊdɪzm̩
95. 'egju
96. tʊ'kɑn
97. 'dɛswɪtɪud
98. 'faɪæt
99. vɪ'rego
100. 'lændɔ

Reading Exercise for All Sounds

1. ə'gri
2. ə'piz
3. ə'fred
4. ə'klem
5. ə'mezd
6. ə'drɛs
7. ə'rɛst
8. ə'lɛkt
9. ə'dʌlt
10. ə'baɪd
11. ə'raɪv
12. ə'laɪz
13. ə'raʊz
14. ə'raʊnd
15. ə'maʊnts
16. 'irə
17. 'eʒə
18. 'plæzmə
19. 'ɛmə
20. 'rʌʃə
21. 'mænə
22. 'drɑmə
23. 'æzmə
24. 'kɑmən
25. 'sæmən
26. 'lɛmən
27. 'opən
28. 'ɔrfən
29. 'ɒfən
30. 'eʒən
31. 'liʒən
32. 'oʃən
33. 'moʃən
34. 'kwoʃənt
35. 'fʌŋkʃən
36. 'fistɛd
37. 'fistɪd
38. 'fistəd
39. 'hetɛd
40. 'hetəd
41. 'bestɪd
42. 'westəd
43. 'testɪd
44. 'rʌstəd
45. 'sizɪz
46. 'tizəz
47. 'fesɛz
48. 'lesɪz
49. 'kɔzəz
50. 'pedʒɪz
51. 'pasəz
52. pə'lis
53. prə'tɛkt
54. pro'vaɪd
55. də'tɛkt
56. tə'ren
57. bə'sun
58. ə'bjuzd
59. kən'vʌlst
60. ə'naʊns
61. sə'kʌm
62. gə'rɑʒ
63. mə'staʃ
64. kən'daɪn
65. də'vʌldʒd
66. kən'faʊnd
67. 'vɑljəm
68. 'nʌpʃəl
69. 'junək
70. 'wʊmən
71. 'hærəs
72. 'holsəm
73. 'kɔkəs
74. 'rɔkəs
75. 'lɛŋθən
76. 'strɛŋθən
77. 'kworəm
78. 'hɛrəld
79. 'grivəs
80. 'bɔlsəm
81. 'reʃən
82. 'ɔkʃen
83. 'trækʃən
84. 'ʌŋkʃən
85. 'sæŋkʃən
86. 'dʒʌŋkʃən
87. 'kwoʃənt

88. 'bɛstʃəl
89. 'kɔrdʒəl
90. 'nɪutrəl
91. 'bʌfəlo
92. 'lɛvətɪ
93. 'junətɪ
94. 'dɛkəret
95. 'ɛvərɪ
96. 'grosərɪ
97. sɪgə'rɛt
98. 'ɑpəret
99. 'ɪləstret
100. 'θɛrəpɪ
101. 'sɪmfənɪ
102. 'hɛkətɑm
103. mægə'zin
104. dɪsə'bil
105. 'kwɑrəntin
106. mɛzə'nin
107. 'dræmətɪst
108. 'ɛkspədaɪt
109. kɑnə'sɝ
110. 'vɛrəfaɪ
111. 'julədʒɪ
112. 'junəvɝs
113. 'mʌltətɪud
114. 'saɪnəkjur
115. 'kwɛrjʊləs
116. 'mɛlədɪ
117. 'rɛmədɪɪŋ
118. 'ɛnvəlop
119. 'sɛləbret
120. 'ɑrkətɛkt
121. 'wʊmənhʊd
122. 'ɛksəkɪut
123. 'dʒuvənɪl
124. 'eprəl
125. 'nesənt
126. o'besəns
127. 'ɛksələnt
128. 'ɪmpotənt
129. 'prɛzədənts
130. lɒŋ'dɪstəns
131. 'pjuɪsəns
132. 'ɪnfəntaɪl
133. 'ɛkspədaɪt
134. 'pærəsaɪts
135. ə'lɛktrɪk
136. də'tɛktɪvz
137. də'rɛktɪvz
138. ə'klaɪmɪt
139. nɪr'vɑnə
140. bə'nænə
141. kən'doləns
142. ə'spaɪrənt
143. kən'vɪkʃən
144. 'ɪmpɪəs
145. 'mɪskrɪənt
146. ɪn'ʃʊrəns
147. sə'dɪʃən
148. kə'redʒəs
149. ɪn'klɛmənt
150. 'tɛnəmənts
151. 'tʊrnəmənt
152. ɪ'lɪuʒən
153. 'kænərɪ
154. 'kwɑndərɪ
155. 'baʊndərɪ
156. 'bɛvərɪdʒ
157. 'mɑkərɪ
158. 'kæmərə
159. 'kɑlərə
160. 'lɪtərəl
161. 'fjunərəl
162. 'næʃənəl
163. 'ræʃənəl
164. 'strɛnjʊəs
165. 'tɛnjʊəs
166. lɒŋ'ʃormən
167. 'ɛnɪwən
168. 'kjupolə
169. kaɪ'mɪərə
170. 'ebl̩
171. 'tebl̩
172. 'pærəbl̩
173. 'lɔdəbl̩
174. 'pasəbl̩
175. aɪ'ræsəbl̩
176. 'vaɪə
177. 'vaɪədʌkt
178. 'viəkl̩
179. 'viəmənt
180. 'ɑrɪə
181. 'hæərɪ
182. 'hɛərɪ
183. 'æərɪd
184. 'ɛərɪd
185. 'skæərɪ
186. 'skɛərɪ
187. 'fɛərɪ
188. 'fæərɪ
189. və'gæərɪ
190. hɪ'dʒaɪrə
191. rə'fɜrəl
192. 'pɝsəkjut
193. hwɛə'rɑv
194. 'hwɛəræz
195. ikə'nɑmɪk
196. æpə'retəs
197. jʊ'tɪlətɪ
198. jʊ'renɪəm
199. 'dɛsəltorɪ
200. 'hɑspɪtəbl̩
201. 'dɛspɪkəbl̩

202. ɪm'plekəbl̩
203. 'romənɪzm̩
204. 'kætəkɪzm̩
205. 'vɪʒənɛrɪ
206. 'tɛləvɪʒən
207. 'mɪnɪətʃʊr
208. 'lɪtərətʃʊr
209. æŋ'zaɪətɪ
210. 'dɪkʃənɛrɪ
211. jʊ'topɪə
212. dɪf'θɪərɪə
213. pɪ'ræmədəl
214. 'kwɑlətetɪv
215. bonə'faɪdɪ
216. 'vaɪsə'vɝsə
217. kə'pɪtʃʊlet
218. θɛrə'pjutɪk
219. prɪ'kɛərɪəs
220. 'praɪmərəlɪ
221. əg'zɛmplərɪ
222. ə'blɪgətorɪ
223. ək'spɛrəmənt
224. ə'stɑnɪʃmənt
225. frezɪ'ɑlədʒɪ
226. 'ɪnterɛstɪd
227. ɔg'zɪljərɪ
228. ɪndɪ'fætəgəbl̩
229. sækrə'lidʒəs
230. kən'grætʃʊlet
231. ɪ'nɛksplɪkəbl̩
232. æd ɪnfə'naɪtəm
233. ək'strɔrdənɛrɪ
234. 'ekɚ
235. 'kwekɚ
236. 'lɑkɚ
237. 'kulɚ
238. 'sʌfɚ
239. 'ʃevɚ
240. 'dʒæbɚ
241. 'ʌðɚ
242. 'sʌðən
243. 'kʌstɚd
244. 'wʌndɚd
245. 'skwɑlɚ
246. 'plʌndʒɚ
247. 'pɝʒən
248. 'hwɪspɚd
249. 'hʌŋgɚ
250. 'pɑvɚtɪ
251. 'ekɚz
252. 'ekərɪdʒ (acreage)
253. 'ekɚ rɪdʒ (*Acre* Ridge)
254. 'lɛvɚz
255. 'lɛvərɪdʒ
256. pə'red
257. pɚ'swed
258. 'pɝ'si
259. pɚ'siv
260. kɝz
261. 'dɪkɚz
262. lɪ'kɝ
263. 'lɪkɚ
264. tɝn
265. 'pætɚn
266. nɝs
267. 'nɝsɚ
268. 'nɝsərɪ
269. 'kɝsərɪ
270. ɪɚ
271. 'ɪərɪ
272. tʃɪɚz
273. 'jɪɚlɪ
274. 'jɪɚlɪŋ
275. 'bɪɚdɪd
276. kə'rɪɚ
277. sə'vɪr
278. ə'rɪrz
279. prɪ'mɪɚ
280. 'primɪɚ
281. bʌkə'nɪɚ
282. 'trævɚs
283. 'kwɔrtɚ
284. æɚ
285. ɛɚ
286. 'æərɪ
287. 'skɛɚ
288. ʃæɚd
289. 'ræɚlɪ
290. dɪ'klɛɚ
291. skwæɚd
292. pre'pɛɚ
293. 'brʌðɚlɪ
294. 'kʌləful
295. 'ʌðɚwaɪz
296. 'θiətɚ
297. 'sɪŋgjəlɚ
298. 'gʌvnmənt
299. 'aftɚwɚdz
300. 'wʊstɚʃɪr
301. sjʊ'pɝfluəs
302. 'pɝkəletɚ
303. ælmə'metɚ
304. əd'vɝtɪzmənt
305. mɪs 'smɪθ
306. mɪ's:mɪθ (see p. 19)
307. 'fɪʃ ʃɛd
308. 'fɪʃ:ɛd
309. ʌ'n:on
310. ʌ'n:idɪd
311. ʌ'n:oɪŋ

312. ʌn'ond
313. mɪ's:ɛnt
314. mɪ's:pɛnt
315. dɪ's:ɝvɪs
316. 'wi sim:ɛrɪ
317. wɪð:ɪs'rɪŋ
318. 'bɪl:aɪktɪt
319. go wɪ'ð:ɛm
320. hɪ wɪ'l:uz
321. ðe bɪhev:ɛrɪ 'wɛl
322. ɪ'm:ɑdɪst
323. nɑ'n:etɪv
324. ʌ'n:ætʃʊrəl
325. kænze's:ɪtɪ
326. ʌ'n:otɪsəbl̩
327. bɔ̃[5]
328. e'lɑ̃
329. ɑ̃'swit
330. ɑ̃'priz
331. sə'vɑ̃
332. ɑ̃n'tɑ̃nt
333. mizɑ̃'sɑ̃
334. ɑ̃pɑ'sɑ̃
335. pɑ̃'ʃɑ̃
336. de'numɑ̃
337. bɔ̃vi'vɑ̃
338. ɑ̃pɛ'naʒ
339. ʃez'lɔ̃
340. kru'tɔ̃
341. gar'sɔ̃
342. ogrə'tæ̃
343. læ̃ʒə'ri
344. ʔit (see p. 14)
345. ʔaɪ
346. 'ʔæksɪs
347. 'ʔetθs
348. 'ʔaʊtsaɪd
349. 'ʔɔkwɚd
350. 'let̬ɝ (see p. 12)
351. 'bɛt̬ɚ
352. 'kæt̩ɪ
353. bɛt̬ɪ
354. bɑt̬l̩
355. sʌt̬l̩
356. 'æktəvet̬ɚ
357. mjurɪ'æt̬ɪk
358. 'tfɑrlz̥ (see p. 12)
359. bɝdz̥
360. biz̥
361. 'lʌvɚz̥
362. 'kɔz̥we
363. 'pɪkl̩
364. 'ʔoʃən
365. 'vɝsɪz̥
366. 'rælfən 'dɛlənɚ
367. 'hɪə rɪ tɪz.
368. wʌnsəpəne 'taɪm
369. 'θɝzdɪ ðə fɪfθəv 'fɛbrʊɛrɪ

370. dontʃʊ wɔntʃʊr 'sæləd?
371. 'ðɛɚ bət fɚ ðə gresəv 'gɑd goz 'gɑd.
372. hjumənzɚ ðɪ onlɪ kritʃɚz hʊ kən 'blʌʃ—ɚ 'nid tʊ.
373. 'petrɪətɪzm̩ əz ðə last rɛfjudʒəvə 'skaʊndrəl.
374. ə'roz baɪ ɛnɪ'ʌðɚ nem, sʌtʃəz 'gæŋgrin,
375. wəd smɛləz 'swit ɪfjʊ dɪdn̩t 'no ðɪ ʌðɚ wɝd.
376. pʊtʃʊr nem ɒn ðə 'dɑtɪd 'laɪn.
377. jʊl faɪnd ðə'mɛvrɪhwɛ rɪf jʊ dʒʌst 'lʊk fɚ ðəm.
378. ðɛrə ronlɪ 'tu taɪpsəv pipl̩—'ðoz hʊ pʊt pipl̩ ɪntʊ tu taɪps ənd ðoz ðət 'dont.
379. ɪtwəzə taɪməv:ɛrɪ 'klin bɑdɪzən dɝtɪ 'maɪndz.
380. hɪ toldəv:ærɪəs:ʌbdʒɪksɪn hwɪtʃɪ wə 'zɪntərɛstɪd.
381. bɝtn̩ daɪ wɛn tə 'taʊn.
382. ʃɪ mæərɪdɪm fɚ 'lʌv—əvɪz'mʌnɪ.

[5] A tilde [~] means that the vowel is produced with nasality (see p. 170).

383. dont prənauns pɪ'ænɪst 'piənɪst.
384. mʌnɪ kænt baɪ 'ɛvərɪθɪŋ—fɚ 'wʌn θɪŋ, 'pɑvɚtɪ.
385. jʊ kænt mekə 'nɑmlɪt wɪðaʊt 'brekɪŋ 'ɛgz.
386. gɛtɪŋ mæərɪd ət 'mɪd sə'mɛstə rɪz pʊtɪŋ ðə 'hɑrt bəfor ðə 'kors.
387. aʊ'r:ɑkɪt lɔntʃɪŋzəfɛkt ðɪ ɔrbɪtəv ðɪ 'ɝθ.
388. bɛt̬ɪ lɪt̬l̩ɪz 'prɪt̬ɪ 'kæt̬ɪ.
389. hɪ kə'n:aʊ se "ə nɔ̃ɪzɪ̃ ɔ̃ɪstɚ" wɪðaʊt ə 'tresəv nezælətɪ,
390. 'bʌt ɪts ðə 'dɑrndɪst ðɪŋ tə traɪ tə wɝkɪntʊ ə kɑnvɚ'seʃən.
391. hɪ lʌvz hjʊ'mænətɪ bət hets 'mɛn.
392. ə'skep vəlɑsətɪ ɪz 'twɛntɪ 'faɪv 'θaʊzənd maɪlz pəraʊɚ.
393. ɪt gozɪntʊ 'ɔrbɪt hwən sɛn'trɪfəgl̩ forsikwəlz ðə forsəv 'grævətɪ.
394. se sɛn'trɪfjʊgl̩, nɑt sɛn'trɪfəgl̩.
395. ɪtsə pɪtɪ ðət juθɪz westɪdɒn 'tʃɪldrɪn.
396. bɛtɑn 'gɑd—jʊv gɑt nʌθɪŋ tə 'luzən dɛ'vrɪθɪŋ tə 'gen.
397. ɔl mɛnə'rikwəl, bət sʌmɚ mo rikwəl ðə 'nʌðɚz.
398. hɪ raɪts:o 'mʌtʃ ðətʃʊd θɪŋk hɪd ræðɚ bɪ 'rɛd ðən 'dɛd.
399. dont kənfjuzə 'nopən maɪnd wɪðə 'nɛmptɪ wən.
400. ðɪ 'izɪɪst ækʃən me'nat bɪ ðə'kwɪkɪst wən.

Reading Exercise for All Sounds

1. 'kɑnsənənts med wɪð:ə 'tʌŋ 'tɪp dʒʌstə'bʌv ðɪ 'ʌpɚ 'gʌm 'rɪdʒ.
2. 'saʊndz 'gretlɪ dɪpɛndəntɒn ðə 'nezəl 'kævətɪ əzə 'rɛzənetɚ.
3. 'saʊndz hwɪtʃɚ 'dɪfəkʌltə 'klasəfaɪ əz 'stɑpsɚ kən'tɪnjʊənts.

1. glaɪdz
2. 'frɪkətɪvz
3. æl'viələz
4. 'plosɪvz
5. 'nezəlz

4. 'saʊndz hwɪtʃ fʌŋkʃənəzə'nɪʃɪetɪŋ ənd 'tɝmənetɪŋ pɑrtsəv 'sɪləbl̩z.
5. 'saʊndz 'nɑt verɪ dəpɛndəntɒn 'lɪp pəzɪʃən.
6. 'saʊndzɪn hwɪtʃ ðə 'brɛθɪz kəm'plitlɪ əb'strʌktɪd.

1. 'frʌnt vaʊəlz
2. 'bæk vaʊəlz
3. 'kɑnsənənts
4. stɑps
5. kən'tɪnjʊənts

7. 'hwɪtʃ pæərəv saʊndz dɪfə'ronlɪ ɪn 'vɔɪsɪŋ?
8. 'hwɪtʃ pæərəv saʊndz dɪfə'ronlɪ ɪn 'plesəvɑrtɪkjəleʃən?
9. 'hwɪtʃ pæərəv saʊndz dɪfə'ronlɪ ɪn 'mænərəvɑrtɪkjəleʃən?

1. ʒ–ʃ
2. k–s
3. l–ŋ
4. n–d
5. ð–ʒ

10. 'hwɪtʃ wɝd bɪgɪnz wɪðə 'vɔɪslɪs 'frɪkətɪv?
11. 'hwɪtʃ wɝd bɪgɪnz wɪðə 'vilɚ 'plosɪv?
12. 'hwɪtʃ wɝd bɪgɪnz wɪðə 'nezəl?

1. jump
2. pneumonia
3. who
4. question
5. then

13. 'hwɪtʃ wɝd 'ɛndzɪnə 'vaʊəl?
14. 'hwɪtʃ wɝdəz 'nɑt kəntenə 'vilɚ 'nezəl?
15. 'hwɪtʃ wɝd 'ɛndzɪnə 'vɔɪst 'kɑnsənənt?

1. sponge
2. trinket
3. anxious
4. conquer
5. strength

16. 'hwɪtʃ wɝdəz 'nɑt kəntenə 'vɔɪst baɪ'lebɪəl 'glaɪd?
17. ɪn 'hwɪtʃ wɝdəz ðə 'sem 'vaʊəl rɪ'pitɪd?
18. 'hwɪtʃ wɝd ɛndzənə 'vaʊəl saʊnd?

1. one
2. swell
3. answered
4. quickly
5. choirs

19. 'hwɪtʃ wɝdɪzɪnkə'rɛkt bɪkɔzə kɑnsənəntɪzo'mɪtɪd?
20. 'hwɪtʃ wɝdɪzɪnkə'rɛkt bɪkɔzə kɑnsənəntɪ'zædɪd?
21. 'hwɪtʃ wɝdɪzɪnkə'rɛkt bɪkɔzə kɑnsənəntɪzʌn'vɔɪst?

1. 'pɪkʌl
2. 'tʃozn̩
3. 'fɪŋɚ
4. briðs
5. rudʒ

22. ɪn 'hwɪtʃ wɝdɪz ðə 'vɔɪstæl'viəlɚ 'plosɪv 'list 'ɔdəbl?
23. 'hwɪtʃ wɝd me sim tə kəntenə 'vɔɪstæl'viəlɚ 'plosɪv dju tə 'vɔɪsɪŋ?
24. 'hwɪtʃ wɝdəz 'nɑt kəntenə 'vɔɪstæl'viəlɚ 'plosɪv?
25. 'hwɪtʃ wɝd kəntenzə 'vɔɪst 'vilɚ 'plosɪv?

1. extraordinary
2. lettered
3. existed
4. rinsed
5. excited
6. finds

ə 'kjurɪəs 'kʌpl̩[6]

ʌndɚ ðɪ 'æʒʊr krautʃtənɪn'dɪspjʊtəbl̩ 'ɪndɪən. hɪz 'fɑrɛd wəz bɪdɪzn̩d wɪðɝbɪdʒ, ən dɪ worə 'skɑrlɪt bɛltəbautɪzæb'domɪn. ðo ɪz kɑndʌktwə zəg'zɛmplərɪ ən 'dɛkərəs, hɪ lɪvd 'vɑlənterəlɪ ɪnək'strɔrdənɛrɪ 'skwɑlɚ.

ðo, laɪkə 'petrɪət, fəmɪljɚ wɪð:ə traɪbəl:ɛdʒəndz hɪz pæərəntsəd tɔtɪm, hɪ nju 'lɪtl̩ bəjɑnd 'lɛdʒəndɛrɪ 'lor, ənd wə'zɪgnərəntivənəvɪz 'nebɚz, ənd 'vaɪsə 'vɝsə.

hɪ nju nʌθɪŋ əv 'lɪtərətʃʊr, ənd vɛrɪ lɪtl̩ əbaʊt fɪ'næns. hɪ wəz 'nɑtənə 'spaɪrənt fɚ 'pɑrləmənt, bətɪ hoptə 'ɛksɔrsaɪz ivl̩ spɪrɪts frəm ðɪ 'irə baɪ ðɪ əd'vɝtɪzməntəvə'nɪndɪən 'sækrəfaɪs. hwən grantədə 'fevɚ, hɪ sɔt ðɪ əpɑθɪ'osɪsəvɪz 'petrən.

ə 'pikəntənd 'kɑntrɛrɪ 'metrən baɪ ɪz saɪd wəzɪz 'haʊswaɪf, tə humɪ gev 'ɔltɚnɪtlɪ ə 'migɚ 'mentənənsənd pə'rɛmptərɪ kə'mandz, fɚ hɪ kənsɪdɚd ðə pə'zɪʃən ɪ'rɛfrəgəbl̩, ðætʊ pɚ'fɛktə wʊmən ʃɪ məst bɪ 'pinəlaɪzd 'æd ɪnfə'naɪtəm. ɒn ðɪs pɔɪntɪ kənsɪdɚdɪzɑrgjʊməntsɪ'rɛfjʊtəbl̩ ənd 'nʌnəvɪzidɪkts 'rɛvəkəbl̩. hɪ əpɪrd tə kæɚ 'lɪtl̩ fɚ haɪməniəl 'hɑrmənɪ. 'hɝ pɪkjulɪærətɪ wəz brɑn'kaɪtəs, hwɪtʃɪ hoptə 'kjur baɪ lɔntʃɪŋ ə taɪnɪ 'ræzbɛrɪ ɪntə ðɪ ɪn'tɝstɪsɪzəvɚ 'lærɪŋks. ðə 'tu medə 'skwɑlɪd bə'tɪntərəstɪŋ 'tæblo.

ðə 'dræmətɪs pɚ'soni əv ðɪs:ə'næərɪo wɚ nemd 'ɛlɪhju (elɪəs 'renənðə 'fes) ənd mɪnɪ'hɑhɑ, hɪz waɪf. hwaɪl ʃi wəz no pɪ'ænɪst, ʃɪ wəzə 'djutəfəl waɪf. hɪ wəz glæd tə hævərəzɪz ko'ædʒətɚ. 'jɛtɪnɚ 'lonlɪ laɪf hɪ wədɒfən 'hærəsɚ wɪð sʌm sɑr'dɑnɪkɪn'kwaɪrɪ ɚ wɪðə 'vɪrjələnt 'θrɛtə pʊtərɪn 'dʒel. ʃi wəd ðɛn 'pleketɪm baɪ kʊkɪŋ fɔrɪm səm 'flæksɪd 'swit pə'tetoz fraɪdɪnolɪo'mɑrdʒərin, hopɪŋ hɪ wəd no lɒŋgɚ tritərəzə pə'raɪə.

ðɪ'sæntik gɝl sætɒfənɒn ðɛr 'pɑtɪo, itɪŋ ə'tæljə'nɑməndz, ənd mjuzɪŋ ovərɛso'tɛrɪk və'gɛərɪz. hɚ 'tɛmpɚ wəzəz 'tʃɛndʒəbələz ðə hjuzevə kə'miljən. ənætətɪudəv 'læŋgərɪndəketədə nidəv kən'doləns, ərəve'lɑpəθɪ, əndɚ 'hæɚ, wornɪn pə'ræmədəl staɪl, medɚ ðə 'saɪnəʃʊrəv ðə 'traɪb. hɚ tætɚdə'meljən hʌzbənd wəd 'laʊndʒɪnɪz 'wʊstɪd 'brɪtʃɪz θruaʊt ðə 'lɪvlɒŋ 'de, sɪtɪŋ 'krɒs 'lɛgədɒnə tɑr'pɔlɪn sprɛdovərɪz ʃez 'lɔ̃ŋ, əndət 'naɪtfɔl hɪ wəd

[6] By permission from G. & C. Merriam Co., publishers of the Merriam-Webster Dictionaries.

bəgɪnənə'drɛs tə hɚ, wɪð:ə grə'mesəzən 'dʒɪbərɪʃəvə 'rʌfɪən. 'ðʌs:

"'ʌg! 'wek tə jʊr 'djutɪ, ənd bɪ ə 'dɑsələnd 'klɛnlɪ skwɔ. brɪŋ maɪ 'ʃɛvrəle 'ʃæsɪ, ənd lɛts rə'liv sʌm 'grænərɪ əvɪts 'prɑdjus."

tə hwɪtʃ:i, wɪð 'grɪm 'relərɪ, rə'plaɪd: "ju 'bletənt 'blægɚd, aɪ 'wont. jʊr 'kɑmbətənt 'mænərən 'trʌkjələnt kə'mandzɚ 'nɑtə'blɪgətorɪ ɒn mɪ. ɪtwəd əg'zɔst maɪ 'strɛŋθən'dɛnɚvet maɪ kɑnstə'tɪuʃən; 'niðɚ hævaɪ 'drɑptə sʌtʃə dɪ'gri əv də'kedənsəz tə bi ə 'kɑmjənɪst."

ðɛnɪ 'kokst: "'du, dɪɚ, əndaɪl gɪv jʊ ə bu'ke əndə 'brotʃəv 'daɪəməndz. ju ʃəl faɪndɪtə 'dʒɑkəndənd 'nɑtə 'dɑlərəs task. juɚ so ə'klaɪmətəd ðət ðə 'naɪtæɚ wəl nɑt 'hɝtʃʊ, ənd jʊɚ 'kɑnvɚsənt wɪð maɪ 'grivəs 'tɛmpɚ hwənə'raʊzd." bət ʃɪ wəzɪm'plekəbl̩.

'brændɪʃɪŋ ə 'fɛrul, hi ðɛn 'ʃaʊtɪd wɪð 'viəməns: "hwɑt! ʃælaɪ 'nɑt hæv prə'sidənsənd 'hɑmɪdʒ baɪ maɪ on 'hɑrθston? aɪl 'titʃʊ ðə rə'mænsəv 'mætrəmonɪ, aɪl titʃʊ tə 'ɝ, əndaɪl gɪv jʊr 'ʃɔrt'laɪvd 'bonzovɚ fɚ 'sɛpəltʃʊr!"

bʌt ʃɪ swɪtlɪ rəplaɪd: "lʊkaʊt fɚ jʊr 'ɔrθoəpɪ, maɪ 'lʌv, əraɪl 'tɛɚ jʊr 'rɪstbænd!"

ðə 'ʃɛrɪfs dɪ'lɛmə[7]

"fɔrmə 'pɑsɪ!" ʃaʊtəd ðə ro'bʌst 'ʃɛrɪf. "ə most 'fɔrmədəbl̩ 'brɪgəndɪzət lɑrdʒ."

"ɪz 'hwɛɚ?" askt ðə kən'trolɚ, laɪɪŋ ɒnə 'nɛkskwɪzɪt 'daɪvæn. hɪ wə zən'dʒɔɪɪŋ ə 'rɛspɪt frəm ðə wərɪzəv fɪ'næns.

"jʊ tʃɪmpæn'zi," rəplaɪd ðə ʃɛrəf, næʃɪŋɪz tiθ, "jʊrɪgnərənsɪz 'læməntəbl̩, ən 'grivəs, ən . . ."

"ɪrə'midɪəbl̩," səplaɪdɪzɪnkɑmpərəbl̩ 'dɛpjʊtɪ, hʊ 'hetɪd ðə kəntrolɚ fɚ 'daɪvɚz kozɪz. wɪðə'nædmərəbl̩ twɪstə hɪz mə'staʃ, hɪ kən'tɪnjud, "ənlɛsaɪ 'ɝ, ðə 'dʒɪbɪt, ənɛlə'fæntɪn 'traɪpɑd, ɪz 'rɛdɪ, ʃɛrəf. lɛts 'ɛnd ðɪs lɑn'dʒɛvətɪ əvaʊɚ bɑrbərəs brɪgənd."

"hɪ minz 'lɛvətɪ," rord ðə kəntrolɚ. bət ðe əd 'lɛft, kærɪɪŋ wɪð gret 'trævel ə tɑr'pɔlɪnəndə 'tipi.

aftɚ pasɪŋ ə 'kɑməndɑntəndɪz 'kor, hʊ ɒfɚd minzəv kən'daɪn

[7] By permission from G. & C. Merriam Co., publishers of the Merriam-Webster Dictionaries.

'pʌnɪʃmənt—bət no 'hɛlpɚ 'vɪtl̩z—ðe 'həltɪd ðɛrək'skɝʒən fɚ 'kjulənɛrɪ 'pɝpəsɪz, əl'biɪt ðe ə'donlɪ 'wʌn 'vɛdʒətəbl̩, səm pɪ'kænz, ə 'sæmən, ən lɪtl̩ 'vɛnəzən.

"wɪ məst rɛsl̩ wɪð:ɪs 'fɝðɚ," bæd ðə 'ʃɛrɪfɪnɪzə'drɛs.

"aɪ," rəspɑndədə 'mɪstʃəvəsə'dʌlt, tʃuɪŋ ɪn 'bɛstʃəl fæʃən, "əlðo 'dʒɛnjʊɪn vɛnəzən wəd bɪ 'prɛfɚəbl̩. ɪn zo'ɑlədʒɪ, aɪ rɪmɛmbɚ, 'vɪsərə wɚ 'nɑt . . ."

"aɪ 'rɛkn̩," kɑmlɪ ɪntərʌptɪd ðɪ ɪn'kɑmpərəbl̩ dɛpjʊtɪ, nɔɪɪŋ, "wɪd bɛtə rɛkə'nɔɪtɚ. aʊ'rɪnfəməs, 'dɛspɪkəbl̩ 'kɑmbətənt . . ."

"'kɑmpətənt," kərɛktəd ðɪ ædʒəl kəntrolɚ, 'hu, kəmplitɪŋ ɪz 'tʃorz, hədə'raɪvd. "jʊr 'ɔrθoəpɪ ɪz . . ."

"'ædmərəbl̩," fɪnɪʃt ðə ʃɛrəf, əl 'rɔɪld. "lɛts krɒs ðɪs 'baɪu."

"'keɑsən 'mɔrgɪdʒɪz!" ʃaʊtəd ðə kəntrolɚ, 'skrætʃɪŋ ɪmsɛlfəz ðe 'fordɪd ðə krik. ðə wɔtɚ həd rɪnstɒfɪz mə'dɪsənəl prɛpəreʃən fə 'rɛksəmə.

"ðə 'kɝsəv ðə 'brɪgənd!" wəz ðə kraɪ, ənd ðe 'sizdɪm. ənə'pɪsl̩ əndə 'kupɑn dɪsklozdɪz dimo'naɪəkl̩ kɑg'nomɪn. maʊntɪŋ ə 'nætʃʊrəl 'deɪs nɪrə krɪ'væs, hɪ gev, sʌmhwɑtə'raɪ, hɪz vɝʒənəvɪz baɪ'ɑgrəfɪ.

hwaɪlə'rɛktɪŋ ðə kærɪ'ætədiz ɒn ðə fə'sɑdəvə kə'θidrəl, hɪ fɛlɪntʊ ðə 'slaʊ əv dɪ'spɑnd bəkozəv 'kɑndʒʊgəl dɪfəkʌltɪz. hɪz kor'tɪɚlaɪk 'ætətjud wəz 'ʃɔrt-'laɪvd, əndɪ 'mærɪdə 'geʃə hʊ hædə pɑ̃ 'ʃɑ̃ fɚ baɪɪŋ pə'ruks əl ðə 'lɪvlɒŋ 'de.

"'ɪmpɪəs," mʌtɚd ðə ʃɛrəf, lʊkɪŋ ə'skænsətɪm, "bə'tɛksplɪkəbl̩. əndʒʊr kən'vɝʒən tʊ ə laɪfəv 'henəs 'kraɪməz sɪ'kweʃəs. naʊ, ə'nɔtɑpsɪ wɪl . . ."

"'no 'æləbaɪ," wɛntɒn ðə brɪgənd, naʊ 'dɑsələ'nʌf, "wɪl kən'don maɪ 'debju ɪntə 'kraɪm. 'hɑspətəbl̩, 'sʌtl̩, aɪ kʊdəv bɪn . . ." hɪ 'dɔbdɪ'zaɪz. ðɪ ɪnkɑmpərəbl̩ dɛpjʊtɪ, dɪs'kʌmfɪtɪd, plʌktə glædɪ'oləsənd 'bɝstɪntʊ ə 'rɪbəld 'sɒŋ. bəkʌmɪŋ 'ænəkdotl̩, ðə brɪgənd toldəvə 'gelə 'ɔrdʒɪ ɪnənə'kʌlt 'kæzm̩, ðə storɪ əlmost kɔzɪŋ ə 'sɪzm̩ ɪn ðə grup.

felɪŋ tə sɒfən ðə 'dʒʊrɪ, hɪ wəzən'daɪtədəzə 'slik 'vɪlən, əz ðɪ ɪ'pɪtəmɪ əvəl 'krɪmənəl də'bri. tʊ ɪz 'vælɪt hɪ bɪkwiðdɪz 'brokən, ðo 'rɛpərəbl̩, 'jɑt. dɛf tə 'əl, hɪ dræŋk 'næfθə tə kjurɪz 'egju ən dɪf'θɪərɪə. 'faɪnəlɪ, bɪtn̩ baɪ rə'mɔrs, əl'rɛdɪ klædɪn 'sɪɚmənts, hɪ kəntræktɪd 'rebɪiz, ænd, mʌtərɪŋ 'dɪfθɒŋz, bɝstɪz 'dʒʌgjʊlɚ 'ven. wɪð gret 'klæŋgɚ, hɪz dɪ'maɪz wəzə'naʊnst. ə 'sɑm wəz sʌŋ əzə 'rikwɪəm baɪ ðə 'pɑsɪ, hwɪtʃ medʌp ðə kɔr'tɛʒ.

CROSSWORD PUZZLE FOR ALL SOUNDS

1	2	3	■	4		5	6	7
8			9		■	10		
11				■	12			
■	■		■	13			■	■
14	15	■	16				■	17
18		■	19			■	20	
	■	21				22		
23			■	■	24			

Note: Write answers in phonetics.

ə'krɒs

1. 'prifɪks minɪŋ "bæd"
4. 'but ʃept 'kʌntrɪ
8. 'most 'ɑd
10. ə 'laɪənz 'saʊnd
11. 'tʃes 'aftɚ
12. θɪŋz jʊ slip ɒn
13. 'nɑt gæðɚd baɪ 'rolɪŋ'stonz
14. 'ʌnstrɛst'pronaʊn
16. əv 'haɪɪst 'wɝθ
18. 'ɛvrɪwən
19. 'ʌŋkl̩z 'waɪf
20. 'ʌnstrɛst fɔrm əv 'wi
21. laɪk ə 'kɪtn̩
23. 'wʊdɪ 'plænt
24. kə'rɛlətɪv əv 'nɔr

daʊn

1. 'klinɪŋ 'tul
2. 'wʌn hu 'ædz
3. kə'lɛkʃən əv 'nemz
4. 'pronaʊn
5. ples ɪn 'kʌstədɪ
6. 'bɝdn̩
7. 'hɪrɪŋ dəvaɪsɪz
9. tə 'prɑsəkjut fɚ 'dæmədʒɪz
12. 'sɪtɪ ɪn mæsə'tʃusɪts
13. ɪn'tɛndɪd
14. 'nɑt 'lɒŋ
15. sɪk
16. nɪɚ
17. wʌn hʊ 'fɪʃɪz
20. prɛpə'zɪʃən
21. 'lɑk 'opənɚ
22. 'lɛg 'dʒɔɪnt

Correct answers to puzzle are on page 328.

Transcription Exercise for All Sounds

1. ə'kɜrəns
2. 'kɔʃən
3. ʌn'sɝtn̩
4. 'hɛroɪn
5. dʒæpə'niz
6. 'kwɛstʃən
7. 'kɑlərə
8. 'pæʃən
9. bə'nænəz
10. 'ɑksədʒən
11. 'enʃənt
12. 'nɑkwɝst
13. 'dʒɝmənɪ
14. 'ɛləfənt
15. 'wofəl
16. 'kæləbret
17. 'wɪljəm
18. ə'stɑnɪʃmənt
19. 'mɔrtɚ
20. 'jʌŋgɚ
21. də'klɛɚ
22. bɪ'ætətɪud
23. bə'sun
24. sə'dɪʃən
25. 'sɪgnəfaɪ
26. 'θɜrobrɛd
27. jʊr'sɛlf
28. pə'redɚz
29. 'romənɪzm̩
30. 'mɒsɪ
31. saɪð
32. kən'faʊnd
33. 'bʌfəlo
34. kən'grætʃʊlet
35. sə'kʌm
36. 'pɝʒən
37. 'junək
38. 'ɛərɪd
39. 'wʊmənhʊd
40. 'julədʒɪ
41. 'eʒən
42. 'mæərɪd
43. 'kætəkɪzm̩
44. jʊ'topɪə
45. 'pasəbl̩
46. kə'redʒəs
47. 'medn̩hʊd
48. sə'raʊndz
49. 'θɜrofɛɚ
50. də'zɑlvd
51. 'bʌnjən
52. dʒə'renɪəm
53. 'ʌðɚz
54. 'vɛnəsən
55. 'ɑpərə
56. ə'laɪəns
57. ɪn'tɛlədʒənt
58. 'ɪntəmɪt
59. 'jʊrəp
60. ʌ'n:otɪst
61. kænzə's:ɪtɪ
62. 'vaɪələts
63. 'sɒŋbɝd
64. 'wɪnsəm
65. əmædʒə'neʃən
66. 'sɛpərɪt
67. 'pasəfaɪ
68. ɔ'dæsətɪ
69. 'æŋgjəlɚ
70. ɔr'net
71. mɪ's:tetmənts
72. 'dɪərɪst
73. sɪ'kjurətɪ
74. 'bɔɪstrəs
75. 'vɛstʃʊr
76. lɪ'kɝ
77. 'felæŋks
78. 'ɑrgju
79. 'sʌfərəbl̩
80. 'ʌnjən
81. dɪsə'bil
82. daɪ'æstoli
83. 'dɛswɪtɪud
84. 'mɪskrɪənt
85. 'kjupolə
86. 'dɛsəltorɪ
87. kən'daɪn
88. nɪ'mɑnɪk
89. mɪ'nʌskjul
90. nɪr'vɑnə
91. aɪ'ræsəbl̩
92. 'hɛkətɑm
93. 'kɑntjʊmilɪ
94. kaɪ'mɪərə
95. 'uzl̩
96. 'pjuɪsəns
97. sə'vɑ̃
98. 'saɪnəkjur
99. 'hɑspɪtəbl̩
100. ogrə'tæ̃

3

Anatomy and Physiology of Speech

The anatomy and physiology of the vocal mechanism will be discussed only to the depth necessary for an intelligent approach to speech training. The advanced student is referred to the references in the Bibliography.

Anatomy as used in this chapter refers to a description of the bones, cartilages ("soft" bones: dense connective tissue more transparent than bone, most of which tends to become bone in the process of fetal development and human aging) and muscles involved in speech. Physiology refers to how these structures operate in the process of speech.

The technical meaning of the following terms used in this discussion should be understood before reading further. Their pronunciation is given in the Appendix.

anterior (also *ventral*): toward the front of the body.
posterior (also *dorsal*): toward the rear of the body.
superior: toward the head.
inferior: toward the feet.

medial: toward or on the midline which divides the body into right and left halves.

lateral: toward the side of the body.

anterolateral: toward the furthest anterior and lateral "corner" of the body.

sagittal section: a slice through a structure dividing it into left and right portions.

frontal section: a slice through a structure dividing it into anterior and posterior portions.

origin (of a muscle): the place at which the muscle connects to the bone or cartilage, (or aponeurosis or tendon of another muscle) that is considered as remaining relatively fixed during that muscle's contraction.

insertion (of a muscle): the place at which the muscle connects to the bone or cartilage, (or aponeurosis or tendon of another muscle) that is considered as the organ to be moved during that muscle's contraction. Obviously, no structure remains completely fixed when a muscle connected to it undergoes contraction, but to the extent that the structure characteristically undergoes less movement than the structure to which the muscle is attached at its other end, the terms *origin* and *insertion* are useful. When both structures move almost equally or under different conditions either may move more than the other, these terms are arbitrary.

agonists: said of two muscles which, for a given function, act cooperatively. Thus, the anterior and posterior fibers of the deltoid muscle in the shoulder operate agonistically to raise the arm laterally.

raphe: the seamlike union of the two lateral halves of an organ, such as the tongue or the muscles in the back of the neck. The line of fusion creates a groove or indentation. *Median raphe* emphasizes that the line of fusion is medial.

symphysis: place of medial fusion of paired bones and cartilages. Thus, the jaw bone (mandible) is formed from a fusion of two bones long before birth, and its symphysis is at the center of the chin.

articulation: a joint between two bones, two cartilages, or a bone and a cartilage. One end of the joint may be a facet (flat surface), a nodule (slightly rounded end), or tubercle (knoblike end). The other end may be a facet or a fossum (depression). Each articulation is lubricated and protected from shock by a capsule, the synovial membrane, containing a fluid, synovia.

The anatomy of the vocal mechanism will be discussed in four parts: (1) the respiratory system, which supplies the air pressure necessary for the creation of vocal sound; (2) the phonatory system, which provides the sound itself; (3) the resonatory system, which alters the sound to produce an individual's characteristic voice quality; and (4) the articulatory system, which effects the changes necessary to produce the various sounds. After the anatomy of each section is presented, the physiology of that system will be discussed. If at any time you are unable to understand a portion of the discussion of physiology, review the pertinent anatomical material until the meaning of that portion becomes clear. The only purpose of the anatomical sections is to enable you to understand the subsequent discussions of physiology.

Anatomy of the Respiratory System

The bony portion of the thorax (chest cavity) consists of twelve thoracic vertebrae,[1] twelve pair of ribs (costae) running from the spine inferiorly around the body, and the sternum (breastplate). The upper seven pair of ribs ("true" ribs) connect directly or by means of very short cartilages to the sternum. The next lower three pair ("false" ribs) connect to the sternum by means of long cartilages. The lowest two pair ("floating" ribs) are shortest and terminate in the abdominal musculature. Most of the thorax lies between the third and eighth ribs. It should be noted that every rib is lower at its anterior end than at its posterior end. Table 3–1 displays the muscles of the respiratory system, the general area in which each is located, the origin, insertion, and shape of each muscle, and the respiratory function effected by contraction. By locating each muscle on the figures listed in the table, a better understanding of the muscular characteristics may be obtained.

[1] The first seven vertebrae (spinal segments) in the neck are cervical vertebrae (C1–C7), the next twelve are thoracic (T1–T12), the next five are lumbar (L1–L5), and the last few (usually 5–7) rudimentary ones form the coccyx (tailbone).

TABLE 3–1

Respiratory Muscles

Muscle	Location	Fig.	Origin	Insertion	Shape	Respiratory Function
*Diaphragm	Above intestines		Beltline	Central tendon	Double-domed (2 hemispheres)	Depresses viscera during inhalation
External intercostals	Between ribs	3–2	Every rib but 12th	Rib below	Narrow band	Elevate ribs and expand rib cage during inhalation
Internal intercostals	Beneath external intercostals	3–1, 3–2	Every rib but 12th	Rib below	Narrow band	Assist external intercostals
Costal levators	On spine		Every rib but 12th	Rib below and two below	Narrow band	Assists intercostals
Serratus posterior superior	Upper back		Vertebrae C7–T2	First few ribs	Narrow band	Assists rib elevation during inhalation
Serratus posterior inferior	Lower back		Vertebrae T11–L2	Lowest few ribs	Narrow band	May assist transverse thoracis
Serratus anterior	Beneath arm	3–1, 3–2	Scapula (shoulder blade)	First 8–9 ribs ventrally	Quadrangular	Can elevate ribs during inhalation if shoulder is fixed
Pectoralis major	Upper chest	3–1, 3–2	Clavicle (collar bone)	Humerus (upper arm bone)	Fanlike	Elevates ribs during inhalation if shoulder is fixed
Pectoralis minor	Upper chest	3–1, 3–2	2d–5th costal cartilages	Scapula	Triangular	Assists pectoralis major
Subclavius	Upper chest	3–1, 3–2	First rib	Clavicle	Cylindrical	Elevates first ribs during inhalation if shoulder is fixed

Latissimus dorsi	Back	3–1, 3–2	Vertebrae T6–L5 and iliac crest	Humerus	Three-pronged	May assist in elevating lower ribs during inhalation if arm is fixed
Sternocleido-mastoid	Side of neck	3–4, 3–5, 3–13	Manubrium (top of sternum) and clavicle	Mastoid process of occipital bone	Two-pronged	Elevates ribs during inhalation by elevating sternum
Scalenus anterior	Side of neck	3–4, 3–5	Vertebrae C3–C6	First rib	Thin, flat	Elevates first rib during inhalation
Scalenus medius	Side of neck	3–4, 3–5	Vertebrae C2–C7	First rib	Long, thin, and flat	Elevates first rib during inhalation
Scalenus posterior	Side of neck	3–4, 3–5	Vertebrae C5–C7	Second rib	Short, thin, and flat	Elevates first two ribs during inhalation
Transverse thoracis	Upper chest		Lower sternum	2d–6th costal cartilages	Narrow band	Depresses ribs during exhalation
Subcostals	Back		Lowest ribs	Ribs above	Narrow band	May assist transverse thoracis
External oblique	Abdomen	3–1, 3–2	Iliac crest and lower abdominal muscle fibers	4th–12th ribs	Broad, flat band	Moves viscera inward and upward during exhalation
Internal oblique	Abdomen	3–2	Same as above	Lower few ribs and pubis	Broad, flat band	Moves viscera inward and upward during exhalation
Transverse abdominis	Abdomen	3–2	Linea alba	Lower six ribs and iliac crest	Broad, flat band	Moves viscera inward and upward during exhalation
Rectus abdominis	Chest and abdomen	3–1, 3–2	Pubis	Lower sternum and 5th–7th costal cartilages	Long, flat	Moves viscera inward during inhalation and depresses ribs during exhalation
Quadratus lumborum	Back		Iliac crest	12th rib and upper lumbar vertebrae	Flat sheet	May depress lower ribs during forced exhalation
Sacrospinalis	Back		Pelvis	Most or all ribs	Three-pronged	Mainly postural but may assist rectus abdominis

* Indicates that the muscle is unpaired. All others are paired.

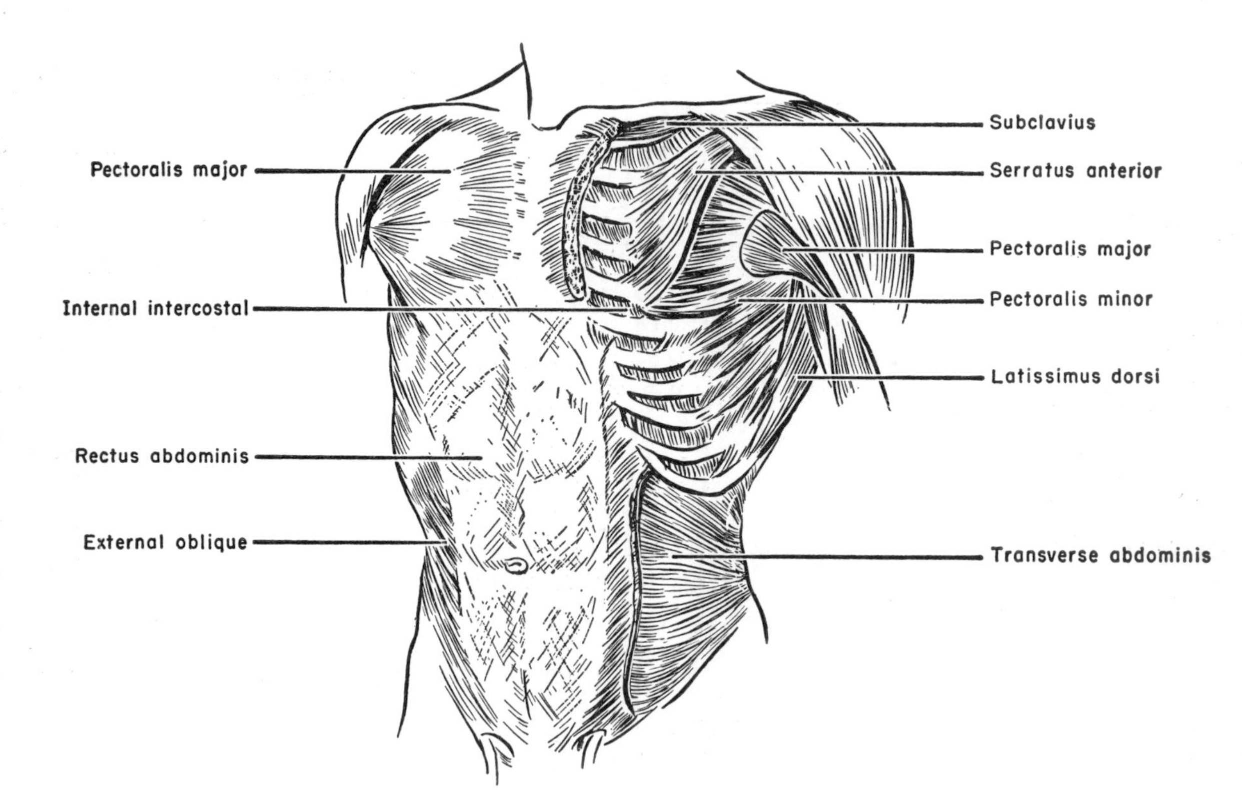

Fig. 3–1. Muscles of the thorax and abdomen.

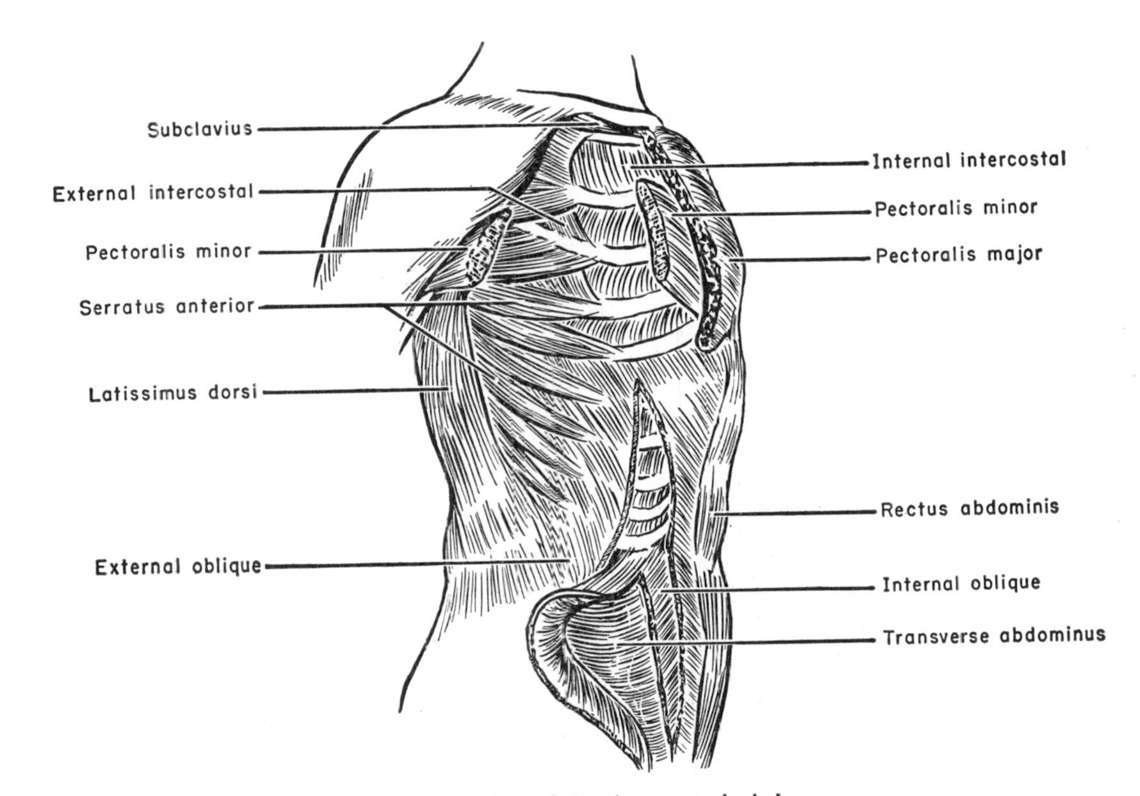

Fig. 3–2. Muscles of the thorax and abdomen.

Physiology of Respiration for Speech

Quiet inhalation is effected mainly by the thoracic muscles, assisted to a slight degree by the scaleni and the sternocleidomastoids. The diaphragm may be tensed, moving the central tendon down and forward 0.5–1.1 inch. Quiet exhalation is accomplished almost completely by the force of gravity when accompanied by relaxation of the muscles mentioned above.

Inhalation for speech may be the same as for quiet inhalation, or a deeper inhalation may bring the other muscles of inhalation listed in Table 3–1 into action.

After inhalation for speech, the rectus abdominis and transverse thoracic muscles begin contraction, and shortly thereafter phonation is begun. The lower ribs are fixated by the abdominal muscles, such as the quadratus lumborum. After almost two seconds of continuous phonation, the diaphragmatic hemispheres begin to rise. The amount of volume change effected in the several regions, viz., clavicular, thoracic, and abdominal, is extremely variable from person to person and is also variable in one person from situation to situation. For example, abdominal movement accounts on the average for 43 per cent of the total volume change, but this may vary 20 per cent either way. During speech the costal muscles and rectus abdominis continue thoracic depression, and the scaleni group provide a chest pulse for each syllable uttered to restore the subglottal (below the folds) pressure lost on the preceding syllable and to regulate the pressure needed for a desired loudness on the forthcoming syllable. At very low speaking rates, the abdomen also pulses for each syllable, but above four syllables per second no such pulsation occurs.

No relation exists between regional predominance (e.g., thoracic, abdominal) and any speaking factor, such as voice quality, loudness, or rate. Moreover, any categorizing of persons in terms of regional predominance is highly arbitrary and, therefore, suspect. The vital capacity of persons (the amount of air which can be expelled following deepest possible inhalation) also bears no relation to speaking ability. Of course, in that type of singing which requires very prolonged continuation of a single sound these findings probably do not apply, but in speech such prolongation almost never occurs. Vital capacity is also not related to intensity or to audibility. Although it might seem that the more air one can take in, the more pressure he can produce, and the greater loudness he can create, subsequent discussion of vocal-fold action should clarify why this is not true. Nor is voice quality, control of force, or any other speech characteristic related to vital capacity.

Since breathing is a vegetative function (on which speech has been superimposed), to teach any system of breathing is impossible, if by system we mean how to breathe, not when. Obviously, one may consciously inhale or exhale at any time. Almost all physiologists are agreed that, even if a system of breathing could be taught, to do so would be extremely dangerous.

The only speech-breathing relationships discovered are that the diaphragmatic hemispheres rise further and more steadily in good speakers than in poor ones, and that in all speakers the hemispheres tend to move higher for loud whispering than for loud production, and to move higher for loud production than for normal production. However, this probably means merely that good speakers tend to utter more words on a single breath than do poor speakers, and that anyone uses his abdominal muscles more when a greater expiration of air is required.

Anatomy of the Phonatory System

The larynx is located in the neck just anterior to the esophagus and connects the lungs to the mouth. Its framework consists of cartilages, viz., the thyroid, cricoid, arytenoid, corniculate, and cuneiform cartilages, and of a single bone, the hyoid. The smaller cartilages are paired; the thyroid and cricoid cartilages and the hyoid bone are unpaired. (These parts of the larynx will be found in Fig. 3–3; other references are explicit.)

The hyoid (upsilon-shaped) is a U-shaped bone lying horizontally at the uppermost part of the neck with its open end directed posteriorly. It is unique in having no direct attachment to other bones or to cartilages, being held in position by muscles and ligaments. It provides a base for the tongue and from it is suspended the thyroid cartilage. Note that the entire

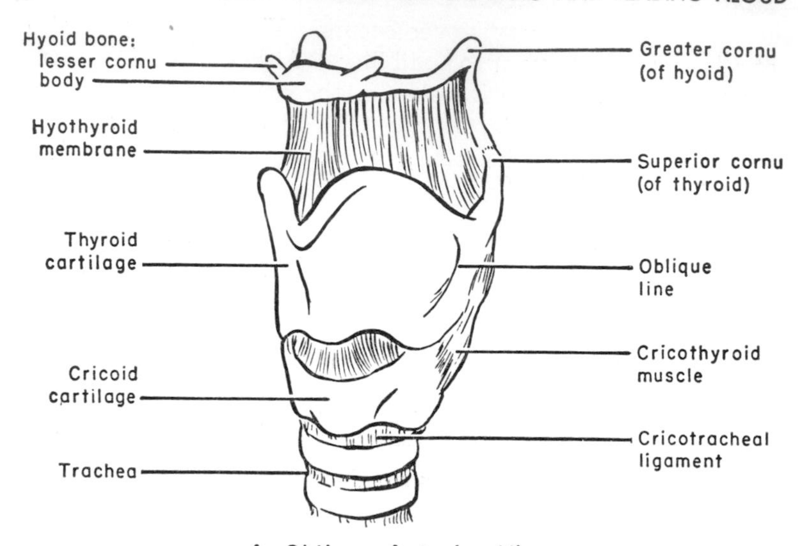

A. Oblique Anterior View

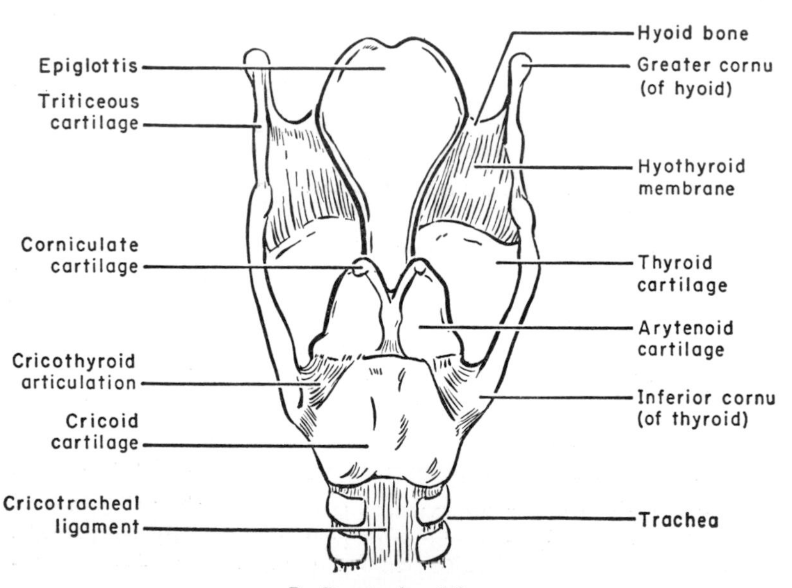

B. Posterior View

Fig. 3–3. Larynx.

larynx is not attached at any point to the spine; it is merely suspended from the muscularly positioned hyoid. This will provide an important consideration in subsequent discussion of voice quality. The hyoid bone consists of a body (the bend of the U), the greater cornua (the two main horns of the U), and the lesser cornua (the two spikes, one on each greater cornu).

The largest of the eight cartilages (three paired and two unpaired) is the thyroid (oblong shield-shaped) cartilage. The lateral ends of the shield are directed posteriorly. The unpaired thyroid consists of two quadrilateral plates, or laminae, fused at the median ventral line. The anterosuperior portion is a notch which protrudes anteriorly to produce the "Adam's apple." The posterior portion of each lamina has a superior cornu which is fused or attached by the triticeous cartilage to the greater cornu of the hyoid bone, and an inferior cornu which articulates in the lateral facet of the cricoid cartilage to form a cricothyroid joint. On either lamina are two tubercles, one at the base of the superior cornu and another between the inferior cornu and the thyroid angle. A ridge, the oblique line, runs along the lamina between these tubercles.

The other unpaired cartilage, the cricoid (ring-shaped) cartilage, is shaped like a signet ring, with the signet portion facing posteriorly. The cricoid arch, or ring portion, consists of two fused laminae, which taper from a height of about one inch at the signet to about 0.3 inch at the ventral fusion. The lateral facet in which the inferior cornu of the thyroid cartilage articulates is located at the junction of the signet and arch. The signet has an inverted V-shaped ridge at the midline, the bases of which are near the posterolateral corners of the signet. The upper border of the signet has a central notch, on each side of which is a smooth surface facing upward and outward.

Each of the arytenoid (ladle-shaped) cartilages has a triangular base and three triangular sides. The apex of each triangle is curved medially and posteriorly. The three sides face laterally, posteriorly, and medially. A small process called the muscle or motor process is at the posterolateral angle of the base. Another process, the vocal process, is at the mediolateral angle of the base. The base of each arytenoid is a concave oval with its long dimension running mediolaterally. The superior surface of the cricoid near the signet slopes laterally downward from the midline, and on each lateral slope is a convex, oval facet whose long dimension runs anteroposteriorly. Since the long dimensions of the arytenoid base and the superior facet of the cricoid are perpendicular to each other, this permits the arytenoids to glide medially and laterally, forward and backward, and to rotate to some extent.

The paired corniculate (horn-shaped) cartilages are small nodules, atop the arytenoid apexes, which form the medio-posterior curves. In addition, most humans have a pair of cuneiform (wedge-shaped) cartilages lying in the aryepiglottic fold to be discussed subsequently.

The epiglottis (behind tongue; see Figs. 3–3, 3–7, 3–9) resembles a shoehorn in shape. It lies behind the base of the tongue and curves forward. The concavo-convex posterior portion contains a tubercle on the midline near the widest portion. The base of the epiglottis is attached ligamentously to the inside of the thyroid just below the notch by the thyro-epiglottic membrane. It is attached, also ligamentously, on the anterior side opposite the tubercle to the body of the hyoid bone (the hyoepiglottic membrane).

The membranous framework of the larynx is an important portion of laryngeal anatomy since the laryngeal duct is formed by these membranes.

The unpaired hyothyroid membrane suspends the entire larynx from the hyoid bone by its connection to the superior border of the thyroid (Fig. 3–3).

The cricothyroid membrane, or conus elasticus, has a thick, central unpaired portion, the central cricothyroid ligament, which connects the central portions of the thyroid base and cricoid arch. The paired lateral portions run ventrally from the posterior surface of the thyroid angle up to the mediolateral angle of each arytenoid. The thick, upper margins of these lateral portions form the true vocal folds (Figs. 3–7, 3–8).

The paired quadrangular membrane, or vestibular membrane, runs from the sides of the epiglottis near its base and from the posterior surface of the thyroid angle posteriorly downward to the mediolateral angle of each arytenoid. The free lower borders of this membrane turn inward to form the false vocal folds (Figs. 3–7, 3–8).

The paired aryepiglottic folds form the superior aperture of the larynx. They originate high at the sides of the epiglottis and slope downward posteriorly to encase the cuneiform cartilages and terminate on the corniculate cartilages (Fig. 3–9).

The cricotracheal ligament connects the base of the cricoid cartilage to the first tracheal ring below (Fig. 3–3).

The hyoepiglottic and thyroepiglottic membranes which support the epiglottis have been mentioned previously.

The muscles which have both their origin and insertion within the larynx (i.e., between the hyoid bone and cricoid cartilage) are termed *intrinsic muscles* of the larynx. These primarily effect fine adjustments in the positioning of the members of the laryngeal framework. Those muscles which have either their origin or their insertion, but not both, within the larynx are termed *extrinsic muscles.* These regulate the overall length and shape of the larynx. The extrinsic muscles are listed in Table 3–2A and the intrinsic ones in Table 3–2B. Locating each muscle on the indicated figure should prove helpful in understanding its function.

Physiology of the Larynx

The larynx is shaped roughly like an hourglass with a bulge in the middle of the constriction. The superior funnel, the vestibule, lies anterior to the esophagus. Its lower portion terminates at the level of the ventricular (false vocal) folds. The space between the ventricular folds and true vocal folds is termed the ventricle. The ventricle bulges laterally to form a small cavity or sinus on each side between the ventricular and true folds which extends upward anterolaterally to a cul-de-sac at the level of the upper border of the thyroid lamina. These sacules are sources of secretions for lubricating the folds. The lower, inverted funnel is termed the conus elasticus and extends from the ventricle downward. At the level of the inferior border of the cricoid cartilage it becomes continuous with the trachea.

TABLE 3–2

Phonatory Muscles

A. Extrinsic Muscles of Larynx

Muscle	Location	Fig.	Origin	Insertion	Shape	Phonatory Function
I. Larngeal Elevators						
Digastric, anterior belly	Under chin	3–4, 3–5	Near symphysis of mandible	Intermediate tendon and body of hyoid	Y-shaped	Retracts jaw if hyoid is fixed; elevates and advances hyoid if mandible is fixed
Digastric, posterior belly	Side of neck	3–4, 3–5	Mastoid process of temporal bone	Intermediate tendon	Y-shaped	Elevates, retracts, and tilts hyoid
Stylohyoid	Parallel to posterior belly of digastric	3–4, 3–5	Styloid process of temporal bone	Greater cornu of hyoid	Slender band	Elevates and retracts hyoid
Mylohyoid	Floor of mouth	3–4, 3–5	Inner aspect of mandible on one side	Inner aspect of mandible on other side and to body of hyoid posteriorly	Sling	Elevates and moves hyoid ventrally and raises tongue if mandible is fixed; depresses jaw if hyoid is fixed
Geniohyoid	Upper surface of mylohyoid		Symphysis of mandible	Body of hyoid	Cylindrical	Elevates and advances hyoid if mandible is fixed; depresses jaw if hyoid is fixed
Genioglossus	Under chin		Superior ventral part of mandible	Hyoid and up to upper surface of tongue	Triangular	Depresses and advances tongue; elevates hyoid

Hyoglossus	Beneath tongue		Body and greater cornu of hyoid	Back and sides of tongue	Flat band	Retracts and depresses tongue
Middle pharyngeal constrictor	Apex of vestibule		Greater cornu of hyoid and stylohyoid ligament	Midline of back wall of mouth	Long, thin	Retracts hyoid and elevates it slightly
			II. Laryngeal Depressors			
Omohyoid	Base of neck	3–4, 3–5	Scapula	Body of hyoid	Two-bellied with fixed intermediate tendon	Depresses and retracts hyoid
Sternohyoid	Beneath omohyoid	3–4, 3–5	Clavicle and manubrium of sternum	Body of hyoid	Flat band	Depresses hyoid
Sternothyroid	Beneath sternohyoid	3–4	Sternum	Thyroid lamina	Long, thin	Depresses thyroid, thus depressing larynx, or may work as agonist of anterior fibers of cricothyroid (q.v., Table 3–2B)
Thyrohyoid	Front of neck	3–4, 3–5	Thyroid lamina	Major cornu and body of hyoid	Flat band	Shortens larynx; depresses hyoid if thyroid is fixed; elevates thyroid if hyoid is fixed, thus raising level of folds

TABLE 3–2—(Continued)

B. Intrinsic Muscles of the Larynx

Muscle	Location	Fig.	Origin	Insertion	Shape	Phonatory Function
Posterior cricoarytenoid	Signet of cricoid	3–9, 3–10	Signet ridge of cricoid	Muscle process of arytenoid	Flat, triangular	Abducts folds
Lateral cricoarytenoid	Arch of cricoid	3–10	Arch of cricoid	Muscle process of arytenoid	Rectangular	Adducts folds; when acting as agonist of posterior cricoarytenoid, tilts arytenoid backward and outward, thus elevating and abducting folds
Thyroarytenoid	Parallel to fold	3–7, 3–10	Posterior surface of thyroid	Lateral edge and muscle process of arytenoid	J-shaped with vocalis at medial end of hook	May shorten folds and assist in adduction
Cricothyroid	Laterally between thyroid and cricoid	3–7	Lower border and lateral surface of cricoid	Inferior border of thyroid from inferior tubercle to base of inferior cornu	Broad, rather thick	Posterior fibers rock arytenoid forward to relax folds; anterior fibers rock arytenoid backward to tense folds; both as agonists elevate cricoid if thyroid is fixed, thus shortening conus elasticus, and depress thyroid if cricoid is fixed, thus lowering level of folds

*Transverse arytenoid	Posterior surfaces of arytenoid	3–9, 3–10	Muscle process and posterolateral edge of one arytenoid	Muscle process and posterolateral edge of other arytenoid	Thick, rectangular	Moves arytenoids medially to close intercartilaginous portion of glottis for falsetto; stabilizes arytenoids
Oblique arytenoid	External to transverse arytenoid	3–9, 3–10	Lower posterior surface of one arytenoid	Apex of other arytenoid	Triangular	Assists transverse arytenoid in its actions
Vocalis	Within vocal folds between conus elasticus medially and thyroarytenoid laterally	3–7	Posterior aspect of thyroid angle	Vocal process and lateral surface of arytenoid	Variably thin to thick	Increases fold tension if thyroid and arytenoid are fixed; reduces fold length by moving thyroid and arytenoid closer together; short (aryvocalic) fibers can tense a portion of fold
Aryepiglottic	Superior continuation of oblique arytenoid	3–9, 3–10	Apex of ayrtenoid	Lateral border of epiglottis	Thin, curved	Stabilizes arytenoid; depresses epiglottis
Thyro-epiglottic	Lateral portion of vestibule	3–10	Inner surface of thyroid near angle	Aryepiglottic fold posteriorly and epiglottis superiorly	Thin, flat	Widens vestibule; may assist in depressing epiglottis
Ventricularis	Lateral portion of vestibule		Lateral border of arytenoid	Lateral border of epiglottis	Thin, flat	Depresses epiglottis

* Indicates that the muscle is unpaired. All others are paired.

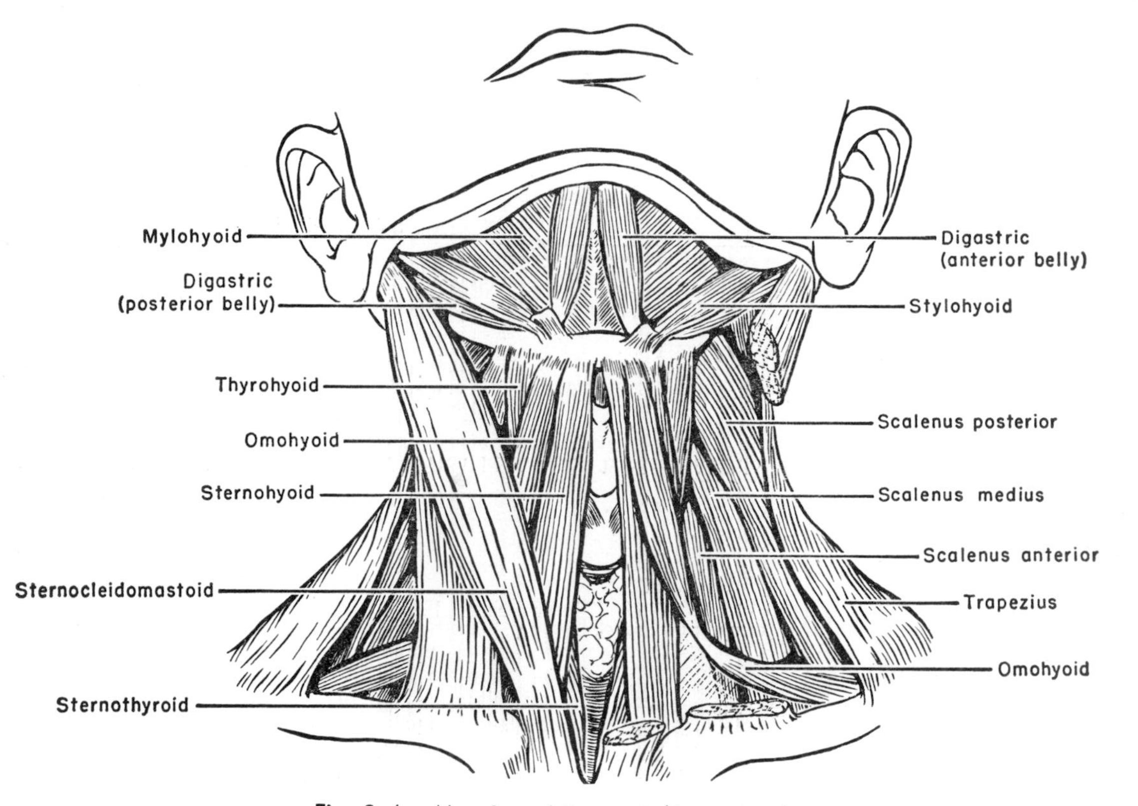

Fig. 3–4. Muscles of the neck (front view).

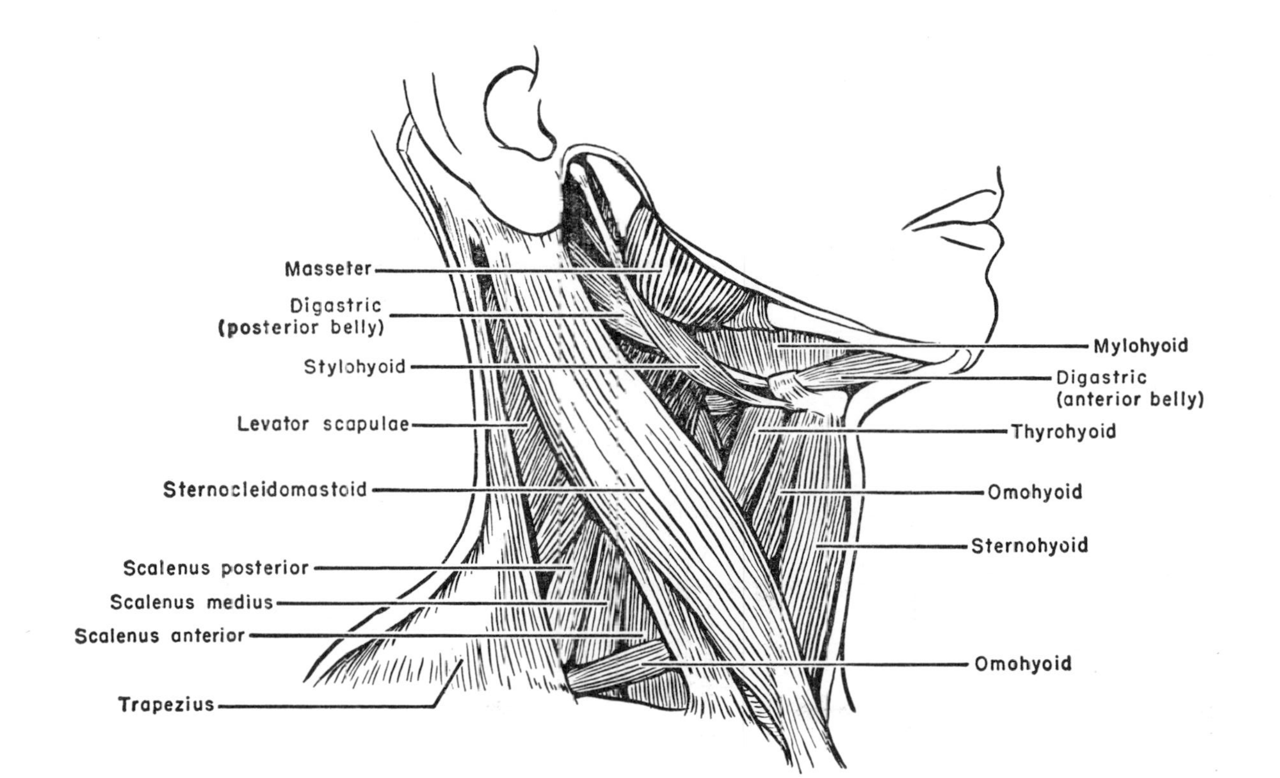

Fig. 3–5. Muscles of the neck (side view).

The ventricular folds are soft, thick, rounded, and somewhat flabby lateral indentations into the laryngeal tract. Each contains the lower, medial border of the quadrangular membrane, a few muscle fibers which are vestigial in some persons and rather well developed in others, and many mucous glands. These

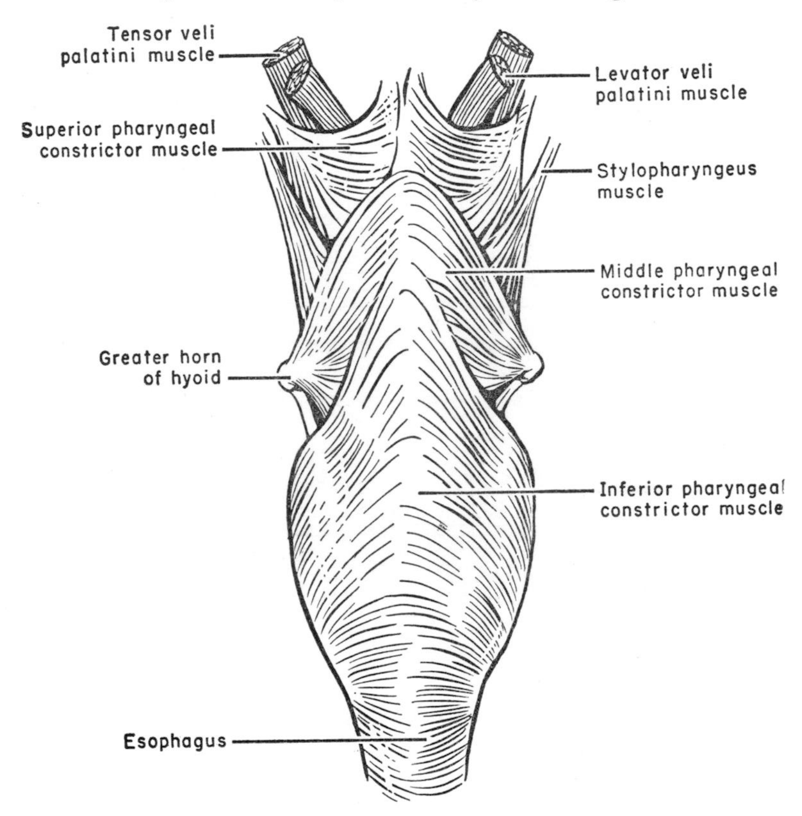

Fig. 3–6. Muscles of the neck (rear view).

folds extend from the thyroid laminae anteriorly to the arytenoids posteriorly, inserting somewhat above the vocalis in the fossa on the medial surfaces of the arytenoids. Thus, the ventricular folds are capable of adduction, in some persons more easily than others, provided the apexes of the arytenoids are moved medially by the oblique arytenoid and thyroarytenoid muscles.

However, once adducted, vibration is irregular, perhaps due to a lack of sufficient tension within the ventricular folds to adduct them in a consistent manner in consecutive cycles. This "flapping" of the ventricular folds may account for what is termed a guttural voice quality.

The vocal or true folds lie parallel and inferior to the ventricular folds and extend from a single origin on the inner aspect of the thyroid angle to the vocal process of the arytenoids.

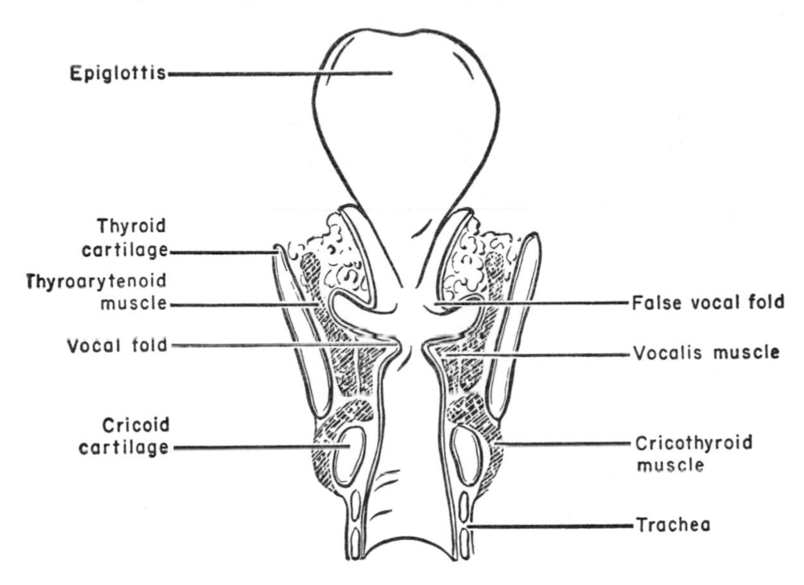

Fig. 3–7. Frontal section of larynx.

They have sufficient vertical thickness to make use of the term "vocal bands" entirely misleading. Their configuration, depending upon manner of phonation, is variable. When viewed as in the case of a frontal section (as in Fig. 3–7), the upper surfaces of the folds may be horizontal or the tips may be elevated slightly or even acutely.

The vertical thickness may also be varied so that the slope of the inferior medial surfaces may be slight or acute. The cross-sectional area of the folds may thus vary considerably, altering the mass. Moreover, the level of the folds may change by action of the extrinsic muscles, the laryngeal elevators raising, and the depressors lowering, the level of the folds. The most medial portions of the vocal folds are covered with the same kind of tissue found on the palms of the hands, stratified squamous epithelium. Thus, the folds are capable of considerable abuse and rapid restoration following such abuse. However, at places of excessive abuse calluses termed nodules may form on the folds. The vocal folds are well lubricated from numerous glands whose secretions flow mainly into the ventricular sinuses and thence onto the folds. These glands are activated by intrinsic muscle

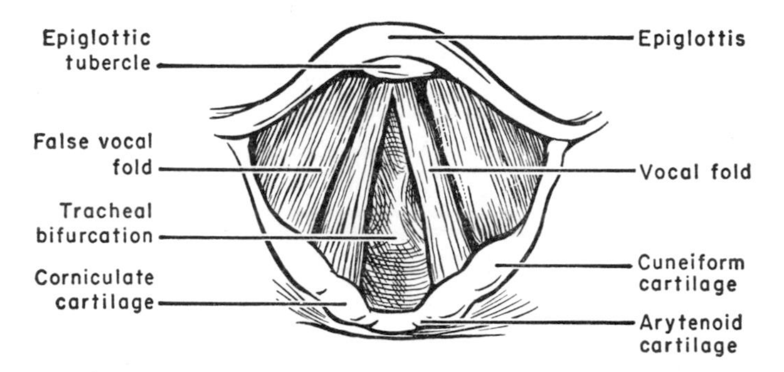

Fig. 3–8. Glottis (superior view).

activity so that lubrication and vocal-fold action are highly correlated.

As seen from above (Fig. 3–8), the space between the vocal folds is termed the glottis. That portion between the anterior juncture and the vocal processes of the arytenoids is termed the intermembranous portion of the glottis. The posterior portion from the vocal processes along the medial surfaces of the arytenoids to the transverse arytenoid muscle posteriorly is termed the intercartilaginous portion of the glottis. Only the intermembranous portion of the glottis undergoes vibration in the production of sound; the intercartilaginous portion can be adducted by the lateral cricoarytenoid and the transverse and oblique arytenoid muscles, thus moving the intermembranous portion of the folds into position for phonation. However,

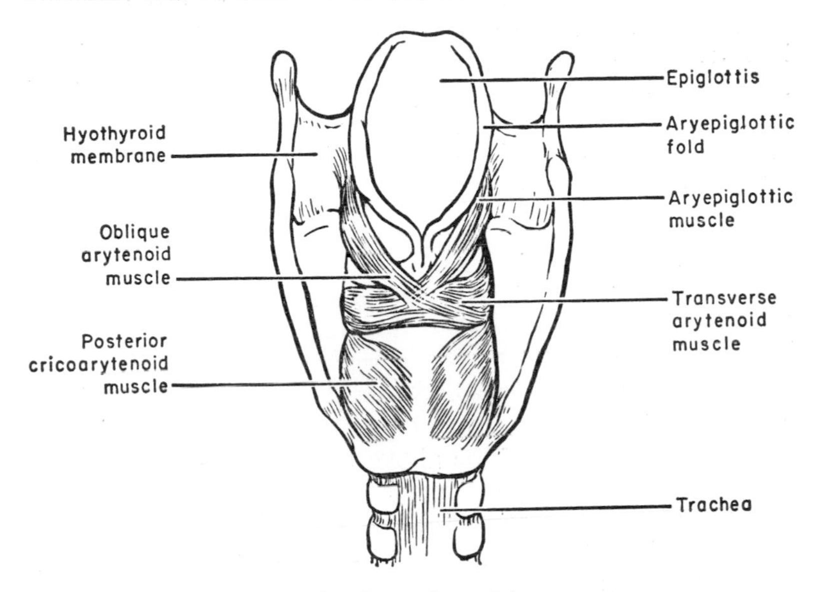

Fig. 3–9. Rear view of larynx.

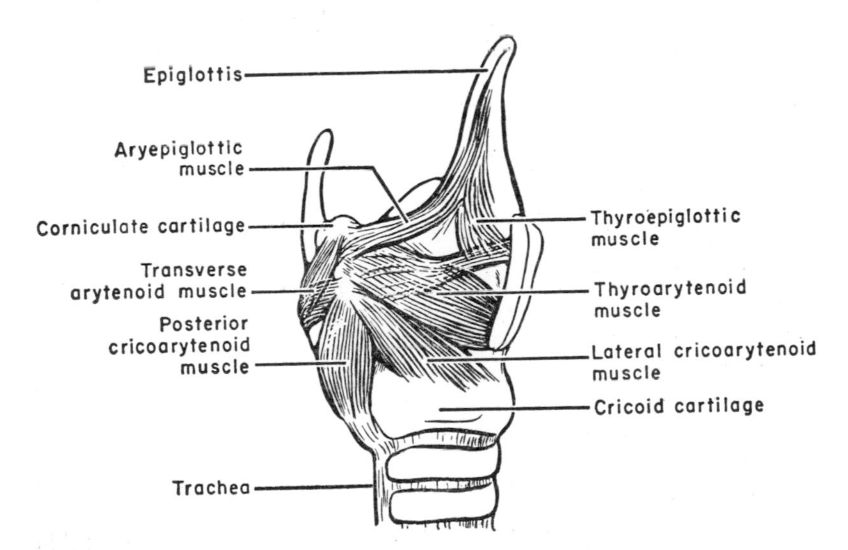

Fig. 3–10. Muscles of the larynx (side view).

phonation can occur without adducting this posterior portion of the glottis to form a complete or almost complete closure. If the intercartilaginous portion of the glottis is not in an adducted position during phonation, the gap between the medial surfaces of the arytenoids is termed a glottal chink. Note that no fibers of the vocalis lie within the intercartilaginous portion of the glottis. The length of the intermembranous portion when the folds are at rest is about 0.6 inch in males and 0.45 inch in females. Thus the folds of males are about one-third longer. The intercartilaginous portion is about one-half this length, or approximately 0.3 inch in males and 0.2 inch in females.

Since the vocalis is capable of segmental contractions due to aryvocalic fibers not extending the entire distance to the thyroid cartilage, one portion of the glottis may close more completely during adduction than any other portion. When this occurs, the place of maximum contact is termed a node; such adduction is called nodular. The shape assumed by the glottis may be any of the following:

a lozenge, as in forced exhalation;
a triangle with the medial arytenoid surfaces parallel to the folds, as in quiet breathing or glottal chink phonation;
an oblate oval, during the portion of a cycle of vibration when the folds are abducted;
a small oblate oval anteriorly, due to aryvocalic closure of the posterior portion of the intermembranous glottis, as in falsetto;
two oblate ovals, due to nodular adduction.

Since the arytenoids pivot so as to move the vocal processes laterally and posteriorly, the length of the folds is greater in abduction than in adduction. Also, since the level of the folds is variable and since the cricoid and thus the arytenoid cartilages do not have to move upward or downward as the thyroid is elevated or depressed, it is conceivable that the vocal folds may be tilted anteroposteriorly, thus effecting alterations in both tension and mass.

The manner in which sound is produced by the vocal folds will be discussed in subsequent chapters.

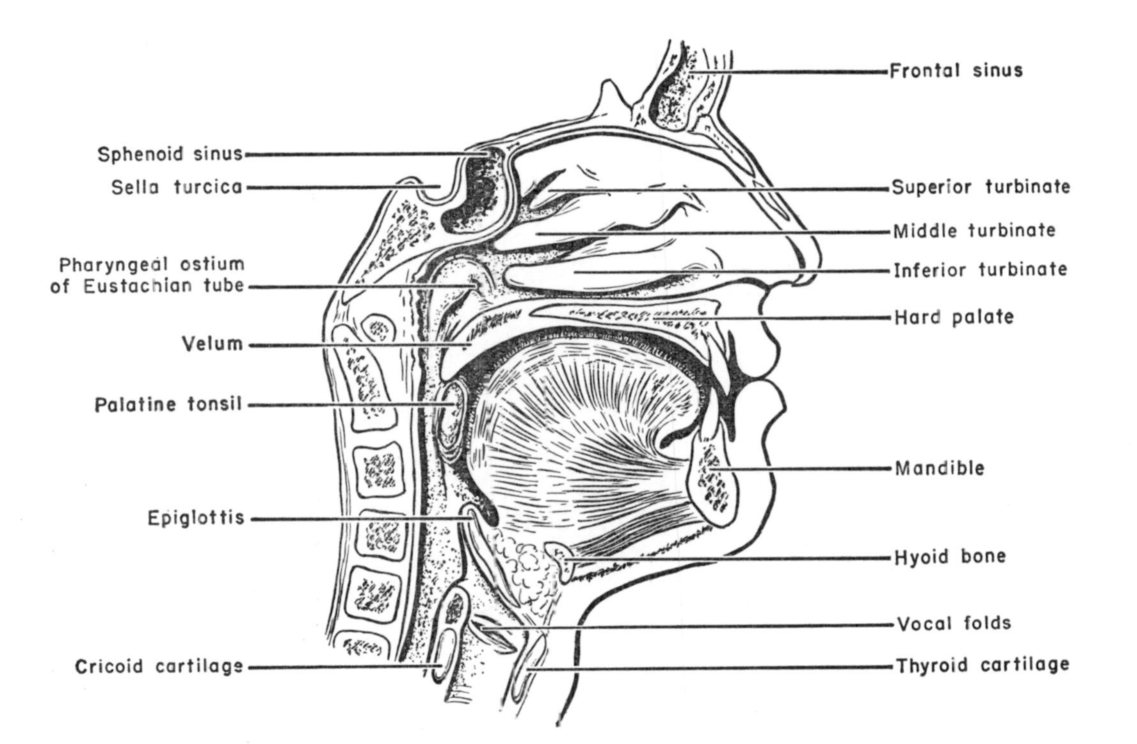

Fig. 3–11. Sagittal section of oronasolarynx.

Anatomy of the Resonatory System

The anatomical features of the skull related to the process of resonation are shown and named in Figures 3–11 and 3–12. For the purpose of considering vocal resonance, however, certain terms related to cavity areas are also needed. These are the oral cavity, oropharynx, nasal cavity, nasopharynx, and laryngopharynx.

The oral cavity is bounded anteriorly by the body of the mandible below and the alveolar processes of the maxillary bone

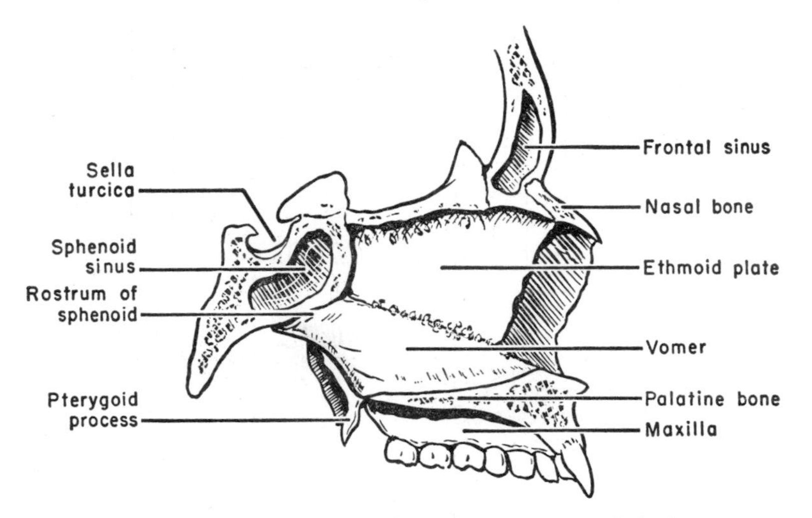

Fig. 3–12. Sagittal section of nasal area of skull.

(premaxillae) above. The upper teeth reside in the alveolar processes of the maxillae; the lower teeth in the alveolar processes of the mandible. Superiorly, the cavity is bounded by the inferior surface of the palatine bones anteriorly and by the velum (soft palate) posteriorly. The anterior border of the palatines is fused with the maxillary bones. The inferior boundary is, of course, the tongue. The posterior boundary is the oropharyngeal cavity.

The oropharynx extends from the fauces (i.e., faucial pillars, cf. Fig. 3–14) anteriorly to the dorsal wall of the mouth pos-

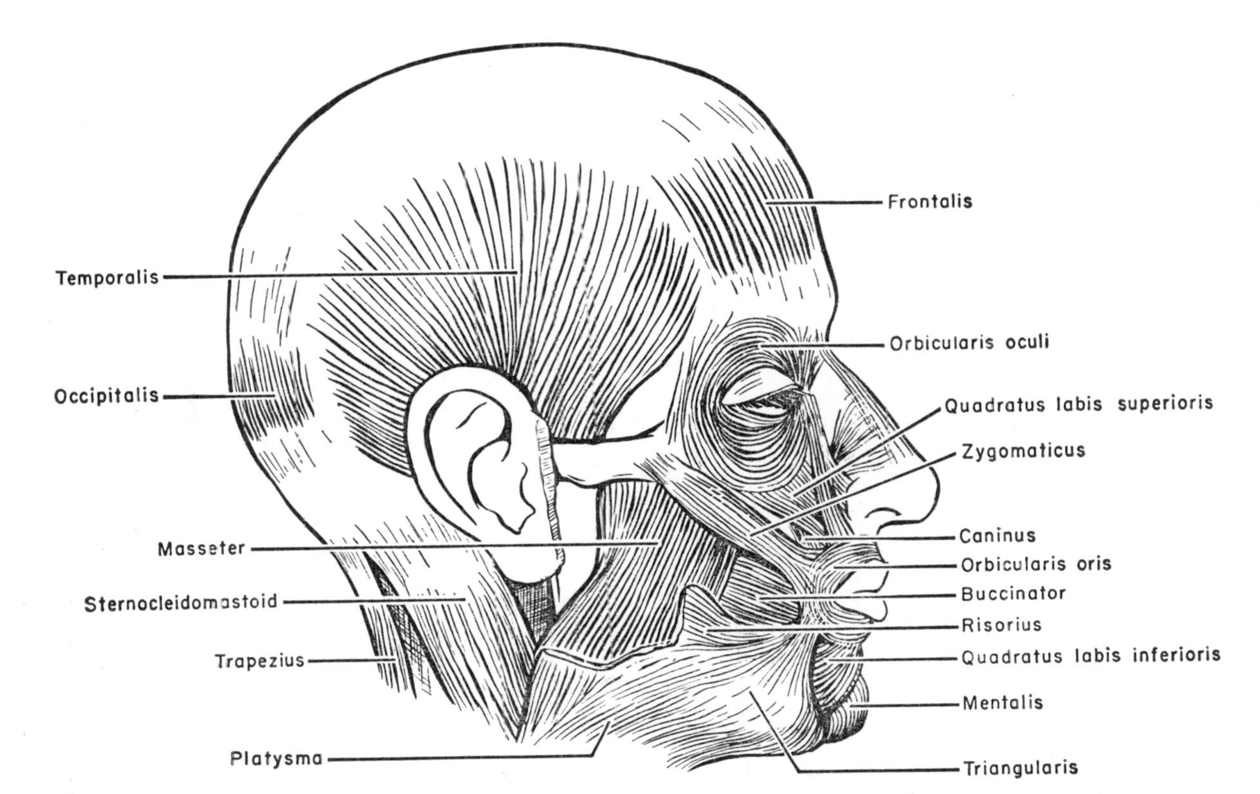

Fig. 3–13. Superficial facial muscles.

teriorly, and from the velum and pharyngeal isthmus superiorly to the level of the hyoid bone inferiorly.

The nasal cavity is formed anteriorly by the nasal bones and the frontal processes of the maxillary bones. The maxillaries also assist in the formation of the lateral portions of the external nose. The more anterior lower portion of the external nose is

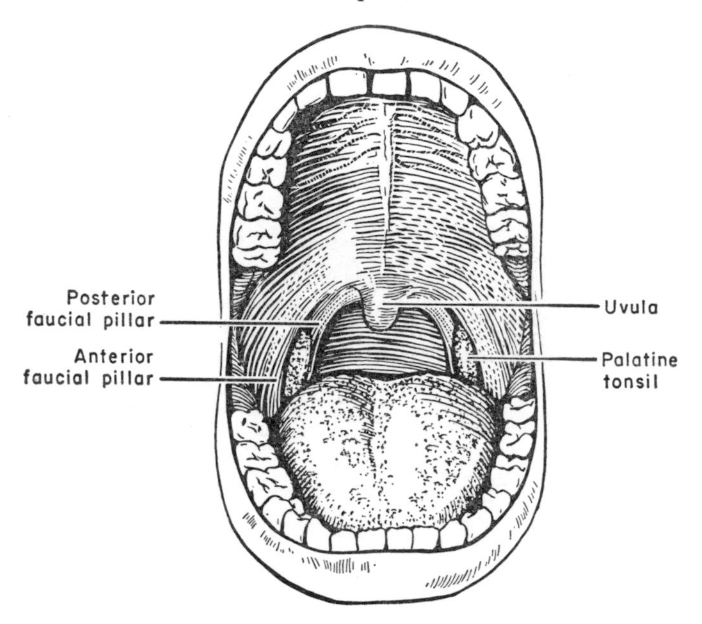

Fig. 3–14. Front view of interior of mouth.

formed by nasal cartilages, viz., the paired lateral, major alar, and minor alar cartilages. The nasal cavity is bounded superiorly by the nasal bones ventrally, the horizontal plates of the ethmoid bone centrally, and the rostrum of the sphenoid bone dorsally. The maxillaries, which on their lower surfaces form the anterior three-fourths of the hard palate, form the ventral, inferior boundary of the nasal cavity. The palatines, which are the posterior one-fourth of the hard palate, form the inferior boundary of the nasal cavity centrally. The posterior portion of the cavity terminates in two relatively small tubes, or choanae, one on each side, which lead to the nasopharynx. The nasal cavity is divided sagittally into two parts by the nasal septum. The septum is formed anteriorly by the crest of the nasal bone and the spine of the frontal bone. The central portion is formed by the vertical plate of the ethmoid bone. The vomerine and sphenoid bones create the septum posteriorly. The ethmoid bone is roughly T-shaped. The upper portion extends horizontally outward on each side from the vertical plate and then downward, ending in a mass of thin-walled sinuses, the paranasal sinuses. This labyrinth folds in medially to produce a pair of oblique shelves on each side which form the upper and middle nasal turbinates, or conchae. A third indentation into the nasal cavity on each side is effected by an independent bone, the inferior turbinate. The three chambers formed on each side of the septum by these indentations from the lateral surfaces inward are termed the superior, middle, and inferior meatuses. Each meatus extends anteriorly from the naris on that side to the choana on that side posteriorly. Thus it can be seen that each side of the nasal cavity can be considered as three chambers which extend anteriorly into one chamber (a naris) and posteriorly into another (a choana).

The nasopharynx is a cube-shaped cavity posterior to the choanae. The lateral walls contain the orifices of the Eustachian tubes. Its posterior wall is a membrane covering the pharyngeal tonsils. The anterior floor is formed by the superior portion of the velum. The posterior floor is the velopharyngeal port, which opens into the oropharynx below. This port may be closed partially or completely, as during swallowing, by elevation and retraction of the velum and uvula against the posterior pharyngeal wall. Some researchers claim that the posterior pharyngeal wall moves somewhat forward to assist in such closure, the resulting bulge being termed Passavant's pad, but whether it is operative in normal individuals has been much disputed. Persons with cleft palates do tend to manifest such activity; the action of a well-developed palatopharyngeus muscle and of the palatal fibers of the superior constrictor muscle does produce considerable forward movement of the posterior wall, but that this action is present in persons with normal vela is as yet unproved.

The lower pharyngeal division, the laryngopharynx, is funnel-shaped. It lies below the oropharynx and extends down to the esophagus at the level of the cricoid cartilage. The anterior surface is formed partly by the posterior wall of the larynx. The lateral surfaces are the aryepiglottic folds, and the posterior surface is the back wall of the esophagus. Note by referring to Fig. 3–11 that the laryngopharynx lies immediately beneath the oropharynx and that the larynx branches out anteriorly before descending. A diverticulum lies just superior to the laryngeal orifice. This is a raised median surface which forms a pyriform sinus or trough on each side, thus deflecting food and liquids around the entrance to the larynx and into the esophagus. Food naturally flows into the laryngopharynx rather than into the larynx due to its location below the oropharynx and to the action of the diverticulum. The epiglottis may assist in preventing entrance of foods into the larynx, but its function is unnecessary since removal of the epiglottis has never been found to cause difficulty in drinking or eating.

Since speech is essentially a function superimposed on organs whose basic purposes are ingestion and respiration, the very same muscles which effect changes in the size and shape of cavities for speech purposes as a result of training are activated unconsciously in vital and vegetative processes. Those which change the configuration and, to some extent, the location of the oropharynx and the laryngopharynx are listed in Table 3–3A as the orolaryngopharyngeal muscles of resonation. Those which operate the velopharyngeal port and alter the configuration and to some extent the location of the nasopharynx and thus the oropharynx are listed in Table 3–3B as the oronasopharyngeal muscles. The superior constrictor muscle of Table 3–3A also belongs in this latter category. Reference to the appropriate figures should prove helpful in perceiving each muscle's function. It should be noted that the levatores veli palatini raise the velum and, once the velum is in this elevated position, the fibers of the tensor veli palatini lie nearly horizontally and can therefore tense the velum. Two pharyngeal muscles listed in Table 3–3B, the palatopharyngeus and the palatoglossus, may assist in velar depression but are probably much more useful in swallowing than in phonation, since gravity and muscle relaxation are probably the most important factors in opening the velopharyngeal port. By visual inspection of a normal mouth one may see the uvula (cf. Fig. 3–14), a pendulous organ hanging from the posterior terminus of the velum. On each side of the oral cavity behind the molars are the anterior faucial pillars. These may obscure the posterior faucial pillars in which the palatopharyngeus lie, since the posterior pillars are parallel to the anterior pillars and do not extend medially to the same extent.

Physiology of the Resonatory System

As has been seen, the larynx, which contains the sound-producing apparatus, the vocal folds, is capable of undergoing considerable alteration in length and to some extent in position and cross-sectional area. The folds themselves may be elevated or depressed. The resonatory cavity between the trachea and the glottis accounts for what is termed infraglottal resonance. The larynx superior to the glottis produces laryngeal resonance. The larynx opens into the oropharynx at the same level as does the laryngopharynx, the latter accounting for esophageal resonance. The oropharynx and oral cavity can, with the entire tongue depressed as in phonating [ɑ], be considered as a single large cavity, but in raising some portion of the tongue, as in phonating any other vowel, two mouth cavities are formed, one anterior and one posterior to the linguopalatal or linguovelar constriction. Thus, "oral resonance" is a term that may be employed only loosely. The oropharynx can be considered as merely a volume addition to the oral cavity during the production of tongue-depressed sounds or to the cavity posterior to the linguopalatal or linguovelar constriction during the production of other sounds. Nasal resonance is effected by the nasal and nasopharyngeal cavities. Although the nasal cavity is to a large degree fixed in size and shape, due to its bony structure, the nasopharynx can undergo variation by changing the amount of velopharyngeal opening. Sound can easily penetrate the palate and velum at all times, so that nasal resonance must occur on all sounds unless the nasal cavity is filled with fluid and, even

TABLE 3–3

Resonatory Muscles

Muscle	Location	Fig.	Origin	Insertion	Shape	Resonatory Function
A. Orolaryngopharyngeal Muscles						
Superior pharyngeal constrictor	Back and side of neck	3–6	Pterygoid and hamular processes, velum, mandible and base of tongue	Posterior median raphe	Broad, quadrilateral	Assists in velopharyngeal closure
Middle pharyngeal constrictor	Slightly lower than above and slightly overlapping	3–6	Greater and lesser cornua of hyoid bone	Posterior median raphe	Broad, quadrilateral and thicker than above	Mainly used in swallowing, but may assist in laryngeal retraction and in reducing volume of laryngopharynx
Inferior pharyngeal constrictor	Slightly lower than above and slightly overlapping	3–6	Lateral surfaces of thyroid and cricoid	Posterior median raphe	Broad, quadrilateral and thicker than above	Mainly used in swallowing, but may assist in laryngeal retraction and in reducing volume of laryngopharynx
Stylopharyngeus	Side of neck	3–6	Styloid process of temporal bone	Posterior border of thyroid cartilage	Oval, tubular	Elevates larynx and laryngopharynx and widens laryngopharynx laterally

B. Oronasopharyngeal Muscles

Levator veli palatini	Choana	3–6	Petrous portion of temporal bone	Posterior portion of velum	Thin, cylindrical	Elevates and retracts velum; widens oropharynx
Tensor veli palatini	Posterior nasal cavity	3–6	Pterygoid plate and underside of sphenoid bone	Anterior portion of velum	Ribboned mass	Elevates and then tenses velum
*Uvular	Back of velum	3–14	Velum	Uvula	Short, thin	Shortens and elevates uvula
Palatoglossus	Within anterior faucial pillar	3–14	Anterior portion of velum	Sides of tongue	Narrow band	Depresses and relaxes velum; elevates side of tongue
Palatopharyngeus	Within posterior faucial pillar	3–14	Velum	Posterior border of thyroid cartilage	Long, thin	Depresses and relaxes velum; elevates larynx

* The uvular muscle is found to vary in individuals; it may be paired or unpaired.

then, audible resonance very conceivably occurs. However, nasal resonance may be increased to the extent that the velopharyngeal port is opened and to the extent that sound is focused towards the nasopharynx. This focusing is accomplished perhaps to the extent that the laryngeal cavity is inclined posteriorly or retracted, since it is obvious from a study of the musculature that such laryngeal changes may occur, but the physiological correlates of nasal resonance are by no means completely understood. It should be noted here that the nares are capable of some constriction, which can affect the nasal cavity acoustically.

Anatomy of the Articulatory System

Except for the mandible, the skeletal framework for articulation has been discussed previously. Articulation is the process of phonating the various consonants; enunciation refers to the phonation of vowels and, since the production of vowels is essentially due to tongue positioning, that subject can be considered as being covered implicitly under the discussion of the physiology of the resonatory system. The articulators, those structures which actively produce the various consonants, are the lips, tongue, teeth, hard palate, and velum.

The tongue is a muscular organ attached posteriorly to the hyoid bone, epiglottis, velum, and laryngopharynx and centrally to the mandible.

The mandible is U-shaped, with a body and two rami. The upper border of the body, or alveolar process, contains two bony plates which form the sockets for the lower teeth. Each ramus is roughly quadrilateral with two superior projections, the anterior or coronoid process and the posterior or condyloid process. The latter articulates in the mandibular fossum of the temporal bone to form a trempromandibular joint. The condyl (rounded head of the condyloid process) is able to slide out of this fossum downward and forward to permit extremely wide mouth opening.

The upper teeth are set in the alveolar processes of the maxillary bone. Some texts refer to the cavity between the inner aspect of the cheeks and lips and the outer aspect of the alveolar processes of the mandibular and maxillary bones as the buccal cavity, but this cavity has here been considered merely as a portion of the oral cavity.

The muscles which are employed most directly in articulation are the facial muscles, the mandibular muscles, and the lingual muscles, listed in Table 3–4. Some muscles which have dual functions have been listed previously. Thus, the mylohyoid, hyoglossus, and genioglossus appear in Table 3–2A as laryngeal elevators, which assumes that the tongue is relatively fixed. However, with the hyoid and mandibular bones relatively fixed, these muscles assist in tongue depression. In like manner, the palatoglossus listed in Table 3–3B assists in elevating the tongue, provided the velum is relatively fixed. In addition, this muscle, together with the palatopharyngeus, which depress the velum are probably active in the articulation of those consonants which require linguovelar constriction. Although the only muscles listed in part II of Table 3–4B as depressors of the mandible are the external pterygoids, it can be seen from Table 3–2A that the mylohyoids, geniohyoids and, to some extent, the anterior bellies of the digastrics also act as mandibular depressors, provided the hyoid bone is relatively fixed.

Physiology of the Articulatory Mechanism

The functions of the articulators will be discussed subsequently under acoustics in Chapter 4, and under voice quality in Chapter 5. It can be seen, however, that the tongue tip may be elevated by the superior longitudinal muscle, that the central portion may be elevated by the inferior longitudinals and the transverse muscles, and that the back of the tongue may be elevated by the styloglossus, the palatoglossus, and the superior constrictor muscles. The tongue as an entity may be shifted anteriorly by the genioglossus and hyoglossus and shifted posteriorly by the styloglossus and the superior constrictor muscles.

TABLE 3–4

Articulatory Muscles

Muscle	Location	Fig.	Origin	Insertion	Shape	Articulatory Function
			A. Facial Muscles			
*Orbicularis oris	Within lips	3–13	None	None	Oval ring	Purses or closes lips
Buccinator	Within cheek	3–13	Maxilla and mandible	Lower fibers into upper lip; upper fibers into lower lip	Broad, flat, and interlaced	Widens and retracts lips
Platysma	Anterolateral part of cheek	3–13	Under skin on chest and shoulder	Mandible and lips	Wide, quadrilateral	Spreads lips and depresses corner of mouth
Risorius	Within cheek	3–13	Masseter muscle	Side of lip	Flat	Widens corner of mouth
Zygomaticus	Within cheek	3–13	Temporal process of zygomatic bone	Lips	Oblong, flat	Spreads lips and elevates corner of mouth
Caninus	Above corner of mouth	3–13	Outer surface of maxilla near canine tooth	Side of lip and lower lip	Flat, triangular	Elevates lower lip and widens corner of mouth
Triangularis	Chin	3–13	Outer surface of mandible	Corner of mouth	Flat, triangular	Depresses corner of mouth and assists in lip closure
Mentalis	Chin	3–13	Outer surface of mandible	Lower portion of orbicularis	Short, flat	Extends lower lip
Quadratus labis superioris	Above upper lip	3–13	Premaxilla and zygomatic bone	Orbicularis oris	Flat, triangular	Elevates upper lip

Quadratus labis inferioris	Chin	3–13	Outer surface of mandible, medial and deep to triangularis	Orbicularis oris	Flat, quadrangular	Depresses and widens lower lip
			B. Mandibular Muscles			
			I. Mandibular Elevators			
Masseter	Within cheek	3–5, 3–13	Zygomatic arch	Ramus and angle of mandible	Flat, thick, and quadrilateral	Elevates lower jaw; fibers can extend or retract jaw
Temporalis	Side of skull	3–13	Temporal fossum	Zygomatic arch, coronoid process of mandible	Flat, triangular	Elevates jaw; posterior fibers retract jaw
Internal pterygoid	Around oral cavity		Pterygoid fossum and medial surface of pterygoid plate of sphenoid bone	Medial surface of mandible near angle	Thick, quadrilateral	Elevates and extends jaw
			II. Mandibular Depressors			
External pterygoid	Around oral cavity		Lateral pterygoid plate and greater ala of sphenoid bone	Condyloid process of mandible	Thick, triangular	Extends and depresses jaw
Mylohyoid	Cf. Table 3–2A					
Geniohyoid	Cf. Table 3–2A					
Digastric, anterior belly	Cf. Table 3–2A					
			C. Lingual Muscles			
			I. Extrinsic Muscles			
Styloglossus	Deep within side of neck		Styloid process of temporal bone	Into tongue from near base to tip	Long, many fibered	Elevates and retracts tongue

TABLE 3–4—(Continued)

Muscle	Location	Fig.	Origin	Insertion	Shape	Articulatory Function
Genioglossus	Cf. Table 3–2A					
Hyoglossus	Cf. Table 3–2A					
Palatoglossus	Cf. Table 3–3B					
II. Intrinsic Muscles						
*Superior longitudinal	Within superior surface of tongue		Base of tongue	Tip of tongue	Long, fibrous network	Elevates tongue tip; thickens and shortens tongue when agonist of inferior longitudinal
Inferior longitudinal	Within inferior surface of tongue		Base of tongue	Genioglossal and hyoglossal muscle fibers and up into inferior body of tongue	Rounded	Depresses tongue; lowers tongue tip; shortens and thickens tongue when agonist of superior longitudinal
Transverse	Throughout tongue except tip		One side of tongue	Opposite side of tongue	String-like; interlaced with vertical fibers	Narrows and thus extends tongue; can bulge midline upward
Vertical	Throughout tongue		Superior surface of tongue	Inferior surface of tongue	String-like; interlaced with transverse fibers	Flattens tongue

* Indicates that the muscle is unpaired. All others are paired.

4

Acoustics of Speech

Anatomy, physiology, and acoustics are the three factors which interact to enable anyone to engage in the process of communicating orally with another, and before we can progress meaningfully to methods of improving this process we must understand precisely the nature and functions of these factors. The first two were treated in the preceding chapter and the last will now be discussed, but this division is quite artificial since these factors are interrelated. However, to discuss all three simultaneously would be confusing. Hence, acoustics per se will be discussed and then, as in the last chapter, interactions will be considered. The most important consideration of such interactions, however, will occur in subsequent chapters. The chapters on voice quality and pitch, for example, cannot be understood except in terms of the interactions of anatomy, physiology, and acoustics. Thus, the primary reason for considering acoustics in this text is to provide understanding of the chapters on voice training.

Obviously, no attempt is made to consider acoustics in anywhere near its entirety; only enough is included to provide an understanding of voice and voice training. Therefore, the subsequent material is to be studied carefully; you should not skip any sections you do not understand but reread them until their meanings and significances become clear. Your ability to answer the questions at the end of each main section can help you to determine the extent to which rereading is necessary. A little extra effort on this chapter can save you considerable time in trying to make sense out of seemingly incomprehensible ideas which are presented later.

1. Waves

The most difficult concept to make tangible in the area of acoustics is that of a wave, but once this concept is grasped the rest of the area becomes lucid without much difficulty. Therefore, you should read this material with care, and progress beyond it only after it is well understood.

Let us assume that seven persons stand in a row, one boy at each end and five girls in the middle. Let us designate the boy on the right as "sender," the one on the left as "receiver," and the five girls between them as the "medium of communication," each girl of which is a "particle" of this medium. Now let's instruct the five "particles" to pass on whatever "message" they receive from the person on their left *as quickly as possible* and to return for another message as quickly as possible. Now, suppose the sender hands the first particle (girl) a piece of chalk. Eventually, the receiver is handed that same piece of chalk. If you were asked "what" was sent, you would reply, and correctly so, that a "piece of chalk" was sent. Now suppose that the sender slaps the palm of the first particle (girl). Eventually, the fifth particle slaps the receiver's palm. Now what was sent? You cannot reply that a "slap" was sent, because a slap cannot be considered a "thing" in the same sense that the piece of chalk is a "thing"; technically, nothing (no "thing") was sent. What was sent was an "act of slapping," which is an activity rather than a thing.

Let us make some other observations about this communication of the act of slapping. Suppose the sender now gives out another slap to the first girl just as soon as her hand returns for the next message. What is now being communicated is a steady repetition of the same activity, the act of slapping. Let us examine this process closely by instructing the girls to freeze in whatever stage of the activity they are in when we shout "Freeze!" What do we see? Are all palms outstretched in the same direction? Quite obviously, they are not. It could be that the first, third, and fifth particles are in somewhat similar positions, as compared with the second and fourth, and that the second and fourth are likewise in similar positions, but different from the odd-numbered particles. If the odd-numbered particles are in identical positions, we say that one *wave* is, say, 6 feet long, or the *wavelength* is 6 feet, which is the distance between the first and third or third and fifth particles.

Now, suppose the *frequency* of slapping is slowed down so that the sender slaps the first particle's palm, say, 2 seconds after she extends it toward him. We notice that the speed with which each particle transmits each slapping remains the same regardless of how many slappings are sent in any given amount of time. That is, whether 2 slappings per second are sent or 1 slapping per second is sent, each wave of slapping travels at the same *velocity* provided we do not try to send them more frequently than the particles can pass them along. Since the velocity is the same regardless of the slapping frequency (number of slappings per second), if the frequency is changed the wavelength must change. This change in wavelength must be the reciprocal of the frequency change. For example, if the frequency is halved, the wavelength is doubled. So, if at 2 slappings/sec. the first, third, and fifth particles are in the same position (our 6-foot wavelength from 1 to 3 or 3 to 5), at 1 slapping/sec. only the first and fifth particles are in the same position and the wavelength is now 12 feet.

It was said that the girls constituted our *medium* of communication. It can be seen that, so long as the medium remains unchanged, the velocity remains constant (regardless of frequency). How might the medium change? The particles might move farther apart or closer together; or, we could add or remove some particles. When we talk about moving the particles in any medium farther apart or closer together, without change in the number of particles, we are speaking of decreasing or increasing the *pressure* of the medium. When we talk of adding or subtracting particles without changing the pressure, we are speaking of increasing or decreasing the *density*[1] of a medium.

One final remark before we leave the analogy of the slappings. We instructed the five girls to transmit the messages they receive as rapidly as possible. Assuming the girls are all anatomically and physiologically identical, we can see that their speed of acting is related both to their muscular strength and the weight of their arms. If their muscles were stronger (more elastic), they would act faster, but if their arms had greater weight (more density), they would act more slowly.

Review Questions

1. Do high-frequency sounds travel faster than low-frequency sounds?
2. Small ocean waves (not breakers) are processes of change. Will a cork riding such waves move in the direction they are moving?

2. *Characteristics of Particles*

From this point on, an analogy different from the girls as particles proves more useful. Henceforth, the analogy portrayed in Fig. 4–1 will be employed. When we speak of a particle we mean something, larger than a molecule, which acts as a unit[2] in three important ways: it possesses an *elasticity* and an *inertia* which can be considered as entities throughout (rather than, say, having an elasticity at the core which differs from that at the crust), and it moves as an entity. Inertia refers to the

[1] Density is the mass divided by the volume it occupies. Since we are speaking of particles, particle density refers to the number of particles per unit volume. Density can be increased, therefore, either by packing more particles into a given amount of space or by packing the same number of particles into a smaller amount of space.

[2] A molecule of air is approximately 10^{-8} cm. in diameter. They are so numerous (averaging about 400 billion billion per cubic inch of air) that they can travel only about 10^{-5} cm. before striking another molecule. Thus, a single molecule's activity may not seem closely related to a sound wave, but any small group of them acts much the same as any other small group; hence the usefulness of the "particle" concept.

amount of work required to disturb a particle. Thus, the heavier it is, the greater its inertia. By elasticity is meant the amount of springiness or energy enabling it to return toward its original position from a disturbed position. Thus, a stiff spring has more elasticity than a lax one. Now let us relate density (usually measured in grams per cubic centimeter) and pressure (usually measured in dynes per square centimeter) to elasticity and

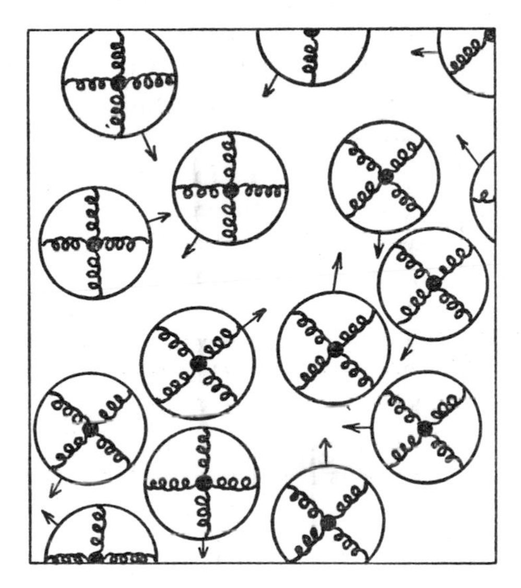

Fig. 4–1. Schematic representation of the concept, *particle*. Solid core represents particle *inertia*. Springs between core and outer surface represent particle *elasticity*. Arrow direction and length represent direction and amount of Brownian movement due to temperature.

inertia. If we increase pressure on particles without altering the density (make the same number occupy less space), we increase their elasticity much as a spring under high pressure will move toward its original position more quickly, once this pressure is removed, than a spring under low pressure. If we increase the density of particles without altering the pressure (make a greater number occupy the same space), we increase their inertia, just as it takes more work to move a third billiard ball by the cue ball hitting a second ball which hits the third ball than by striking the third ball with the cue ball directly.

However, we have thus far been considering pressure and density as unrelated when, in fact, within a given medium they are so closely related that the effect of one cancels the other. That is, if we double the pressure we double the density. This makes sense because when we say we double the pressure we can imagine compressing a unit of volume into a volume half as large. Thus, we now have twice as many particles per unit volume, or twice the density, in this compressed volume. We see that compression, then, increases the elasticity, which would in turn increase the velocity, but we also increase the density so as to reduce the velocity, and both theoretically and experimentally the effect of one cancels the effect of the other. Thus, we see that, as we go from one gas to another as media we may change density and pressure disproportionately, but *within a single medium* velocity is *not* affected by pressure or density alterations.

It should not be imagined that particles are stationary until a sound (a change in pressure) disturbs them. They are constantly moving about and, of course, striking one another. This Brownian movement is affected by temperature. That is, the higher the temperature, the more active the particles become; and the work required to accelerate an object is related to its velocity, being greatest when the object is at rest. We all know how much easier it is to push an automobile the faster it is moving. In like manner, a wave passes from one particle to the next at a higher velocity the faster the particles are moving prior to being disturbed by the wave. Thus, since temperature regulates the activity of particles, the only determinants of the velocity of a wave are which medium it is propagated in and the temperature of that medium.

Review Questions

3. Can high or low frequencies (i.e., waves that are, respectively, very short or very long) more readily produce ice falls from glaciers?

4. The solid line in the figure below represents pressure variations on a particle due to a passing sound wave. The dashed line represents

particle displacement. At what moment (A, B, C, or D) is the particle displacement (a) maximal in the direction of wave travel? (b) maximal in the opposite direction? At what two moments is the particle velocity (c) greatest? (d) least?

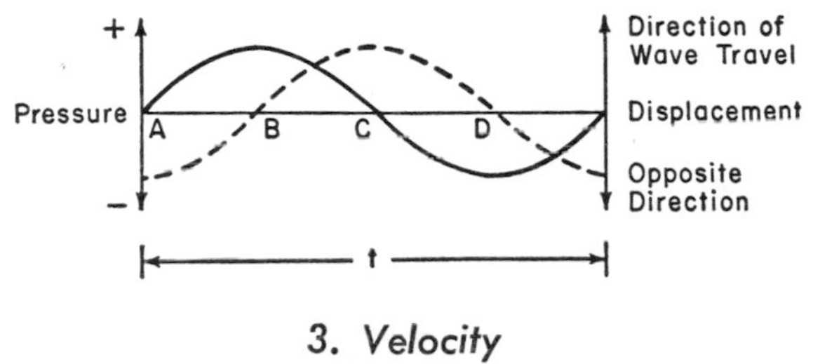

3. *Velocity*

When we speak of "velocity" we may refer to either of two different but related phenomena. *Particle velocity* refers to a movement which is continually changing. A particle disturbed by a wave is displaced in the direction of the ongoing wave, its elasticity then pulls it in the opposite direction, and it oscillates thus for a length of time determined by its inertia and elasticity, so that the less its inertia and the greater its elasticity, the longer it continues to oscillate. The extent of this particle displacement is but a very minute fraction of a millimeter, and even at very high frequencies the particle moves far less than a millimeter in a second. To get a better idea of the difference between the distance covered by a particle and that covered by a wave, if we assume a particle to move as far as .00001 foot (an extremely generous assumption) during each cycle, at a frequency of 1000 cycles per second (cps) it would move back and forth 36 feet in an hour, while a sound wave travels about 4,000,000 feet in that time.

The other velocity, the one in which we are usually more interested, is the *wave velocity*. We have already seen that a change in frequency does not change the velocity. We have also considered how wavelength explains this lack of change. The formula which expresses this relationship for a given medium of constant temperature is:

$$v = f \times \lambda \qquad (1)$$

where v, velocity, and λ (lambda), wavelength, are both measured in the same units (say v in feet/sec. and λ in feet), and f is the frequency or number of waves per second.

Review Questions

5. If you could observe a particle in motion due to disturbance by a sound wave, could you determine in which direction the wave is traveling?

6. Airplanes must travel faster at lower altitudes to reach the speed of sound (called Mach 1). Why?

7. Do we cease to hear a sound the instant the source ceases to produce sound?

8. Why is a whistle or horn on a passing train higher pitched as it approaches and lower as it recedes? Does the passenger on the train observe this phenomenon?

9. The velocity of sound is determined by which of the following: (a) its frequency, (b) the amplitude of particle displacement, (c) its intensity, (d) particle velocity, (e) temperature of the medium?

10. Within a uniform medium, if a sound is doubled in frequency: (a) its amplitude is halved, (b) its velocity is doubled, (c) its velocity is halved, (d) its wavelength is halved, (e) its period (time required to complete one wave) is doubled.

4. Sound Waves and Sound

Loosely speaking, sound waves are waves in any medium whose frequencies are such that they are capable of being heard. Technically speaking, however, sound waves are those frequencies between certain limits within which the phenomena observed may all be explained by the same concept of wave propagation. Thus, other types of waves are bundles of energy (e.g., light waves), or they travel through a vacuum (e.g., radio waves) or they are reflected differently (e.g., radar waves). *Sound* is the psychological perception of sound waves. Thus, we can resolve quite simply the classic poser of "Does a falling tree make a sound if no ear hears it?" The answer is that it creates sound waves, but it does not make a sound.

5. Air as a Medium

Sound waves can obviously be propagated through liquids and solids, but we are most concerned with their propagation through air.

Air is a combination of several gases, each of which, being a different medium, has a different velocity of propagation. It would be unrealistic to suppose that this combination of gases is identical at all places and times in our atmosphere, and thus we should not expect a single answer to the question of what the velocity of sound in air is. These differences are not large enough to concern us here, but they do account for slight differences among researchers in computing the velocity of sound waves in air.

We have mentioned that temperature affects the amount of disturbance of particles. At absolute zero (−273° C), this movement theoretically ceases. Both theoretically and experimentally, it has been shown that velocity is proportional to the square root of the absolute temperature (0° C = 273° Absolute). Hence, for a rise in temperature from 0° C to 1° C, the velocity would be $\sqrt{(273 + 1)/273}$ times the velocity at 0° C. At t° C, then, the velocity would be:

$$v_t = v_0 \sqrt{\frac{273 + t}{273}} \tag{2}$$

where v_0 is the velocity of a sound wave at 0° C.

The velocity of a sound wave in air at 0° C is about 331.5 meters/sec. = 1087 ft./sec. = 741 mph. Thus, to find the velocity of a sound wave at 72° F, we would convert Fahrenheit to centigrade by subtracting 32° and multiplying the remainder by 5/9, to yield 22° C. Inserting this in Equation 2 we have

$$v_{22^\circ} = 741 \sqrt{\frac{273 + 22}{273}} = 770 \text{ mph}$$

Now we are ready to examine more precisely why velocity is unrelated to pressure and density. In a gas:

$$v = \sqrt{k \frac{p}{\rho}} \tag{3}$$

where p and ρ (rho) are, respectively, the undisturbed pressure and density, and k is a quantity related to the specific heats of the gas. Since the velocity of sound remains unchanged in a medium so long as the temperature remains unchanged, it would seem that a change in pressure changes the density. Experiments do in fact bear this out nicely. Thus, if the pressure on a gas is doubled, we pack twice as many particles in the same space, thus doubling the density, so that the ratio p/ρ remains the same and the velocity changes only with respect to the change in temperature. Hence, we do not need to know the pressure and density of a gas to know the velocity of a wave in it; we need only to know its temperature.[3]

Review Questions

11. Assume that we have a sound source in a room that produces the same frequency regardless of the medium in the room. If you entered the room when it contained, first, helium and oxygen and, second, normal air at that same pressure, and if sound travels faster in the first case, would the frequency of the sound that you hear be different in the two cases?

12. Why do supersonic jets have to be built stronger to fly polar routes?

13. What is the velocity of sound in air at 0° F?

6. Simple Harmonic Motion

Assume a light source, a wheel with a shaft, and a paper screen (which, for the moment, is *stationary*), arranged as in Fig. 4–2. The shadow traced on the screen as the wheel revolves starts at the center position, moves toward the reader, stops for an instant, passes back through the center, moves away from the reader (back into the plane of the illustration), stops for an instant, and then passes back through the center to repeat this pattern again. The path traced by the shadow of the ball is called *simple harmonic motion.*

If the paper screen in Fig. 4–2 is made light-sensitive and

[3] The foregoing is true for all of our purposes, but it should be noted that, at very low temperatures (say below −100° C), especially at extremely high pressures (say from 25 to 250 times atmospheric pressure), bewildering changes in velocity have been observed.

Also, it was implied that particle displacement is independent of velocity, but this is true only if this displacement is rather small. In an explosion the particles are displaced quite drastically, and thus the velocity near the source of an explosion or a high-energy spark is much greater than at a distance from this disturbance.

the equipment set up in a dark room, a single line is traced. To see exactly how this line is traced, let us pass the light-sensitive paper behind the revolving ball at a constant speed. A curve like that in Fig. 4–3 would then be traced. It can be seen that at A the ball is at center, at B it is at one extreme, at C it passes back through center, at D it is at the opposite extreme, and at

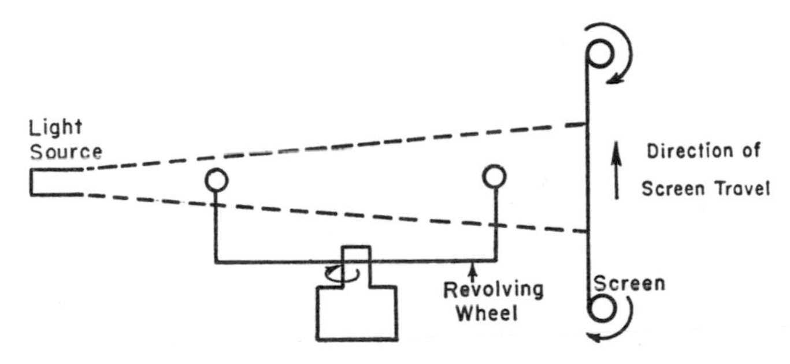

Fig. 4–2. Device for tracing a shadow that moves with simple harmonic motion.

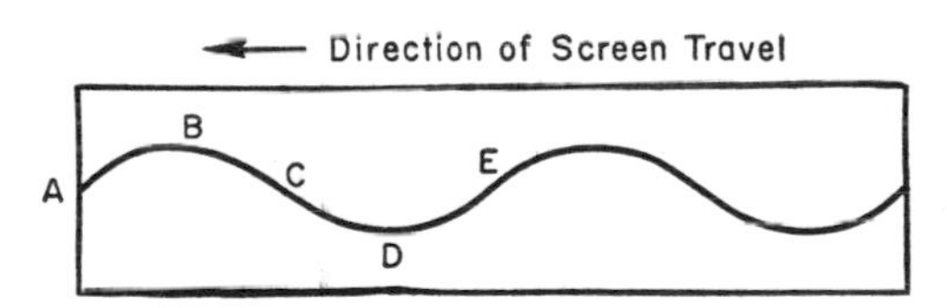

Fig. 4–3. Path traced by shadow on screen as in Fig. 4–2 as screen moves perpendicular to shadow's axis.

E it is back to the same position as at A. Thus it has completed *one cycle* or *one full wave* in going from A to E.

If we consider that the wheel revolved 360°, i.e., made one complete revolution, in tracing the line from A to E we can say that AB is 90°, AC is 180°, and so on.

The type of motion shown in Fig. 4–3 describes (1) the simplest possible particle activity (in which the vertical scale represents amount of longitudinal particle displacement), or (2) the pressure on a particle over a certain amount of time, or (3) an instantaneous picture of the relative pressures of a series of adjacent particles. In any case, the motion described is called *simple harmonic motion,* and the curve itself is called a *sinusoidal curve.* When applied to sound waves in any of the three above uses of the term, it is called a *sinusoidal wave.* A wave is sinusoidal regardless of width or amount of ascendancy. A number of such waves are shown in Fig. 4–4.

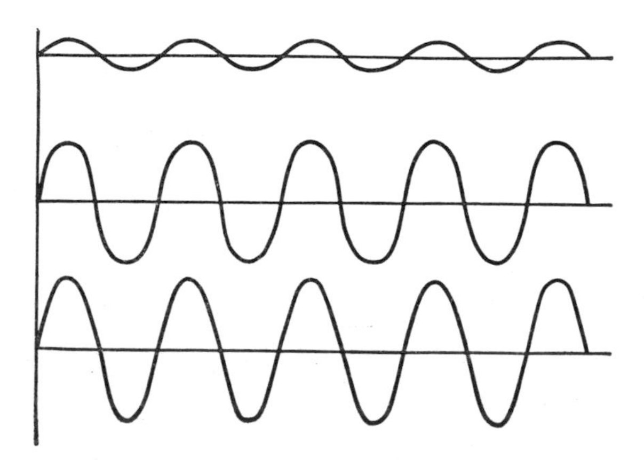

Fig. 4–4. Three sinusoidal waves.

Review Questions

14. Is a pendulum's movement simple harmonic motion?

15. In viewing cowboy films we sometimes notice the wheels on a moving wagon seem to stop, turn slowly, or turn backward. Why? (*Hint:* a motion picture is a series of still pictures.)

7. Phase

Now suppose we place two balls opposite each other on the apparatus, as shown in Fig. 4–5. The resultant tracings on a sheet of paper moving at a constant rate would be as in Fig. 4–6.

The two waves are said to be 180° *out of phase.* Suppose these were two sounds of equal intensity traveling in the same direction from the same source. It can be seen that their forces are at all times opposite and the resultant effect on any particle would be zero, or as if neither sound existed.

Phase, then, refers to the time difference between two waves and this time difference is expressed in degrees of identical length (hence, identical frequency), (e.g., $90° = \frac{1}{4}\lambda$, $180° = \frac{1}{2}\lambda$).

The way we are able to detect the direction of sounds is not only by a difference in intensity at our two ears, but by the degree to which the sounds at the two ears are out of phase. A

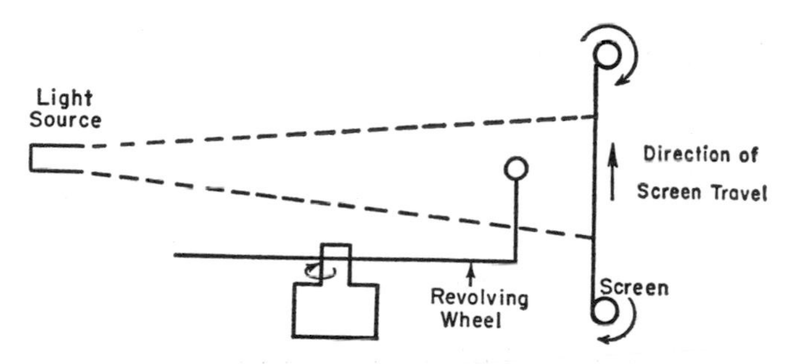

Fig. 4–5. Device for tracing two shadows simultaneously, each of which moves with a simple harmonic motion.

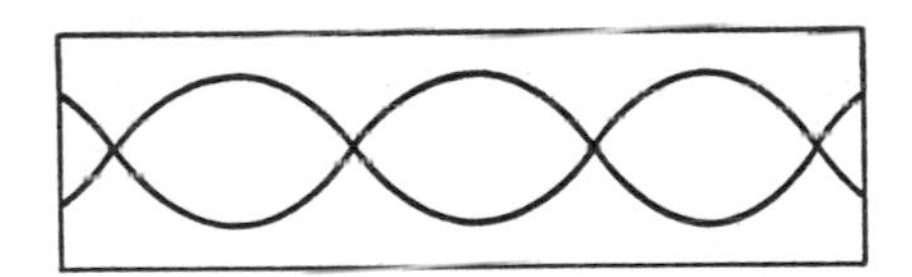

Fig. 4–6. Paths traced by shadows on screen as in Fig. 4–5 as screen moves perpendicular to shadows' axes.

knowledge of phase enables us to locate objects, to design musical instruments and sound reflectors, to plan the acoustical characteristics of concert halls, to help the blind move about safely, and in many other ways.

Review Questions

16. Exactly how does phase enable us to tell the direction of a sound source?

17. Portable radios are usually not permitted near persons who are broadcasting. Why?

18. True stereophonic sound requires recording from two microphones placed in the ears of a manikin's head and listening to the recordings via earphones. Why?

8. *Reflection*

Sound is a wave of pressure traveling through space in time, or at any point in space it is a changing of pressure with time, and thus we would expect pressure waves to be reflected in a manner different from other types of waves such as light waves.

The manner in which a *sound wave* is reflected at a plane surface can be understood from examining Fig. 4–7. A sound originating at A would be reflected from plane X along the path of a wave originating at a point A_1 in the same position as A on the opposite side of the plane.

Thus, it can be seen that at any point B_1, B_2, or B_3 on the wall the reflected wave is in phase with the incident wave.

One might wonder why a reflection occurs at all. At any point on the surface of the plane the pressure increments and decrements are exactly in phase with the incident wave and, since sound is such pressure variations, we can consider the wall as the source of the reflected wave much as each particle in any wave can be considered as the source of the wave received by the next particle. Since these fluctuations in pressure are not absorbed by the plane, they create a reflected wave. We have assumed plane X to be rigid. This is a rather safe assumption about most solids, such as walls, furniture and the like, since we would not expect particles traveling with energies of less than a billionth of a billionth of one horsepower per $cm.^2$ to do much moving of any objects that they strike.[4]

[4] A "sonic boom" is quite another matter. When an aircraft travels at the speed of sound, the particles are compressed against the front of the aircraft and the medium begins to act more rigidly than elastically, and when such "booms" break windows it is due to this inelastic bunching.

Upon consideration it can be realized how altitude, aircraft speed above the velocity of sound, wind direction, wind velocity, aircraft size, and fuselage and wing tapering all affect the pressure against a window, not to mention such characteristics of the window as thickness, thickness variance, size, stresses applied in installation, glass quality, etc. It should also be noted that the aircraft drags the lower edge of this pressure cone behind it rather than in front of it because it is traveling faster than sound.

However, a reflection at an orifice is quite different from a reflection at a rigid plane. Assume a wave is traveling through a tube when it encounters an open end. To simplify matters, further assume that the undisturbed pressure in the tube and

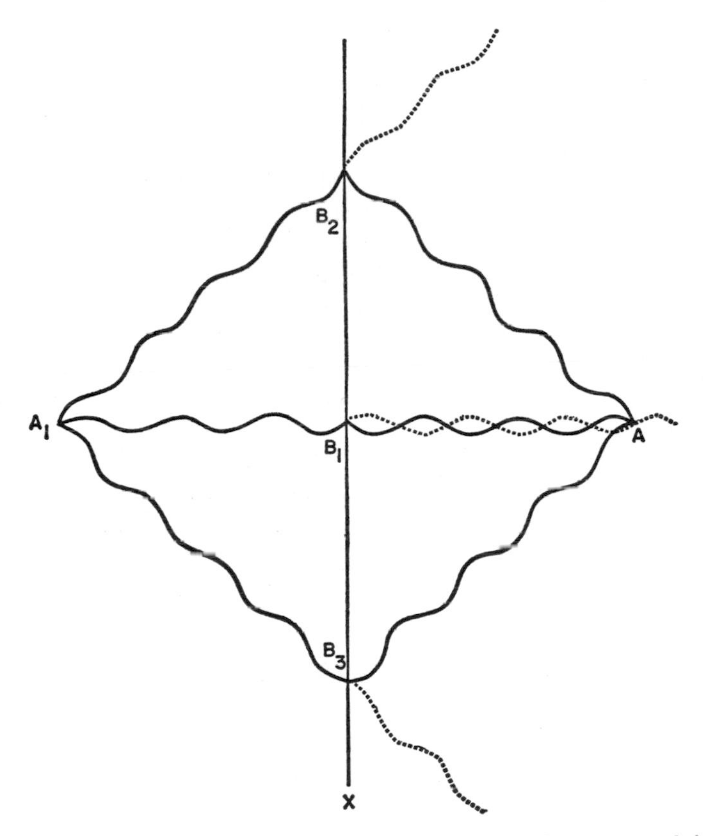

Fig. 4-7. Nature of the reflection of a sound (A) at a wall (X).

outside are the same and that the temperatures at both places are equal. It might seem that the wave would simply be propagated out of the tube. However, this would require less pressure at the open end than the lowest pressure in the tube, but we said that the normal pressure in the tube and outside were the same.

To see what happens when sound in a tube encounters an open end consider a wave, W, propagated through a tube as in Fig. 4–8. As the point of maximum (above atmospheric) pressure (+) reaches the open end, P_1, it encounters a pressure (atmospheric) which is less and so can continue outward to P_2. But when the maximum pressure reaches P_2, P_1 is at atmospheric pressure (0) and P_0 is below atmospheric pressure (−). Hence, the condensation at P_2 expends itself toward P_0, setting up a reflected wave.

It might be wondered how much of the pressure at P_2 escapes outward and how much is reflected. This, of course, depends upon the narrowness of the tube and the wavelength, since the distance from P_1 to P_2 is one half-wavelength. The greater this length, the greater is the force of return. Also, the smaller the

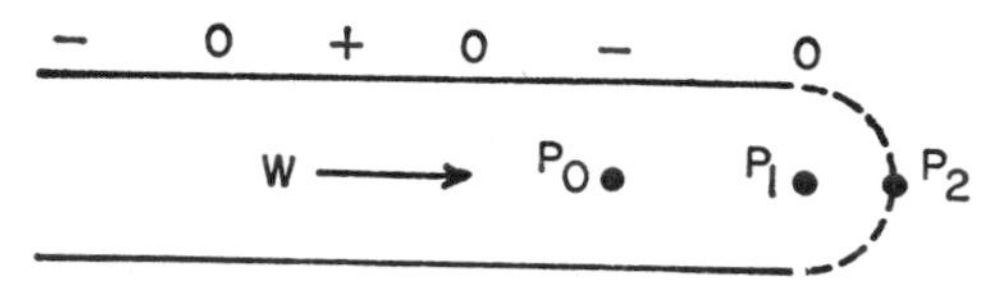

Fig. 4–8. Nature of the reflection of a wave (W) at an open end (P_1) of a tube.

opening, the better is the reflection. The theoretical percentage of dissipation loss for a tube of radius R, where R/λ is much less than 1 foot, is:

$$\text{Per cent dissipated} = \frac{800\pi^2R^2}{\lambda^2} \tag{4}$$

To understand the extent of dissipation better, suppose the medium is air and the temperature is 72° F. Using Equation 2, we previously found the velocity to be 770 mph, which is 1129 ft./sec. Suppose we introduce into the tube a sound whose frequency f is 1000 cps. Then $\lambda = v/f =$ 1129 ft./sec. divided by 1000 cycles/sec., or 1.129 ft. per cycle, or one wave is approximately 13.5 inches. If R is $\frac{1}{2}$, $R/\lambda = \frac{1}{2}/13.5$ or $\frac{1}{27}$ and, using Equation 4, about 11 per cent would be dissipated and 89 per cent reflected. For the same tube and a frequency of 100 cps, $R/\lambda = 1/270$ and the loss is far less than 1 per cent!

Review Questions

19. Why do the notes played by one instrument in an orchestra not cancel the notes played by another instrument?
20. Why must infantrymen not march in step across a bridge?
21. A singer may shatter a mirror by singing a certain note. Explain.
22. A bomb explodes near a house, but the broken window panes lie *outside* the house. Explain.

9. *Intensity*

The more energy a sound source imparts to particles, the greater are the pressure variations in the wave, and the greater the amount of particle displacement. Thus, Fig. 4–9 reveals

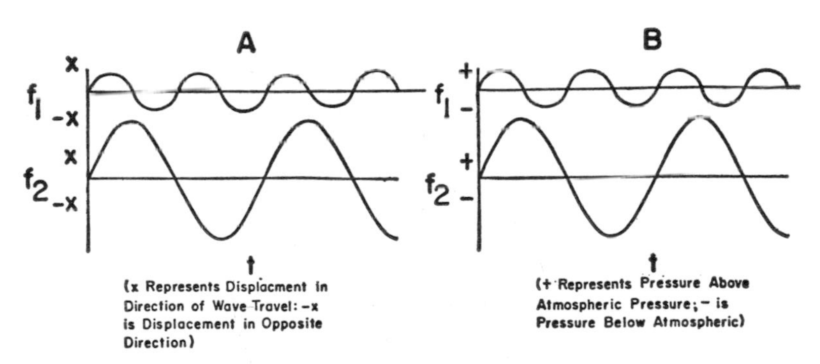

Fig. 4–9. (A) Particle displacement and (B) pressure changes for two frequencies (f_1, f_2).

the magnitude of particle displacement and (in B) the amount of pressure change of two sounds of different intensities. The difference between the terms *intensity* and *pressure* is that pressure is the ability to do work whereas intensity is the amount of work done. Intensity is related to the square of the pressure ($I = kP^2$, and in an uninterrupted or plane progressive sound wave, $I = P^2$). Hence, to do twice as much work we need to square the pressure applied.

Review Questions

23. Is intensity related to amplitude? If so, how?
24. Why isn't the intensity of four violins playing together sixteen times as great as one alone?

10. Harmonic Analysis

So far, we have been speaking of sounds whose pattern of pressure variations is sinusoidal. We are now ready to perceive that *any* waveform which is exactly repeated from cycle to cycle can be considered as being composed of a number of such sinus-

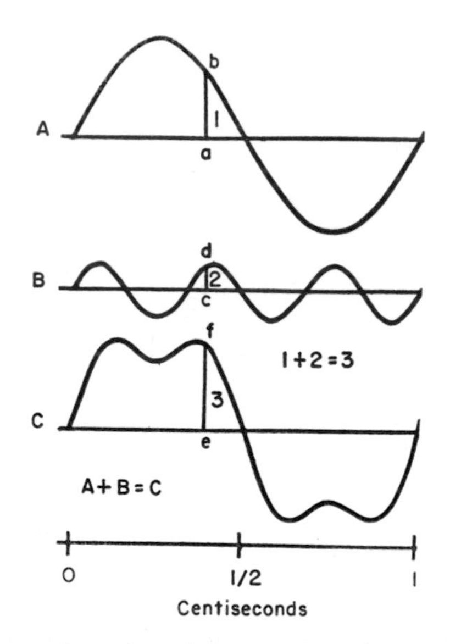

Fig. 4–10. A complex wave (C) as a sum of sinusoids (*A* and *B*).

oidal waves. Moreover, the frequencies of these components are integral multiples of the frequency of the given wave. Waveform *C* of Fig. 4–10 can be treated as if it consisted of the two frequencies of 100 cps and 300 cps, labeled *A* and *B*, in the

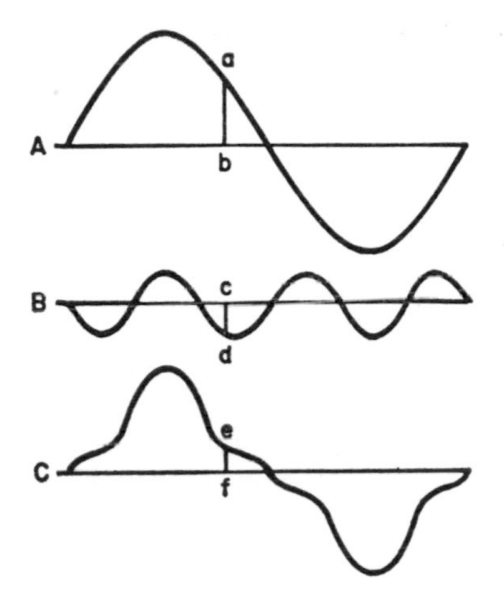

Fig. 4–11. The same complex wave shown in Fig. 4–10, but with sinusoids out of phase.

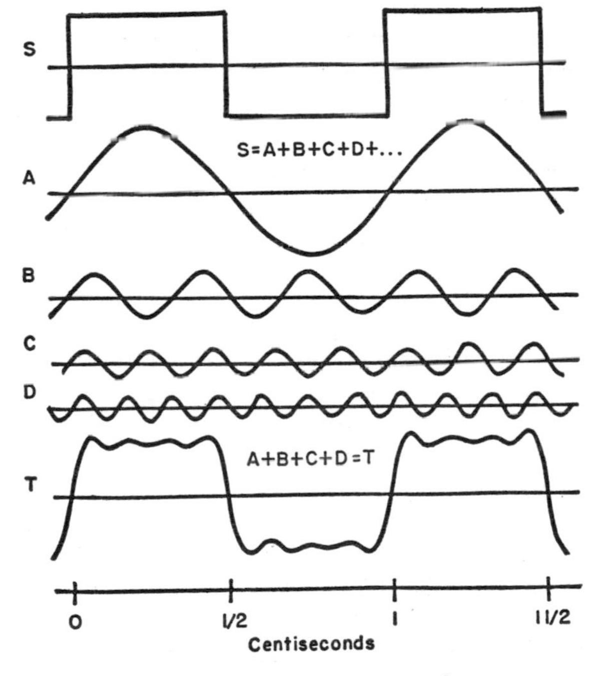

Fig. 4–12. Four sinusoidal components of a square wave.

figure. Hence, all we need to specify such a complex waveform is to state the amplitude and phase relationship of each sinusoidal component. Thus, waveform *C* could have been created by two tuning forks, one tuned to 100 cps and a less powerful one tuned to 300 cps, both of which are struck simultaneously (0° difference in phase). It could also have been created by a diaphragm which is made to vibrate according to the pattern shown in *C*, but in either case the sound produced would be the same. If we adjust *B* so that, instead of crossing the axis simultaneously with *A*, while heading in the same direction, it crosses headed in the opposite direction (180° difference in phase), the resultant waveform would be the one shown in Fig. 4–11.

In Fig. 4–12, even the waveform labeled *S*, called a *square wave*, may be considered as consisting of an infinite number of sinusoidal components, four of which are shown. In like manner, the *rectangular wave* shown in Fig. 4–13 could be completely specified by a table which lists the frequency, relative amplitude, and phase relationship of each component. However, differences in phase among various components of a complex wave are usually not perceived (unless a component's phase relationship undergoes change as we listen to it). Hence, we usually ignore phase and represent the components of a complex wave by use of a graph which provides the same information that would be provided by a table. Such a graph, shown in Fig. 4–13, is called a *line spectrum*.

We have seen that complex waveforms are capable of being considered as if they are composed of various sinusoidal components. However, it is important to note that the frequencies of the various components bear a distinct relationship to the frequency of the complex wave. Each component is a *whole-number multiple* of the frequency of the complex wave. The frequency of the complex wave is called the *fundamental* frequency of the complex wave. The sinusoidal component whose frequency is exactly the same as the frequency of the complex wave is called the *first partial*. The second partial is a sinusoidal wave that is twice the frequency of the fundamental, the third partial is a sinusoidal wave three times the frequency of the fundamental, and so on. Hence, if a complex wave occurs 100

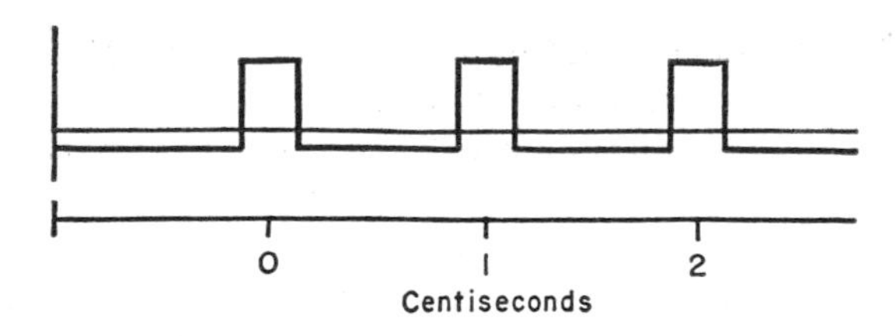

Partial	*f*	Amplitude	Intensity	db Down
1	100	1.000	1.000	0.0
5	500	0.983	0.967	0.2
10	1000	0.935	0.876	0.7
15	1500	0.858	0.737	1.3
20	2000	0.757	0.573	2.4
25	2500	0.636	0.405	3.9
30	3000	0.505	0.255	5.9
35	3500	0.368	0.135	8.7
40	4000	0.234	0.055	12.6
45	4500	0.109	0.012	19.2
50	5000	0.000	0.000	∞
55	5500	0.089	0.008	21.0

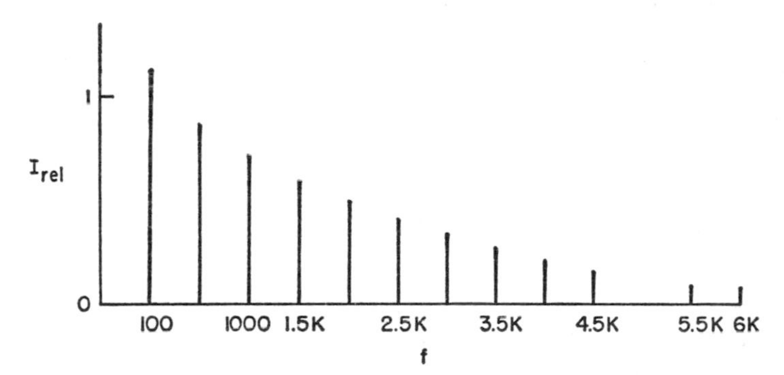

Fig. 4–13. Waveform, relative partial energy (abbreviated table), and line spectrum of a rectangular wave of 100 cps.

times per second, the frequency of its 55th partial is 5500 (or 55 × 100) cps.

Partials are useful because waveforms are not necessarily altered by changes in frequency. Hence, a waveform can be considered as composed of relative amplitudes of various *partials* (rather than various frequencies) because a change in the frequency of the wave would not change the relative amplitude of, say, the 55th partial although the frequency of the 55th partial would necessarily change.

It should also be noted that a waveform can *not* contain any components that are not *whole-number* multiples of that wave's fundamental frequency. If a component that is not a whole number multiple were added to a given waveform, it would be seen that this so-called *inharmonic partial* would prevent adjacent cycles from being identical in waveform. The waveform would vary from cycle to cycle because, in effect, a partial whose phase (starting time) is constantly changing has been introduced. Hence, when we say that we have a complex wave that is repeated cycle after cycle, the fact that it is repeated excludes all consideration of components that are not whole-number multiples of that wave's frequency.

Review Questions

25. Which of the following is not true? (a) The 6th partial is twice the frequency of the 3rd. (b) The 8th partial is four times the fundamental. (c) The 8th partial minus the seventh partial equals the funda-

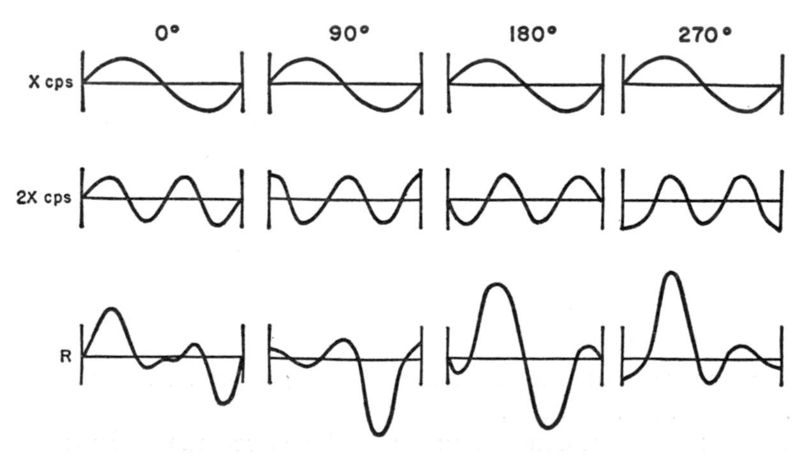

Fig. 4–14. Resultant waveform (*R*) of a complex tone consisting of two frequencies differing variously in phase.

mental. (d) The 5th partial is the sum of the 2nd and the 3rd. (e) The 2nd partial is twice the frequency of the first.

26. What is the fundamental of a complex wave whose harmonic analysis shows energy at 44, 110, and 176 cps?

27. From a study of Fig. 4–14, what single factor makes it impossible to draw the waveform from a knowledge of the amplitude of every partial?

28. How would you account for the fact that a pilot of a twin-engine aircraft can keep both engines turning at the same number of revolutions per minute without consulting any gauges?

11. Resonance

From the foregoing you can see that, when two waves of the same frequency and intensity travel in the same direction in phase, their pressures combine. This is shown in Fig. 4–15A.

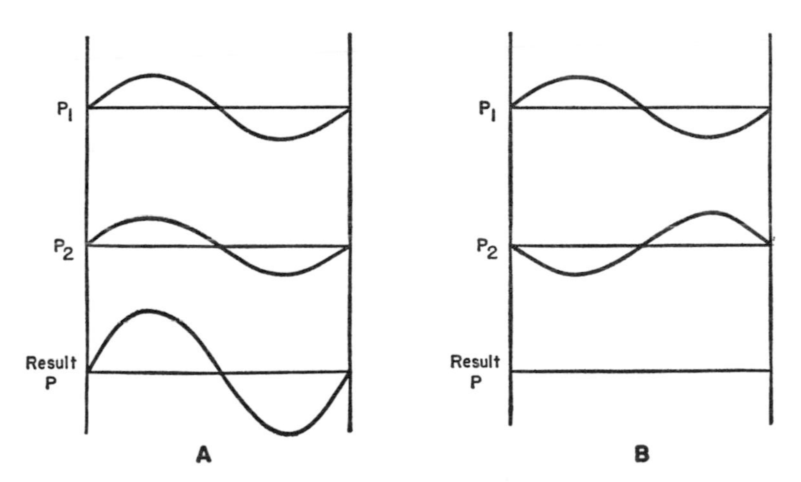

Fig. 4–15. Waveform dependency upon phase relationships.

When they are out of phase (180° phase difference), their pressures also combine, but since one is positive (above atmospheric pressure) and the other is negative (below atmospheric pressure), their pressures cancel or annul each other (Fig. 4–15B). Thus far we have considered waves traveling in the same direction. What happens when they travel in opposite directions?

We might consider the activity that a particle undergoes

when it is disturbed by two sounds of the same frequency and intensity traveling in the same direction. In that case, at any moment the pressure is twice the pressure of each sound, and the particle moves in the same direction as if only one wave were disturbing it, but it moves out a greater distance but not twice the distance (since this would require squaring rather than doubling the pressure). Now if these two waves are traveling in opposite directions *out of phase,* when one wave is trying to displace the particle in one direction the other is trying to displace it that same distance in the opposite direction. Thus, the particle remains *stationary* (except for its usual thermal activity) but the pressure on that particle is twice the pressure exerted by either wave. Figure 4–16 attempts to indicate this.

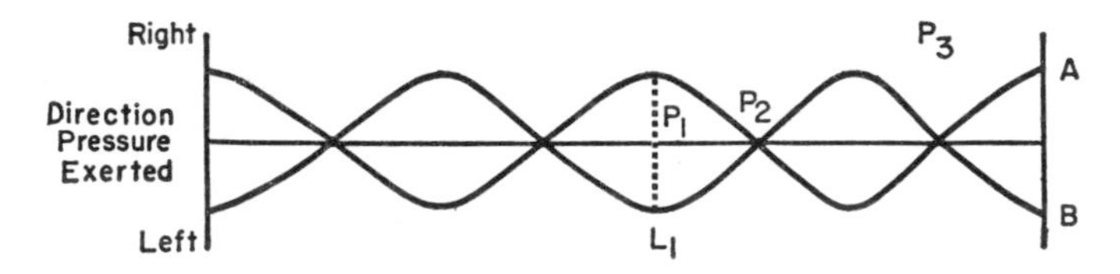

Fig. 4–16. Particle pressures due to waves traveling in opposite directions.

Consider particle P_1, which is at the center of what is termed a *displacement loop.* The pressure exerted by wave A tends to move it to the right while the pressure exerted by wave B tends to move it to the left. Thus it remains stationary, but the pressure on that particle above atmospheric pressure is represented by the length of the line L_1. It can also be seen that particle P_2 is equally stationary but the pressure on it equals atmospheric pressure, or the pressure on such a particle as P_3. P_2 is said to be at a *displacement node.*

Now let us consider three ways in which we can produce these stationary waves, i.e., to obtain two waves of equal frequency and intensity traveling in opposite directions. Consider Fig. 4–17.

If we place a sound source at O and it enters the cavity at A, it will be reflected at B without change in phase. Hence, we need the incoming wave to create a displacement node at B.

The reflected wave will return to A where it will again be reflected (except for energy lost according to Equation 4), but with change in phase. Hence, to reinforce the wave from O the length of the tube (L) should be such that a displacement node occurs at B and the midpoint of a displacement loop occurs at A. If we

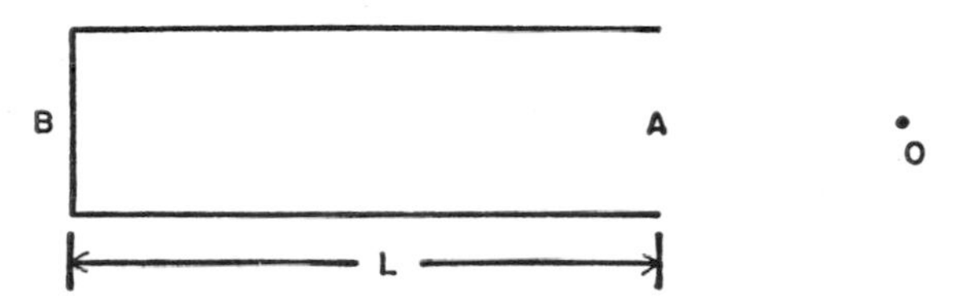

Fig. 4–17. Sound from source O enters tube of length *L*.

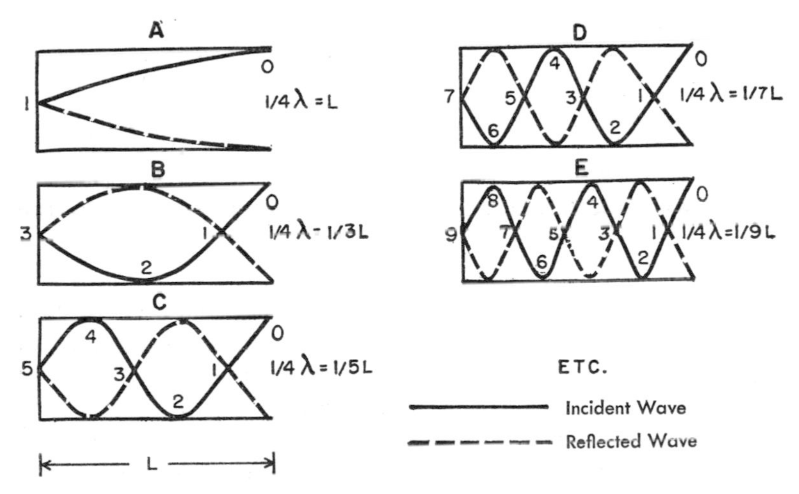

Fig. 4–18. Stationary waves capable of being contained in a tube open at one end ($\frac{1}{4}\lambda$ between any two consecutive numbers).

represent these waves in this cavity as in Fig. 4–16, remembering that we are representing longitudinal pressures on particles rather than particle displacement, we arrive at the figures shown in Fig. 4–18.

You can see that the lowest frequency has a wavelength $\lambda = 4L$ or that $L = \frac{1}{4}\lambda$. The higher frequencies have wavelengths of $4/3L$, $4/5L$, $4/7L$, etc. Thus, if the lowest frequency to which the tube is tuned is 100 cps, the other frequencies it would reinforce are 300 cps, 500 cps, 700 cps, 900 cps, etc. or any odd whole-number multiple of this *fundamental.*

The fundamental (f_1) is called the *first partial.* The second partial refers to a frequency twice that of the fundamental, the third to $3f_1$, and so on. Hence, we say that a tube open at only one end reinforces only the odd partials of the frequency to which it is tuned.

We have used the terms *stationary wave* and *reinforce,* but it is now time to reflect on their meanings with more precision. Consider the arrangement shown in Fig. 4–19. Suppose the tuning fork vibrates at a frequency to which the length of the

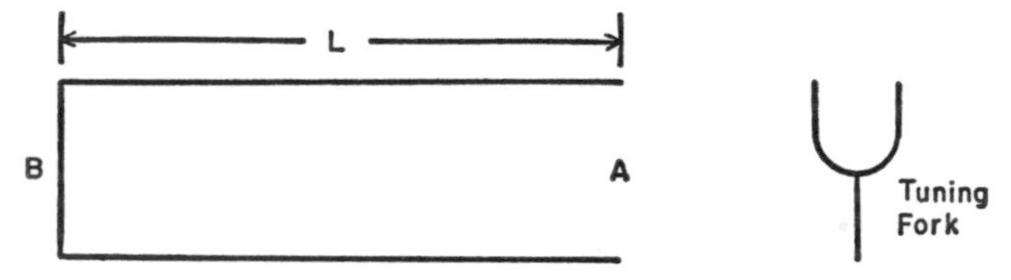

Fig. 4–19. A tuning fork vibrating at that frequency whose $\lambda = 4L$, where L is the length of the cavity to which it is exposed.

tube is tuned. We mean that, for this medium and temperature, if the λ of the created sound is X, the tube is $X/4$ in length. When the wave reflected at B returns to A, it undergoes reflection with phase change. We might think of it bulging out, as in Fig. 4–8, so that the fork is best prepared to push the wave back into the tube when it is best prepared to be pushed. The analogy of pushing a child in a swing is suitable here. We accomplish most with least effort by beginning each push as the swing reaches its crest; although we could accomplish some work by pushing somewhat earlier or later, our efforts would to some extent be wasted. Hence, when we speak of a tuned cavity, we should realize that, although one group of frequencies will fit best, frequencies near these will be somewhat effective. Thus, we could graph the reinforcement characteristics of the cavity shown in Fig. 4–19 as in Fig. 4–20. If we assume that

$v = 1100$ ft./sec., for an f of 100 cps, $\lambda = 11$ feet and L must be $\frac{1}{4}\lambda$, or 2.75 feet.

Reinforcement does *not* imply that more sound energy is created; it simply means that energy is taken from the source more efficiently. Thus, reinforcement does not create energy but consumes it rapidly. To illustrate this, strike a tuning fork and listen to see how long you can hear it. This will probably be about one minute. Now fill a tube with water until the tube is tuned to the fork, and place the fork above the tube after striking it. It will probably become inaudible in less than one-fourth the previous time (depending on the sharpness of tuning, the

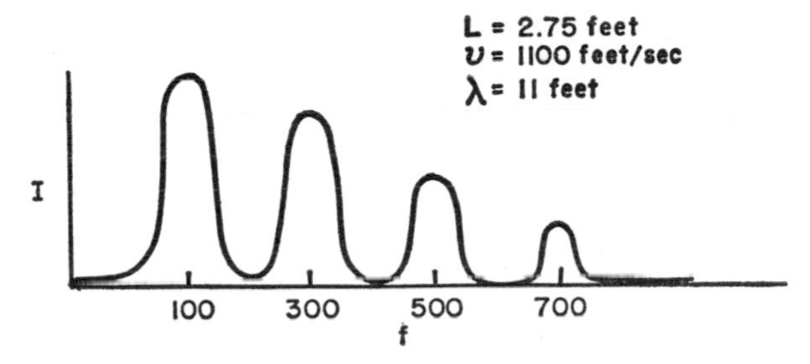

Fig. 4–20. Reinforcement characteristics of the tube shown in Fig. 4–19.

dimensions of the tube, and the internal losses of energy in the fork). Thus, the tube actually drew energy from the fork forcing the fork to expend its energy faster than it would have in the absence of any cavity to which it is tuned. A distinction should be made here between cavities which *reinforce* sound and those which *filter* sound. Look at Fig. 4–21. Although the relative frequency response of the two cavities is identical, the cavity in A merely permits certain frequencies to pass from the source to the outside air[5], while the cavity shown in B reinforces, rather than merely passes, the frequencies from the source to which this is tuned. *Resonance* refers to the fact that a cavity is tuned to one or more frequencies of a source

[5] According to dissipation-loss theory discussed earlier (see pp. 108–9).

which, if the source is outside the cavity, reinforces those frequencies best and, if the source is within the cavity, filters or prevents passage of those same frequencies to the outside least.

As will be seen later, the vocal cavity is a filtering system rather than a reinforcing system. Hence, the acoustic energy is greater at the folds rather than at the lips. To cite a musical analogy, we are discussing the essential difference between a flute

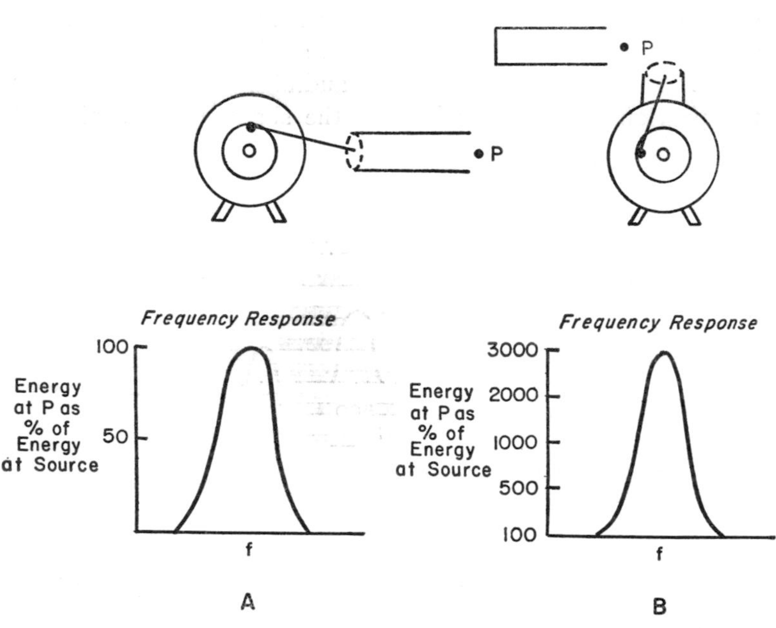

Fig. 4–21. Frequency response differences between (A) filtering and (B) reinforcement.

across which air is blown and a horn into which air is blown. Obviously, more energy is used in playing the horn.

One additional important factor needs to be considered here, and that is that a stationary wave is not created instantly. The previous figures, such as Fig. 4–18, have represented the stationary waves formed after a considerable—and, for our purposes, an important—interval of time. A more accurate portrayal of this time might be shown by Fig. 4–22. It can be seen that, at first, the energy is taken from the fork to build up the maximum pressure node provided by the diameter of the tube and that, once this limit is reached, the energy is taken from the fork to replace both the dissipation loss at the open end and the energy being expended in vibrating the tube. The latter is the principal source of the resonated sound, since we have employed a much larger surface area (the outside of the tube) to disturb air particles than that of the original source (the fork). Thus, the larger the diameter of the tube for a given length, the longer is the time required to build up a stationary wave to maximum, and the

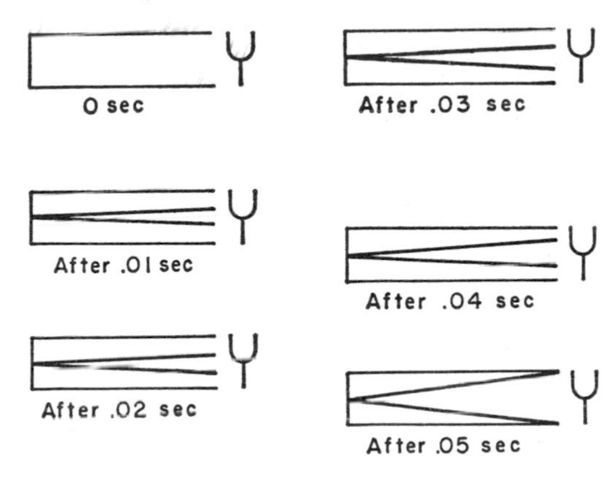

Fig. 4–22. Creation of a stationary wave as a function of time.

greater are both the dissipation loss and the energy required to maintain the created stationary wave.

Let us now progress to a consideration of resonance in a tube open at both ends. Here we want a tube whose length permits a displacement loop at both ends, as in Fig. 4–23.

As in our previous calculations, we can see that the λ of the various partials are $2L$, L, $2/3L$, $\frac{1}{2}L$, $2/5L$, etc., or $2/1L$, $2/2L$, $2/3L$, $2/4L$, $2/5L$, etc. Hence, the corresponding multiples of the fundamental to which it is tuned are 1, 2, 3, 4, etc., or *all* whole number multiples of the fundamental. The reinforcement characteristics of the tube in Fig. 4–23 are indicated in Fig. 4–24. Again assume $v = 1{,}100$ ft./sec., so that an f of 100 cps has $\lambda = 11$ feet, and L then equals $\frac{1}{2}\lambda$ or 5.5 feet.

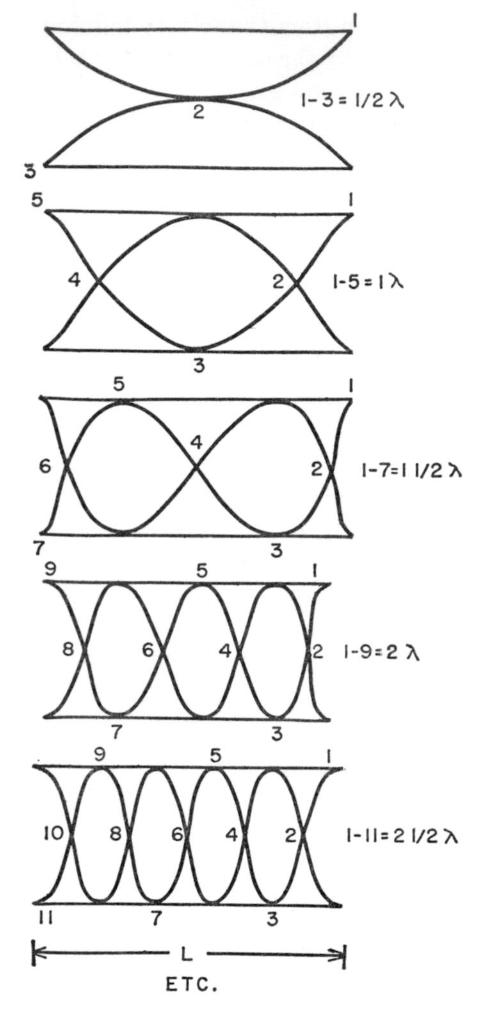

Fig. 4–23. Wavelengths contained in a tube open at both ends (¼λ between any two consecutive numbers).

A third type of cavity differs in several respects from the two previously considered, and for our purposes this last type is the most important. Consider the cavity shown in Fig. 4–25A.

If this cavity receives an incoming wave at the orifice, the

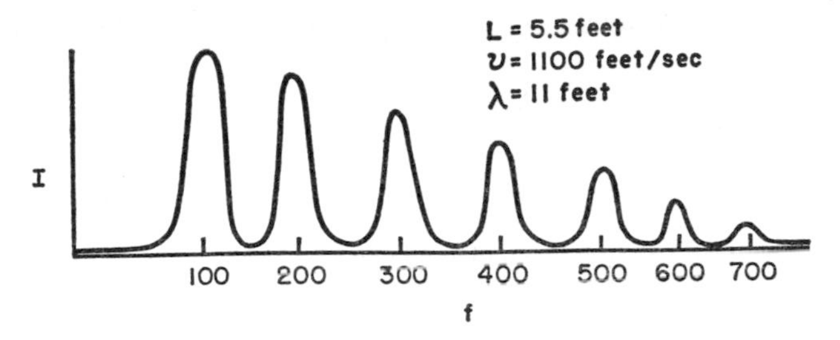

Fig. 4–24. Reinforcement characteristics of the tube shown in Fig. 4–23.

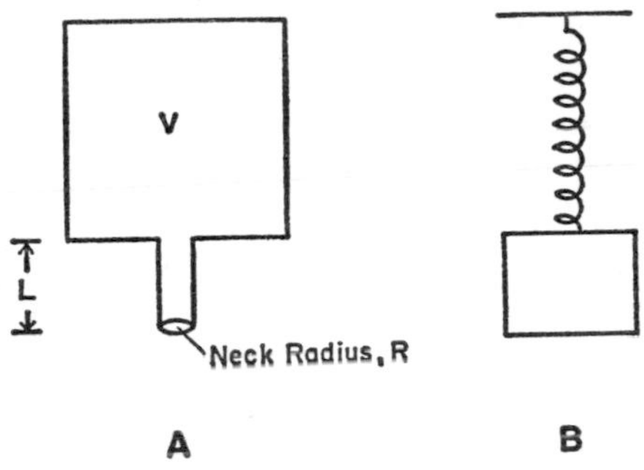

Fig. 4–25. (A) Helmholtz cavity and (B) its physical representation.

maximum inertia will occur in the neck[6] and the maximum elasticity will occur in the cavity. We can represent this by the spring and weight shown in B.

The cavity shown in Fig. 4–25 is called a *Helmholtz resonator*. Its frequency is dependent upon the volume of the cavity, V, the characteristics of the neck, and the velocity of sound.

This frequency can be computed by:

$$f = \frac{v}{2\pi}\sqrt{\frac{c}{V}} \tag{5}$$

[6] Inertia is a resistance to motion, and particles with less velocity have more inertia. Since the particles in the cavity move much less rapidly than those in the neck, the cavity can be thought of as a relatively inert mass affected only slightly by the violent changes in direction and velocity of the particles in the neck.

where v is the velocity of sound in cm./sec., V is the volume in cm.^{3}, and

$$c = \frac{\pi R^2}{L + \frac{\pi R}{2}}$$

where R and L are the radius and length of the neck in centimeters.

Thus you can see that the frequency to which a Helmholtz resonator is tuned increases as the cavity volume decreases, as neck radius increases, or as neck length decreases. That is, the longer the neck the lower the frequency, the narrower the neck the lower the frequency, and the larger the volume the lower the frequency. To illustrate the usefulness of a Helmholtz resonator, consider the length of the tube required to resonate a frequency of 100 cps. For a tube open at both ends, we found $L = 5.5$ feet and, for a tube closed at one end, $L = 2.75$ feet.

Now suppose the tubes employed above were circular and had a diameter of 10 cm. (3.9 inches). This value would not affect our previous calculations. Assume now that we take the tube that is open at one end and seal the open end with a lid in which we have a circular orifice 0.5 cm. in diameter. It is now a Helmholtz resonator where neck length is zero for all practical purposes, $c = 2R = d = 0.5$, and $V = \pi R^2 L$ or $L = V/\pi R^2 = V/78.54$. Hence, $100 = 34900/6.28 \sqrt{0.5/V}$. Solving, $V = 1543$ cm.^{3} and $L = 19.65$ cm. or 7.7 inches. Thus a tube with this orifice can reinforce the same frequency as a tube without it more than four times as long.

Review Questions

29. A Helmholtz resonator's frequency is determined by which of the following: its (a) shape, (b) total volume, (c) neck length, (d) neck constriction, (e) volume of the cavity portion?

30. A tubular cavity closed at one end and tuned to a fundamental frequency of 100 cps will reinforce which of the following frequencies: (1) 150 cps, (2) 200 cps, (3) 250 cps, (4) 300 cps, (5) 450 cps?

31. What type of tubular resonator can reinforce all of the following frequencies: 220, 440, and 770 cps? What is its length if the velocity of sound in the medium employed is 1100 ft./sec.?

12. Classification of Sounds

Sounds can be classified as *periodic* or *aperiodic*. A periodic sound is one whose waveform is repeated cycle after cycle. Because it is repeated, we can determine the time required to complete one cycle or to pass one wave, and this time required to complete one cycle is the *period* of that sound. Periodic sounds are of two types, *pure tones* and *complex tones*. A pure tone consists of only one frequency; hence its waveform is sinusoidal, i.e., a simple harmonic motion. A complex tone is composed of

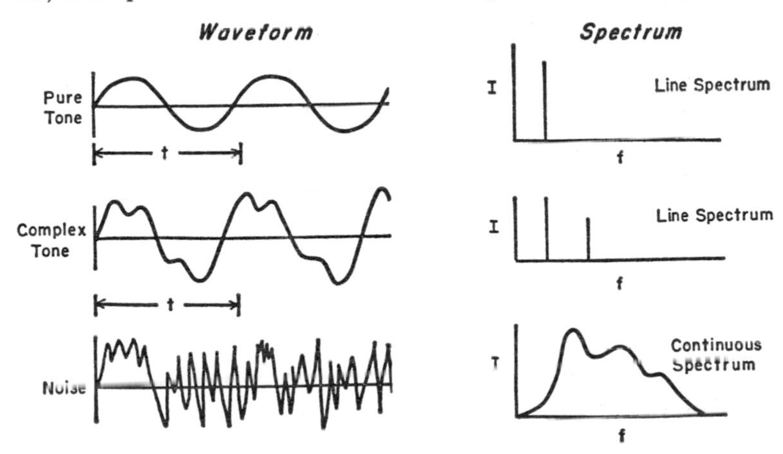

Fig. 4–26. Waveforms and spectra of pure tones, complex tones, and noise.

two or more frequencies, the largest common denominator of which is the fundamental. As shown in Fig. 4–26, both a pure tone and a complex tone may be represented by its waveform or its line spectrum. However, it should be remembered that the line spectrum does not provide information about phase.

Aperiodic sounds are also of two types, *transient sounds* and *noise*. A transient sound may be of very brief duration, such as a gunshot, or it may consist of a complex tone plus inharmonic partials so that only, say, every hundredth wave is similar, or the components of the complex tone may undergo continuous phase changes during production.

Noise is a randomness in both frequency and the energy of each frequency. Notice in Fig. 4–26 that periodicity of noise is meaningless, since there is no regularity in time (distance) between axis crossings. Noises are classified as to bandwidth, or the lowest and highest frequencies which randomly occur. The noise of widest bandwidth is called *white noise,* or *white thermal noise,* (by analogy with white light), meaning that all frequencies in the range of human hearing randomly occur with random energies. Other noises, narrower in bandwidth, are characteristic of various sound sources, such as when air escapes from a balloon, when we blow through pursed lips, or when we make the various consonantal noises of [p, t, k, θ, ʃ, s, h].

It should be noted that resonance cavities can reinforce certain frequencies of noise, as in blowing across the end of a tube. Hence, resonance is not restricted to periodic sounds.

The human ear is capable of hearing sounds with frequencies as high as 16,000 cps, and some persons can perceive frequencies as high as 22,000 cps. The lowest perceptible frequency is about 16 cps. Below this frequency, waves of sufficient amplitude may be audible but they tend to be perceived as painfully loud clicks or bursts of noise rather than as tones. Why they are painful will be discussed later, but that they are perceived as pulses seems obvious upon considering that one can almost count the cycles as they occur. The range of hearing, then, is over a frequency range of at least 1000:1 (from 16,000 to 16 cps). Frequency relationships cannot be easily perceived over such a huge range unless the relationships are expressed as ratios. For example, if baseball games had such scores, it would not be obvious at a glance, when Team A beat Team B by a score of 3840 to 376 and C beat D by a score of 890 to 55, that C's victory was the more decisive since it scored more than 16 times as many runs as D while A scored only about 10 times as many runs as its opponent. Moreover, humans tend to compare frequencies geometrically rather than arithmetically. For example, 1000 cps seems just about as far above 500 cps as 32 cps seems above 16 cps, although these arithmetic differences are 500 and 16 cycles.

A ratio scale implies the utilization of logarithms, the frequencies being converted to their logarithmic values. A logarithm (log) of a number is the exponential power to which a given base must be raised to yield that numerical value. One such system of logarithms, called common logarithms, is based on the number 10. Thus, if n is the logarithm of x to the base 10 (abbreviated $n = \log_{10} x$), this means that $x = 10^n$. Hence, if $x = 100$, $\log_{10} x = \log_{10} 100$ (meaning the power to which 10 must be raised to yield 100) $= 2$; if $x = 10{,}000$, $\log_{10} x = 5$.

Since the frequency relationship most easily perceived is an octave, which is a ratio of 2:1, a meaningful logarithmic base for comparing frequencies is the number 2. Look at the scale in Fig. 4–27.

A logarithmic scale is useful in many respects, one of which is that a frequency ratio is merely a logarithmic difference. For example, $128:32 = 2^7 \div 2^5 = 2^{7-5} = 2^2$ or 4:1. If the range of human hearing is divided into only 14 octaves, we err in the

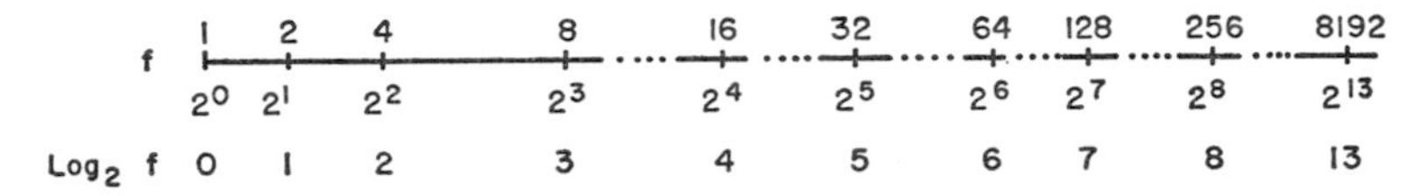

Fig. 4–27. Scale displaying f and $\log_2 f$ relationships.

opposite extreme, having too few units rather than too many. Hence what we need are octaval subdivisions. Again we divide each octave into 6 *equal* units, where equality means equal *ratios*. Hence, we use $\sqrt[6]{2}:1$ as our ratio; and $\sqrt[6]{2} = 1.122$. Thus, for the octave between 100 cps and 200 cps, the 6 intervals would be 112 (100×1.122), 112 to 126 (112×1.122), 126 to 141 (126×1.122), 141 to 159, 159 to 178, and 178 to 200. These divisions of an octave are called *tones*. Some of these intervals still seem too great so, in like manner, these are subdivided into *semitones:* $\sqrt[12]{2}:1$, or 1.059:1. In the previous example, the frequency between 112 and 126 cps that divides this interval of a tone into two semitones is 119 (which is 112×1.059, or $126 \div 1.059$) cps.

To construct a musical scale, then, all we need do is decide on one frequency as our base from which to determine all octaves, tones, and semitones. Three such standards are $A_4 = 450$ cps (concert pitch), $A_4 = 440$ cps (philharmonic pitch), and $A_4 =$

435 cps (international pitch). The subscript refers to the fourth octave above octave zero, which is the lowest octave that can be heard. Hence, when $A_4 = 440$ cps, $A_0 = 27.5$ cps. In music, an octave contains eight notes, from A through G to A, such that from B to C and from E to F the intervals are semitones, the other five intervals being full tones. Hence, when $A_4 = 440$ cps, $C_4 = 261.6$ cps and $C_0 = 16.35$ cps, as shown in Table 4–1.

TABLE 4–1

Tones Employed in Philharmonic Pitch

Interval	Tone	Frequency
	C_5	= 522.8 cps
½ Tone		
	B_4	= 493.7 cps
1 Tone		
	A_4	= 440 cps
1 Tone		
	G_4	= 392 cps
1 Tone		
	F_4	= 349 cps
½ Tone		
	E_4	= 329.4 cps
1 Tone		
	D_4	= 293.6 cps
1 Tone		
	C_4	= 261.6 cps
	C_3	= 130.8 cps
	C_2	= 65.4 cps
	C_1	= 32.7 cps
	C_0	= 16.35 cps

It is important to remember that the terms *octave* and *tone* refer to *intervals between* frequencies and not to the actual frequencies themselves. Terms such as *note*, *pure tone*, and *complex tone* refer to frequencies and not to intervals between frequencies.

Pitch is a psychological phenomenon, referring to the perceived highness or lowness of sounds. It correlates with frequency in that, for pure tones, a higher frequency will generally have a higher pitch. The next question would obviously be what is the precise nature of this relationship. As nearly as can be determined it is neither truly logarithmic, nor lincar, but somewhere in between. Intensity has little effect on pitch, although duration tends to affect pitch perception in cases of extremely short duration, the very brief durations being perceived only as "clicks." However, in general we can term pitch the psychological correlate of frequency of pure tones without having to consider such additional variables as intensity and duration. For complex tones having few partials, we tend to associate pitch with the frequency of the fundamental, even when the fundamental frequency is relatively low in intensity and, for certain situations, even when the fundamental frequency is not physically present (i.e., has zero energy). For highly complex tones, as is the case with human speech, we tend to associate pitch with the distribution of energy among partials. For example, if in a highly complex tone the energy in lower partials is reduced and this energy is distributed among the higher partials, the complex tone will then be higher pitched, although the actual frequencies containing energy remain unchanged. This phenomenon is important for voice training.

Review Questions

32. Why do we have difficulty distinguishing between a sound that fluctuates in frequency and one that fluctuates in intensity?
33. What type of sound is created by a drum?

13. Loudness

Intensity refers to the average[7] power of a sound, and is usually expressed in microwatts (millionths of a watt) per square centimeter ($\mu W/\text{cm.}^2$). Speech power is so minute that Fletcher has estimated that it would take 500 persons talking continuously for a year to produce enough energy to heat a cup of tea. However, the range of intensities which the normal ear can detect is from about one ten-billionth of a millionth of a watt ($10^{-10}\mu W$) at the threshold of audibility up to about one thousandth of a watt ($10^{3}\mu W$) at the threshold of auditory pain. This represents an enormous range of $10^{13}:1$ or ten trillion to one. Moreover, loud speech is about one million times as intense as whispered speech. To comprehend such a range, we must again (as we

[7] This average is computed by taking the square root of the mean of the squares of each infinitesimally small portion of a cycle.

did with frequency) resort to the use of logarithms. The conventional logarithmic base for expressing intensity is the *bel* (after Alexander Graham Bell). Since the range of $10^{13}:1$ is only 13 bels, we subdivide each bel into ten equal units, each of which is called a decibel (abbreviated db). Hence, 1 db is a ratio of $\sqrt[10]{10}:1$ or 1.259:1. To state it another way, a db is 10 times the common logarithm of the ratio of two intensities. All that we then need to express any intensity in decibels is to agree upon a reference intensity. This arbitrary reference point is $10^{-10}\mu W/\text{cm.}^2$) (which is $10^{-16}W/\text{cm.}^2$). Hence, the *intensity level* (I.L.) of a sound is the ratio of its intensity to this reference intensity expressed in db. For example, a sound of $10^{-3}\mu W/\text{cm.}^2$ has an intensity level of 70 db ($10^{-3}:10^{-10} = 10^7:1 = 7$ bels $=$ 70 db).

Sound energy is more directly measured, not in terms of the work it does (its intensity), but in terms of the pressure it exerts (its sound pressure). Since intensity is proportional to the square of the pressure, sound pressure relationships are also expressed in db. However, since we defined a bel as a 10:1 relationship for intensities, we must use the ratio $\sqrt{10}:1$ for sound pressure to hold db's of intensity and sound pressure at approximately the same values.[8] Thus, two sounds which differ by 10 db in sound pressure have a pressure ratio of 3.16:1. To express the sound pressure (P) of any sound in db we must again have a reference point. This arbitrary value is .0002 dyne/cm^2. The pressure ratio of any sound compared to this base expressed in db is that sound's *sound pressure level* (S.P.L.). Thus, a sound which has an S.P.L. of 70 db has a pressure of .0044 dyne/cm.^{2} This is obtained by 70 db $=$ 7 bels $= 7(3.16):1 =$ $22:1 = .0044/.0002$.

Intensity, energy, and power are measured in 10-log units, and pressure, displacement, voltage, and current are measured in 20-log units. Table 4–2 is sufficient to solve many problems without the necessity of employing elaborate logarithmic computations.

For example, given two intensities such that one is 40 times

[8] These values would be identical in a perfectly free sound field where no reflection, absorption, or turbulences occurred.

as intense as another, we find their db difference from 40:1 = 4:1 × 10:1. Since we are dealing with logarithms, to multiply we add, and since we are dealing with intensities, we use 10-log units. Hence, 40:1 is a db difference of 6.02 + 10.00 or 16.02 db.

To cite a reversed situation, suppose two sounds differ by 25 db in S.P.L.: what is the ratio of their pressures? Here we find two or more 20-log units (since we are dealing with pressure ratios) whose sum is 25, e.g., 6.02 and 19.08. Hence, their pressure ratio is approximately 2:1 × 9:1, or 18:1.

TABLE 4–2

Ratio and db Relationships in 10-Log and 20-Log Units*

Ratio	Log of Ratio	Decibels in 10-log units (*I*, I.L.)	Decibels in 20-log units (*P*,S.P.L., displacement)
2:1	.301	3.01	6.02
3:1	.477	4.77	9.54
4:1	.602	6.02	12.04
5:1	.699	6.99	13.98
6:1	.778	7.78	15.56
7:1	.845	8.45	16.90
8:1	.903	9.03	18.06
9:1	.954	9.54	19.08
10:1	1.000	10.00	20.00

* To multiply ratios, add db; to divide ratios, subtract db; to raise ratios to a power, multiply db by exponent; to take root of ratios, divide db by exponent.

We are now ready to consider the effect of various frequencies and intensities on the perceived loudness of sounds. Figure 4–28 represents a synthesis of many researchers' findings as to the thresholds of audibility and pain. An examination of the figure reveals that:

1. Frequencies between about 2000–4000 cps require least sound pressure for audibility.
2. Frequencies at the extremes of human hearing require most sound pressure for audibility.
3. The threshold of pain is rather independent of frequency.

4. The greatest range of audible pressures (roughly 150 db) is between approximately 1000–4000 cps.

Other than the two reference levels previously mentioned ($10^{-16}W/\text{cm.}^2$ and .0002 dyne/cm.^{2}), a useful base is the threshold of audibility at that frequency. This is called *sensation level* (S.L.). That is, a frequency having 0 db S.L. lies on the threshold of audibility, and one of 10 db S.L. has a sound pressure of 10 db compared to this reference pressure.

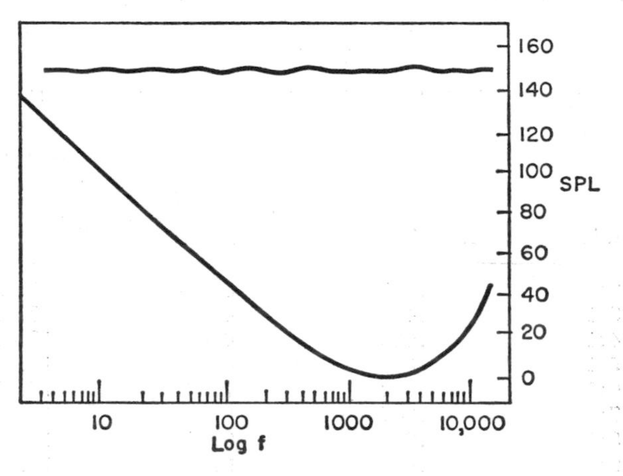

Fig. 4–28. Approximate threshold of audibility (lower curve) and threshold of pain (upper curve) summarized from the data of Bekesy, Sivian, and White, Waetzmann and Keibs, Wegel, Steinberg, Montgomery and Gardner, Silverman, Harrison and Lane, and others.

When subjects listen to a 1000-cps pure tone of a given intensity and are asked to adjust another frequency so that it is equal in *loudness* to that reference tone, the results can be considered a table of equal loudness contours. Such a table is graphically portrayed in Fig. 4–29. From this table we see that, if we compare midfrequencies to extreme frequencies in the audible range, much less increase in intensity is required to increase loudness at extreme frequencies than at midfrequencies.

The question of whether loudness is a function of duration has also been considered. In general, we can say that sounds of constant intensity build in loudness extremely rapidly and then

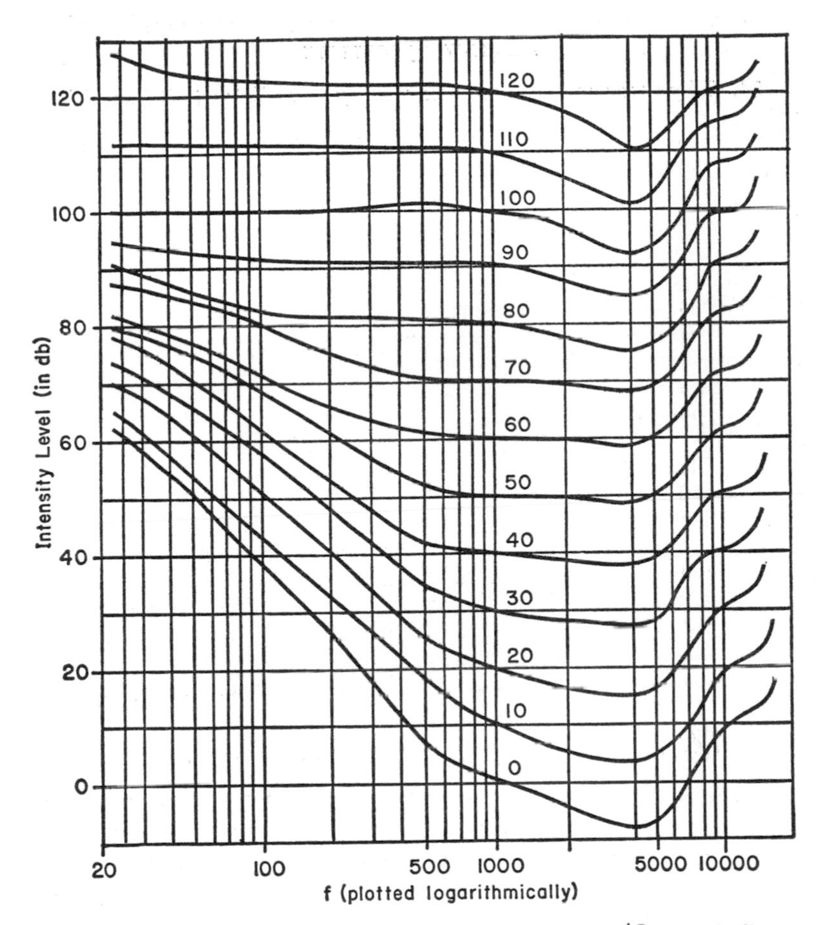

Fig. 4–29. Table of equal loudness contours. (Curves indicate intensity required for any frequency to be as loud as 1000-cps tone at each intensity level. For example, a 100-cps tone must be about 38 db more intense than a 1000-cps tone for both to be barely audible.)

decline. The peak for frequencies in the range of speech is reached after approximately one-fourth second of duration.

To conclude from these findings, then, we can say that *loudness is a function of frequency, intensity, complexity, and duration,* rather than simply a function of intensity alone.

Review Questions

34. Why does a sound change its quality as we listen to it from different distances?

35. Why is loudness of a voice heard through a door not proportional to the size of the crack around the door?

36. If at 2500 cps the threshold of pain is 140 db S.P.L. and the threshold of audibility is −4 db, what is the ratio of the two pressures?

37. *Reverberation time* is defined as the time required for a sound to drop in intensity 60 db lower than it was when the source ceased sounding. What proportion of the original energy remains?

38. If we speak of the range of sounds in conversational speech as 40 db, what ratio of intensity do we imply between the loudest sound and the softest sound? How many times as much sound pressure exists (at the same point in the medium) on the loudest as compared to the softest sound?

39. If the displacement of a particle in a sound medium is 20 millimicrons at 15 db S.P.L., what will be the displacement when the sound pressure level is 35 db?

40. If only 4 per cent of the energy of a sound is transmitted through a wall, the wall introduced a loss of ____ db between the speaker and a listener on the other side of the wall. If an additional 12 per cent is absorbed at the wall, what is the difference in db between the wave incident upon the wall and the wave reflected from the wall?

41. A sound whose S.P.L. is 60 db has a pressure of ____ $dyne/cm.^2$

14. Acoustic Characteristics of the Vocal Folds

Assume that a speaker's vocal folds are abducted as in quiet respiration and that he desires to produce a voiced sound. He induces tension in the adductive (lateral cricoarytenoid, arytenoid, and vocalis) muscles to close the folds. Let us call this tension on the folds induced prior to phonation *phonatory tension.* The air pressure is then increased subglottally until subglottal air pressure overcomes the combined resistance of phonatory tension and supraglottal air pressure, at which moment the folds part.

Now that the folds are abducted, four forces combine to close them again:

1. Phonatory tension, previously mentioned
2. *Elastic tension* of the folds, which is the extra tension induced by the folds being stretched apart

3. Reduced subglottal air pressure, due to loss of air while the folds are open
4. The *Bernoulli effect*

The Bernoulli principle is that pressure decreases at a constriction in a tube as the rate of flow through the constriction increases. Thus, when subglottal air pressure succeeds in abducting the folds, air begins to flow between the folds. This increased flow decreases the pressure at the glottis (which, even at maximum abduction, is a laryngeal constriction), causing the folds to be "sucked" together. An example of this principle can be observed in the rubber device used to produce a "Bronx cheer." It consists of a mouthpiece attached to a sleeve composed of two rectangular strips of rubber fused along the longer sides. Blowing into the mouthpiece parts the two strips, increasing airflow and, therefore, reducing air pressure, which returns the two strips together. The more forcefully we blow into the tube, the more rapidly do the two strips come together.

The four forces, then, act to close the folds *against* that force by which subglottal exceeds supraglottal pressure. As the supraglottal pressure decreases (due to the rarefaction behind the wave of condensation) and subglottal pressure increases (due to the folds closing), the rate of fold closure may be reduced just prior to fold contact. The rate of adduction is therefore not a constant; the rate decreases as the moment of impact of one fold against the other approaches. The degree of deceleration of adduction prior to impact is a function of the extent to which phonatory tension exceeds subglottal pressure. If phonatory tension exceeds subglottal pressure to such a minimal extent that the folds remain abducted for a relatively long portion of the period, the volume of air expended will be relatively great so that no excess of subglottal over supraglottal pressure can occur until after the folds are closed. If, however, phonatory tension exceeds subglottal pressure to such a great extent that the folds begin to close as soon as abduction occurs, the folds remain open only a small fraction of each period, the loss of subglottal air volume is extremely small, and the subglottal pressure can offset the falling supraglottal pressure in time to ease fold closure at moment of impact.

In summary: The folds are abducted in each cycle when subglottal air pressure exceeds phonatory tension; they are adducted in each cycle by phonatory tension, elastic tension, reduced subglottal air pressure, and the Bernoulli effect; and resistance to closure at moment of impact increases as the proportion of each cycle that the folds remain abducted decreases.

Since sound is pressure change with time and we are interested in the actual sound produced by the vocal folds, it can be seen that the waveform of supraglottal pressure is proportional to the rate and extent of fold opening and closure.[9] Thus, the vocal-fold wave should be very similar to that shown in Fig. 4–30. The horizontal axis represents air pressure in the absence of the wave. A portion of any wave will lie below this axis because any condensation must be followed by a rarefaction, due to the elasticity of the medium.

Van den Berg, who has heard the vocal-fold wave by means of a microphone inserted above the folds of a hemilaryngectomized person, describes it as buzzer-like in quality. Let us see why this is so. If we analyze a buzzer, it is simply a flexible arm attracted to an electromagnet when the voltage in the electromagnet is sufficiently high. Hence, Fig. 4–30 could describe the movement of the free end of the flexible arm, since in any cycle it is stationary until attracted suddenly to the magnet. When this voltage is reduced it returns to its original position, and remains there until the next voltage peak is reached.

Any complex tone may be analyzed into the pure tones of which it is composed and their relative intensities. However, because this analysis can be made is no justification for assuming that these pure tones were combined to produce the complex tone. To expose this fallacy by analogy, milk consists of water,

[9] Thus far, we have discussed phonation as if fold action were unaffected by the supraglottal pressure variations produced in the act of phonation. Such, indeed, seems to be the case. For example, the Sonovox is a "gimmick" used in radio and television commercials and by some laryngectomized persons. It is a buzzer-like sound source which is held against the throat while the articulatory organs move to shape words (as in dumb show rather than whispering). The resultant speech is highly intelligible. One would be on tenuous ground indeed in defending the notion that such speech affected the nature of the vibrations of such a sound source.

calcium, etc., but the cow that produced it did not take pure calcium, add water to it, and so forth, to produce milk. Such futile reasoning has led more than one researcher to wonder which parts of the vocal-fold activity produce which frequencies. Both lateral and longitudinal rippling along the folds have been observed, but these are totally unnecessary to account for the fact that the vocal folds are a complex sound source. This is explained merely by saying that the folds act as a valve whose

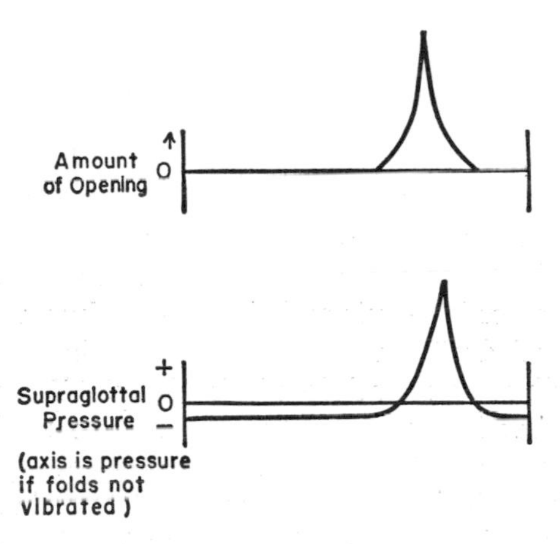

Fig. 4–30. Representation of vocal-fold adduction and abduction and resultant pressure changes during one cycle of phonation.

cycle of opening and closing is not a simple harmonic motion. Since they open late in each cycle, they function so as to produce a wave much like the rectangular wave shown in Fig. 4–13.

Since the folds produce a complex sound, our next matter for concern is the relative frequencies and intensities of this sound source. This first partial or fundamental is obviously the frequency of opening and closing, so that, if the folds open 100 times/sec., the fundamental frequency of the complex tone produced is 100 cps. The relative intensities of the other partials have been shown experimentally to decrease exponentially for higher partials so that

$$I_n = n^{-3.07} \tag{6}$$

where I_n is the intensity of the nth partial expressed as a fraction of the intensity of the fundamental (i.e., $I_1 = 1$).

Thus, we have the relative intensities of partials 1, 2, 3, . . . approximately equal to $1/1^3$, $1/2^3$, $1/3^3$, $1/4^3$, . . . , or 1.000, 0.125, 0.037, 0.016, 0.008, 0.005, 0.003, 0.002, ... This value of $n^{-3.07}$ is not, of course, an absolute one, and various researchers report somewhat different exponential values. This is partly due to the rates of opening and rates of closing of the folds being different for different speakers and for the same speaker at different frequencies and intensities,[10] but it is also related to the amount of time the folds are open in each cycle. If the proportion of time the folds remain open in each cycle is reduced, the relative intensity of higher partials is increased. Hence, louder tones have more energy in higher partials. Table 4–3 shows the frequency-energy distribution for two rectangular waves (rough approximations of the glottal wave), one of which has a duration of $\frac{1}{10}$ cycle and the other a duration of $\frac{1}{50}$ cycle. Do *not* be misled into assuming that a drop in intensity of 20 db or even 30 db means much loss in *loudness*. Remember that, as partial number increases, frequency increases; referring to Fig. 4–29 you can see that a huge loss in intensity may be more than offset by the gain in loudness because the higher partial (e.g., the 20th partial of a 200-cps complex tone) requires far less intensity to be perceived as equally loud.

It has been shown experimentally that the actual amount of time the folds are open in each cycle is independent of frequency so that the proportion of each cycle during which the folds are open increases linearly with frequency. Hence, the higher one's frequency, the more the time his folds are open tends to equal the time his folds are closed. This means that a higher pitch involves a less rich voice quality (i.e., less energy is distributed

[10] Tiffin, Saetveidt, and Snidecor found for a frequency of 150 cps, the absolute exponential value was 2.95, for 200 cps, 3.18, for 250 cps, 3.35, and for 300 it dropped to 2.85. The lower the absolute value of the exponent, the smaller is the divisor and the larger the proportion of energy in a partial; hence these data indicate that, as fold frequency increases, the higher partials have more energy until the fold frequency is doubled. Probably at that time the folds are lengthened and the folds are able to adduct more readily.

TABLE 4–3

Abbreviated* Distribution of Energy in Rectangular Waves of Different Durations

Partials 2, 3, 4, 6, 7, etc., not indicated

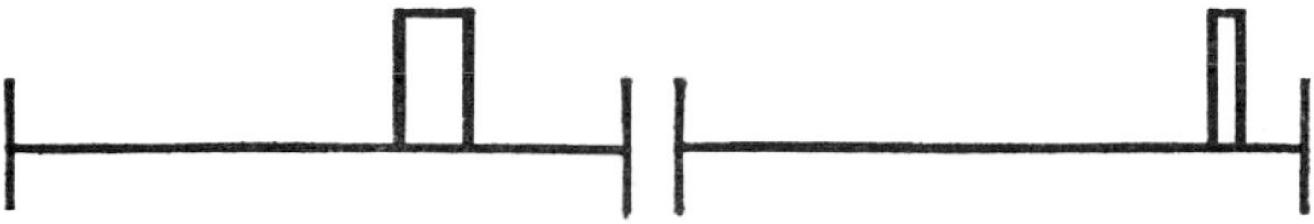

1/10-Cycle Duration				1/50-Cycle Duration			
Partial	Relative Amplitude	Relative Intensity	db down	db down	Relative Intensity	Relative Amplitude	Partial
1	1.000	1.000	0	0	1.000	1.000	1
5	0.647	0.419	3.8	0.15	0.966	0.983	5
10	0.000	0.000	∞	0.7	0.874	0.935	10
15	0.216	0.047	13.4	1.3	0.736	0.858	15
20	0.000	0.000	∞	2.4	0.573	0.757	20
25	0.129	0.017	17.7	3.9	0.404	0.636	25

among higher partials). A louder voice, however, means a richer quality because more energy will be present in higher partials. These findings are important for our subsequent consideration of voice quality and loudness.

Review Questions

42. Why does a good speaker tend to use less air the louder he talks?
43. What conditions must be fulfilled for the folds to produce a sinusoidal wave (pure tone)?

15. Acoustic Characteristics of Vowels

Obviously, the sound produced by the vocal folds is not the same as the sound emanating from the lips. This is due to the filtering which the sound must undergo. We are now ready to examine how these filtering cavities function so as to modify the initial sound.

Figure 4–31A is an outline of the orolaryngeal cavity. Study this figure with reference to Fig. 3–11, so that you can identify the precise nature of the structures which produce that characteristic shape. Obviously, tongue position can modify the shape of this cavity but, for purposes of simplification, let us assume that the tongue is fixed in the position shown in Fig. 4–31A.

The vocal tract as represented in two dimensions in Fig. 4–31A is an obviously complicated physical structure even though the figure does not include such additional complications as the variance in width and the damping characteristics of the walls of the tract. For purposes of scientific study of the acoustic characteristics of the vocal tract, such complications do have to be considered. In such research, the tract is approximated by considering it as a tube composed of many sections, the acoustic

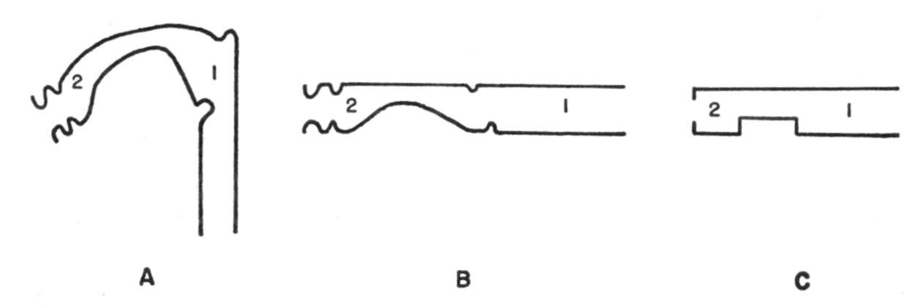

Fig. 4–31. (A) Orolarynx and (C) its acoustical representation.

characteristics of each section being dependent upon its width and length and the width and length of adjacent sections. For purposes of voice training, however, the vocal tract can be loosely approximated by assuming that *the cavity from the vocal folds to the lips is essentially two Helmholtz cavities coupled in series.*

One such resonator extends from the folds to the linguopalatal constriction (number 1 in the drawings) and the second extends from the linguopalatal constriction to the lips. Since the acoustic characteristics of Helmholtz resonators are generally dependent upon cavity volume rather than cavity shape, we may ignore the bend in the cavity shown in Fig. 4–31A. This yields the simpler diagram of Fig. 4–31B. In like manner, the reflections of the incident sound wave and turbulences produced by the epiglottis, uvula, and teeth may be ignored and the gradual constriction imposed by the tongue may be treated as if the constriction were sharp. This yields the representation of the vocal cavity shown in Fig. 4–31C which, for practical purposes, is acoustically similar to the original Fig. 4–31A.

Now let us examine carefully this acoustic representation of the orolaryngeal tract. It is reproduced in Fig. 4–32 with the cavities and dimensions indicated in detail.

The first important characteristic to observe is that *three Helmholtz cavities are involved.* The third is formed by the lips

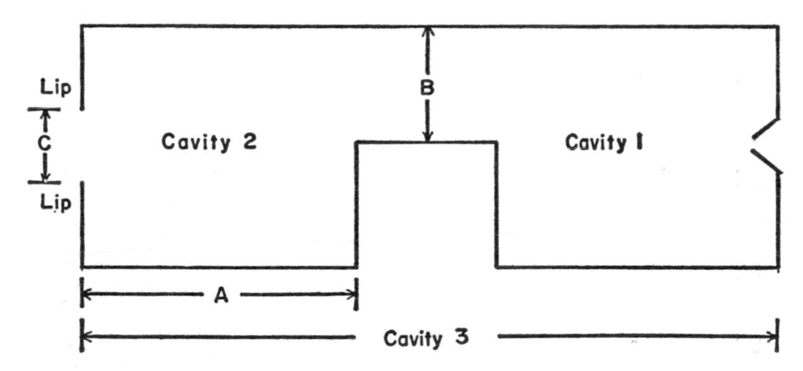

Fig. 4–32. Schematic representation of the acoustic variables of the orolaryngeal tract.

as its constriction, and its volume is the entire orolaryngeal cavity.

The tongue can produce a constriction in a position either more forward or more retracted than the one shown. This longitudinal variable is indicated on the figure as dimension A. The amount of linguopalatal constriction is indicated as dimension B, and the amount of lip opening as dimension C.

We are now ready to explore the acoustic and physiological relationships involved in the production of vowels. In preparation for this we should review three points:

1. The vocal folds produce a complex wave the partials of which decay in intensity roughly according to the reciprocal of the cube of the number of the partial.
2. The larger the cavity of a Helmholtz type filter the lower the frequencies that it will pass.

3. A given Helmholtz filter will pass frequencies on either side of that to which it is exactly tuned, but with less effectiveness.

Research has shown that vowels are characterized according to the distribution of energy at various bands of frequencies. Each such band is called a *formant*. Figure 4–33 shows the

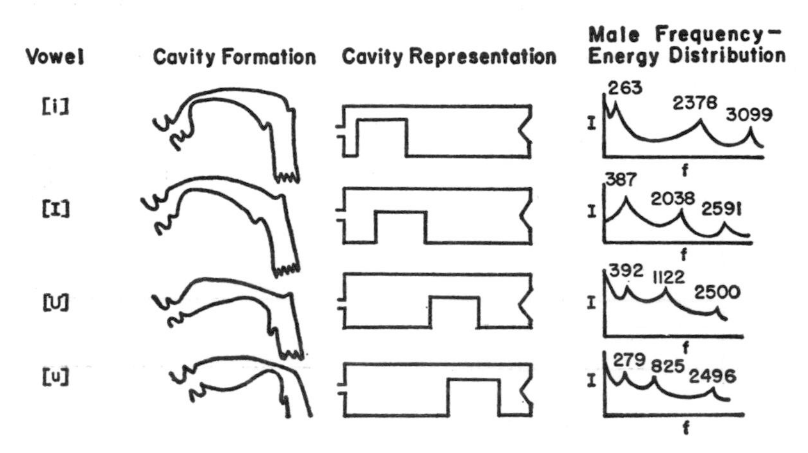

Fig. 4–33. Frequency-energy distributions and cavity configurations for the production of various vowels.

formants involved in male production of the vowels [i], [ɪ], [ʊ], and [u].

The peak frequency of each formant is indicated, but good male production of these vowels is not of course dependent upon producing formants at these precise frequencies. Obviously, a change in fundamental frequency will affect the frequency-energy distributions, if we assume that the cavities remain unchanged. This assumption seems reasonable, or we would have to suppose that as a person spoke at different frequencies he would have to enunciate the same vowel with different tongue positions. The extent to which formant frequencies may be changed without effecting a change as to which vowel is produced may be inferred from Fig. 4–34 and Tables 4–4 and 4–5.

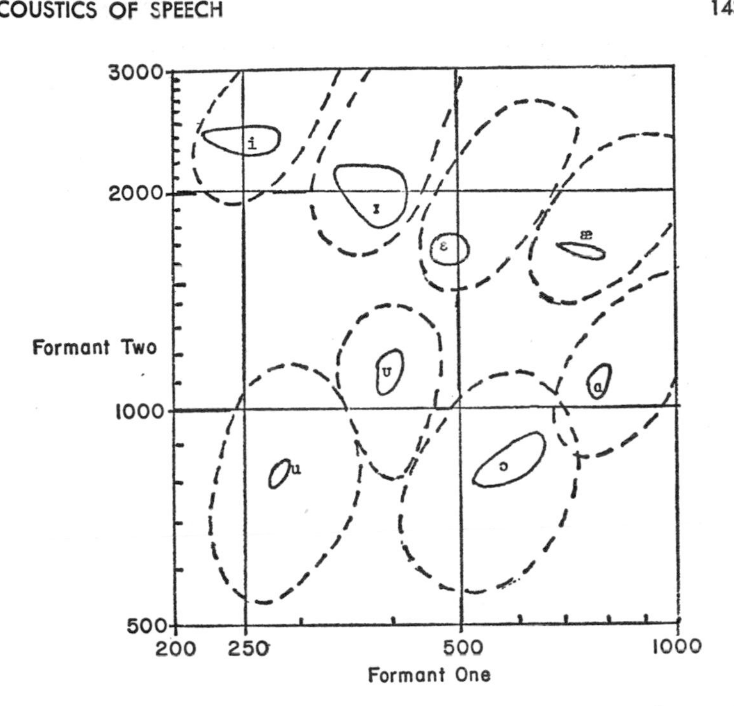

Fig. 4–34. Frequency areas for preferred samples of vowels of men (solid lines) and of men, women, and children combined (dashed lines) from Tables 4–4 and 4–5.

TABLE 4–4

Mean Frequencies for Formants 1 and 2 of Men, Women, and Children in Producing Various Vowels*

Formant	Population	[i]	[ɪ]	[ɛ]	[æ]	[ɑ]	[ɔ]	[ʊ]	[u]
1	Men	270	390	530	660	730	570	440	300
	Women	310	430	610	860	850	590	470	370
	Children	370	530	690	1010	1030	680	560	430
2	Men	2290	1990	1840	1720	1090	840	1020	870
	Women	2790	2480	2330	2050	1220	920	1160	950
	Children	3200	2730	2610	2320	1370	1060	1410	1170

* From the data of Fairbanks and Grubb.

The distribution data from vowel productions of men, women, and children are shown as dotted areas in Fig. 4–34 and the means of these are shown in Table 4–4. Notice that this figure is a plot of formant one vs. formant two. In general, these two frequencies are sufficient for vowel recognition, as research on synthetic (electronically produced) speech has indicated. The third formant may be useful in distinguishing between [ʊ] and [ɝ], but is otherwise not essential information.

As shown in Table 4–4, males have the lowest and children the highest formant frequencies, so that the lower left portion of

TABLE 4–5

Mean Frequencies for Formants 1 and 2 of Men*

Formant	Production†	[i]	[ɪ]	[ɛ]	[æ]	[ɑ]	[ɔ]	[ʊ]	[u]
1	Average	270	390	530	660	730	570	440	300
	Preferred	263	387	493	733	775	600	392	279
2	Average	2290	1990	1840	1720	1090	840	1020	870
	Preferred	2378	2038	1660	1654	1064	846	1122	825

* Men's average productions from the data of Fairbanks and Grubb; men's preferred productions from the data of Peterson and Barney.

† Average formant frequencies include all productions; preferred formant frequencies include only those productions that listeners with phonetic training judged to be best.

each dotted area in Fig. 4–34 refers to males and the upper right portion to children. The slight overlapping on certain vowels, then, are male productions of one vowel with children's production of another, e.g., children's [ɔ] (680 and 1060) and males' [ɑ] (730 and 1090), but these similarities are clearly differentiated by our perception of the octave difference in their fundamentals (about 130 versus 260).

These data are for all productions that were attempted. However, when phonetically trained persons identified male productions, the results shown in Table 4–5 were obtained. The solid area in Fig. 4–34 represents those productions they identified correctly most frequently.

We are now ready to make some general statements about the acoustic characteristics of vowels. One such statement is that the fundamental frequency and the first- and second-formant frequencies are generally sufficient to specify any vowel. Second, the specific peak frequency of any formant can be varied so as to make the vowel more intelligible and, specifically, this means a more precise production of the second-formant peak frequency (cf. Fig. 4–34). Third, the striking similarity between tongue constriction and formant frequencies (comparing the vowel classification of Table 2–1 to Fig. 4–34) suggests quite strongly two physiological and acoustic interrelationships. First, as the amount of constriction increases, the first-formant frequency decreases. This is obviously due to the fact that, as the constriction of a Helmholtz resonator is increased, the frequency to which it is tuned decreases (see page 124). Second, front vowels have higher second formants than do back vowels. One might well suspect that the first formant is provided by the linguopalatal constriction and the second formant is provided by the cavity anterior to this constriction. Obviously the fundamental frequency is passed by the entire tract from folds to lips. Little experimental evidence exists as yet to substantiate clearly the seeming relatedness suggested above, but until such substantiation is provided it would not seem unwise to suppose that these relationships exist. If we are to assume a perfect relationship between tongue placement and formant frequencies, however, additional research seems indicated to investigate why [ʊ] has a higher second formant than would be expected. Future radiographic studies may lead to the discovery that in producing [ʊ] the linguopalatal constriction is made in a more anterior position than in the production of [ɔ] and [u]. Additional research should also be directed toward investigating the physiological and acoustic characteristics of [o], [e], [a], [ɒ], and [ɜ]. The first two are more difficult to analyze than the vowels previously investigated because of the tendency of the tongue to rise during sustained production. The latter three are difficult to analyze because of their relative infrequency of occurrence. Hence, there may be disagreement among auditors as to which are the most intelligible productions of these sounds.

Just as [ʊ] seems to have a higher second formant than one would suppose, so [ɔ] has an unexpectedly low second formant. However, this may be due to greater tongue retraction. Certainly [ɒ] and [ɔ] should be investigated together to resolve this anomaly.

Exactly how the auditory mechanism (including the brain) functions to enable us to interpret certain frequency-energy distributions as phonemes to the exclusion of others is still much of a mystery. One theory is that recognition requires specific frequencies. Another is that identification depends upon certain frequency relationships, perhaps the second formant/first formant ratio. Neither theory has been able to explain fully all the facts. Still another explanation is tenable. It is that the brain monitors incoming *changes* in frequency-energy distribution and certain *patterns* of change are recognized, not only as specific vowels, but as syllables, words, or even phrases. We may learn first to recognize dynamic auditory behavior over short intervals of time and then increase our recognition span by combining several learned patterns into a larger *gestalt.* What needs to be said here is that no inference should be drawn from what is said anywhere in this text that vowels and consonants are the basic psychological units involved in speech recognition. In fact, we have much evidence to indicate that this is untrue. In work with synthetic speech, merely gliding into the second formant from a higher or lower position is perceived as if the vowel were preceded by two different consonants. At this time, however, about all that can be said accurately is that speech is a dynamic phenomenon and is perceived as such. The study of unvarying frequency-energy distributions may be useful in speech training but is scarcely a methodology for providing theoretical knowledge of perceptual behavior. The dynamic information provided is quite complex. Even our most sophisticated electronic computers, when taught to perceive dynamic variations, are far inferior to the average person in speech recognition. This does not mean that the foregoing discussion of vowel formants is pedagogically of little worth, however. For example, speech training could be considerably improved by the provision of a reasonably priced vowel recognizer, and the only reason such a device is not presently available is that of cost. However, recent developments in electronics should make the production of such a device economically feasible in the near future.

Review Questions

44. Is vowel recognition related to the relative amount of energy within certain frequency ranges?

45. Why is singing of operatic arias less intelligible than speaking the libretto, although in singing the rate is much slower?

16. Acoustic Characteristics of Consonants

As implied in the foregoing section, consonants are perceived not only as various frequency-energy distributions but according to the transition of such energies into subsequent, and out of preceding, vowels, so that there is considerable truth to the statement that a vowel's formant transitions provide much of the information as to which consonant precedes or follows that vowel. An obvious example of this occurs in the case of syllabic consonants. For example, say [hi] and then say [hit] without making a plosive release on the [t]. It is quite obvious that, even without the plosive release, the second production was [hit] rather than [hi]. Hence, we could say that we perceived the existence of [t] from the nature of the dynamics of [i].

An extremely useful device for dynamic speech analysis developed in recent years is the sound spectrograph. It records a two-second sample of speech on a single loop of tape. This recording is played over and over into a narrow (50-cycle) band-pass filter. The output from the filter is printed on a piece of paper placed on a drum which revolves with the loop so that, as the frequency of the filter moves upward, the marking pen moves upward on the drum. A greater signal intensity causes the pen to mark more darkly. A diagram of this device is shown in Fig. 4–35.

Visible reproduction of continuous speech by this method provides such intelligibility that with a moderate amount of experience one can inspect the markings and determine what was recorded with near-perfect accuracy.

You should remember that the acoustic information provided in this chapter was not merely for the purpose of gaining a better understanding of consonants and vowels. Indeed, its primary function insofar as this text is concerned is to provide a clear

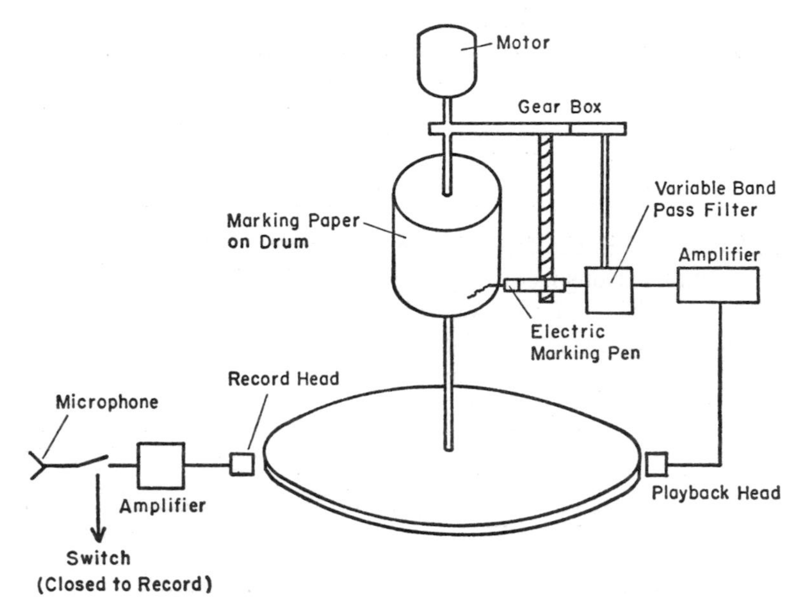

Fig. 4–35. Schematic representation of a sound spectrograph. (Courtesy of Kay Electric Co., Pine Brook, New Jersey)

understanding of the following chapters on voice quality, pitch, intonation, and loudness. In reading those chapters, you might benefit from a review of related sections in this chapter when matters discussed subsequently seem difficult to understand.

Review Questions

46. Are consonants or vowels usually more intense?
47. What type of sounds (periodic, transient, etc.) are [s] and [z]?
48. When a person speaks while breathing a helium-oxygen mixture, his voice sounds much higher pitched. If we make the rather safe assumption that his vocal folds vibrate at practically the same fre-

quency and complexity in both air and helium-oxygen, how do you account for the fact that, for example, a low-pitched male can sound even higher pitched than a child?

Answers to Review Questions

1. No. Velocity is independent of frequency.

2. No, the cork would merely ride in place unless blown by the wind. Any small portion of water through which a wave passes undergoes a circular motion in a vertical plane which is what the cork would ride.

3. High frequencies can more readily produce ice falls because, having shorter wavelengths, they can penetrate cracks better.

4. (a) at C, (b) at A, (c) at B and D, (d) at A and C.

5. Since a particle travels back and forth longitudinally in the direction of the wave, you could tell that its axis of movement pointed either to the source or to the direction in which it was going but you could not tell which was which. Even this much knowledge assumes that the particle was not disturbed by a wave reflected from an object but one emanating directly from the source.

6. The temperature is much higher at lower altitudes, hence the velocity of sound is greater. Density and pressure are *not* the cause.

7. No. The time lag is that required for the last wave to travel from the source to our ears.

8. The velocity of the approaching wave is added to the velocity of the train and, since the wavelength is unaffected by the train being in motion and $v = f\lambda$, as v increases f increases. Put another way, as the train approaches, more waves per second reach our ears. However, a person on the train moves at the same speed as the sound source, so he perceives no such frequency change.

9. (e) temperature of the medium.

10. (d) its wavelength is halved.

11. No. Your ear would receive the same number of cycles per second that were sent by the source. However, since the velocity of sound is higher in the helium-oxygen mixture, the wavelength of the sound is greater.

12. The air is much colder so the speed of sound is less. At that speed the particles lose elasticity and "bunch up" on the plane's leading edges.

13. $0° \text{ F} = -18° \text{ C}$, so $-18° \text{ C} = 741 \sqrt{(273 - 18)/273} = 741\sqrt{.934} = 741\ (.966) = 716$ mph.

14. No. However, the shadow cast by a light source directly above or below it would be.

15. A motion picture camera takes pictures at, say, 16 frames per second. If the wheel were to revolve 16 times a second or any integral multiple of this, it would be photographed in the same position each

time so that it would appear to be motionless. However, what produces this particular *stroboscopic effect* is that a spoke is photographed at such a rate that it is always where another spoke had been in the previous frame.

16. The time of arrival at the two ears is different, unless the sound is directly in front or directly behind us. We can tell whether the sound source is to our left or to our right by intensity differences at the two ears. We can tell whether it is directly in front or directly to the rear by turning our head. Indoors, of course, reflections from walls also provide directional cues.

17. If the radio is tuned to the broadcaster's station, its radio's sound is picked up and retransmitted. This increases the amplitude of the transmitted wave, which is also picked up and retransmitted, etc. so that the result is, almost instantly, a signal of greater intensity than the transmitting facilities can handle.

18. If the microphones were x distance apart and the two loudspeakers were that same distance (where $x \neq$ head thickness), the phase differences at the two ears would be highly distorted. Even the absence of the manikin's head makes an appreciable difference since high f's "bend around" objects better than low f's.

19. This requires two waves traveling in exactly the same direction at exactly the same frequency and intensity with 180° phase difference, an unlikely situation.

20. The frequency of their cadence may be equal, or nearly so, to one of the bridge's natural frequencies, which would add amplitude upon amplitude with each step until the bridge collapsed.

21. The mirror's natural frequency of vibration (due to its particular elasticity and inertia) and the frequency of the note are equal, so that each successive wave reinforces the last until the mirror shatters.

22. The wave of condensation bulged the panes inward *against* the inertia of the glass, but the elasticity of the glass *cooperated* with the wave of rarefaction to bulge the panes outward.

23. Yes. Amplitude is directly related to pressure. Hence, intensity is related to the square of the amplitude.

24. If they sounded each note exactly in phase the amplitudes would add and, since $I \propto A^2$, they would be 16 times as intense, but imperfect tuning and non-identical bowing prevent this.

25. (b).

26. 22 cps, the largest common divisor.

27. Every different phase of every partial would produce a different waveform.

28. One explanation is that, when they are turning at exactly the same frequency, no beat of an inharmonic partial will be heard. For example, if the speeds of the two engines before adjustment are 30 and 31 revolutions per second, a droning once each second will be heard.

29. (c), (d), and (e).

30. (4).

31. The fundamental or 1st partial is the largest common divisor, so the fundamental is 110 cps and these frequencies are the 2d, 4th, and 7th partials. Only a tube open at both ends can reinforce even-numbered partials. The length of the tube must be 10 feet (1100 ÷ 110) if it is to reinforce the fundamental and all integral multiples of it. If it were 5 feet long, we could reinforce 220 and 440 cps, but not 770 cps.

32. Because a varying frequency varies the pressure pattern at the eardrum and is perceived much as if it were an intensity variation.

33. A transient type of aperiodic sound.

34. The decrease in intensity of each component will cause it to fall below the threshold of audibility at a certain distance.

35. The sound wave travels through the door, changing from air to wood to air as its medium.

36. 144 db $= 6(20) + 2(12)$, or $10^6(4^2):1 = 16{,}000{,}000:1$.

37. 60 db is an intensity ratio of $10^6/1$ so the intensity remaining is one millionth (10^{-6}) of the original.

38. 40 db $= 10^4/1 = 10{,}000/1$ or $I_L/I_S = 10{,}000/1$; $I_L/I_S \propto P_L^2/P_S^2$ so that $P_L^2/P_S^2 \sim 10{,}000/1$ or $P_L/P_S \sim \sqrt{10{,}000/1}$ or 100:1.

39. Pressure and displacement are measured in 20-log units, so a 20-db difference in pressure represents a ratio of 10:1, or the displacement becomes 200 millimicrons (which incidentally, is only .00007874 inch).

40. $100/4 = 25/1 = 6.99 + 6.99 = 13.98$ db; $12\% + 4\% = 16\%$. $100\% - 16\% = 84\%$. $100/84 = 10 \times 10 \div 7 \times 6 \times 2 = 10.00 + 10.00 - (8.45 + 7.78 + 3.01) = 0.76$ db.

41. 60 db represents a pressure ratio of 1000:1. Hence, $x/.0002 = 1000/1$, or $x = .2$ dyne/cm.^{2}

42. His folds remain closed longer in each cycle, so that there is much less time in which air can escape.

43. The folds must be open exactly one half of each cycle, time spent in abduction must equal time spent in adduction, and their rate of opening must decrease as the folds open and their rate of closure must increase as the folds close. An approximation of these conditions tends to occur at extremely high frequencies (falsetto) when only the anterior portions of the folds are abducted.

44. Yes

45. Consonant-vowel and vowel-consonant transitional cues are almost imperceptible, due to relatively long vowel duration.

46. Vowels.

47. [s] is aperiodic noise; [z] is a combination of noise and periodicity.

48. The cavities in the vocal tract are tuned to pass higher partials of the same complex tone because the velocity of sound is increased (as in v of Equation 5). In the case of vowels, for example, all formants are shifted upward on the frequency spectrum although the fundamental remains unchanged.

5

Voice Quality

Voice Quality Defined

Voice quality refers to those characteristics of voice which prevail regardless of the vowels or syllables uttered, the frequency or intensity of the sounds produced, or the rate of speaking. Anatomically and physiologically, one's voice quality is determined by the size and shape of his vocal tract and resonating cavities and by the manner of vocal-fold action. Psychologically, one's voice quality is that which provides the most information regarding his identity. Acoustically, it rests on differences in distribution of sound energy on the same vowel from speaker to speaker.

An *habitual voice quality* refers to the voice quality a person tends to employ regardless of context. In the case of an actor, it would refer to the basic voice quality he chooses in playing a role. When a person deviates from good voice quality to emphasize certain words in certain ways, each quality thus employed is an *emphatic voice quality* and, when employed, will be termed the use of a particular voice quality for word emphasis.

Good Voice Quality

Although we shall understand better what good voice quality is by considering subsequently all that it is not, we should begin by defining the term positively. Good voice quality is the result of:

1. Tonicity in the vocal folds, sufficient to keep the folds closed long enough in each cycle to produce a highly complex tone at any desired intensity and frequency level.[1]
2. Vertical positioning of the glottis at a level which provides maximum coupling with the filtering tract.
3. Horizontal positioning of the tongue so that the resulting intelligibility, audibility, and perceived personality will be most favorable.
4. Proper utilization of the nasal cavity.
5. A proper amount of sympathetic resonation.

To speak of "goodness" of habitual voice quality does not mean to imply any arousal of aesthetic appreciation of the speaker's voice. Rather, it is a neutral term implying the absence of perceived personality characteristics which most persons would deem unfavorable. In like manner, the other voice qualities discussed subsequently are faulty in three senses:

1. If they are habitual voice qualities, the resultant perceived personalities of speakers would be considered as unfavorable to those speakers.
2. If they are habitual voice qualities, their use for word emphasis is rendered ineffective.
3. If used for word emphasis, they provoke connotations different from those intended.

Voice Qualities Due to Faulty Vocal-Fold Action

The action of the vocal folds in producing good voice quality was discussed in Sect. 14 of Chapter 4. Two other types of action are possible, producing what will be termed a *breathy* quality or a *tense* quality.

Breathiness is defined as the minimal degree of phonatory tension necessary to achieve adduction of the folds once sub-

[1] Quality is most closely related to the outline of the wave envelope on a line spectrum. However, if this envelope is shifted along the frequency scale, a change in quality is perceived. This could be attributed to the threshold of audibility being nonlinear so that, if loudness rather than intensity or pressure were held constant, a perceptual change in quality might not occur.

glottal pressure forces their abduction. Put more simply, it is the least vocal-fold tension needed to counteract a given subglottal air pressure to close the folds every time they open.

First, let us consider breathiness when produced with a very slight excess of subglottal over supraglottal air pressure. In such a case, relatively little phonatory tension is induced and very little air pressure is needed to abduct the folds in each cycle. They therefore open relatively early in each cycle. Once the folds are opened, the degree or elastic tension assisting their closure is relatively small. This is because degree of elastic tension is proportional to degree of phonatory tension, just as the elasticity of a bowstring that is pulled, say, 6 inches increases as we increase the tautness of the bowstring prior to its being pulled. Because of the relatively small amount of subglottal air pressure required to open the folds, it can be seen that the folds remain open until enough air has been expelled to produce a drop in subglottal pressure sufficient to adduct the folds. Since little subglottal air pressure was employed, the *rate* of airflow is rather low but, because the folds are abducted throughout most of the cycle, the *amount* of air expended is relatively great. The force counteracting adduction at moment of impact is a rise in subglottal air pressure. However, so much air was lost during the cycle that the subglottal pressure cannot be restored in time to provide much deceleration of adduction. In the case of breathiness at a low subglottal pressure the rate of adduction is so gradual without such deceleration that the force of impact is small.

Consider, however, the case of breathiness produced at a much higher intensity (great excess of subglottal over supraglottal air pressure). Again no greater phonatory tension is induced than is needed to adduct the folds, although subglottal air pressure and phonatory tension are both considerably increased. The result is a much greater force of closure because elastic tension is now increased. Moreover, the folds have remained open, as before, throughout most of the cycle, so that a great loss of subglottal pressure has occurred which cannot be restored in time to brake the extremely rapid rate of closure. Hence, breathiness produced at higher intensities (relatively greater subglottal air pressure) not only increases the speaker's expenditure of air but causes his folds to come together quite forcefully and, due to a repetition of this mode of impact with every cycle, may eventually injure his folds. The portion of each fold which comes in contact with the opposite fold is protected by a heavy layer of squamous epithelial tissue, the same type of tissue found on the palms of our hands. The normal color of the glottal edges of healthy folds is therefore the same as the color of our palms, a pinkish white. Squamous cells are capable of considerable abuse before damage occurs, and damaged cells can be sloughed off and rapidly replaced by new cells. However, the extent of vocal-fold abuse occasioned by hours of breathy phonation at an intensity above that of normal conversation is frequently more than the folds can tolerate. The prognosis is obviously that, in the first few minutes, they change in color from pinkish white to bright red (due to the rush of blood to the area to repair shock damage) just as excessive clapping would affect our palms. Then, if that intensity continues, they become traumatized and bleed. It is no wonder that research shows that breathy speakers have an unusually high incidence of complaints of sore throats and that their folds are the prime site of their respiratory infections, and temporary loss of voice ensues. What better locus of infection could bacteria, microbes, and viruses require? Finally, laryngeal carcinoma (cancer of the larynx) is found almost exclusively in persons with a voice quality which had been breathy before surgeons removed their folds and whose occupations required considerable phonation above normal conversational intensities (e.g., athletic coaches, schoolteachers, and shop foremen).

Breathiness should not be confused with *whispering.* In whispering, the folds are abducted prior to phonation and remain apart as long as whispering occurs. The air rushing through the laryngeal tract produces a broad band of noise, and the oronasopharynx passes to the outside those frequencies to which it is tuned much as it would if the source were a highly complex sound. In breathiness, however, the folds are adducted prior to phonation, and they open and close cyclically during phonation to produce a periodic sound.

The complexity of the glottal tone in the production of a breathy voice quality is much less than that in a good voice quality because in breathiness the open quotient (proportion of each period during which folds are open) is extremely high. Hence, breathiness is more nearly a pure tone (i.e., very few partials contain much energy) superimposed upon the broad and rather intense band of noise created by air rushing through the vocal tract during the time the folds are open.

The perceived personality of an habitually breathy speaker is that of a person who is weak physically, mentally, and morally. For example, spinelessness, torpidity, stupidity, and libidinousness[2] are words which might be used to characterize him. Whether or not he behaves or characterizes himself thus is of course a mere chance phenomenon.

Breathiness for emphatic usage connotes softness, lightness (in weight), weakness, awe, love, childish exuberance, passionate intensity, and admiration. For example, say the following italicized words breathily and the other words with a good voice quality:

1. The kitten's fur is *soft.*
2. It didn't weigh as much as a *feather.*
3. I'm *tired* this morning.
4. The majesty of creation filled him with *awe.*
5. She's really in *love.*
6. I do *so* want to do it.
7. I *admire* him very much.

Reread these sentences, using a breathy voice quality on *every* word. Notice that connotational value on the italicized words is almost entirely lost.

Hence, we are now ready to reach an important conclusion: *If one has a voice quality other than good, he must acquire a good voice quality habitually before he can effectively use other voice qualities emphatically.*

Connotations of words can be indicated vocally only by

[2] Although a female's breathy voice is generally considered by males to be seductive, probably this is merely a logical conclusion from the premise that, if she is physically, mentally, and morally weak, she would not resist one's amorous advances.

deviations from good voice quality and by loudness, pitch, and duration. As will be seen, increased and decreased loudness can suggest only relative importance or unimportance; loudness or softness and prolonged or abbreviated duration can suggest only relative importance or unimportance, length, or size; and pitch can suggest highness or lowness. But each voice quality evokes several connotations, and combinations of voice qualities dozens of other possibilities. Moreover, the combination of voice qualities with pitch, loudness, and duration can effect literally hundreds of connotations. Hence, a speaker with a voice whose quality is not good is extremely handicapped in his ability to connote his intentions while, at the same time, he is perhaps unintentionally connoting to strangers a personality that he probably considers alien to him.

Breathiness occurs far more commonly in females than in males. This is probably because males generally are better able to use their bodies for physical tasks more efficiently; and this, in turn, may come about because in our society they more frequently engage in strenuous physical activities.

Speech is a physical task that requires sustained rather than intermittent effort. It is therefore more closely related to slow lifting, as in chinning on a bar, than to quick lifting, as in wrestling. Slow lifting requires sustained good posture; quick lifting requires moving from one position of good posture to another as quickly as possible. Since the larynx receives no direct support from the spine, it must be positioned by a steady and, therefore, well-controlled tonicity in every extrinsic and intrinsic muscle of the larynx, but especially in the pharyngeal constrictors, since these are the only direct laryngeal connections to the spine.

Good posture can be defined in various ways, all generally referring to the same condition. It can be defined as an equal division of body weight front and rear, left and right, by a plumb line suspended from the center of the hyoid arch. It can be defined as maximal ability to recover balance from an unbalancing force. And it can be defined as maintenance of tonicity, rather than of laxness or tension, in all muscles.

Good voice quality cannot be produced without good posture.

Breathiness is the voice quality we produce in positions of poor posture with muscle relaxation. Try leaning off balance to your left or right in a relaxed manner and then count. A breathy quality will be produced.

A person whose quality is breathy must learn to achieve good posture and then to utilize that posture to remove breathiness. The latter is much easier to accomplish since, with good voice quality, the louder one talks the less air he uses but, with breathy voice quality, the louder one talks the more air he uses. Hence, placing a palm in front of the lips during phonation of a vowel enables us to perceive any trace of breathiness because we can feel air being expelled from the mouth. Try this while counting at a somewhat louder than conversational level. Do not try to "hold the sound in," as this may result in a throaty voice quality. (If you are breathy, see page 167–168 on this point.)

Any or all of the first four exercises that follow, together with all of the remaining three, should enable a breathy speaker to learn the kinesthetic sensation of good posture, and can result in good voice quality being produced.

Exercises to Remove Breathiness

1. Stand erect with shoulders held back and rise *very slowly* on the balls of your feet. Let your heels descend quickly, and repeat this process several times. Concentrate on the lifting feeling in your calf and thigh muscles. Now, as you come up slowly, say the word "one" loudly with your palm held in front of your lips. If you feel any air being expelled, try again until you feel no air. Now, as you go up on the balls of your feet, say the word "two," but be extremely careful not to overaspirate the plosive [tᴴu]. This means that you should get to the vowel as quickly as you can. You should feel very little air on your palm as a result of the plosive release. Continue counting very slowly from one to ten until you can say each vowel with good voice quality and with no overaspiration on "two" or "ten."

2. Stand behind a chair and grasp the seat lightly with your fingers. Keep your knees straight and lift the chair *slowly*. If it feels heavy, you are lifting incorrectly, with the muscles in your arms and back rather than with the muscles in your legs. Lift the chair again, and count as above while you lift. Try to capture both the feel and the sound of the good voice quality produced.

3. Have someone hang on your shoulders behind you. Now count as indicated in Exercise 1.

4. Place your hands on the top, rear portion of your thighs and "lift yourself upward" as you count.
5. When you can produce a good voice quality while counting without resorting to any forced good posturing as in the previous exercises, try counting with good voice quality as you sit in a chair and as you rise. Notice that you cannot sit leading with your tailbone nor rise leading with your chin without producing a breathy quality. Practice until you can sit and rise gracefully and non-breathily.
6. Practice reading a paragraph with good voice quality throughout. Now underline several words and try to be breathy only on those words.
7. Try to count backward from "ten" to "one," being extremely loud on "ten" and less loud on each number without becoming breathy on the lower numbers.

The above exercises do not of course remove breathiness but they provide the prerequisite for such removal. The habitual adoption of any different vocal behavior requires an ability to produce the desired vocal behavior effortlessly (albeit consciously), and emotional disgust with the way one presently speaks or a feeling of success when one speaks the new way. You can learn to reinforce your new mode of speaking by clearing your throat and beginning again when you hear yourself being breathy in daily conversation. You should compliment others when they improve and, for your own benefit, hope that they compliment you in turn. Unfortunately, intellectual conviction that one's speech can be improved is not sufficient motivation for acquiring new patterns of vocal behavior; dissatisfaction must be felt rather than deduced.

It should be added that mere drill will not produce better speech. A story told to illustrate this is that of the man who spent years with various voice teachers trying to remove his nasality. He was telling his friend of his most successful experience, wherein the teacher drilled him for six months on only one sentence, "A noisy noise annoys an oyster," so that he had learned to say it without a trace of nasality, which he proceeded to do three times rapidly. "But," he told his friend despondently, "[ĩts ðə 'dǣmdĩst θĩŋ tə trãĩ tə w3̃˞k ĩntũ ə kãnvɚ̃'sẽʃən]."

Tenseness is the opposite of breathiness in terms of amount of phonatory tension employed. Whereas in breathiness only that amount of phonatory tension is induced that will provide cyclic adduction of the folds, in a tense voice quality the phonatory tension induced is sufficient to adduct the folds in each cycle at an extremely rapid rate. This means that, for a tense voice quality, abduction occurs extremely late in each cycle, rate of abduction and rate of adduction are both very high, and the open quotient is extremely small—hence, expenditure of air is extremely small and the pressure loss can be partially restored so that fold velocity at moment of impact is relatively low.

Good voice quality is defined as medial between the extremes of breathiness and tenseness. The upper part of Fig. 5–1 compares these three vocal-fold actions by plotting degree of glottal opening at each moment in a characteristic cycle. (The duration of open time on all but breathiness is highly understated to reveal detail.)

A tense voice quality requires more subglottal air pressure for abduction than good voice quality requires, and good voice quality requires more air pressure for abduction than breathiness requires. However, less air is expended in tenseness than in good voice quality because the folds are closed more rapidly. The acoustic difference between tenseness and good voice quality is that the former waveform is narrower and more rectangular and the latter is more sawtoothed. Although tenseness is richer in terms of distribution of intensity over higher partials, the perception of such a sound tends to be more that of a train of pulses than a richness of quality. In fact, four greater degrees of tenseness have been termed, respectively, *huskiness*, *harshness*, *hardness*, and *stridency*. Their vocal-fold actions are represented in the lowest part of Fig. 5–1. Huskiness is perceived even more as a train of pulses than is tenseness. Harshness sounds like a rubbing of coarse sandpaper. Hardness (a raucous, grating quality) and stridency (usually characterized as metal clanging against metal) are extremely rare in occurrence and are usually pathological in nature. That is, the lack of relationship mentioned in Chapter 1 between both behavioral and self-characterized personality and speech ceases to be true at abnormal extremes. It should not be surprising, therefore, that hard or strident voice qualities tend to be found in psychotic or highly neurotic individuals.

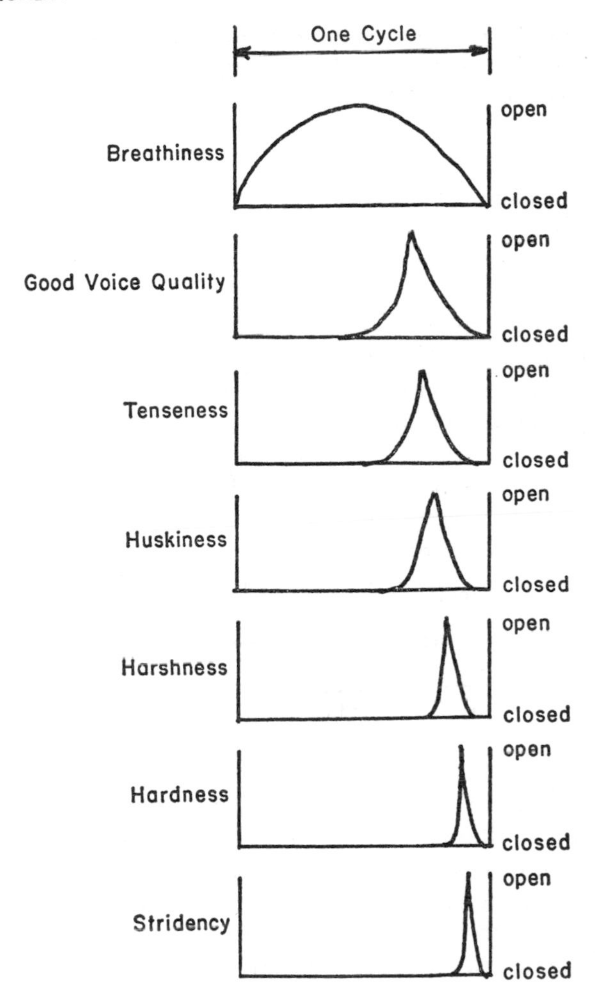

Fig. 5–1. Representation of vocal-fold action for different amounts of vocal-fold tension (extent of abduction assumed to be constant).

A person with tenseness as his habitual voice quality tends to be perceived as uncooperative, ill-tempered and emotionally insecure. Moreover, his voice produces tension in the listener. We can usually avoid association with persons who have tense voices, but in many cases the speaker may be a superior (e.g., teacher, employer, or supervisor), and the tension cannot be completely relieved by avoidance. In such situations, we tend to seek scapegoats on whom to release our tension. Hence, the consequences of a tense voice quality cannot be fully assessed although they are doubtless great.

As a deviation from habitual voice quality, tenseness is useful for word emphasis to connote tenseness, irritability, anger, cruelty, rudeness, frustration, or arresting importance.

Tenseness can be reduced by thumb and finger massage of the neck along each side of the thyroid cartilage during sustained phonation on a vowel. At some point in time the tenseness will seem to become a good voice quality and, with greater relaxation, a breathy quality will appear.

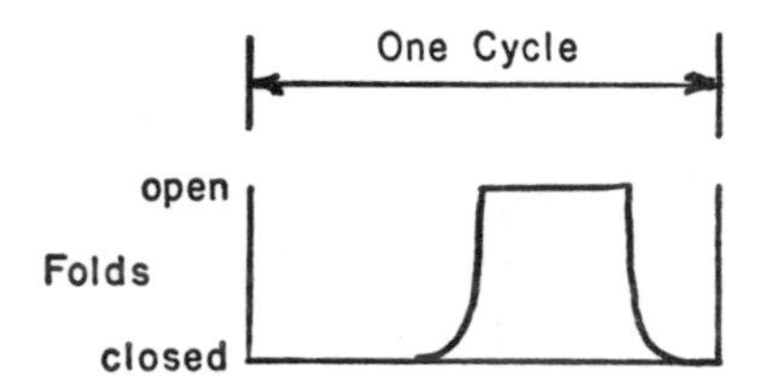

Fig. 5–2. Representation of vocal-fold action in breathy-tense production.

Tenseness and breathiness have been defined as extremes of vocal-fold tension. However, they can be produced or at least simulated simultaneously. One possible explanation of how this is accomplished is shown in Fig. 5–2. Here the folds are opened *fully* by great subglottal air pressure, but the Bernoulli effect is least operative because laryngeal constriction at the glottis is minimal. Hence, air escapes for a longer portion of each period to produce the noise characteristic of a breathy voice quality, and the high rate of opening and closure produces that characteristic of a tense voice quality.

Thus, we could say that, to produce a breathy voice quality you should have poor posture and relax the larynx, to produce a tense voice quality you should have good posture and tense the larynx, and to produce both simultaneously you should have poor posture and tense the larynx.

The personality and emphatic connotations of a breathy-tense voice quality have not as yet been investigated, but it seems reasonable to assume a resultant of the two. Thus, for habitual usage the perceived personality should be that of a nervous, weak individual, and emphatic usage should connote a person at the breaking point.

Voice Qualities Due to Faulty Glottal Level

Figure 4–32 reveals that, if the level of the glottis is depressed by excessive tension on the infrahyoid and infrathyroid muscles, the overall cavity volume of the largest Helmholtz filter—that between glottis and lips—will be increased. The greater the volume of a Helmholtz cavity, the lower are the frequencies it will reinforce or, since we are concerned with filtering rather than reinforcement, the lower are the frequencies it will pass.

Now suppose we assume a complete absence of any linguopalatal constriction and that the vocal folds produce a sawtooth wave. Hence we have a complex sound source to be filtered through a single Helmholtz tube. Further assume that the loudness of all lower partials is the same. This is not necessarily a distortion of truth because, although partial amplitude decays exponentially in terms of partial number (see page 137), loudness increases with frequency in the range of which we are speaking (the first 8 to 10 partials of any vocal-fold frequency) as indicated in Fig. 4–29. Hence, we are merely assuming that particular vocal-fold frequency and sound pressure for which the rate of gain in loudness exactly offsets rate of decay in amplitude for every lower partial.

As indicated in Fig. 5–3, a relatively low glottal level will enable the Helmholtz tube between folds and lips to have the frequency response indicated by the dashed line, thus passing partials 1 and 2 best. A relatively high glottal level would produce the frequency response indicated by the dotted line, thus passing partials 3, 4, and 5 best. Between these extremes is a glottal level that will produce the response indicated by the solid line, passing partials 1, 2, 3, and 4 best.

Obviously, as glottal level is lowered, a larger percentage of the energy in the lower partials of the glottal tone is passed but a larger percentage of the energy in the higher partials is filtered out (or damped). This is a *flat voice quality.* If the glottal level is raised, a larger percentage of the energy in higher partials is passed, but more energy in the lower partials of the glottal tone is filtered out. This is a *thin voice quality.* Good voice quality is therefore a compromise, in terms of glottal level, between

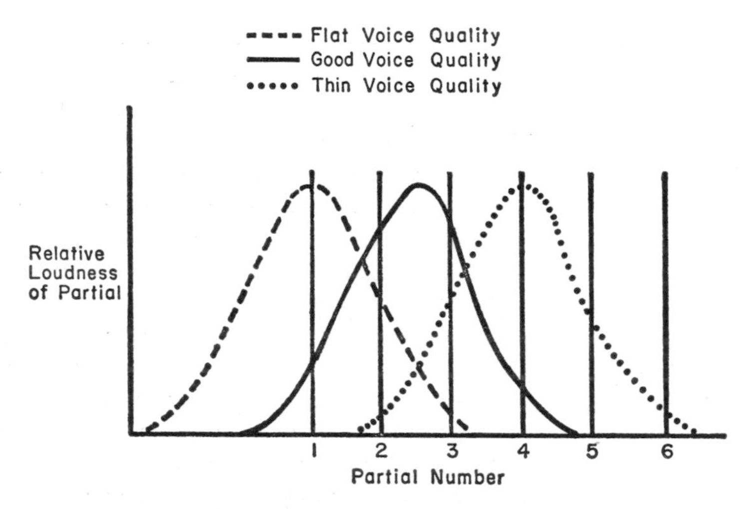

Fig. 5–3. Effect of glottal level on transmission of lower partials of glottal tone (assuming equal loudness at the glottis of all lower partials and no linguopalatal constriction). Proportion of any vertical line below each frequency response curve indicates relative amount of that partial's loudness at the lips.

these extremes. At that level, we say that maximum coupling between sound source and filters is achieved.

It might easily be imagined that there is one and only one glottal level that is appropriate for each person, depending upon the volume of his vocal tract, but this is not the case. At every different vocal-fold frequency, a different glottal level tends to be employed. This is probably due to our recognition of others' voices in terms of their complexity rather than their frequency. If this were not so, at every different frequency we would sound like different persons. Hence, each of us tries to provide the same complexity by reinforcing the same partials at every frequency. As our frequency rises, therefore, our glottal level rises, and as we go down in frequency our glottal level descends. A flat voice quality, then, is produced by a glottal level that is too low at every frequency produced, and a thin voice quality is produced by a glottal level that is too high at every frequency produced.

The treatment of glottal level has thus far ignored cavity constrictions and other actions which produce the various sounds and syllables of speech. This point of view is valid because glottal level has no necessary effect on phonetic or syllabic quality. For example, a vowel produced thinly will have more energy in the second formant than the same vowel produced with a flat voice quality, but the actual formant frequencies are dependent upon the frequency of the glottal tone; so that, although the second formant may be more intense with a thin quality, it may still be the same second-formant frequency.

You can easily produce flatness and thinness by placing your thumb and forefinger on the superior margin of each ala of your thyroid cartilage and pushing downward for flatness or beneath each ala and pushing upward for thinness while you sustain phonation of [ɑ]. Do not try to manipulate the thyroid from the front but from the sides. Since pitch is a perception of sounds in terms of their highness and lowness, you may perceive flatness as lower pitched, thinness as higher pitched, and between these extremes you will note a greater richness of tone. If this rich tone is your normal quality, your voice is neither thin nor flat. Although flatness and thinness tend to be perceived as pitch differences, you should fully realize that the acoustic difference lies, not in frequency, but in the distribution of energy among the partials (complexity). It is possible to be flat or thin at any frequency, although obviously flatness is more apparent at low frequencies and thinness is more apparent at high frequencies, and we tend to elevate the glottis to reach higher fundamental frequencies and to depress the glottis to reach lower fundamental frequencies.

Perhaps the fact that pitch can be made to seem higher or

lower by manipulating either fundamental frequency or glottal level accounts for much of the disagreement between teachers, who insist that some persons need to lower their pitch, and researchers (who have examined only fundamental frequency expressed in tones), who insist that the only direction in which a person's pitch should shift is upward.

You can easily differentiate between a change in frequency and a change in quality by using a microphone and a cathode ray oscilloscope (CRO). Sustain phonation on a vowel at one pitch level until you can adjust the synchronizing circuit on the CRO so as to hold the waveform on the scope. Slide upward in frequency and observe that the wave is no longer held by the scope. Readjust synchronization to hold your waveform on the scope. Now produce that same vowel at that same pitch with a flat voice quality. If the wave changes its shape but remains fixed because the period is unchanged, you have altered quality rather than frequency. To determine whether someone other than yourself is flat or thin, rather than deviating in frequency, no such device is needed. If, when he sings up a musical scale with a musical accompaniment, he obviously hits each note (as most persons can), his quality rather than his frequency is at fault.

Although breathiness and tenseness may be produced simultaneously, obviously flatness and thinness cannot. However, a person may use a flat voice quality for some words and a thin voice quality for others. If he does this as an intonational device (see page 202 on ditonal intonation), then his problem is basically one of pitch rather than of voice quality. If, however, he seems to jump back and forth haphazardly from one quality to another, his problem is essentially one of voice quality.

An habitually flat voice quality suggests a person who is vapid (unenthusiastic by nature) and phlegmatic (unemotional by nature). Flatness used for word emphasis, deviating from an habitually good voice quality, connotes flatness, laziness, boredom, cruelty, or mild displeasure, e.g., "He squashed it *flat,*" "*Don't bother me,*" "*Stop that.*"

The perceived personality of one with a thin voice quality is that of a person who is immature and insecure. On words, thinness conveys thinness, weakness, apology, tenuousness, indecision, or doubt; for example: "He's *skinny*," "This coffee is *weak*," "I'm *sorry* it happened," "It *could* be true," "I don't *know*."

If flatness or thinness cannot be overcome temporarily by manual manipulation of your folds, try to speak with an orotund voice quality (on the latter, see pages 175–177) and then reduce the extent of duration on continuant sounds. Why this is helpful in overcoming flatness or thinness will be understood once an understanding of the nature of orotundity has been achieved.

Voice Qualities Due to Faulty Tongue Positioning

In terms of the acoustic representation of the vocal tract shown in Fig. 4–32, assume that the tongue position shown in Fig. 5–4A is employed to produce a particular vowel, [ʌ]. Further assume that the tongue is shifted posteriorly without altering the degree of linguopalatal constriction, as indicated by the dotted line in Fig. 5–4B. This would obviously produce a different vowel, because the volume of the cavity posterior to the linguopalatal constriction (referred to hereafter as the posterior cavity) is decreased. Since the vocal tract, for voice training purposes, may be considered a pair of Helmholtz cavities in series, and since a Helmholtz cavity's resonant frequency increases as volume or amount of constriction decreases, it can be seen that a decrease in the volume of the posterior cavity will raise that cavity's resonant frequency. However, we can compensate for this by increasing the linguopalatal constriction (raising the tongue) as shown in Fig. 5–4C. Now that the resonant frequency of the posterior cavity is the same as it was prior to tongue retraction, the volume of the cavity anterior to the linguopalatal constriction is increased. This lowers its resonant frequency, but we can again compensate by reducing the lip constriction (by opening the mouth wider) as shown in Fig. 5–4D, so that the same frequencies can be resonated by the configuration shown in Fig. 5–4A or 5–4D.

Hence, the same vowel can be produced with a different voice quality by retracting and elevating the tongue (by increased tension in the styloglossal muscles) and by opening the lips wider. Such a quality is termed *throatiness.* It can be produced by opening the mouth widely, which causes the tongue to be elevated and shifted posteriorly, or by elevating and shifting the tongue posteriorly, which forces the lips to be opened more widely to produce the same vowel.

It should also be remembered that a greater dissipation (i.e., less reflection) occurs at an orifice if its radius or cross-sectional

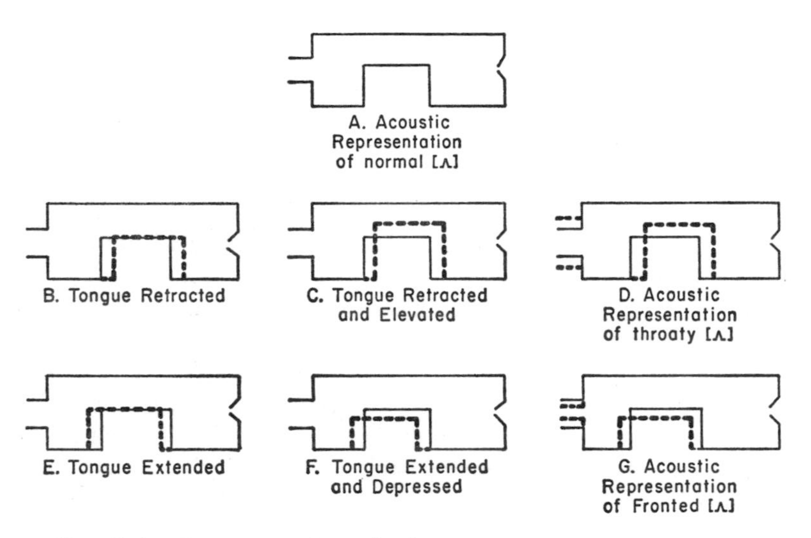

Fig. 5–4. Representation of relative tongue position and extent of lip opening in the production of the same vowel with (A) normal, (D) throaty, and (G) fronted quality.

area is increased. Hence, with the mouth opened more widely, more sound energy is directed outward and less is directed back into the vocal tract. This point will be considered subsequently, but it should not be concluded from the preceding that loudness of a person's voice is necessarily increased when he opens his mouth more widely.

If we now assume the opposite mode of tongue positioning, by increased tension in the genioglossus so as to shift the base of the tongue anteriorly as in Fig. 5–4E, the posterior cavity's volume is increased. This lowering of the posterior cavity's frequency response can be offset as shown in Fig. 5–4F by lowering the tongue (reducing linguopalatal constriction) sufficiently to raise the resonant frequency to its previous level. The higher resonance produced by the anterior cavity's reduction in volume is restored by increasing the lip constriction, as shown in Fig. 5–4G. Thus we can say that the same phoneme can be produced as shown in Figs. 5–4A, 5–4D, and 5–4G; or, indeed, with the tongue positioned anywhere along the anterior-inferior to posterior-superior axis in such a way that, as the tongue is positioned lower and more forward along this axis for a given vowel, the lips are opened less widely.

Now consider the case of the tongue positioned extremely forward and low in the mouth. Back vowels are dependent upon degree of lip opening and, for the higher back vowels, [u], [ʊ], and to some extent [o], the lips are open only slightly in normal production. By pursing the lips, however, we can increase the volume of the anterior cavity without shifting the tongue posteriorly. Hence, with the tongue shifted anteriorly, the lips tend to be pursed for [o], more so for [ʊ], and even more so for [u].

The voice quality occasioned by anterior positioning will be termed a *fronted voice quality*, or *fronting*. It is also called "clipped" or "overprecise" speech, but these terms tend to imply a negative value judgment which speakers with that quality—such as Britishers—would tend to dispute.

Acoustically, as a vowel is produced further toward the throaty end of the fronted-throaty continuum, the number of, and proportion of energy in, higher formants increases and the energy in lower formants decreases. This greater richness of higher formants with increased throatiness is probably due almost entirely to the simultaneous reduction in total cavity volume and increase in mouth opening, both of which shift the frequency response of the total vocal tract upward to a far greater extent than that provided by a rise in glottal level, which produces greater thinness along the flat-thin continuum.

From what has been said about sound energy dissipation at the lips being directly related to width of lip opening, it can be seen that fronted speech is less intense than is good voice quality at the same glottal intensity, which in turn is less intense than throaty speech at the same glottal intensity. However, fronted speech is more intelligible and throaty speech is less intelligible than speech of good voice quality because more lip action is involved to provide both better visual cues and more precise articulation. Practice saying "principles of political economy" with a throaty, good, and fronted voice quality. Notice that even the consonants [p] and [t] seem to be clearer on the fronted production.

Throatiness as an habitual voice quality connotes stupidity. It is even used theatrically to indicate imbecility. For word emphasis it connotes retraction, recession, or mild surprise, e.g., "He moved *backward*," "It went *down*," "*Oh?*"

Fronting as an habitual quality connotes a person who is punctilious, supercilious, and disdainful. It should be remembered that perceived personality due to speech characteristics is doubtless culture-related. No one could maintain that, where the people of an entire region or country very commonly uses a certain voice quality, the same personality stereotypes will be found. Fronting used for word emphasis connotes precision, exactness, importance, or irritability, e.g., "*Two o'clock*," "There were *five* of them," "*Stop* it *immediately*."

Obviously, throatiness and fronting cannot be simultaneously produced.

Voice Qualities Due to Faulty Resonation

The two voice qualities produced by excessive resonation are *nasality* and *orotundity*. Insufficient resonation is essentially attributable to an excessively rapid rate and will be considered subsequently in the chapter on rate.

Nasality involves excessive utilization of the nasal tract as a resonating chamber. This can of course occur on the production of any voiced continuant but, like all other voice qualities, is most noticeable on the production of vowels.

The oral cavity is separated from the nasal cavity anteriorly by the palatine bones and posteriorly by the velum, both of which are covered inferiorly and superiorly by membranes. The thickness of this wall between nose and mouth is only about one-fourth inch, so it is reasonable to assume that sound energy passing through the mouth cannot be prevented from entering the nose; the amount can only be reduced or increased.

The velum (soft palate) can be raised and retracted to seal or constrict the velopharyngeal port, and for many years it was believed that nasality was due to insufficient closure of this port. However, research has shown numerous examples of a satisfactory quality being produced with an open port. Hence, constriction of the velopharyngeal aperture is probably only one of several methods of attenuating nasal resonance. Another possibility is mere velar elevation rather than elevation and retraction. This would reduce the volume of air in the nasal cavity and thus shift the resonant frequencies of the nasal cavity upward out of the range characterized perceptually as nasality. Another possible method is retraction of the inferior portion of the larynx by increased tension on the inferior pharyngeal constrictor, which would aim or direct the laryngeal sound energy more inferiorly toward the oral cavity rather than more superiorly toward the nasal cavity. Perhaps regulation of nasal resonance is attributable to some degree of each of these three actions rather than to any one of them alone.

The nasal tract, as mentioned in Chapter 3, consists of three tubes on each side (the superior, middle, and inferior meati) which converge anteriorly into a naris (nostril) and posteriorly into a choana. Hence, from back to front we have two tubes becoming six tubes becoming two tubes again. Obviously, none of these tubes is constant in cross-sectional area throughout its length; nevertheless, we can consider their shape as much more tubular than globular, so that we may characterize the nasal tract acoustically as a single tube rather than as a Helmholtz structure when a good voice quality (normal oral resonation) is produced. Although the nasal cavity is segmented longitudinally and is a curved labyrinth containing fluid and walls that absorb sound energy, these characteristics may be ignored for purposes of voice training since the frequency response of such a tube is primarily a function of tube length rather than diameter or linearity. If these longitudinal divisions were removed, we would obviously have a greater amplitude of resonant frequencies, but the frequencies themselves would not be greatly altered.

With normal oral resonation, then, the nasal cavity should function as a tube open at both ends to permit passage of higher partials of the glottal tone. For example, assume the length of the tube to be 0.5 foot and the velocity of sound to be 1100 ft./sec. In that case, the tube would maximally pass all frequencies that are integral multiples of 2200 cps (since $f = v/\lambda$ or 1100/0.5). Thus, we could say that the nasal tract in normal production permits passage of some higher partials in the glottal tone.

However, in nasal production of vowels the nasal cavity is less a resonating tube and is much more a volume addition to the orolaryngeal filtering tract, so that we might characterize nasality as due to an enlarged oronasolaryngeal cavity. In that case it can be seen that the higher frequencies which would have been passed in normal production are now attenuated and the lower partials are now more completely allowed to pass. But this sounds like a description of flat voice quality. Wherein lies the difference? First, the volume addition effected by glottal depression is much less than that which can be accomplished by velar depression, so that a nasal voice quality should have even more midfrequency richness than a flat voice quality. Moreover, the anterior nasal port is open, so that we have a reflection which provides an ability to pass certain higher frequencies not occasioned in flat voice quality.

Since nasality on vowels involves an increase in the intensity of certain frequencies due to greater use of nasal resonance, this can result in increase of formant energies, of formant bandwidths, of the energy in regions between vowel formants, or any combination of these, as determined by the fundamental frequency of the speaker, the complexity of his glottal wave, and the acoustic characteristics of his nasal and other cavities. A vowel is probably perceived as nasal in terms of formant bandwidth and interformant energy: the broader the formants and the greater the energy between formants, the greater is the perceived nasality.

If we constrict the anterior port consciously or with our fingers as we nasalize a vowel, a *twangy quality* will be produced. This is a damping of those partials of the glottal tone which would have been passed with the tube open at both ends and a passing of others which would have been damped. To use the previous

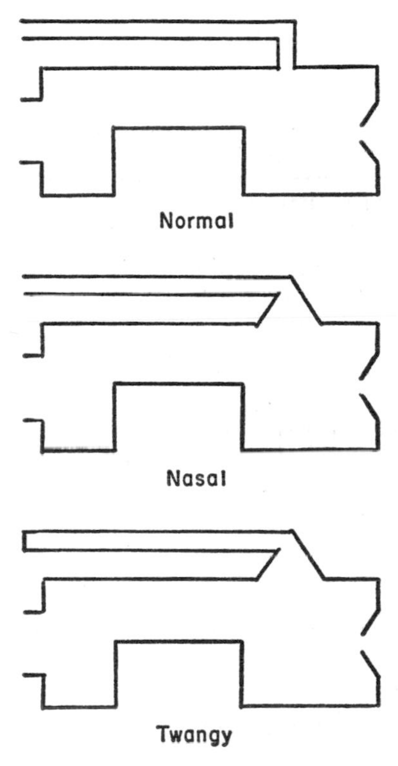

Fig. 5–5. Acoustic representation of normal, nasal, and twangy productions of a vowel.

example of the tube, open at both ends, passing frequencies at or near 2200, 4400, 6600, . . . cps, that tube, closed at one end, would pass frequencies of 1100, 3300, 5500, . . . cps. Figure 5–5 illustrates these cavity differences acoustically. It should be noted that a nasal cannot be articulated with a twangy quality since, if both the nasal and oral cavities are simultaneously sealed off, no sound will be produced.

An habitually nasal voice quality suggests a person who is dull, lazy, and argumentative. Nasality as a device for word emphasis connotes repugnance (e.g., ['næ̃stĩ]), ugliness, boredom, complaint and self-deprecation.

Reduction of habitual nasality requires a knowledge of phonetics sufficient to understand the acoustic difference between the normal and nasal production of any vowel and to recognize the greater tendency of nasality to occur on vowels adjacent to nasals.

The following exercises are designed to assist in removal of nasality. If any vowel is nasalized, remove it from its context and say the word omitting the nasal, trying to produce a non-nasal quality on the vowel. Repeat it several times and then quickly add the nasal, listening to keep the vowel quality as much unchanged by the addition as possible. Then try to say the word in context in that same way. The procedure would be represented as follows for Exercise C, Sentence 1, if nasality occurred on the last word.

1. [kæn jʊ dʊ ɪt 'na͠ʊ]
2. [na͠ʊ]
3. [aʊ, aʊ, aʊ, aʊ, naʊ]
4. [kæn jʊ dʊ ɪt 'naʊ]

Exercises for Reducing Nasality

A. Practice reading the following sentences with a mirror held under your nostrils so that it will become frosted if nasal emission occurs.

1. How do you do?
2. Please take this chair by the fireplace.
3. Did she believe what you said?
4. Her father surely tries to let her do what she likes.
5. Few of us will be there if the party starts after three o'clock.

B. Practice reading the following sentences (without a mirror), and try to avoid nasalizing the italicized vowels.

1. N*ow* is the hour.
2. S*a*m believes it.
3. S*i*nk it.
4. N*u*ts were asked for.
5. *I*nk spilled everywhere.

C. Try to avoid nasality on the italicized vowels.

1. C*a*n you do it n*ow*?
2. He m*a*de her a pr*o*mise.
3. S*o*me day s*oo*n he m*ay* c*o*me.
4. M*a*n.
5. N*a*ncy.
6. S*i*ng*i*ng.
7. N*o*th*i*ng.
8. M*o*nday.
9. M*o*n*ey*.
10. M*o*nks.
11. A n*u*mber of girls m*i*ngled with the boys.
12. M*a*ny m*e*n studied it.
13. What c*a*n *o*ne *a*nswer wh*e*n his *a*nxiety is k*ee*n?
14. M*a*ny m*i*nutes passed.
15. S*o*me *a*ngry m*e*n m*a*ngled h*i*m.

D. Read the discussion of denasality on page 178 and then repeat the above exercises to see how well you can nasalize the nasals while not nasalizing vowels.

Orotundity is the voice quality characterized by a high degree of sound reinforcement. It is the same quality that occurs in singing a vowel at an unvaried pitch rather than speaking that vowel at that pitch for the same duration.

Orotundity is accomplished physiologically by many actions, all of which serve to increase the volume and surface tension of the vocal tract. The faucial pillars can move laterally (by relaxation of the palatoglossus, palatopharyngeus, salpingopharyngeus, and stylopharyngeus), the mandible can be lowered, the velum can be raised, and the laryngeal tract can be minimally constricted (by relaxing the pharyngeal constrictors). As the cross-sectional area of the vocal tract is thus increased, the walls of the cavity become more rigid so that less sound energy will be absorbed by the cavity walls and more will be reflected. Thus far the vocal tract has been considered as a filtering device for attenuating certain partials of the glottal tone. Such filtering can only reduce the intensity of a sound. Reinforcement increases the intensity of a sound.

Two media may be employed to produce such reinforcement. The more important medium of course is air; the pressure variations in the vocal tract cause the body structures to vibrate, much as a tuning fork will vibrate in the presence of a sound to which it is tuned. This is termed *sympathetic vibration.* The other medium is the body itself, so that fold vibrations can vibrate the dense, adjacent tissues directly, much as the base of a struck tuning fork can vibrate a table top when the base is placed against it. This is called *forced vibration.* It is doubtful if much head and chest vibration can be attributed to forced vibration any more than a violin's sound can be attributed to the direct contact of the ends of each string with the body of the violin. An example of this increased sympathetic resonance occurring in orotundity is the rather common observation that a person standing in deep water can speak naturally but can sing by no means as well as on dry land.

Orotundity requires, of course, sufficient duration of continuant sounds to enable sympathetic resonance of bones and cartilages to occur, but mere prolongation of continuants is not sufficient for the production of orotundity. Cavity enlargement and surface tension which increase the ability of sound energy in the vocal tract to set the dense tissues of the head, neck, and chest into sympathetic vibration are essential. Thus, orotundity is not equivalent to prolongation of continuants although such prolongation is required to produce orotundity.

As stated previously, attempting orotundity can occasionally reduce flatness. This may be due to muscular activity which enlarges the oral cavity, counteracting some of the muscle activity which depresses the glottis. However, orotundity and flatness may be produced simultaneously. A simultaneously orotund and nasal quality probably would be achieved by less velar elevation than in orotundity alone. It is obviously difficult to combine extreme breathiness and orotundity. Generally, then, the only voice qualities which cannot be produced simultaneously are the flat-thin and throaty-fronted combinations.

The perceived personality of a speaker with an habitually orotund quality is that of a person who is authoritarian, idealistic, artistic and proud. Other terms used to describe orotundity are "preacher voice" or "ministerial tone." Orotundity with a Spanish intonation (see page 202) is called a "sing-song" or "school-teacherish" quality. For word emphasis, orotundity connotes multidimensionality, expansiveness, richness, positiveness, or vast importance. Since opportunities for such connotations occur frequently, orotundity is an extremely useful emphatic quality.

Unlike voice qualities mentioned previously, orotundity is more consciously acquired, and may be removed by a mere decision to do so. However, in some persons this quality may be desirable, as the following anecdote unfortunately true, implies. Several ministers were told in a speech class how to communicate effectively without orotundity and returned to their pulpits to do so. Many of them subsequently reported that they encountered extreme dissatisfaction in their congregations, the typical objection being the statement that "We come to church to be inspired, not to be made to think."

Pseudo Voice Qualities

Breathy, tense, flat, thin, throaty, fronted, nasal, and orotund voice qualities are independent of the sounds produced, although they are more distinguishable on vocalic than on consonantal continuants. However, certain modes of articulation may be so frequently employed, because of the frequency of occurrence of the consonants involved, that the resultant speech seems to be more a voice quality than a manner of articulation. Such modes of articulation will be termed pseudo voice qualities. The two pseudo voice qualities to be considered here are *simulated breathiness* and *denasality*.

Although breathiness is useful theatrically to connote certain personality characteristics frequently found in characters in plays, that voice quality employed on a stage has insufficient intensity for intelligibility in such situations unless the audience is quite near (as in arena theatre) or electronic amplification is employed, and to speak at the requisite intensity would, as stated previously, tend to traumatize the folds. Hence, trained actors tend to simulate breathiness. Simulated breathiness is an unvoicing of consonantal continuants and an overaspirating of plosives and fricatives in initial syllabic positions. Thus, the following phonetic distinction could be made:

Breathiness: [pli̥z 'du̥ɪ̥t]
Simulated breathiness: [p^{H}liz̥ 'd^{H}uɪt]

Breathiness is frequently employed where the communication is electronically amplified or reproduced, as in speaking on the radio or in making recordings. This is because (1) microphones are designed to be very sensitive to pressure variations and very insensitive to pressure blasts, and (2) unless the entire electronic system has high fidelity, high frequencies are greatly attenuated. Since breathiness consists of considerable air pressure and randomly occurring high frequencies, both tend to be lost in the electronic system. However, using breathiness in such situations is a makeshift procedure which is obviously inferior to using good voice quality. About the only merit of such advice is that it achieves some perceptual improvement in little time with practically no training.

Denasality is insufficient nasal resonation on nasals, i.e., on [m], [n] and [ŋ].[3] It is due to reduced air volume in the nasal cavity, as when a person has a cold or draining sinuses or when the velum is excessively elevated and retracted.

Denasality connotes little in terms of personality, being indicative more of a person who has a cold than of one with certain traits.

Nasality and denasality frequently occur in the same individual. This is perhaps due to his feeling that he has sufficiently advertised the existence of a nasal by nasalizing the adjacent vowel. A person who is working to overcome nasality should, therefore, examine the degree to which he nasalizes nasals and, if this seems insufficient, he should strive to hold nasals longer than he habitually holds them.

[3] Denasality may be considered a distortion of other sounds as well, and thus deserving classification as a voice quality per se. The distinction can be illustrated by having someone with a good voice quality read each sentence of Exercise A, page 179, once normally and once while holding his nose without obstructing his mouth. If you can distinguish correctly, in 15 of 20 cases, when he is and is not holding his nose, you would probably prefer to classify denasality as a voice quality per se.

Voice Quality Exercises

Practice reading the following selection with each of the voice qualities identified numerically under A, then with each pair listed under B, then with each combination listed under C. The best method for combining qualities is to produce first the requisite vocal-fold action (breathiness, tenseness), to superimpose upon this the requisite glottal elevation (flatness, thinness), to add the requisite tongue positioning (throatiness, fronting), to add the type of resonation required (nasality,[4] orotundity), and lastly to achieve the required articulatory action (simulated breathiness). In the combinations under B and C, the sequence of numbers indicates the relative degree of that quality to be employed. Thus, an *N* in an *Nxx* combination requires nasalizing all continuants, an *xNx* requires nasalizing many vowels, and all vowels adjacent to nasals, and an *xxN* combination implies nasalizing only vowels adjacent to nasals.

> "When the sunlight strikes raindrops in the air, they act like a prism and form a rainbow. The rainbow is a division of white light into many beautiful colors. These take the shape of a long round arch, with its path high above, and its two ends apparently beyond the horizon. There is, according to legend, a boiling pot of gold at one end. People look, but no one ever finds it. When a man looks for something beyond his reach, his friends say he is looking for the pot of gold at the end of the rainbow."

A.

1. *Breathy* (B)
2. *Tense* (Te)
3. *Flat* (Fl)
4. *Thin* (Th)
5. *Throaty* (Thr)
6. *Fronted* (Fr)
7. *Nasal* (N)
8. *Orotund* (O)
9. *Simulated breathy* (Sb)

B.

1. BFl	11. SbTe	21. TeN
2. FlB	12. FrSb	22. FrFl
3. BTh	13. FlThr	23. OTh
4. ThB	14. NTh	24. ThrTe
5. BThr	15. TeB	25. ThSb
6. FrB	16. FlN	26. NThr
7. BN	17. OTe	27. SbFl
8. NB	18. BSb	28. ThrO
9. OB	19. FrTh	29. FlO
10. TeFl	20. ThTe	30. ThThr

[4] The twangy quality is omitted in the belief that the perceived personality and connotations resulting from such word emphasis are very similar if not identical to those occasioned by nasality.

C.
1. BNFl
2. ThSbB
3. TeFlN
4. NThrO
5. OTeFr
6. ThrOSb
7. SbThThr
8. TeFlFr
9. ThrOFl
10. FrSbTe
11. OFrTe
12. ThTeB
13. FrBTh
14. SbThN
15. FlBTe

D. Read the selection as indicated below, using good voice quality on all words except those marked with letters above them. On those words produce the qualities indicated.

O Fr B
"When the *sunlight* strikes *raindrops* in the *air,* they act like a
O O Fr Th Th
prism and form a *rainbow.* The rainbow is a *division* of *white light*
B O O O
into many *beautiful colors.* These take the shape of a *long, round*
B Th Th Fl O
arch, with its *path high above,* and its two *ends apparently* beyond the
Te Fr O
horizon. There is, according to legend, a *boiling pot* of *gold* at one end.
Fr B N
People look, but *no* one ever finds it. When a man looks for some-
Te
thing beyond his reach, his *friends* say he is looking for the pot of gold
N Fl
at the *end* of the *rainbow.*"

6

Pitch and Intonation

PITCH

1. *Anatomical, Physiological, and Acoustic Relationships*

The frequency of the voice, or vocal frequency, refers to the fundamental frequency of the vocal folds, i.e., to the number of openings or closings of the folds per second. The pitch of the voice can refer to perception of its highness or lowness, but it is also commonly used to refer to notes and intervals on a musical scale, so that we speak of a pitch of C_4 or F_3 or of a pitch rise of three tones. However, pitch as used in this chapter will refer only to the *fundamental frequency of the vocal folds.*

In this sense of the term, pitch is affected by three interrelated anatomical and physiological characteristics of the folds: their mass, length, and tension. The mass of the folds may be increased physiologically by reduction of tension in the vocalis muscle, or by reduction in either the length or tilt of the folds. Tilting of the folds refers to elevation of the medial superior surface of each fold above the level of the lateral superior surface. As tilting increases, the consequence is a decrease in the medial angle between the superior and inferior surfaces, and hence in the mean cross-sectional area of the folds. Thus the mass of the folds, which is the mean cross-sectional area times length, decreases as tilting increases. The probable explanation of this tilting of the folds is that the greater subglottal air pressure necessary to overcome the increased fold tension at higher pitch pushes their medial surfaces upward before abduction. The mass of the folds may be increased anatomically by normal growth or by glandular or nasal secretions onto the folds. The folds may be lengthened by reducing tension in the vocalis or by increasing tension in either the cricothyroids or in both the lateral and posterior cricoarytenoids. The folds may be tensed by lengthening or by increased tension in the vocalis.

It may seem that pitch should decrease as the folds are lengthened much as the shorter the string of a harp the higher its pitch, but this would be true of the folds only if the vocalis muscle were to undergo proportional relaxation. Usually, however, the opposite seems to occur, like stretching a harp string to make it longer. Thus, the vocalis tenses to provide slight increments (glides) in pitch. Large increments in pitch (jumps) are achieved by lengthening the folds so that, if vocalis tension remains constant, the added length achieves greater tension in the folds. Obviously, the mass of the folds does not remain unaffected by these changes in tension and length. When length is held constant, less tension produces greater mass. When tension is the same for two different lengths, the greater length will produce more mass. Hence, we can say that as pitch rises the folds become more tilted, and sharp rises are achieved primarily by fold lengthening whereas gradual rises are achieved primarily by fold tensing.

Obviously, since three variables are involved (mass, length, and tension), a particular vocal frequency may be produced in various ways, by altering the proportion of each. One determinant of the proportions employed is the intensity desired. As will be seen in the chapter on loudness, a greater intensity is effected by holding the folds closed longer and returning them to the closed position more quickly in each cycle. This requires greater phonatory tension. Hence, if the same pitch can be produced with relatively more mass and less tension or less mass and more tension, the latter will tend to be employed for the more intense production.

Natural growth was mentioned as a factor affecting length and mass of the folds and, consequently, pitch. The mean frequencies of males aged 8, 10, 14, and 18 are, respectively, 297, 270, 242, and 137 cps. Thus, the male voice drops about an octave between the ages of 10 and 18. Since fine manipulations of the folds are required to effect pitch changes, it is not amazing that so-called "voice breaks" occur in children. However, such breaks are not coincident merely with puberty but occur at every stage of growth. These breaks are usually about one octave, breaking upward when low pitches are attempted and downward when medium pitches are attempted. They occur about as often in males as in females but are perhaps more noticeable in males because the actual pitch of their voices changes more in the same amount of time. At age 8 both sexes have about the same pitch level but at adulthood females have lowered their pitch about two tones while the pitch of males has dropped about one octave, or three times as far.

As was seen previously in the chapter on voice quality, pitch may be perceived as being higher without changing vocal-fold frequency, due to glottal elevation. However, this constitutes a change in pitch as defined psychologically rather than, as defined in this chapter, purely physically, since glottal elevation is effected by extrinsic laryngeal muscles which do not necessarily affect intrinsic muscle tension.

2. Psychological Relationships

Pitch may be thought of as an absolute or relative level, as an absolute or relative range capable of being produced, or as an absolute or relative range habitually achieved. Certainly we make many judgments about speakers on the basis of their delivery, and our consideration here is what pitch characteristics, if any, are related to characteristics which accurately describe the person as he sees himself, as others see him, or as his behavior reveals him to be. For our purposes we will need to use only two terms: *producible range* and *used range*.

A person's producible range comprises the frequencies he can accurately produce when a frequency-producing stimulus is provided. For example, a person might listen to a clarinet and try to sing each note with the instrument as it went up the scale. Beauty of production would not be important; accuracy would be the sole criterion. That is, did his folds vibrate at the same fundamental frequency as the stimulus provided? If he produces 33 successive notes accurately and each 8 notes spanned one octave, we say that his producible range is 24 tones (4 octaves).[1] If, however, we record a sample of his speaking or reading and analyze it to determine the highest and the lowest frequencies he produced, the span in tones between these extremes represents his used range. Thus, if the highest frequency he used was 480 cps and the lowest was 120 cps, we would say that his used range was 12 tones (2 octaves).

Each of these ranges, producible and used, can be considered in terms of its *level* or its *extent*. Extent of range refers to how many tones are spanned; level refers to the relative height of this span. Thus, words like soprano, mezzo-soprano, alto, tenor, baritone, and bass refer to different levels of range and, since these are musical terms, they tend to refer to level of producible rather than to level of used range.

Our first consideration is which, if any, of these pitch characteristics (extent of producible range, level of producible range, extent of used range, and level of used range) is related to any characteristics of the three types of personality, behavioral, self-characterized and perceived, and precisely what is the nature of these relationships.

One question, then, is whether any traits of self-characterized or behavioral personality correlate more than by chance with any pitch characteristics. The answer seems to be only sex: whether the speaker is male or female. A large number of characteristics have been examined, including sales ability, truth-telling or lying, and even physical characteristics (when the speakers are

[1] If a whole-tone scale had been employed, 25 successive notes one tone apart would be equivalent to 24 tones. The extra note is due simply to the fact that notes refer to *frequencies* and tones refer to *intervals* between frequencies whose ratio is 1.122:1.

not seen), and any accuracy greater than chance has yet to be obtained. Hence, any relationship between pitch characteristics and behavioral or self-characterized personality traits is purely coincidental.

In terms of perceived personality, however, certain close relationships are found to exist. But with respect to level or extent of producible range, no relationships with perceived personality have been found. For example, neither the frequency of a male's lowest producible pitch nor his classification, on the basis of producible range, as a tenor, baritone, or bass seems to have any relation to his ratings on masculinity, interest, aggressiveness, intelligence, speaking ability, or similar traits. Since level of used range is dependent upon level of producible range, and since level of producible range is not found to be related to any type of personality or personality characteristic other than sex, it is logical to conclude that level of used range is similarly unrelated. However, in terms of relationships between used range and perceived personality, relationships are meaningful and clear. The greater the extent of used range, the more favorably will the speaker be looked upon. Table 6–1 presents a summary of several relationships which have been found. It is based on various studies which seem to show that, the more variety in pitch one uses, the more personable and interesting he seems.

One other interesting pitch-personality relationship has been found. It involves the concept of habitual pitch level, which is the pitch a particular person uses most frequently; it is usually the pitch at which he initiates ideas and at which he terminates unemphatic, simple statements. The finding is that an almost perfect relationship exists between the level of habitual pitch in producible range and extent of used range. *The higher the habitual pitch level, the more pitch variety one uses, and vice versa.*

The question of how high one can set his habitual pitch in his range is probably restricted by voice quality. So long as habitual pitch can be raised without resulting in a thin voice quality, the higher it is set, the better. Research has shown, however, that this *optimum pitch level* is reached by males whose habitual pitch level is such that approximately one-fourth of their pro-

TABLE 6–1

Relationships Between Perceived Personality Characteristics and Amount of Pitch Variety Employed (Used Range)

HIGHLY RELATED CHARACTERISTICS

Male Speakers	Female Speakers
Effective in speaking	Effective in speaking
Extroverted	Extroverted
Jovial	Jovial
Enthusiastic	Careful
Energetic (vs. lazy)	
Artistic	
Good-looking	
Good sense of humor	
Talkative	

MODERATELY RELATED CHARACTERISTICS

Male Speakers	Female Speakers
Active (vs. passive)	Talkative
Sensitive	Convincing
Kind	
Emotional	

ducible range in tones is below this level or, conversely, the speakers rated as most effective employ an habitual pitch level which is 25 per cent of the way up their producible range. Females have an optimum pitch level at approximately 20 per cent of their range. In general, female speakers as a group are rated as less effective than males as a group whether the auditors are males, females, adults, children, experts, or laymen. Since absolute pitch level and used range are the only two sex-linked vocal characteristics, and since absolute pitch level is not related to speaking effectiveness, it seems reasonable to suppose that this general male superiority in effectiveness can be attributed almost entirely to male achievement of a higher optimum pitch level.

Several possible ways of locating one's habitual and optimum pitch levels exist, all of which are equally effective. However, in this regard, one highly erroneous concept is held by many singing voice coaches. This is the notion that, as one sings up the scale, when he reaches his optimum (or his habitual) pitch level, a perceptible "swell" in richness or intensity will occur. Research has shown this not to be true. All of the following, however, are equally effective as determinants of optimum pitch level for males:

1. The frequency one-fourth of the way up his producible range including falsetto,
2. The frequency one-third of the way up his producible range excluding falsetto,
3. Two full tones below his middle note excluding falsetto, and
4. Five full tones above his lowest sustainable note.

For females, optimum pitch level is:

1. The frequency one-fifth of the way up her producible range including falsetto,
2. The frequency one-fourth of the way up her producible range excluding falsetto,
3. Three full tones below her middle note excluding falsetto, and
4. Four full tones above her lowest sustainable note.

Generally, a person can produce a range of 20 tones, a fifth of which is in falsetto. Falsetto frequencies are clearly recognizable because of a qualitative difference. Falsetto is produced by the arytenoideus bringing the posterior portion of the folds together and the posterior fibers of the vocalis being tensed so that only the anterior portion of the folds vibrate. Such vibrations are far less complex than at lower frequencies because the relatively small mass and the great tension of the folds produce a more rhythmic (harmonic) manner of opening and closing. The glottal tone in falsetto therefore consists of fewer partials than at lower frequencies, and in certain cases a pure tone may even be achieved.

3. *Achieving Greater Pitch Variety*

To derive maximal benefit from an increment in pitch variety, it is not sufficient merely to have greater variety in pitch; pitch should vary meaningfully. Hence, if you are capable of producing a wide range of pitches with flexibility and ease, you should be concerned with improving your intonation rather than simply using more pitch variety.

However, persons who do not use much pitch variety are generally incapable of readily producing a wide range of pitches with flexibility and ease. This is *not* because they are "tone deaf." Obviously, merely from what has been said previously about the acoustic characteristics of vowels, anyone who can hear a difference—with or without a hearing aid—among such words as "put," "peat," "pit," "pert" possesses an amazing, albeit normal, amount of pitch discrimination. "Tone deafness" should not be applied to a person's hearing mechanism but to his speaking mechanism. It may be true to some extent that some persons have never been trained to differentiate between frequency and intensity so that, when instructed to sing up the musical scale, they merely sing the same note more loudly. Such instances are much rarer than is commonly believed and, if correction involves careful discrimination between frequency and intensity, the task of singing up the scale will be readily accomplished. Another rare exception is the individual who sings up the scale but is occasionally "off key." This is because he has never been required to adjust his vocal frequency to the frequency of a stimulus. Informing such a person that he is below or above his intended objective as each note is played will soon enable him to produce notes accurately under stimulus conditions.

In both of these cases, rare though they are, the difficulty is not an inability to hear but an inability to perceive differences when perceptible differences occur. Ninety-five per cent of a group can produce a wide variety of pitches accurately. At least four per cent will not readily be able to span more than a few tones, but not for the foregoing reasons. The cause is one of insufficient tonicity in the frequency-regulating musculature. Asking such individuals to sing up a scale is analogous to asking a person whose leg has just been removed from a cast to dance. His muscles did not deteriorate in the cast; they lost tonicity. The remedy is exercise. In the same manner, a person who cannot produce a range of at least two octaves is unable to do so because he habitually uses only one frequency (a monotone), a range of only a few tones, or two frequencies about an octave apart. He needs to exercise his laryngeal musculature until he is able to produce a range of as many tones as he is capable of spanning without extensive training. That is, in a day or two he can learn to produce a range of, say, three full octaves. Weeks of additional training might enable him to add one or two lower and two or three higher frequencies to his producible range, but for speech purposes such extensions are quite unnecessary (because extent of used range is not related to extent of producible range). Hence, any person lacking in muscular tonicity should be given what little training is necessary to enable him to produce at least two octaves, but training any other person to extend his producible range will not by itself increase or enable him to increase his used range. If his range is already satisfactory, covering at least three octaves including falsetto, he should learn to use greater variety in pitch by drilling on intonation. For persons whose ranges are quite limited, drills to extend their producible range provide the fundamental requisite for benefiting from drills on intonation.

The following exercises, therefore, are designed for persons whose producible ranges are very limited. Mastery of them provides the prerequisite for benefiting from the subsequent discussion and drills on intonation. All students, however, should perform the first exercise to be sure their range is not limited.

Exercises for Extension of Producible Range

1. Notice that a piano has a succession of two black keys together and three black keys together. Any "C" is the white key just below the two black keys. "Middle C" is the one whose black keys above it are in the center of the keyboard. Strike "middle C" and phonate or sing [ʌ]. Continue upward, striking only the white keys, and phonate or sing [ʌ] at the same pitch as the note produced. You will reach a point at which your voice has a "crack" or "squeak" rather than the quality of the previous note. You are now entering your falsetto range. With a little practice you should be able to include at least two notes above this one in your range. If you cannot do so immediately, begin again at "middle C" and proceed upward until you can produce at least three notes in falsetto. Do this at least three times to be sure that these falsetto notes are the only ones you can readily produce; a fourth or

fifth may be found to occur. Remember which is your highest producible note. Now return to "middle C" and proceed downward. Do not be perturbed if you find that you must retract your jaw or depress your larynx to produce lower notes. Do this three times to be sure you have reached the nadir below which you cannot go without additional training. Remember which is your lowest producible note. Now phonate or sing [ʌ] upward from your lowest to your highest producible note. If you cannot begin at your lowest note, repeat the descending scale until you can do so. Now phonate or sing [ʌ] downward from your highest to your lowest producible note. Again, if you cannot begin at your highest note, practice the ascending scale until you can.

2. If you have not been able to perform all of these tasks without effort or repetitions, perform the following exercises after you can phonate or sing both upward and downward throughout your range. Drill on the sentences numbered below until you can speak each at a *normal rate* in each of the following ways.

a. Begin at your lowest producible pitch and say each successive syllable at a higher pitch, ending on your highest producible pitch.
b. Begin at your highest producible pitch and step gradually downward syllable by syllable to your lowest producible pitch.
c. Begin at your lowest producible pitch, work upward to your highest producible pitch on about the middle word, and then work downward again to your lowest producible pitch at the end.
d. Begin at your highest producible pitch, work downward to your lowest producible pitch on about the middle word, and then work upward again to your highest producible pitch at the end.

1. Now is the time for all good men to come to the aid of those who want to stay free.
2. He brought his aunt to her big house to meet them when they came.
3. I don't know why he tries to work so fast.
4. I heard him shout that he could come.

INTONATION

1. Definitions

Several terms must be clearly defined before we discuss intonation. The first term is "concept." For our purposes, a *concept* is defined as one or more syllables which communicate a single mental image of a person, thing, state, or action. The following are examples of single concepts according to this definition:

1. America (as the name of a country)
2. the United States of America (as the name of a country)
3. spread out (as in "They were spread out")
4. light blue (as a color)
5. ex-governor (as a title)

The following are *not* single concepts by our definition:

1. America (as an answer to "Where do you live?" Since it also conveys another concept, viz., "I live in_____")
2. the United States of America (as in "Heretofore we have been disunited; today we are truly_____")
3. spread out (as in "He took the_____")
4. light blue (meaning light rather than dark and blue rather than some other color or meaning light and blue)
5. ex-governor (as in "The one we have now is honest, but the _____")

Hence, it can be seen that a concept may be an affix (*ex-*), a simple noun (*typewriter*), a compound noun (*electric typewriter*), or a nominative substantive (*the thing you type on*), a simple verb (*ask*), a compound verb (*had asked*), or a participle (*raising a question*), an adverb (*speedily*) or an adverbial phrase (*as fast as greased lightning*), an adjective (*soft*) or an adjectival phrase (*soft as silk*), or a prepositional phrase (*in the box*).

The next term requiring careful definition is *idea*, and we must distinguish clearly between the two terms, concept and idea. An idea is two concepts, one of which is subjective and the other predicative; either may be explicit or implied. Neither punctuation nor number of words is a reliable indication of what constitutes an idea.

The following are examples of ideas, with the two constituent concepts underlined where both are explicit:

1. The boy ran down the street.
2. He said, "Hello."
3. "Stop that!"
4. "Are you sure?"
5. "O.K.?"
6. The constitution of the United States of America was adopted in 1796.

Any idea may be *unemphatic, emphatic,* or *interrogatory.* The following are examples of each type:

Unemphatic

1. Today is Tuesday.
2. Be quiet.
3. You did.

Emphatic

1. Today *is* Tuesday!
2. Be quiet!
3. You did!

Interrogatory

1. Today is Tuesday?
2. Be quiet?
3. You did?

Ideas may be combined in many ways, several of which are important for our purposes. Two or more ideas may be *independent, parallel, dependent,* or *parenthetical.* The following are examples of each type:

Independent

1. Tom went to the show. He was gone about two hours. He walked home.
2. Tom went to the show and he was gone about two hours and then he walked home.

Parallel

1. Tom and Jane went to the show.
2. Tom went to the show and to the grocery store.
3. Tom or Jane went to the show.
4. I believe in right; I also believe in justice.
5. I believe in right and in justice.
6. He is a tall, dark-complexioned, stately individual.
7. Maine, Vermont, and New Hampshire are in New England.
8. He said it proudly, disdainfully, even haughtily.
9. "Hog-butcher, tool maker, stacker of wheat, builder of the nation's railroads . . ."
10. He ran and jumped and leaped and skipped across the rocks.

Dependent

1. I believe in justice tempered with mercy.
2. He planned to go, but he couldn't.
3. It is generally true. However, there are exceptions.
4. I believe in security; I disbelieve in security at any price.
5. I believe in security, but not at any price.

Parenthetical

1. Tom, not Jane, went to the show.
2. Mr. Smith, our milkman, is ill. (*Note:* "Mr. Smith, our milkman is ill" is two independent ideas.)
3. My brother, who lives with us, decided to move. (*Note:* "My brother who lives with us decided to move" is one idea.)

One additional term needs to be defined before we can get to matters of intonation, that of *most-important-word.* This term always refers to ideas rather than to concepts. Since an idea consists of two concepts, the most-important-word is all of the words contained in the more important concept or that portion of those words which conveys the salient information identifying that concept. Monosyllabic words whose only vowel should be schwa or r-colored schwa are obviously not most important. In the following, the most-important-word of each idea is italicized:

1. George ate a *peach.*
2. He lay *prostrate* on the ground.
3. How do you *do?*
4. Today is *Monday* (in reply to "What day is it?").
5. Today *is* Monday! (in countering someone's claim otherwise).
6. *Today* is Monday (in reply to "Which day is Monday?").
7. He is a citizen of the *United States* of *America.*
8. He works as a *night watchman* in a *factory* (meant as equivalent to the compound noun, *factory night watchman*).
9. He is an *alumnus* of the *University* of *Iowa.*
10. *Come in.*

So far we have defined concept, idea, and most-important-word. However, before we can use these terms to discuss intonation, we must differentiate among intonation, inflection, and accent.

Inflection refers to patterns of pitch change during the production of a single syllable that is not an entire idea. Thus, inflection would not refer to a pitch change on "Oh?" because the syllable is the entire idea. Any syllable that is a portion of an idea may be *inflected* (pitch changes) or *uninflected* (pitch does not change).

Accent refers to relative degrees of loudness, duration, and pitch height employed to indicate the relative importance of various syllables within a single word. As an example, the following are accented differently: de*fense*, *de*fense.

Intonation, as we use the term, refers to patterns of pitch change on ideas. Such changes involve inflections (changes within syllables) and *steps* (changes between syllables).

The various symbols to be employed are shown in Table 6–2.

TABLE 6–2

Intonational Symbols Employed in the Text

Symbol	Employed on	Indicates
	Ideas	Producible range (upper and lower lines are highest and lowest producible pitches, respectively)
	Syllabic consonants, or monosyllabic words containing [ə] or [ɚ] as only vowels	Minimal duration and/or intensity at that pitch level
	Single syllable or monosyllabic word	Duration, at a single pitch level, corresponding to extent of line length
	Single syllable or monosyllabic word	Rate and extent of upward inflection by slope (rate of change) and vertical length (amount of change) of line, respectively; length of line indicates duration
	Single syllable or monosyllabic word	Rate, extent, and duration of downward inflection
	Single syllable or monosyllabic word	Rate, extent, and duration of upward followed by downward inflection

Intonation refers, at least for American English, to pitch patterns which reveal the length and purpose of each idea and the relationships among ideas. When we say that intonation reveals the length of ideas, we mean that the pitch patterns tell us where an idea begins and where it ends. When we say that intonation reveals an idea's purpose, we mean that its pitch patterns tell us whether and to what extent it is unemphatic, emphatic, or interrogatory, and what kind and extent of speaker mood or emotion is implied. When we say that intonation reveals relationships among ideas, we mean that the pitch patterns tell us: whether two or more ideas are independent or in parallel; whether one is dependent and, if so, which one; or whether one is parenthetical and, if so, which one; and for any of these, intonation reveals their relative importance. Usually this latter function refers only to those ideas contained in a single sentence. As will be seen, rate and intensity are usually employed to indicate the relative importance of ideas which are contained in different sentences. These functions of intonation are highly culture-related, so that intonation in other languages may convey those same kinds of information differently, or convey different kinds of information, or both. Hence, one other kind of information can be conveyed, and that is whether the language being spoken is the speaker's native language or an acquired one. This is generally so because persons learning a foreign language seldom pay sufficient attention to its intonational characteristics and tend to superimpose their native intonations onto the vocabulary of the foreign language. In fact, no matter how accurately a foreigner pronounces each word, he will still reveal that he is a foreigner if he uses his native patterns of intonation.

Using the foregoing vocabulary, we are now ready to consider how intonations convey each type of information to native Americans.

2. Denotations of American Intonations

The characteristic intonational pattern of American English is as follows: *The first syllable of an idea is uttered at habitual pitch level, and the pitch of each successive syllable tends to be higher, with the highest pitch on the most important syllable of the most-important-word in that idea.*

If the idea is unemphatic, the pitch returns downward from that point to habitual pitch level on the last syllable in that idea. This return is stepped downward if the most important syllable is not the last syllable; if the last syllable is the most important, the return is inflected. The relative height of the most important syllable of the most-important-word above habitual pitch level (first syllable) indicates extent of concern. Hence, the five unemphatic ideas in Table 6-3 might be said to indicate, in descending order, excitement, enthusiasm, interest, unconcern, and boredom.

Emphatic ideas do not return to habitual pitch level from the most important syllable of the most-important-word but terminate at a level which, compared to this highest pitch position, indicates less emphasis the more closely termination approaches habitual pitch level. Thus, maximum emphasis would have no downward stepping or inflection whatsoever. As can be seen in Table 6–3, of the five emphatic statements each is therefore more emphatic than the one below. We might describe them as implying, respectively, intransigence, certainty, confidence, doubtlessness, and a lack of complete assurance.

Interrogatory ideas terminate at a level which is higher than the level of the most-important-word, and the higher the terminal pitch above the highest pitch of the most-important-word, the greater is the dubiety expressed. We might describe the five interrogatory ideas in Table 6–3, therefore, as expressing, from top to bottom, slight uncertainty, doubt, disbelief, incredulity, and great astonishment.

See how well you can illustrate the proper intonations of the following sentences. After you have completed your work, check your answers below.

1. "*Hello.*"
   a. enthusiastically
   b. unconcernedly
2. "The dress is *yellow.*"
   a. interestedly
   b. confidently
   c. doubtfully

3. "It's *three o'clock.*"
   a. boredly
   b. irrefutably
   c. incredulously

ANSWERS

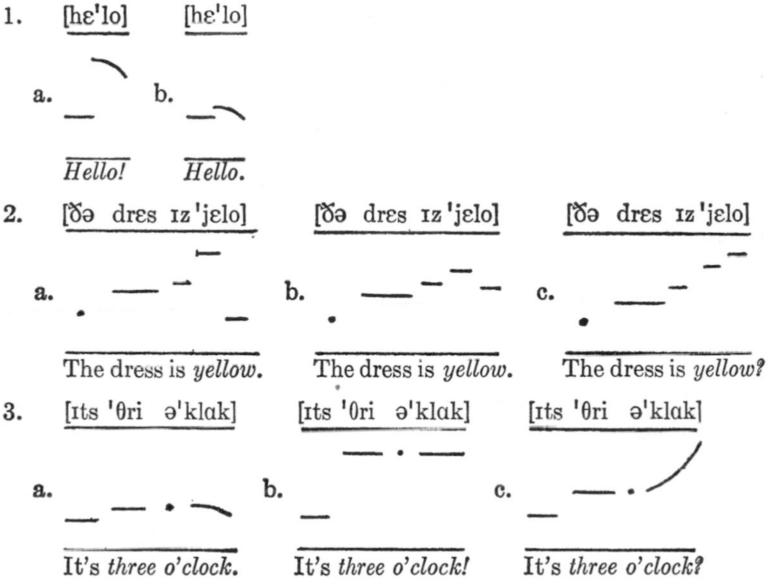

1. [hɛ'lo] [hɛ'lo]

a. b.

Hello! *Hello.*

2. [ðə drɛs ɪz 'jɛlo] [ðə drɛs ɪz 'jɛlo] [ðə drɛs ɪz 'jɛlo]

a. b. c.

The dress is *yellow.* The dress is *yellow.* The dress is *yellow?*

3. [ɪts 'θri ə'klɑk] [ɪts 'θri ə'klɑk] [ɪts 'θri ə'klɑk]

a. b. c.

It's *three o'clock.* It's *three o'clock!* It's *three o'clock?*

Intonation is also used to indicate relationships of ideas, as indicated in Table 6–4. Independent ideas are obviously intoned independently. Parallel ideas are intoned as similarly as possible, and the parallel elements are intoned at the same, highest pitch level. Dependent ideas are intoned so that the contrasting terms are intoned at the same, highest pitch level. A parenthetical idea is intoned with pauses separating it from the basic idea and at a lower pitch level if, as is usually true, the parenthetical idea is less important. If the parenthetical idea is more important, it is intoned at a higher level than the basic idea. This means, then, that the parenthetical idea or the basic idea is initiated at a level which is higher or lower than habitual pitch level. Moreover, the pitch level on the last syllable before the parenthetical idea is the same as the pitch

TABLE 6–3

Characteristic Intonational Patterns of American English

(Most-important-word italicized)

Unemphatic Ideas	Emphatic Ideas	Interrogatory Ideas
[aɪ sɛd ˈpeʃəns ɪz rɪkwaɪrd]	[aɪ sɛd ˈpeʃəns ɪz rɪkwaɪrd]	[aɪ sɛd ˈpeʃəns ɪz rɪkwaɪrd]
I said *patience* is required.	I said *patience* is required!	I said *patience* is required?
[təde ɪz ˈtɪuzdɪ]	[təde ɪz ˈtɪuzdɪ]	[təde ɪz ˈtɪuzdɪ]
Today is *Tuesday*.	Today is *Tuesday!*	Today is *Tuesday?*

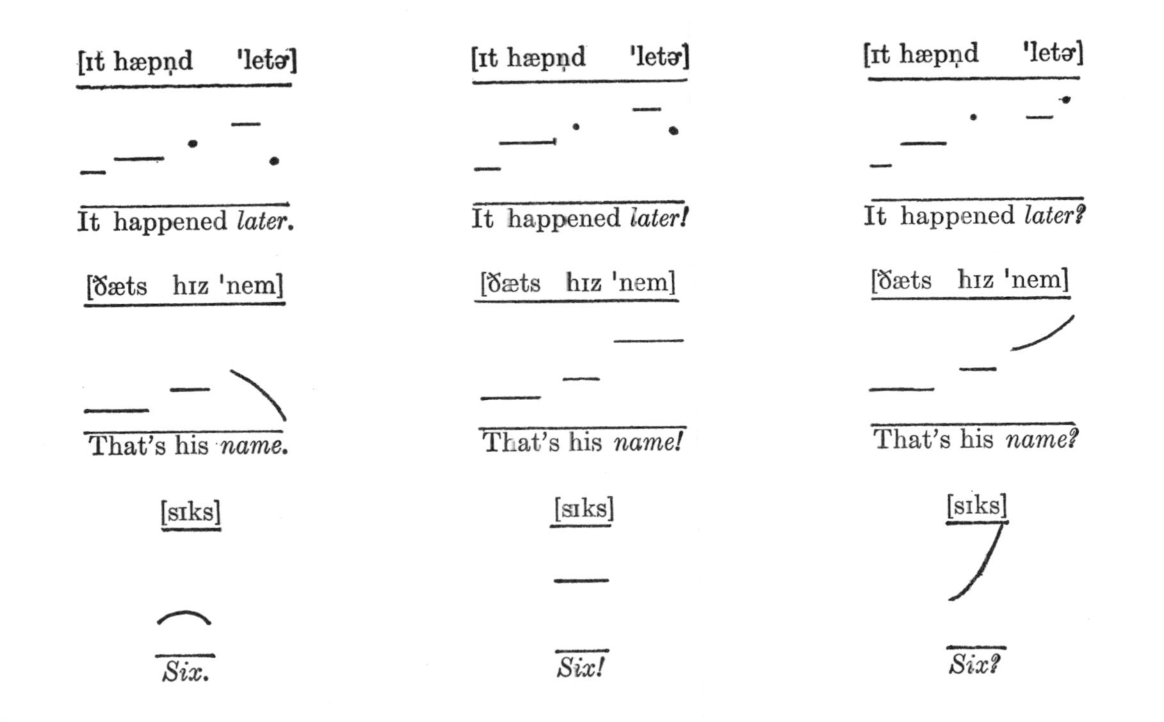
[ɪt hæpn̩d 'letɚ]
It happened *later*.
[ðæts hɪz 'nem]
That's his *name*.
[sɪks]
Six.
[ɪt hæpn̩d 'letɚ]
It happened *later!*
[ðæts hɪz 'nem]
That's his *name!*
[sɪks]
Six!
[ɪt hæpn̩d 'letɚ]
It happened *later?*
[ðæts hɪz 'nem]
That's his *name?*
[sɪks]
Six?

TABLE 6–4

Intonational Indication of Ideational Relationships

Parallel Ideas	Dependent Ideas	Parenthetical Ideas
[ˈtɑm ənˈdʒen wɛn tə ðə ʃo]	[hi ˈplænd tə go bət hɪ ˈkʊdnt]	[mɪstɚ smɪθ aʊr ˈmɪlkmæn ɪz ˈɪl]
Tom and *Jane* went to the show.	He *planned* to go, but he *couldn't.*	Mister Smith, our *milkman*, is *ill.* (*meaning* "Mr. Smith—who, incidentally, is our milkman—is ill.")
[tɑm ˈæn dʒen wɛn tə ðə ʃo]	[aɪ bəlivɪn səˈkjurətɪ bət nɑt ət ˈɛnɪ praɪs]	[mɪstɚ smɪθ aʊr ˈmɪlkmæn ɪz ˈɪl]
Tom *and* Jane went to the show.	I believe in security, but not at any price.	Mister Smith, our *milkman*, is *ill.* (*meaning* "The particular Mr. Smith who is ill is our milkman.")

level on the first syllable following the parenthetical idea. Table 6–4 shows this identity of pitch level and the two cases, in which the parenthetical idea is either less or more important than the basic idea.

3. Connotations of American Intonations

It has already been mentioned in previous sections that extent of pitch variety connotes many characteristics of perceived personality, that the width of an intonation connotes the speaker's degree of concern or unconcern, and that the height of an intonation's ending connotes the speaker's degree of assurance or doubtfulness. Several unique pitch characteristics are, however, indicative of specific emotions and will be mentioned here.

Fear is characterized by use of an extremely high pitch level, an extremely wide pitch range, and extremely wide pitch shifts between concepts or ideas.

Anger employs an extremely wide pitch range on all kinds of inflections and intonations.

Contempt is connoted by extremely wide inflections at ends of concepts and ideas, by a pitch level lower than habitual pitch level, and by many upward inflections within concepts and ideas.

Grief consists of a vibrato or tremolo together with an extremely narrow pitch range, a slow rate of pitch change on inflections, and many small changes in pitch.

4. Other Common Intonational Patterns

It was mentioned earlier that, when non-native Americans speak English, their intonations not only reveal that they are foreigners but frequently indicate their nationality. The following are examples of a few of these foreign intonations.

The characteristic intonation of *English* as spoken in England is a rise in pitch to the *first important word* in each idea. Emphatic ideas terminate at a level that is slightly higher than habitual pitch level, and interrogatory ideas terminate higher than emphatic ideas, but a rising inflection is used only to indicate great anxiety or loss of self-control. For this reason alone, then, to the English we Americans tend to seem brash, extroverted, excitable, and forward. In like manner, we would employ their intonations only if we wanted to seem reserved, insouciant, or disdainful, so that we should not be surprised to find ourselves stereotyping Englishmen as introverted, haughty, and phlegmatic. The truth is probably that intonational characteristics bear no closer relationship to national characteristics than do pitch characteristics to behavioral personality.

Spanish intonations are characterized by a rise to maximum pitch height on approximately the *middle* word in each *syntactical unit.* The unit may be a single word, a compound noun or an adjective, a subject, a predicate, a clause, or a phrase.

French is characterized by a *high-to-low* intonation on each *syntactical unit.* Perhaps nothing so identifies a person speaking French as an American as his tendency to reverse this high-to-low intonation, saying "*Merci,*" "*Bon jour,*" and other phrases using a low-to-high intonation.

Gaelic, Yiddish, Southern Negro speech, and Southern Mountain speech, as well as many other languages and dialects, employ intonations which are more sung than spoken, in that the vast majority of pitch changes are inflected rather than stepped. Any such mode of speech clearly labels one as either a non-native American, as one who speaks an American dialect, or else as one who is considered to be patronizing. Unusual pronunciations of various words would serve to identify the speaker as a foreigner; an absence of such mispronunciations would tend to make one perceived as patronizing:

Two other common intonational patterns are due, not to the speaker being a non-native American, but to his ignorance of the precise nature of American intonations. These two patterns are *ditonal* and *monotonal.*[2] By ditonal is meant that the speaker tends to utter all syllables but the most important ones at very much the same pitch level and to utter the most important

[2] The root word *tone* in these words refers to a single frequency as in the terms *pure tone* and *complex tone.*

syllables at a single, higher pitch level. Instead of intoning ideas by stepping up and down, he tends to wait until he arrives at an important syllable before taking the first step upward. A monotonal speaker says all syllables at very much the same pitch level and, in his attempts to intone, he tends to use changes in intensity and duration rather than changes in pitch. Saying that monotonal and ditonal speakers are ignorant of the precise nature of American intonations does not mean that they are incapable of perceiving the significances of others' intonations; it means that they do not perceive that others are employing pitch rather than intensity or duration as the principal instrument for producing intonations.

5. Improving Your Intonations

Several researchers have found extent of intonations closely related to ratings of speaking ability. Hence, not only is intonational skill important for denoting and connoting your intentions, but greater skill should enable you to be perceived as a better speaker.

First, you should be able to produce a wide range of pitches readily and with ease, which implies that you must have mastered the pitch exercises presented previously. Next, you should examine your ability to locate ideas, important words, and the most-important-word in each idea. Finally, you should practice reading sentences and paragraphs with the use of proper intonations. The following exercises, then, are aids to improvement in intonation. According to the questions in column 1, mark each response in column 2 by setting off each idea with a vertical bar (|), by underlining each important word, and by placing a vertical arrow (↑) before the most-important-word in each idea. After you have completed Exercise A, compare your markings with those given in the Answers below. If you made ten or more errors on Exercise A, do Exercise B. If you made fewer than ten errors, practice reading Exercise A as marked in the Answers, making sure that you begin each idea at optimum pitch level. That is, read each idea several times, initiating it at a higher level each time until you produce the widest intonation between initiation and the most-important-word without resorting to a thin voice quality. Then read Exercise B on that page to be sure that you can consistently use your optimum pitch level.

Exercise A

Column 1	Column 2
("What did she eat?")	1. She ate an apple, a pear, and a banana.
("He did it.")	2. Are you sure he did it?
	3. Some men are born great, some achieve greatness, and some have greatness thrust upon them.
("What is patriotism?")	4. Patriotism is the last refuge of a scoundrel.
	5. Humans are the only creatures who can blush, or need to.
	6. There are only two types of people: those who divide people into two types and those who don't.
("What is the relationship between mass and time?")	7. Mass approaches infinity as time approaches zero.
("When will it happen?")	8. It'll happen on Thursday.
("When will it happen?")	9. It may happen on Thursday.
("When will it happen?")	10. Probably Thursday but possibly Friday.

Exercise B

Column 1	Column 2
(on greeting someone at a door)	1. Come in.
("Give me an example of an adage.")	2. Liquor loosens the tongue.
("Will Mary be there?")	3. No, Mary and Tom.
("Will Mary be there alone?")	4. No, Mary and Tom will be there.
	5. He's penny wise and pound foolish.
("What is meant by the divine right of kings?")	6. Pope says it's the right divine to govern wrong.
("What would you like?")	7. Coffee with cream.
("Do you want your coffee black?")	8. No. Coffee with cream.

9. "Let me not to the marriage of true minds/Admit impediments." (Shakespeare's sonnet on the theme, "True love is constant.")
10. "To die: to sleep; no more." (from Hamlet's soliloquy)

Answers to Exercise A

1. She ate an ↑apple,| a ↑pear,| and a ↑banana.|
2. Are you ↑sure he did it?|
3. Some men are ↑born great,| some ↑achieve greatness,| and some have greatness ↑thrust upon them.|
4. Patriotism is the last refuge of a ↑scoundrel.|
5. Humans are the only creatures who can ↑blush,| or ↑need to.|
6. There are only ↑two types of people:| those who divide people into two types and those who ↑don't.|
7. Mass approaches ↑infinity as time approaches ↑zero.|
8. It'll happen on ↑Thursday.|
9. It ↑may happen on Thursday.|
10. ↑Probably Thursday| but possibly ↑Friday.|

Answers to Exercise B

1. Come ↑in.|
2. ↑Liquor loosens the ↑tongue.|
3. ↑No,| Mary and ↑Tom.|
4. ↑No,| Mary ↑and Tom will be there.|
5. He's ↑penny wise| and pound ↑foolish.|
6. ↑Pope says it's the right divine to govern ↑wrong.|
7. ↑Coffee with ↑cream.|
8. ↑No. Coffee ↑with cream.|
9. "Let me ↑not| to the marriage of ↑true minds|/Admit ↑impediments."|
10. "To ↑die:| to ↑sleep;| ↑no more."|

7

Loudness

1. Physical Correlates of Loudness

Loudness is a psychological term that refers mainly to intensity. However, as implied in the chapter on acoustics, loudness is not a function of intensity alone. Moreover, loudness is not related to intensity either arithmetically or logarithmically. For a given frequency, as intensity is steadily increased on a logarithmic scale, loudness increases slowly at first and then more and more rapidly. In fact, a tone at 100 db is perceived as three times as loud as a tone at 80 db but, in going from 40 to 60 db, loudness does not even double. In either example, however, intensity increases one hundred fold, so one could not conclude that increments in loudness are capable of being achieved economically.

As shown in Fig. 4–29, it is evident that, for a given intensity, loudness is greatest in the middle range of frequencies and least at the two extremes. Hence, frequency is an important correlate of loudness. In terms of vocal output, this means that, given two equally intense complex tones whose fundamentals are 150 cps and 300 cps and whose partial energies are equally distributed, the 150-cps tone may tend to be less loud because its fundamental frequency is lower, but the 150-cps tone contains twice as many partials in the midfrequency range so that it may even be louder than the 300-cps tone. That is, between 1000 and 4000 cps, the 150-cps tone contains 20 partials (7th through 26th) whereas the 300-cps tone contains only 10 (4th through 13th). Thus, complexity is a correlate of loudness, especially in terms of the amount of energy present in frequencies within the midrange of hearing.

Also mentioned in Chapter 4 was the fact that duration affects loudness. Loudness rises sharply during the first one-fourth second, but thereafter is not affected by duration. This means that speech at a rate such that continuants are not sustained for at least one-fifth second will be less loud than speech at a somewhat slower rate.

But intensity, frequency, complexity, and duration are not the only physical characteristics related to loudness. So far we have been speaking of sound as if it were measured at the lips. It can be seen that the distance and position of the auditor from the speaker as well as the acoustic characteristics of the room are also important factors influencing loudness.

Obviously, as distance increases, intensity—and therefore loudness—decreases. Moreover, the lower and higher frequencies will fall below the threshold of audibility sooner than the midrange of frequencies so that at a more distant position the less loud tone is also less rich (seems less complex).

If almost all of the speaker's sound energy emanates from his lips (rather than via sympathetic resonance as in orotunidty), sound will travel away from the speaker's head in spherical waves, with maximum intensity directly in front of the speaker and least intensity directly to his rear due to the barrier of the speaker's head. The greater the proportion of oral emission, then, the less spherical and more narrowly conical will be the distribution of speech intensity. Hence, for the same glottal intensity, fronted speech is louder than throaty speech for listeners in front of the speaker.

Sound reflects best from smooth, hard surfaces. Porous surfaces such as acoustic wallboard trap high frequencies because their shorter wavelengths penetrate the pores and return so delayed as to be out of phase. In like manner, drapes trap longer wavelengths (lower frequencies) and reflect them out of phase. Moreover, neither of these materials is very rigid so that some sound energy is dissipated in moving the drapes or spongy wallboard. Hence the combined intensity of the incident and reflected waves in a room that is highly sound absorbent results in less loudness than in a room that is more reflective. However, in a room that is more reflective, the incident waves are delayed so that, with extreme delay as occurs in a large, or long or high-ceilinged room, an echo is produced. For speech purposes this means that, in a room that is small and highly sound reflective, you need speak less loudly and more rapidly than in a room that is large and highly sound absorbent. Architectual acoustics requires, therefore, some compromise between these extremes which is eminently suited to the intensities, frequencies, complexities, and duration of sounds typically produced in that room, to the size and distribution of the audience, and to the location of the speakers or performers. Ideally, the audience should be packed as closely as possible so that the differences in loudness for the nearest and most distant audience member is as small as possible. A highly reflective wall should be just behind the speaker, the room should be just large enough to contain the number present, and the room surfaces should be reflective enough to add as much increment in intensity as possible as quickly as possible. Since we never encounter the ideal, we can only learn to cope with the real more ideally. The remainder of this chapter is concerned, directly or indirectly, with methods of achieving that end.

2. *Audibility Versus Intelligibility*

Audibility for a single listener is a disjunctive term, implying that a sound is either heard or not heard. It does not mean that sounds are correctly heard. Thus, 50 per cent audibility means that half of the sounds or words produced were heard. Intelligibility for a single auditor is also a disjunctive term, implying that an audible sound is either correctly or incorrectly heard. A 50 per cent intelligibility score means that half of the sounds or words the speaker produced were correctly identified. Audibility and intelligibility in terms of an audience of more than one person refer to the number of persons for whom the communication is audible or intelligible.

Many times we tend to think that we are inaudible when we are unintelligible. Thus, a person who finds that he is not being understood tends to react by speaking more loudly. This frequently fails to alleviate the problem and may even aggravate it. Let us consider separately which vocal characteristics reduce audience audibility and which reduce audience intelligibility so that a more satisfactory adjustment can be made when all we know is that we are not being understood.

Insufficient audibility is due to insufficient intensity. Thus, breathiness reduces audibility. We tend to use less loudness to terminate sentences, a so-called "fading," and, since much of the meaning of ideas in English tends to be revealed in the last word or last few words, a pattern of decreasing intensity throughout sentence length is quite the opposite of what should be desired. It might be thought that this is due to the speakers' "running out of breath." However, nonbreathy persons can easily phonate twenty-five average-length words at a moderate pace on a single, moderately deep inspiration, and one seldom encounters that many consecutive words without at least one meaningful pause somewhere in the passage. But a breathy speaker, especially if he must speak at a louder than normal conversational level, may easily "run out of breath" after a mere half-dozen words. Hence, pausing to inhale is merely a makeshift remedy. A better voice quality would not only achieve greater audibility but improved receptivity. Fading may be due, if not to breathiness, to excessively deep inspiration preceding phonation. Many tyro swimmers make this mistake and find that not only does the extra air escape almost immediately but the remaining air tends to escape more rapidly as well. Consequently, taking deep breaths between phonations achieves the opposite of the desired goal of overcoming fading. A better device would be not to breathe as deeply.

Insufficient intelligibility is due to insufficient precision in enunciation and articulation. Flatness, thinness, throatiness, and tenseness distort vowels (and, to some extent, consonants) and reduce intelligibility. Some languages, such as the Semitic, involve only consonants as identifying elements, and the vowels commonly employed vary drastically from region to region and from time to time. English is somewhat similar in that far more of its word differences are due to consonantal than to vocalic differences. For English, then, reduced intelligibility is usually due more to misarticulation than to misenunciation. However, knowledge of phonetics serves to improve the production of both consonants and vowels.

Intelligibility may also be reduced by using loudness instead of pitch for intonation. Saying the most important word in each idea loudly rather than at high pitch results in a noticeable loudness pattern and a monotonous pitch, both of which reduce attentiveness and, consequently, intelligibility.

A speaker who consistently speaks with excessive loudness or softness may have a hearing loss. Another symptom of impaired auditory acuity occurs in learning phonetics, especially if nonsense words are dictated and the person repeatedly confuses such sounds as [ʃ], [θ], and [s]. However, we are not concerned here with physical defects, so that the only cause of a message being delivered with consistently excessive or insufficient loudness by a normal (non-speech-handicapped) person is his lack of sufficient experience in certain speech situations.

The question, then, is: In which situations are normal persons apt to overestimate or to underestimate their loudness at their auditors' ears? Obviously, we monitor our loudness by listening to ourselves, but it is not so obvious that we hear ourselves in at least three ways: by *bone conduction* within the head, by *diffraction* through the air around the head, and by *reflection* from walls and objects in the room. Bone conduction passes mostly lower frequencies best, diffraction passes higher frequencies best (because shorter wavelengths can "bend"), and reflection passes midfrequencies best (because extreme frequencies fall below threshold sooner with intensity decay). Hence, no two media convey to us the same information about our speech. Let us visualize several situations, then, in which we might speak with excessive or insufficient loudness because we depend on all three channels of information to monitor our loudness and the reception through any one of them may be unusually good or poor. If the room is highly sound absorbent, we may tend to speak excessively loudly because of the attenuated reflection we receive. If the room reflects sound back to us from such nearby objects as a ceiling room divider, we tend to speak with insufficient loudness. If our voice quality is flat our bone conduction is greater so that we tend to speak with insufficient loudness. If our voice quality is thin, diffraction increases so again we tend to use insufficient loudness. If we must speak in noisy situations, we tend to speak more loudly, rather than at a different pitch which would be more intelligible because its frequency range is different from that of the interfering sound. Thus, in the presence of squealing noises as on a subway, streetcar, or train, a lower pitched voice should be more intelligible; in the presence of rumbling noises as in automobiles or propeller-driven airplanes a higher pitched voice should be more intelligible. Therefore, in every speech situation in which we must compete with other sounds and noises or in which our auditors reveal that they cannot hear or understand us (by saying so or, more commonly, by first leaning forward, bending an ear, or turning the "better" ear toward us), we should determine how best to make our speech more intelligible, not unthinkingly with increased loudness. Moreover, the use of greater loudness in such situations is seldom successful because, after a few louder or more intelligible remarks, we lapse into trusting our own ears again. A better remedy is to reduce the source of interference, move closer to the audience, or in extreme cases move the audience into a more compact and less distant unit or adjourn to a different room. Loudness is seldom faulty because we fail to adjust to situations that reduce intelligibility; it is usually faulty because we adjust to such situations habitually rather than intelligently.

3. *Methods for Increasing Intelligibility*

We come, therefore, to a list of possible ways to increase intelligibility. Which should be employed in any specific situation should depend upon an appraisal of the causes of reduced intelligibility and the consequences of each compensatory action.

1. *Reduce the intensity of the interference:* e.g., shut the door or window or move the audience.

2. *Improve audibility for your auditors;* e.g., move closer to them, move them closer together, close the curtain behind you, adjust drapes or rearrange the seating.

3. *Increase your intelligibility:* e.g., use a fronted voice quality, prolong voiced consonants and speak at a slower rate.

4. *Increase your redundancy.* Redundancy is the extent to which an audience can predict what is said from what has been said. It can be measured scientifically by substituting a blank space for every fifth word in a manuscript of a speech and having persons insert in these blanks what they think was omitted. The average percentage of correct insertions serves as an index of that material's redundancy.

Redundancy is a complex function of such factors as word familiarity, context, iteration, sentence order, and sentence length. However, in situations of reduced intelligibility we can increase redundancy by delineating important words more emphatically, by repeating or rephrasing, and by using different levels of abstraction (for the latter, see pages 310–313). Such methods may increase intelligibility more than will a mere increment in loudness. Moreover, loudness sufficient for adequate intelligibility in the presence of noise is difficult to listen to for more than a short while because it is, after all, an additional assault upon our ears. As an example, factory workers generally enjoy listening to music while they work, but they tend to prefer not to listen to news broadcasts under such conditions rather than to increase the volume of the speaker's voice.

5. *Speak louder*, if all else fails.

4. Use of Loudness for Emphasis

Loudness, like voice qualities, may be used effectively for word emphasis. Increased loudness on a word conveys an impression of great importance, loudness, strength, size, or assurance. It is usually employed with a higher pitch or extended duration to delineate one or another of these impressions more precisely.

Loudness may also be used to indicate the relative importance of ideas. Most of us tend to use at least three loudness levels. The minimum level is seldom employed. It should be audible on the least loud word, and is used on monologues, personal asides, and expected or obvious remarks such as common amenities, clichés, casual comments, and the like. The maximum level is also seldom employed and tends to be our way of vocal italicizing. We can easily extend our range of vocal intensity by raising the maximum level, but little merit seems to inhere in such a practice. On the contrary, we tend to adjust our listening to a certain general level much as we adjust the volume control on a radio, and then we tend to be annoyed by frequent excursions greatly above this level or below the level of easy audibility.

This is not to say that the physical range of intensities within a single sentence is not extremely great. Indeed, intensity may easily vary as much as 40 db, which means that the most intense syllable is ten thousand times as intense as the least intense syllable. However, this range—huge as it is physically—is hardly noticeable. Perhaps this is due to the least intense words being so commonplace that they are unconsciously inferred more than they are perceived. When least intense words are acoustically distorted, as by electronic filtering, the distortions tend not to be readily observed. It may be that we listen almost entirely to key words, much as telegrams are written, and the elapsed time between such words identifies the other words. For example, cover the parenthetical words on the right below, and mumble one "hm [hm̩]" for each blank space, and notice how readily you can correctly insert the omitted words in the following:

1. I'll do it _____ _____ morning.	(in the)
2. He gave it _____ me.	(to)
3. Tom _____ Mary came to see me.	(and)
4. How _____ _____ do?	(do you)
5. I had a wonderful _____.	(time)
6. Sincerely _____, Mary Smith.	(yours)
7. Look before you _____.	(leap)
8. Today _____ Thursday.	(is)
9. Happy New _____.	(Year)
10. One, two, _____.	(three)

In conclusion, we can say that, properly used, loudness is a vocal device to emphasize words in certain ways and to indicate greater and lesser importance of various ideas. Loudness is improperly used if the speaker uses loudness as an intonational device, if he tends to become inaudible at the ends of statements, if he attempts to speak louder in the presence of noise when the signal/noise ratio[1] can readily be increased by other means, or if he attempts to speak louder when he is easily audible but insufficiently intelligible.

[1] db difference between the peak (or average) pressure (or intensity) of a message and the peak (or average) pressure (or intensity) of interfering noise.

8

Rate

One of the most important aspects of effective delivery is rate. To speak meaningfully about this vocal factor we must avoid obscurity, which requires, unfortunately, precise definitions for many words. If you have vague or different concepts of the terms subsequently to be introduced, you should refer again to the definitions when any discussion employing those terms is not clearly understood.

Rate

The average number of words per minute (wpm) of a speaker's total impromptu (unrehearsed) output or of any sample of that output is defined as that person's speaking *rate*. This means that, if we were to record the number of words a person uttered throughout one typical day, to compute the number of seconds those utterances consumed, and to divide the former by one-sixtieth of the latter (to convert seconds to minutes), we would have an estimate of his mean wpm, or rate. Let us say, for example, that this estimate is 124.3 wpm for John and 138.6 wpm for Mary. Then, if these seem to be rather typical speaking experiences for both, we are justified in assuming that Mary generally speaks faster than John.

However, a person's rate provides no indication of how much variety in wpm he employs. That is, John and Bill may both speak at 124.3 wpm; but Bill varies the speed of his individual utterances extremely and John practically not at all. Knowing the fastest and slowest rates employed may provide some index of this variety, but this index is generally an unreliable one. Thus, John may have spoken as rapidly as 180 wpm and as slowly as 100 wpm, but these extremes occurred rarely; whereas almost anything Bill said varied in rate from, say, 110 to 138 wpm although he never attained John's maximum and minimum. Nevertheless, we would admit that Bill speaks with a more varied rate than does John. Of course, if we were running an experiment we might use a meaningful statistical index such as the standard deviation of each, but this is so precise that it is psychologically imperceptible. In fact, it might easily be argued that the concept of wpm also belongs in this category.

Hence, let us abandon the concepts of mean and standard deviation of a person's rate and employ less precise but more meaningful terms. To do this requires construction of an arbitrary reference rate which is rather consistently employed in certain situations. Persons who speak the same language tend to be most alike in their speaking rate when the rate is determined most by the speed with which they conceive of what they are to say and determined least by the capacity of their auditors to understand what they say. Thus, the reference rate should occur in impromptu rather than rehearsed situations. Moreover, the diction (words employed in speaking) should be words with which both speaker and audience are quite familiar. These requirements are most commonly occasioned in the type of speaking activity called *chatting*.

One chats about inconsequential, mundane, and transitory matters, as in commenting about the weather ("I hope it doesn't rain today."), making simple requests ("Please pass the salt."), uttering amenities ("Thank you."), describing sensory experiences ("Her dress was blue and she wore a white hat with little blue flowers on it."), and the like. Most of us chat at a rather unvaried and rapid rate (approximately 225 wpm, if we exclude time between ideas, but approximately 150 wpm if we include pauses between ideas). This tendency toward greater uniformity in this speaking situation is due to the fact that the most-important-words in each idea seldom have their continuants prolonged and that the pauses between ideas not due to listening to the person with whom we are conversing are usually only long enough for us to think of the next inconsequential remark.

Let us now define six rates in terms of chatting: *same* (150+ wpm), *slightly slower* (135–149 wpm), *somewhat slower* (120–134 wpm), *slower* (105–119 wpm), *much slower* (90–104 wpm), and *very much slower* (below 90 wpm). To obtain a clearer idea of these rates, you might try counting aloud while using a watch to time yourself.

Tempo

Since no one at present knows how to provide training in delivery when a person is engaged, impromptu or extempore, in speaking because the speaker's attention is required on his content in such situations, we can provide training only in the more formal and less common speech situations of delivering from memory or of reading, with the expectation that habits will be acquired which can then be transferred to the more common types of delivery. That is, if you drill on certain vocal factors while rehearsing a speech, a poem, a literary prose selection, or a scene from a play, the learned techniques may become habitual so that, when you deliver the speech or read the poetry or prose or present the play to an audience, not only may your performance be improved because of such drill but these learned techniques will tend to be applied to anything you say to anyone at any time. Voice quality, pitch, and loudness, previously discussed, and the factor of pronunciation subsequently to be discussed, may all be improved by drilling on nonliterary materials; and the principles of intonation may also be acquired in this way. However, the factor of rate is integrally bound up with content and, since we cannot drill on content that is created during the process of speaking (impromptu and extemporaneous speaking), previously prepared content should be used in working to improve rate. Moreover, with respect to rate, literary selections have the same characteristics as nonliterary materials, together with some additional ones; the use of literary selections for drill materials thus provides a valid and more comprehensive grasp of this aspect of delivery.

Moreover, literary material is unified; it has a beginning and an end. To speak of a single rate comprising several topics tends to be meaningless; for literary material, however, to speak of *tempo* as an average rate at which the entire selection is read is not only valid but useful. If the selection is an excerpt from a larger work, such as a scene from a play, an abridgment of a poem, or a fragment of a novel, it can be said to have a tempo, provided this excerpt is unified in meaning and mood.

Determinants of Tempo

When we say that a certain tempo is appropriate for delivering a particular literary selection to a specific audience, our criteria for determining this appropriateness should be the material's depth, conciseness, and mood, and the audience's capacity for comprehending this material. By depth is meant the relative difficulty of the average person in any audience in understanding this type of content as compared to other types, and this is essentially a function of the amount of independent thinking required of him. Thus, theological matters are, as a general area of discourse, more difficult to understand than, say, matters relating the beauties of nature, just as an enthymeme is more difficult to perceive than a syllogism. Conciseness refers to the relative brevity or wordiness in communicating the ideas in the selection. This factor is influenced by such subfactors as:

- Redundancy (the ability to predict the next word from the foregoing context)
- Iteration (the frequency of repetition or restatement in other words)
- Abstractness (how general or unspecific is the content)
- Illustrativeness (the frequency of specific examples, instances, illustrations, etc.)
- Circumlocution (the extent to which many words are used as equivalents of few words, e.g., "not capable of being disputed" for "indisputable")

Literalness (the degree to which words are used literally rather than figuratively, e.g., "The moon shines" rather than "Diana sheds her light")

The mood, or the particular, basic emotion which the speaker wishes to simulate for his audience, is also a determinant of tempo, so that, for example, if he intends to project a serious demeanor, he will utilize a slower tempo than he would when he simulates a frivolous demeanor. The audience's capacity for comprehending the communication is different from its capacity for understanding. Understanding refers to an auditor's ability to know the meaning of what is said and is related to the factor of conciseness mentioned above. Comprehension refers to the ability to know the significance or importance of what is said and is related to each auditor's extent of familiarity with the subject of the communication, not in terms of the amount of thought required as is meant by the term depth, but in terms of the absolute extent of his knowledge. Thus, for example, a speech on "Problems Involved in Harnessing Thermonuclear Energy" delivered both to college seniors in physics and to physicists might be the same speech if all of the words employed were equally understood by both groups, but the seniors might prefer that the speaker had spoken more slowly because they did not grasp all of the implications of what had been said. Another illustration might be a problem in arithmetic delivered orally to persons who had just been introduced to the procedures required and to those who had considerable experience in using these procedures. Tempo, then, should be faster for literary material which is easily understandable by anyone, wordy (i.e., highly redundant, repetitive, circumlocutory, and literal), light in mood, or with which the audience is very familiar.

In the subsequent discussion we will refer to various tempi by the same terms that we apply to rate, viz., same (as chatting), slightly slower, somewhat slower, and so on

Pace

The relation of the rate of a segment of a literary selection to the tempo of that selection is termed that segment's pace.

Pace refers to the rate of delivering a single line of poetry or of a single idea of prose. "Idea" is defined in Chapter 6 (cf. "Intonation," pages 190–193).

To read a line or idea at *moderate* pace is equivalent to reading it at the tempo of that selection. A *fast* line or idea is to be read at a rate that is faster than the tempo, and a *slow* line or idea at a rate slower than the tempo.

Determinants of Pace

Once the tempo has been determined, the pace of a line of poetry or an idea of prose is determined, compared to other lines or ideas in that selection, by that line or idea's relative depth, conciseness, and connotations. The first two of these were discussed under "Tempo." Whereas the entire selection has an overall mood, each structural unit of this whole may be said to contain implications rather than moods. Thus, the one word "Hello" could be uttered in such diverse ways as to imply unexpectedness, boredom, adoration, cheeriness, or disgust. To the extent that additional time is required to communicate the implicit content in addition to the explicit content, we might say that, in general, the greater the amount of implicit communication to be conveyed in uttering a line or idea, the slower its pace.

Two methods for correct regulation of pace are by regulating the number and duration of pauses and by regulating the amount of prolongation of continuants in important words.

Pauses

The first method for regulating pace is by regulating the number and duration of pauses. For our purposes, eight different kinds of pauses will be discussed: the *terminating*, *transitional*, *anticipatory*, *deliberative*, *separational*, *parenthetical*, *incoherent*, and *caesural* pauses.

The terminating pause follows the completion of an idea and is used to indicate how long the audience should consider that idea. Its purpose is not to reveal where the idea ends; intonation indicates that sufficiently. It is also not for the purpose of breathing; any type of pause may secondarily fulfill that function.

A transitional pause occurs, for example, at the end of a paragraph in prose or at the end of a stanza or other unit of poetry, such as the octave of a Petrarchan sonnet, and signifies the completion of a unified series of ideas. In reading a poem to a class such a pause would occur both before and after mentioning the author and title of the poem, and following completion of the reading.

An anticipatory pause occurs within an idea rather than between ideas, is immediately preceded by relatively unimportant words, and is followed immediately by one very important word or several words which represent a single concept, such as a compound noun or nominative substantive (e.g., "the Soviet Union" or "acquisitiveness but not inquisitiveness"). An example of an anticipatory pause is, "The only word that accurately describes him is (pause) phlegmatic."

A deliberative pause also occurs within an idea, is immediately preceded by a very important word or phrase such as would follow an anticipatory pause, and is followed immediately by relatively unimportant words. An example would be: "Phlegmatic (pause) is the only word that accurately describes him."

A separational pause would, if it did not occur, communicate the alternative meaning in an ambiguous context. Examples are: "He wants some . . . ice for his experiment (to avoid implying "some mice"); "Move the green . . . one back"; "Some men can do; those who can't . . . teach"; "Look! . . . Out the window!"; "I believe; . . . you do too."

Parenthetical pauses have been discussed previously (cf. "Intonation," page 197).

An incoherent pause occurs when a speaker searches, perhaps unsuccessfully, for an appropriate word, and indicates that such a search is going on. Two examples are: "It's called a . . . I forget the name"; "I suppose that he . . . No, I'm sure that he did it." The aposiopesis, to be discussed subsequently, is a poetic use of the incoherent pause.

A caesura is a pause in the last line of poetry or last idea of prose which, together with a falling pitch on the last syllable of the last word of the literary selection regardless of conventional intonation, indicates completion (removal of all deficiencies) or conclusion (statement of the ultimate goal of the communication, summarization, and the like). Thus, each poem, book of an epic poem, or chapter of a book or act or other unified segment of a play should contain one and only one caesura. Some blank verse playrights such as Shakespeare indicate this need for a caesura by the use of a rhymed couplet in otherwise unrhymed verse. Neither the caesura alone nor the falling pitch on the last syllable of the last word alone conveys this information; both are required. Generally, skilled poets make the caesura serve as another type of pause as well, e.g., as anticipatory.

From this point on a relatively short pause will be indicated by a single vertical bar (|) and a relatively long pause by a double vertical bar (||). Thus, the effect of the caesura can be illustrated by reading the following aloud:

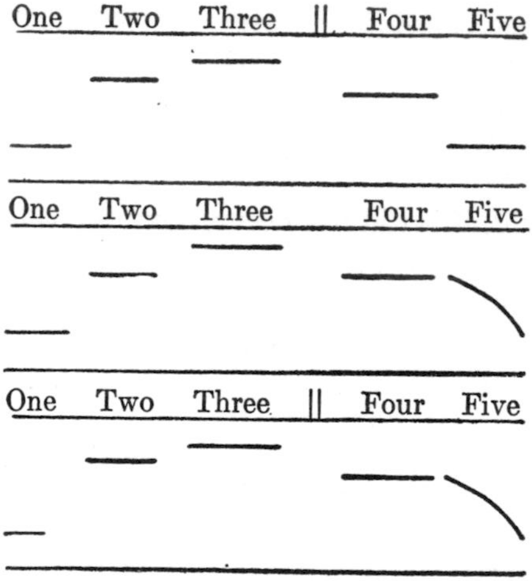

One Two Three || Four Five

Caesura without falling pitch

One Two Three Four Five

Falling pitch without caesura

One Two Three || Four Five

Caesura with falling pitch

Pace in Poetry

Poetry generally makes a more cogent and imagistic appeal, both emotional and intellectual, to the auditor or reader than does prose, and this greater cogency and imagery affects the pace more drastically in poetry than in prose. The devices which provide cogency and imagery are not only more frequently employed in poetry than in prose but some are almost unique to poetry. However, before we examine some of these devices in detail some definitions are needed.

Meter is the percussive, temporal framework upon which any literary communication is structured. The only percussive possibilities are time beats and stress beats. Thus, the *one*-two-three, *one*-two-three meter of a waltz consists of one stress beat followed by two time beats. Incidentally, the tempo determines how many units of a particular meter will occur in a given time. Since the syllable is the basic vocal unit of speech (the phoneme is the basic linguistic unit), accented or unaccented syllables can occur on either stress beats or time beats. A *metrical foot* is the repetitive unit of meter, weaving stress and time beats in the characteristic pattern.

Since the English language seldom provides three or more consecutively unaccented syllables, the only metrical feet employed in English poetry are those containing two or three beats, one of which is stressed. An *iamb*, or iambic foot, is a time beat followed by a stress beat (˘ ´, ta-*tum*). A *trochee*, or trochaic foot, is the reverse of an iamb (´ ˘, *tum*-ta). An *anapest*, or anapestic foot, is two time beats followed by a stress beat (˘ ˘ ´, ta-ta-*tum*), and a *dactyl*, or dactylic foot, is the reverse (´ ˘ ˘, *tum*-ta-ta). A line of poetry consists of a number of feet, such as monometer (one foot), dimeter (two feet), trimeter, tetrameter, pentameter, hexameter, and so on.

In some poetic forms, this basic pattern is modified. One such modification is the use of a *spondee*, or spondaic foot (´ ´, *tum-tum*). Thus, the form might be iambic hexameter with the final iamb replaced with a spondee. This variant is employed frequently enough to deserve a label, the Alexandrine. The spondee may also be used to achieve metrical variety between lines as well as within lines, as by using a spondee only on the final feet of alternate lines or on the final couplet of each stanza. Another modification is the use of *masculine* or *feminine lines*. A masculine line is one which ends on a stress beat and a feminine line is one which ends on a time beat. Thus, iambic or anapestic verse may be varied by the use of feminine lines, and trochaic or dactylic verse by the use of masculine lines. Thus,

> The quality of mercy is not strained;
> It droppeth as the gentle rain from heaven . . .

employs a feminine ending on the second line, and therefore introduces an additional time beat.

Sense stress refers to the accenting of syllables for the communication of meaning, e.g., "ex-*act*-ly," "I *was go*-ing, but *now* I *can't*," etc.

An *ictus* is a coincidence of metrical and sense stress. A *non-ictus* is sense stress which is metrically unstressed, as on the word "not" in the two Shakespearian lines above. A metrical stress which has no sense stress is merely a weak form.

A *run-on line* is one in which the idea's completion fails to coincide with the end of a poetic line:

> Whether 'tis nobler in the mind to suffer
> The slings and arrows of outrageous fortune . . .

Usually a run-on line is used to break the monotony of ideas all of equal metrical length. However, one type of run-on line, called enjambment, serves the purpose of permitting closely related words to fall in different lines, a device which, perhaps together with the use of rhyme or partial rhyme, points up the relation between them:

> To make a prairie it takes a clover and one bee—
> One clover, and a *bee*, and *revery*.
> The revery alone will do
> If bees are few.

Rhyme

Rhyme is the correspondence of terminal sounds in lines of verse. Rhyme is employed (1) to emphasize line length (i.e., the number of feet in each line), (2) to arouse esthetic pleasure by the use of sound patterns, and (3) to support by the arrangement of rhymes a feeling of unity (e.g., five lines rhymed *aabba*). Like meter, rhyme is generally meant to be felt, not perceived. An exception to this for meter would be, say, a ballad with very trivial and perhaps redundant content (e.g., "My Darling Clementine") or a poem with an intentional excess of ictuses to imply hoofbeats, bells tolling (e.g., Poe's "The Bells"), or other situations. An exception to this for rhyme would be verse (verse refers to the use of a poetic form to appeal primarily to the intellect; poetry's appeal is primarily emotional), especially if one important characteristic of the verse is the cleverness of the rhyme, as in the verse of Ogden Nash.

Hence, rhyme should generally not be stressed to call attention to the rhyme as such. Thus, in general, good poetry seems to avoid a frequent occurrence of two very important words being rhymed. In the reading of poetry, then, you should avoid using the same, nonhabitual voice quality, such as breathiness, or increased loudness, on a rhymed pair of words to avoid calling attention to the rhyme per se.

Internal rhyme is used usually to effect a sense of variety in line length, as in Coleridge's "Rime of the Ancient Mariner":

> The fair breeze *blew*, the white foam *flew*,
> The furrow followed free;
> We were the *first* that ever *burst*
> Into that silent sea.

which varies the iambic tetrameter-trimeter to imply a dimeter-dimeter-trimeter form.

Although rhyme generally refers to an identity of vowel and consonant sounds in the last syllable of rhymed lines, other types of rhymes or partial rhymes are frequently employed. For example, *assonance* is an identity of vowels only (n*a*m*e*, s*a*k*e*); *consonance* is an identity of consonants only (na*m*e, co*m*e); *half-rhyme* rhymes only one syllable of disyllabic words (n*am*ely, *aim*ing); *double rhyme* rhymes the last two syllables (b*e* n*amed*, d*e*cl*aimed*); and *triple rhyme* the last three syllables (c*an* be n*amed*, m*an* decl*aimed*).

Generally, the greater the number of rhymed syllables and the closer the rhymed words to one another, the greater is the tendency for the poetry to jingle. Frequent rhyming may be desirable for verse but is seldom useful for poetry unless its basic value is its imagistic word play. As previously stated, an occasional rhyme in otherwise unrhymed verse is useful as a caesural device, and thus may be found at the ends of conclusive scenes in many blank verse plays. In like manner, in a rhyme scheme in which rhymed alternate lines precede rhymed adjacent lines, the latter tends to seem conclusive, and is therefore used to end a poetic segment such as a stanza.

Numerous rhyme schemes have been used so frequently that some of them have a special nomenclature: the Shakespearian sonnet (three independently rhymed quatrains plus a final couplet); the Petrarchan sonnet (two rhymes in the octave, *abbaabba,* plus two or three in the sestet, but no final couplet, as in C. H. Sorley's "Two Sonnets on Death"); rhyme royal (seven iambic pentameter lines rhymed *ababbcc,* as in Chaucer's "Clerk's Tale"); *ottava rima* (eight iambic pentameter lines rhymed *abababcc,* as in Byron's epic poem, *Don Juan*); rounds of various types (rondeau, rondeau of Villon, rondel and roundel) in which the last words in the first two lines are the only rhymes used (e.g., Swinburne's "Roundel").

Pace in Free Verse and Prose

Free verse, or *vers libre,* is free in the sense that it is not restricted to a regular metrical framework, but it is more restricted than prose in that its *cadences* are patterned. That is, different meters are combined or a rhythmical pattern is used instead of a regular meter. This is effected by a pattern of idea lengths or word groupings. An example of free verse is the following:

O Sweet Spontaneous Earth—e. e. cummings[1]

O sweet spontaneous
earth how often have
the
doting

        fingers of
prurient philosophers pinched
and
poked

[1] Copyright, 1923, 1951, by E. E. Cummings. Reprinted from his volume *Poems,* 1923–1954 by permission of Harcourt, Brace & World, Inc.

thee
,has the naughty thumb
of science prodded
thy

beauty , how
often have religions taken
thee upon their scraggy knees
squeezing and

buffeting thee that thou mightest conceive
gods
(but
true

to the incomparable
couch of death thy
rhythmic
lover

thou answerest

them only with
spring)

Free verse, in terms of its regularity of metrical structure, lies between metrical poetry and unstylized prose, and we can sometimes differentiate between free verse and poetic prose only arbitrarily or by accepting the author's stated purpose. For example, the following selection is prose insofar as that is what its author would probably maintain that he wrote, but it has been set in type in free verse form. It is doubtful, however, that the typographic form is a valid criterion for oral reading since the cadences should be apparent in either case.

The Body of An American—John Dos Passos[2]

We are met today to pay the impersonal tribute;
the name of him whose body lies before us took flight with his imperishable soul . . .

[2] From *U.S.A.*, by John Dos Passos. Copyright by John Dos Passos. Published by Houghton Mifflin Co.

as a typical soldier of this representative democracy he fought and died believing in the indisputable justice of his country's cause . . .

John Doe's

heart pumped blood:

down in the clearing in the Oregon forest where the punkins were punkincolor pouring into the blood through the eyes and the fallcolored trees and the bronze hoopers were hopping through the dry grass, where tiny striped snails hung on the underside of the blades and the flies hummed, wasps droned, bumblebees buzzed, and the woods smelt of wine and mushrooms and apples, homey smell of fall pouring into the blood,

and I dropped the tin hat and the sweaty pack and lay flat with the dogday sun licking my throat and adamsapple and the tight skin over the breastbone.

The shell had his number on it.

The blood ran into the ground.

The service record dropped out of the filing cabinet when the quartermaster sergeant got blotto that time they had to pack up and leave the billets in a hurry.

The identification tag was in the bottom of the Marne.

The blood ran into the ground, the brains oozed out of the cracked skull and were licked up by the trenchrats, the belly swelled and raised a generation of bluebottle flies,

and the incorruptible skeleton,

and the scraps of dried viscera and skin bundled in khaki

they took to Chalons-sur-Marne

and laid it out neat in a pine coffin

and took it home to God's country on a battleship

and buried it in a sarcophagus in the Memorial Amphitheatre in the Arlington National Cemetery

and draped Old Glory over it

and the bugler played taps

and Mr. Harding prayed to God and the diplomats and the generals and the admirals and the brasshats and the politicians and the handsomely dressed ladies out of the society column of the *Washington Post* stood up solemn

and thought how beautiful sad Old Glory God's Country it was to have the bugler play taps and the three volleys made their ears ring.

Where his chest ought to have been they pinned

the Congressional Medal, the D.S.C., the Medaille Militaire, the Belgian Croix de Guerre, the Italian gold medal, the Vitutea Militara sent by Queen Marie of Rumania, the Czechoslovak war cross, a wreath sent by Hamilton Fish, Jr., of New York, and a little wampum presented by a deputation of Arizona redskins in warpaint and feathers. All the Washingtonians brought flowers.

Woodrow Wilson brought a bouquet of poppies.

In more prosaic (less regularly cadenced) prose, the pace of ideas depends, as previously stated, upon each idea's relative depth, conciseness, and connotations; but in such prose as that above, one of the principal determinants of these three factors is the literary purpose of each idea, such as general statement, specific narrative statement, direct observation to reader, dialog, transitional statement, parenthetical statement, and similar considerations.

Poetic Devices

One factor which affects the pace of a line of poetry was said to be its connotations. One obvious connotation is the emotion intended, such as the manner in which you intend to convey an idea: joyfully, regretfully, matter-of-factly, etc. However, other information can be implicitly conveyed in reading both poetry and prose by certain devices which, because they are far more frequently employed in poetry, are termed poetic devices. Such devices may be considered to be of two kinds, intellectual implications and aesthetic implications; this distinction is important for oral reading purposes since the former obviously require more time for their reception than the latter, and thus generally require an even slower pace than ideas with merely sensory implications, if we assume that the depth and conciseness are the same. Some commonly employed poetic devices which are classed as aesthetic are rhyme, meter, caesura, alliteration, homophony, and onomatopoeia; simile, metaphor, trope, metonymy, hyperbole, litotes, oxymoron, and aposiopesis are considered intellectual in character. Rhyme, meter, and caesura have previously been discussed and, therefore, will not be redefined.

Alliteration is the repetition of a consonant or of consonants with an identical classification (manner, voicing, place, or duration) in several consecutive or successive words, e.g., "li*f*e's *f*it*f*ul *f*ever." Notice in this example that the labio-dental phoneme, both voiced and voiceless, is repeated. In the example, "fat black bucks," the alliteration is primarily one of voiceless plosives, but the initial voiceless fricative certainly adds to this effect. The aesthetic effect of alliteration can and should be intensified vocally by the use of such devices as fronting (see pages 167–170), overaspiration (see pages 19–20) or orotundity (see pages 175–177). In general, alliteration of continuants tends to invite a slower pace and of stops a faster pace.

Homophony is the repetition of a vowel, or of vowels of similar length, in several consecutive or successive words. Generally, the back vowels, diphthongs, and [i] are long vowels, the front vowels other than [i] are short, and the central vowels are intermediate in duration. Tennyson's "Ulysses" illustrates short-vowel homophony in the first few lines and long-vowel homophony in the fifth line:

> *I*t l*i*ttle prof*i*ts that an idle k*i*ng,
> By th*i*s st*i*ll hearth, among these b*a*rren cr*a*gs,
> M*a*tched w*i*th an *a*g*e*d wife, I mete and dole
> Unequal laws unto a savage race,
> That h*o*ard, and sl*ee*p, and f*ee*d, and kn*o*w n*o*t m*e*.

Onomatopoeia is the use of words whose sounds suggest their sense, e.g., babble, mama, bobwhite. In the following classic example, the word "cuckoo" not only has an aesthetic appeal because of its onomatopoetic effect but has an intellectual appeal because it is a *double entendre*, being a play on the word "cuckold."

Song (From *Love's Labour's Lost*)—Shakespeare

> When daisies pied and violets blue
> And lady-smocks all silver-white
> And cuckoo-buds of yellow hue
> Do paint the meadows with delight,
> The cuckoo then on every tree,
> Mocks married men; for thus sings he,
> 'Cuckoo!
> Cuckoo, cuckoo!' O word of fear,
> Unpleasing to a married ear!

Onomatopoetic words usually affect pace in terms of the duration employed by the original producers of such sounds, the result usually being a slower pace, as in the *buzzing* of bees."

The rational or intellectual poetic devices are obviously of varying depth, and this depth is generally related to the type of device employed. Similes, metonymies and hyperboles are usually easiest to communicate; metaphors, tropes, apostrophes and litotes are intermediate in difficulty and aposiopeses and oxymorons are quite difficult to convey.

Similes and *metaphors* are comparisons that are, respectively, stated or implied. The simile is an explicit and obvious analogy, as in Proverbs, "As cold water to a thirsty soul, so is good news from a foreign country." A metaphor's comparison is unstated, e.g., "the ship plows the sea," "a volley of oaths." A *trope* goes a further step in analogy by making a comparison which, considered explicity, is patently impossible. The poetry of Wallace Stevens is an exponent of this device, e.g., "concupiscent curds," "bawdy strings," "the dew of old devotions."

A *metonymy* is a suggestive word used for a more explicit word or phrase, e.g., "RHIP," which is an acronym of "rank has its privileges" (meaning that persons of higher rank have more privileges). Incidentally, the type of metonymy which uses the part to represent the whole is termed a synecdoche, e.g., "She bought a fall cotton."

An *hyperbole* is an exaggeration usually employed to emphasize the abnormality or uncommonness of the thing or event, e.g., "a thousand pardons," "to take infinite pains." A *litotes* is, in a sense, the opposite of an hyperbole, being an understatement to imply the opposite of what is said, and is usually phrased negatively, e.g., "Not a few praised him," "He is certainly not the wisest of men."

An *oxymoron* is a coupling of bipolar words, usually an adjective with a noun or an adverb with a verb, to imply an shift of the word modified in the direction of the modifier, e.g., "a cruel kindness," "Faith unfaithful kept him falsely true." In the second example, "unfaithful" modifies "faith" to imply faith with remissions or misgivings and "falsely" modifies "true" to imply imperfection or inconstancy.

An *aposiopesis* is a sudden breaking off to indicate interruption by another or by oneself because of the impossibility of mere words completing the idea, or to imply sudden realization, as in "John: 'If you're trying to . . . ' Mary: 'Of course I am!'"

"And if we fail . . ." Or in dramas a character, suddenly realizing all that has been happening, says, "And all this time you've been . . . God, what a fool I've been."

Analysis of Poetic Pace

We are now ready to apply the foregoing discussion to the specific poems which follow. The proper procedure embraces several steps.

1. Read the entire poem several times to determine the *theme*. The theme is one sentence which accounts for the existence of every line in the poem. Unless the poem is extremely recondite (e.g., T. S. Eliot's "The Waste Land") or esoteric (e.g., L. R. Lieber's *The Einstein Theory of Relativity*), it can be said that the poem has only one theme at any level of abstraction. By different levels is meant, for example, that the four themes, "If you try to kill someone, you will go to prison," "Murderers get their just reward," "Crime doesn't pay," and "God vents His wrath on sinners," may all be considered as the same theme except for their different degrees of generalization. Another way to define theme is to differentiate between plot and theme: the plot describes what happened; the theme states what the plot signifies. Excepting differences in level of abstraction, and poetry which is extremely recondite, or esoteric, we can say, then, that the theme of any poem is an indisputable question of fact. Moreover, that a noun or nominative substantive cannot ever be considered as a theme is impossible to emphasize sufficiently. "Love" or "beauty" or "America" or "Communism" is never a suitable theme for any work of literary art. These might be the subjects of themes; the question we should raise is: What are the predicates?

2. Determine the *mood*. The mood is the particular emotion you intend your audience to believe you are experiencing. It is not necessarily the same as the emotion you want them to experience. For example, your mood may be matter-of-fact, but they may be shocked at your matter-of-factness. The mood can be described with an adjective, a group of adjectives, or an adjectival phrase, e.g., "happiness tinged with regret." Unlike the theme,

the mood of a poem is entirely a question of value. That is, each reader is entitled to his own interpretation. Some writers of texts on oral interpretation maintain that the author's intended mood is the one to convey. Putting ethical considerations aside, this would mean that a recent successful Broadway comedy should have been produced as a serious play indicating horror at the levity with which we treat murder and death. To say that *Hamlet* should not be done as a melodrama is to revere Shakespeare inordinately; to say that it cannot be done as a melodrama is obviously untrue. All we should honestly say is that we have reservations that it can be done well. To state the matter ethically, in the determination of mood, you are obligated to the author to be as faithful to your interpretation as he was faithful to his. The same consideration arises with respect to cutting. It is unethical to cut in such a way as to distort the author's theme, but to cut for the purpose of intensifying one's concept of the mood is not only ethical but should be desirable.

3. Assuming that the audience is known, the *tempo* can next be determined, since it is a function of the selection's depth, conciseness, and mood, and of the audience's capacity for comprehending it. Remember to use the words "same" (as chatting), "slightly slower," etc.

4. Underline every important word (see page 203) and doubly underline those words, if any, which state the theme or approximate the thematic statement closely. Many poems do not contain a thematic statement anywhere in the poem.

5. Indicate the intonational peak of each idea by placing a vertical arrow (↑) before the most-important-word in each idea page 203).

6. Indicate pauses by a single vertical bar (|) for a relatively short pause and a double bar (||) for a relatively long pause. Be sure that every pause can be classified as terminating, transitional, anticipatory, and so on. Thus, for example, no pause should occur at the end of a line merely because it is the end of a line; and no pause should occur between such words as "said" and "replied" and what was said or replied merely because a comma is used (e.g., *not*: "I met a traveler from an antique land, Who said: |Two vast and trunkless legs of stone . . . ")

7. If you would use any voice quality other than good voice quality or any increment in loudness on any underlined word, or any combination of these, indicate this by placing the appropriate symbols over that word, viz., *B* (breathiness), *OA* (overaspiration), *N* (nasality), *Te* (tenseness), *F* (flatness), *Th* (thinness), *Fr* (fronting), *Thr* (throatiness), *O* (orotundity), and *L* (extra loudness):

OL
gigantic

8. Since the pace of each line is affected by the number of metrical feet it contains, the number of words underlined, the vocal devices employed, and the number and length of pauses in the line, the pace of each line can now be determined. Indicate the pace of each line by placing an *S*, *M*, or *F* at the beginning of each line to indicate a pace that is, respectively, slower, equal to, or faster than the indicated tempo. With poor poetry variety can be arbitrarily imposed, but it is better to accept what degree of variety it inherently affords and to strive to maximize the virtues it provides in other ways. Obviously, the number of slow lines should equal the number of fast lines. An excess of slower lines indicates the need for selecting a slower tempo; an excess of faster lines indicates the need for selecting a faster tempo.

It should be mentioned here, perhaps iterated throughout this text, that this seemingly mechanical approach to oral reading does not imply that any oral reading is merely skill and requires no art. It is true that most of the matters referred to above are simply skills, but even the artist must master these skills if his art is to be more than perfect faith in his natural perfection. It is one thing to violate rules purposely and another to violate them from ignorance of their existence. However, the matter of violating rules seldom confronts most of us. A far more important consideration is that we learn to master the skills so that we can employ them habitually and thus free ourselves to devote our maximum attention and consideration to more artistic matters. In oral interpretation, the latter are mood, connotations, and the audience's reception of and reaction to ideas. A person with only one voice quality, or rate, or any other vocal characteristic, is hardly free. Rather than this seemingly mechanical approach restricting or interfering with his chosen style of delivery, it frees him by providing him with choices on matters where choice is important. Only a person of little or no talent has his style cramped by learning rules; a truly talented individual masters the rules and, if he needs to, invents new ones.

With this consideration in mind, then, the following are examples of the above method of preparation. The audience for which their preparation was intended is a group of college speech majors.

||Poem No. 62—e. e. cummings||[3]

THEME: I celebrate your birthday because it reminds me of how ever-fortunate I am in loving you.
MOOD: Sincerely affectionate
TEMPO: Somewhat slower

M Your ↑birthday comes to tell me ↑this—|

F Each ↑luckiest of lucky days

S I've ↑loved,| ↑shall love,| ↑do love you,| ↑was

M And will ↑be and ↑my birthday is.||

||Poem—Emily Dickinson||

THEME: Punctiliousness is better than blind faith in a crisis.
MOOD: Seriously didactic
TEMPO: Slower

M ↑Faith is a fine invention

F For gentlemen who ↑see;|

S But ↑microscopes are prudent|

M In an ↑emergency!||

[3] Copyright, 1958, by E. E. Cummings. Reprinted from his volume *95 Poems* by permission of Harcourt, Brace & World, Inc.

||Alone—Siegfried Sassoon||[4]

THEME: Solitude in old age reveals all life excepting faith to be a sham.
MOOD: Regretfully pensive
TEMPO: Slower

M	"When I'm ↑alone"|—the words tripped ↑off his tongue
F	As though to be alone were nothing ↑strange.|
M	"When ↑I was young," he said;| "when I was ↑young . . ."||
S	I thought of ↑age,| and ↑loneliness,| and ↑change.|
M	I thought how ↑strange we grow when we're alone,|
F	And how ↑unlike the selves that ↑meet and ↑talk,
F	And blow the ↑candles out, and say good ↑night.||
S	Alone . . .| The word is life ↑endured| and ↑known.|
M	It is the ↑stillness where our ↑spirits walk|
S	And ↑all |but inmost ↑faith| is overthrown.||

Rate Faults

In spite of analysis such as the above, together with rehearsal, during which the proper emotions are summoned up and the vocal techniques used to represent these emotions are memorized, you may still tend to present your selection with a faulty rate. Ten such possible faults are described below. Making yourself conscious of their existence may tend to remove the possibility of their occurrence.

1. Reading to Meter. Reading to meter describes an almost unvarying coincidence of metrical and vocal stress with consequent strong-form errors (on this point, see pages 265–267), insufficient variety in pace, and unnecessary pausing at the end of each poetic line. Obviously, no one who has experienced much formal training in oral reading would commit such an error at every opportunity, but even a few lapses produce a jingling effect. The best general guide, when three consecutive

[4] From *Collected Poems* by Siegfried Sassoon. Reprinted by permission of The Viking Press, Inc.

metrical stresses are vocally stressed, is to ask yourself if you would read it with those stresses if the communication were prose instead of poetry. Where the tendency is strong to pause at the end of each line, write out the material as if it were prose until that tendency can be avoided. Look at the following selection and see if you can answer the ten questions listed below. Check your answers with the correct answers on page 248.

||When I Was One-And-Twenty—A. E. Housman||[5]

1	*M*	When I was ↑one-and-twenty
2	*F*	I heard a ↑wise man say,|
3	*S*	"Give ↑crowns and ↑pounds and ↑guineas
4	*M*	But ↑not your heart away;|
5	*M*	Give ↑pearls away and ↑rubies
6	*F*	But keep your fancy ↑free."
7	*F*	But I was one-and-twenty,
8	*M*	No use to talk to ↑me.|
9	*F*	When I was one-and-twenty
10	*F*	I heard him say ↑again,|
11	*M*	"The heart out of the bosom
12	*S*	Was ↑never given in vain;
13	*S*	'Tis ↑paid with sighs a-plenty|
14	*S*	And sold for ↑endless rue."|
15	*M*	And I am ↑two-and-twenty,|
16	*S*	And ↑oh,| 'tis ↑true,| 'tis true.||

QUESTIONS

1. Not every ictus is underlined in line:
   (a) 13 (b) 14 (c) 16
2. Every ictus should be underlined in line:
   (a) 5 (b) 8 (c) 11

[5] From "A Shropshire Lad"—Authorized Edition—from *Complete Poems* by A. E. Housman.

3. A non-ictus occurs in line:
   (a) 2 (b) 11 (c) 12
4. A feminine ending occurs in line:
   (a) 10 (b) 11 (c) 12
5. An unnecessary pause occurs in line:
   (a) 4 (b) 10 (c) 13
6. A necessary pause is omitted in line:
   (a) 3 (b) 6 (c) 7
7. A run-on line occurs in line:
   (a) 5 (b) 7 (c) 11
8. Wrong word emphasis occurs in line:
   (a) 2 (b) 8 (c) 10
9. Alliteration occurs in line:
   (a) 3 (b) 6 (c) 14
10. Homophony occurs in line:
   (a) 3 (b) 4 (c) 5

2. Wrong Theme. Frequently a key line is overlooked, and the theme is, as a result, incorrectly inferred. To use the previous poem as an example, one may say that the theme is "Don't give your heart away." However, this fails to account for the second stanza, which says that the heart is not given away but is bartered for suffering. Thus, a more comprehensive, and therefore more accurate, thematic statement, assuming that the second stanza properly belongs in this poem, is: A youth's loving is repaid with remorse." Obviously, a change of theme could lead to a change of mood and thus to a change in tempo. Even if no change in mood occurred, at least the pace of those key lines becomes slower. To be sure that you have stated the theme correctly, test every line in the poem to see if it contributes to your stated theme. Test yourself by seeing how well you can state the theme of the following poem. Compare your statement to the theme suggested on page 248.

Breakfast—Wilfrid Gibson[6]

We ate our breakfast lying on our backs
Because the shells were screeching overhead.
I bet a rasher to a loaf of bread

[6] From *Collected Poems 1905–1925,* by Wilfrid Gibson. Reprinted by permission of the author's representatives and of Macmillan & Co., Ltd.

That Hull United would beat Halifax
When Jimmy Stainthorpe played fullback instead
Of Billy Bradford. Ginger raised his head
And cursed, and took the bet, and dropped back dead.
Because the shells were screeching overhead.

3. Too Fast Tempo. Usually, the rate at which an audience can receive the explicit and implicit content of a communication is overestimated rather than underestimated. That is, you may plan to read a selection at a somewhat slower tempo (than chatting) but actually read it at only a slightly slower tempo. This is probably due to your having rehearsed the material to the extent that it is almost memorized and that you are readily aware of its every nuance. Thus, you unconsciously read it as if you were speaking impromptu, i.e., saying ideas at the rate at which they occur to you. This normal tendency to deliver rehearsed material at the rate at which its contents occurs to you must be consciously resisted. Some actors seem to read their lines faster at each rehearsal. To enjoin them to speak more slowly either produces an artificially unvaried, slow tempo or a momentary slowing up followed by a quick return to the previously rapid tempo. Directors speak of "the illusion of the first time." That is, forget that you have heard what you are saying and listen to yourself as if you had never heard these words before. Such an attitude is difficult for some to master, the more so perhaps because it seems so artificial. However, if this is your problem you must learn to accept this artifice as desirable. Ignore the inner voice that cries, "Your tempo is too slow." Of course it is too slow for you; you have heard these words before. Keep reminding yourself that, for your auditors, you hope, it *is* new.

4. Insufficiently Varied Pace. We said previously that the rate fault of reading to meter tended to produce an insufficiently varied pace. A tempo that is too fast due to rehearsal making the content quite well known to the reader will also tend to produce an insufficiently varied pace, the lines being read too rapidly because rehearsal made their content so well known to the reader. A third case occurs if a great change of pace from line to line tends to seem grotesque. Any good acting by a trained actor is artificial, if by that we mean that he is not actually living his part. How could we expect an actor to "live the part" throughout, say, two hundred consecutive performances without suffering greatly from the consequences of such self-torture? The trained actor suffers during rehearsal and then remembers the physical manifestations of his suffering and summons up these manifestations of his suffering by means of cues in much the same way that he remembers his lines. In like manner, the trained reader must learn to vary his pace during rehearsal so that the pace of each slow and fast line is commensurate with its content (depth, conciseness, and implications) and to adhere to that pace throughout each reading. Thus, for some the admonition to pretend that this is the first time that you are listening to what you say may prove helpful; others are advised to remember the techniques learned in the process of rehearsal and to deviate from such remembered techniques only deliberately for experimentation directed toward greater improvement. When habits countervail learned techniques, more rehearsal is indicated.

5. Incorrect or Slighted Caesura. No matter how many pauses may occur in the last line of your selection, the feeling of completion is provoked by a falling pitch on the last syllable and the final pause before ending the last line. Generally, the farther this final pause is from the end of the line, the smaller the caesural effect it will have. Try to see if the caesura can also serve as another type of pause (e.g., anticipatory or deliberative). Avoid an arbitrary caesura unless a pause between any two words in the last line seems as meaningful as a pause anywhere else. An excellent method for locating the most effective place for a caesura is to read the last line or last two lines with a different caesura employed on each trial. And, as with the faults previously discussed, the tendency to abbreviate this period of silence by hastening on to the selections's resolution should also be avoided. Silence within speech is, perhaps next to a scream, the most attention-arresting of all vocal devices. Learn to relish its use by observing its effect on others. Delight in manipulating others is not restricted to tyrants; why else do we all speak?

6. Excessive Emphasis on Nominatives. Because poetry employs poetic devices and because these devices are employed most frequently on nouns, the verbs, adverbs and predicate adjectives which usually convey the major import of the ideas tend to receive less emphasis. For example, in "When I Was One-And-Twenty" (page 237) it could easily be maintained that the most important words are "paid" and "sold" and their objects "sighs-a-plenty" and "endless rue." However, the ear can easily be distracted by the homophonic "crowns and pounds" and the alliteratives "fancy free," "to talk to," "two-and-twenty," and "'tis true, 'tis true." To use another example, consider these sentences:

1. The meal is finished.
2. The big meal is finished.
3. The fine feast is finished.

Obviously, in the first sentence the important word is "finished," unless it occurs in the rare context of answering someone who knew something was finished, but not what. The same is true of the second sentence, provided it was not a reply to the question of which meal was finished. However, in the third sentence we tend to lose sight of the word "finished" because of the alliteration. To retain emphasis on "finished" would require a rising inflection throughout, which would probably necessitate some conscious effort toward this end in rehearsal. Generally, if poetic devices are good, they are able to call sufficient attention to themselves without sacrificing any communication of meaning. As a general rule, then, avoid the use of intonation to indicate poetic devices.

7. Identical Repetition. A poet seldom repeats a word or words merely to call added attention to their meaning. Generally, if a word is repeated, it is either because the sound of the word is meant to be stressed (e.g., "Cuckoo, cuckoo, cuckoo," "Boomlay, boomlay, boomlay, boom!") or that the two uses mean something different from either alone (e.g., "the death of Death," "ages and ages"). Hence, a refrain which occurs several times in any poem with an intellectual content exceeding that of a ballad will, upon analysis, be found to contain sufficient opportunity for variety in word emphasis. Moreover, if the same line occurs, say, four times, it probably contains at least four important words, and a good general rule to follow is to emphasize these words sequentially, i.e., accent the first important word in the first occurrence of that line, the second important word in the second occurrence, and so forth. To illustrate: The fourth and sixth lines of each stanza in the following poem are practically identical, yet notice the variety achieved by vocally emphasizing the italicized words.

Non Sum Qualis Eram Bonae Sub Regno Cynarae—
Ernest Dowson

Last night, ah, yesternight, betwixt her lips and mine
There fell thy shadow, Cynara! thy breath was shed
Upon my soul between the kisses and the wine;
And I was *desolate* and sick of an old passion,
  Yea, I was desolate and bowed my head:
I have been *faithful* to thee, Cynara! in my fashion.

All night upon mine heart I felt her warm heart beat,
Night-long within mine arms in love and sleep she lay;
Surely the kisses of her bought red mouth were sweet;
But I was desolate and *sick* of an old passion,
  When I awoke and found the dawn was gray:
I have been faithful to *thee*, Cynara! in my fashion.

I have forgot much, Cynara! gone with the wind,
Flung roses, roses riotously with the throng,
Dancing, to put thy pale, lost lilies out of mind;
But I was desolate and sick of an *old* passion,
  Yea, all the time, because the dance was long:
I have been faithful to thee, *Cynara*! in my fashion.

I cried for madder music and for stronger wine,
But when the feast is finished and the lamps expire,
Then falls thy shadow, Cynara! the night is thine;
And I am desolate and sick of an old *passion*,
  Yea, hungry for the lips of my desire:
I have been faithful to thee, Cynara! in *my* fashion.

8. Insufficient Variety in Types of Word Emphasis. Read just the fourth and sixth lines of each stanza in the Dowson poem above, using highest pitch and greatest duration on the underlined words. Observe how much variety is introduced merely by these two vocal devices. However, a reading which employs only these two types of word emphasis, viz., duration and intonation, employs only two essential means of emphasizing words. Words may also be emphasized by using voice qualities other than good voice quality (e.g., nasality, breathiness, thinness, or flatness) and by increased loudness. However, this type of emphasis is not possible if loudness or any voice quality other than a good one is employed on almost every word. Thus, for example, in the chapter on voice quality it was mentioned that breathiness for word emphasis tends to connote physical, mental, or spiritual weakness, indecision, or awe. Yet if a person is breathy on almost everything he says, the use of breathiness to emphasize such words as "tired," "perhaps," or "lovely" escapes our notice as an emphatic device. In like manner, a person who tends to use loudness on almost every important word fails to connote power and massiveness on words such as "bold" and "noisy." The fault of insufficient variety in types of word emphasis, then, is usually due to a person's habitual mode of speaking being an undesirable stereotype (such as breathy, nasal, insufficient pitch variety, up in pitch for word emphasis, etc.) or to a lack of concern for variety in word emphasis. Both are probably due to a lack of voice training; the first indicates a lack of training to achieve good voice quality, pitch variety, loudness, and rate, and the second indicating a lack of training in the employment of various voice qualities and loudness as emphatic devices. To check the extent of your own variety, read the following catalogues twice, first, as if you were asked merely to read off the list to someone and, second, as if you were instructed to make each item sound as different as possible from the other items. The more your first reading tends to sound like a reading of mere numbers, the more you need to work for greater variety in word emphasis. The procedure of labeling the type of emphasis you plan to employ on certain important words, as outlined on page 234, is a helpful one not only for achieving greater vocal variety in rehearsed delivery but for inculcating a habit to carry over into everyday speech.

1. soft, sticky, dirty mint candy
2. thin, long, straight, hard, wet stick
3. brave, inquisitive, eager, intelligent, likeable man
4. triangles, squares, circles, ovals, rectangles
5. boxes, cans, cartons, jars, canisters, bags
6. father, sister, uncle, mother, cousin, brother
7. Chicago, Philadelphia, New York, Los Angeles, Houston, Miami
8. "Gently they go, the beautiful, the tender, the kind;
   Quietly they go, the intelligent, the witty, the brave."

9. Mood Distracting from Meaning. On certain poems, the use of a voice quality other than good voice quality throughout the entire poem rather than for occasional word emphasis may be considered as appropriate, but the risks involved are great. Generally, if the poem has insignificant or puerile content and its values are principally emotional, this mode of delivery may be suitable. However, when discernment of the mood requires clear understanding of the meaning, the use of a single voice quality such as breathiness or nasality tends to make all important words sound alike and thus restricts their ability to denote. Thus, for example, thinness may be appropriate on R. L. Stevenson's "The Swing" or orotundity on certain poems by Lear, such as "Calico Pie," but consider the following poems, reading them first with the voice quality indicated and then with a good voice quality modified only on a few words with other voice qualities.

To Celia—Ben Jonson

(Orotundity)

Drink to me only with thine eyes,
  And I will pledge with mine;
Or leave a kiss but in the cup
  And I'll not look for wine.
The thirst that from the soul doth rise
  Doth ask a drink divine;
But might I of Jove's nectar sup,
  I would not change for thine.

I sent thee late a rosy wreath,
  Not so much honoring thee
As giving it a hope that there
  It could not withered be;
But thou thereon didst only breathe
  And sent'st it back to me;
Since when it grows, and smells, I swear,
  Not of itself but thee!

Sonnet No. 43—Elizabeth Barrett Browning

(Breathiness)

How do I love thee? Let me count the ways.
I love thee to the depth and breadth and height
My soul can reach, when feeling out of sight
For the ends of Being and ideal Grace.
I love thee to the level of every day's
Most quiet need, by sun and candle-light.
I love thee freely, as men strive for right;
I love thee purely, as they turn from praise.
I love thee with the passion put to use
In my old griefs, and with my childhood's faith.
I love thee with a love I seemed to lose
With my lost saints—I love thee with the breath,
Smiles, tears, of all my life!—and, if God choose,
I shall but love thee better after death.

10. Improper Pausing. Any pause which is not readily perceived as purposeful (viz., terminating, transitional, anticipatory, deliberative, separational, parenthetical, incoherent or caesural) tends to provoke confusion. Two such confusing uses of pauses are to set off nonparenthetical remarks and to indicate equivalence. A nonparenthetical remark is a word or phrase which is essential to the main idea. In the following poem, see if you can locate the two incorrect, nonparenthetical pauses. Check your answer on page 248.

Stopping by a Woods on a Snowy Evening—Robert Frost[7]

Whose woods these are I think I know.|
His house is in the village though;|
He will not see me stopping here
To watch his woods fill up with snow.|

My little horse must think it queer|
To stop without a farmhouse near|
Between the woods and frozen lake|
The darkest evening of the year.|

He gives his harness bells a shake
To ask if there is some mistake.|
The only other sound's the sweep
Of easy wind and downy flake.|

The woods are lovely,| dark and deep,|
But I have promises to keep,
And miles to go before I sleep,|
And miles to go| before I sleep.|

For some persons the tendency to use punctuation as a guide to pausing is irresistible. However, commas are generally used to set off quoted or paraphrased remarks from the sentence fragment which identifies the speaker, but a pause merely to differentiate between the speaker and his remark is seldom effectual and is another kind of nonparenthetical pause. As an example, read the following excerpt from Kenneth Fearing's "American Rhapsody (4)"[8] with and without the indicated pauses, and notice that the words "they say" are obviously the subject of the sentence only when no pause occurs; with such pauses these words sound parenthetical, becoming tantamount to "at least that is what they say."

"(They say, you know, that first you hear voices. And then you have visions,| they say. Then,| they say,| you kick and scream and rave.)"

[7] From *Complete Poems of Robert Frost.* Copyright 1923 by Holt, Rinehart and Winston, Inc. Copyright renewed 1951 by Robert Frost. Reprinted by permission of Holt, Rinehart and Winston, Inc.

[8] From *Collected Poems,* by Kenneth Fearing, published by Random House.

An equivalence is a word or group of words which is intended to convey the same meaning as another word or group of words which precedes or follows it. Such a situation frequently occurs in a parenthetical remark, but for our purposes we should consider equivalence as something different from parenthesis. To illustrate, the following are parenthetical remarks, even if it is true that the parenthetical portion is equivalent to the subject or predicate of the main idea:

1. The president during the Civil War, Abraham Lincoln, was a Republican.
2. The psychological correlate of intensity, loudness, obviously requires an auditor for it to be said to occur.
3. Rhythm, the pulling away from and returning to meter, should have an aesthetic rather than an intellectual appeal.

In each of these examples the words between commas are truly parenthetical and, as previously mentioned, require pauses to set them off and, incidentally, a change in intonational level. However, consider the following equivalent statements:

1. He crept, catlike, into the room.
2. He believed, completely and with no misgivings, in her fidelity.
3. To prate, saying much about nothing, is termed garrulity.

In these examples we could say that the words between commas are intended to be something more than mere definitions, that is, comparison, analogies, extensions, or qualifications; but in the first three examples such words are purely definitional. When pauses are used for such nondefinitional matter, the listener strives to apply some meaning to the material set off by the pauses, and the more clearly nondefinitional the content, the more confused he becomes. To use a famous example, consider the difference in meaning provoked by pausing or not pausing at the end of the fifth line:

Soliloquy from *Hamlet*—Shakespeare

1 To be, or not to be: that is the question:
2 Whether 'tis nobler in the mind to suffer
3 The slings and arrows of outrageous fortune,
4 Or to take arms against a sea of troubles,

5 And by opposing end them? To die: to sleep;
6 No more; and by a sleep to say we end
7 The heartache, and the thousand natural shocks
8 That flesh is heir to.

Some reknowned actors have used a long pause at the end of the fifth line. This implies, if anything, a resoluteness which belies the meaning of the entire passage. Moreover, it reverts attention to the troubles mentioned earlier (no more suffering the slings and arrows of outrageous fortune) and distracts our attention from the subject of sleep which both precedes and follows this remark. When it is understood that "To die: to sleep; no more" implies that dying is nothing more than sleeping, the words "no more" qualify the comparison of dying and sleeping, and all that is necessary is a separational pause sufficiently long to prevent implying "to sleep no more." We thus have these possibilities:

1. "To die:|| to sleep;|| no more": *Dying is like sleeping; it ends our troubles.*
2. "To die:|| to sleep; no more": *Dying ends our sleeping.*
3. "To die:|| to sleep;| no more": *Dying is nothing more than sleeping.*

Answers to Questions on Pages 237–238

1. a	6. b
2. b	7. c
3. a	8. b
4. b	9. b
5. b	10. a

Answer to Question on Page 238

The theme of the poem is: "Death in war is an untimely incident." Any predicative substitute is satisfactory as long as it suggests an event that is important and frequent but unexpected. Thus, "tragic" would be inappropriate, but "a shocking commonplace" would be satisfactory.

Answer to Question on Page 245

"To stop without a farmhouse near" and "dark and deep" are not parenthetical. Hence, the pause before each of these is incorrect.

9

Pronunciation

Class Influences on the Words We Use

Pear, a British psychologist interested in speech, comments that, whereas Britishers make many class distinctions on the basis of speech, they tend to perceive American speech as more homogeneous except for regional variations. ". . . yet two American social psychologists assure me that over there [in America] class differences in speech are easily perceptible, with more reluctance than in England to acknowledge their existence."

Although research on class differences in American speech is nil, let us venture to examine whether differences exist and what effect this can have on work at speech improvement.

It seem safe to say without statistical substantiation that we can and do recognize the speech of teen-agers, gangsters, laborers, intellectuals, and other groups. We observe that teenagers use slang, that they make one word substitute for countless others, and are fond of tacking on meaningless phrases at the ends of ideas. Gangsters have their own argot and tend to be laconic rather than voluble. The speech of laborers is characterized by some profanity, faulty grammar, and words that are much more specific than abstract. Intellectuals use many big words to express even trivial ideas, prefer wit to humor, and would rather say the unconventional even at the risk of saying something stupid. That group differences in speech exist in America seems obvious; the extent to which these different groups are classes depends upon attitudes of those in each group toward those in other groups.

If we ask ourselves three questions about such attitudes, we may acquire considerable understanding of speech classes in America in spite of having no research:

(1) What is the attitude of members of a group toward one of another group who speaks as they do?
(2) What is the attitude of members of a group toward one of their own members who speaks like members of another group?
(3) Does any group consider the speech of another group to be superior to its own?

In answering the first question we must consider, for example, the attitude of teen-agers toward parents talking like teen-agers, of intellectuals toward laborers talking like intellectuals, and so on. In the first example, teen-agers might be flattered by parents trying to speak like teen-agers, but their respect for such parents would probably be less. In the second example, intellectuals would probably not be flattered by laborers using intellectual speech conventions, but they might think more highly of such laborers.

In answering the second question we must consider such situations as the attitude of teen-agers toward a teen-ager talking like an intellectual or the attitude of intellectuals toward an intellectual talking like a laborer. In either case, the group would tend to disdain a member for adopting the speech of another group.

Let us define a group as a speech class, and as a speech class which is lower than another, when its members look upon a member of the higher class who speaks like them with both flattery and disdain. We then might rank laborers' speech below bureaucratic speech, and bureaucratic speech below intellectual speech. Possibly we should rank teen-agers as a speech class above penal inmates and foreigners but below laborers, in terms of their speech attitudes. In this sense, then, many groups in America consider certain groups to have speech that is inferior to their own, but they may not realize that other groups may also look upon the speech of their group with disdain. What we have then is a hierarchy of speech classes, admittedly not clearly defined, in which each class is far more aware of its own superiority in speech than of any speech which is superior to its own. When Americans are exposed to the speech of those in a higher class, they tend to rationalize their own speech by claiming that other ways of speaking are artificial while theirs is natural and, therefore, right.

The next question, and the only important one for our purposes, is: What risks does a person run who attempts to adopt the speech mode of a higher class? The answer seems to be that, if he rightfully belongs to that class as evidenced by his age, occupation, wealth, education, nationality, region, etc., he runs practically no risk at all. If he speaks like those of any class below the one to which he rightfully belongs, however, he risks disdain by those in every class. If his speech is higher than his present station, he must weigh the disfavor of his peers against the favor of the higher classes or else employ a different speech mode in talking with those in different classes.

Admittedly, then, we all recognize what we consider to be good speech (our own) and worse speech, and if we are forced to view such a hierarchy dispassionately, we may admit a possibility of the existence of better speech. The final question is: In what aspects of speech do these class differences primarily reside? Research and our own experience reveal that, in terms of voice quality, pitch variety, intonation, loudness, and rate, all classes have practically identical standards. Nasality may be more frowned upon in some speech regions than in others, but this may simply be because nasality is to some extent regional, and our regions are also classes in that we tend provincially to assume that the speech of our own region is obviously more correct than the speech of any other. But we have had no reason to consider the existence of class (or regional) differences in discussing voice quality, pitch variety, and other factors because of the vast homogeneity of attitude on such matters. However, in terms of pronunciation and diction (word usage), class differences exist to such an extent that some rational consideration of them must be made. Anyone who treats of speech improvement in these two areas without defining what he means by improvement can only imply either a boundless conceit which assumes that all should talk as he does because he does it so well or else implies that values are facts and must be swallowed without question.

Both pronunciation and diction are integrally related to class, and mere lamentations about the existence of such classes will not dispel them. To discuss the pronunciation and diction of Easterners, cowboys, teen-agers, laborers, intellectuals, or of any other group would prove of little worth for voice training of any group other than actors. However, pronunciation and diction will be examined to see if any modes are esteemed by all, regardless of class, and, if so, what these modes might be.

Each of us has certain pronunciations he dislikes and words or phrases he abhors, and, perhaps more than we would like to admit it, these prejudices are due to the class to which we belong. The purpose of this chapter and the one following is not to encourage you to change your speech to that of a higher class, but to help you to acquire principles and standards for choosing in those aspects of pronunciation and diction which are to a large extent independent of group affiliation i.e., that are logically rather than merely emotionally desirable. Where this cannot be done, class distinctions will be made, not with the hope of urging you to speak like those in a higher class, but in the conviction that knowledge of such differences is worthwhile even if no immediate use for such knowledge can be seen. Again, this stems from the belief that one who chooses among several possible words or pronunciations is freer than one who is a captive of one, and one who chooses on the basis of principles and standards which he has logically derived in the freest one of all.

Need for a Pronunciation Standard

Pronunciation, when compared with other factors of vocal delivery, such as voice quality, pitch variety, intonation, loudness, and rate, is a relatively unimportant factor. That is, it is far more detrimental in most speaking situations to have a faulty voice quality than to mispronounce many words. However, as will be seen later, many situations do exist in which faulty pronunciations can result in disapprobation of the speaker and, as we will see, since these situations are generally extremely important to the speaker, pronunciation is an important area in speech improvement. However, pronunciation as mere word study tends to produce affectations of delivery; it is essential that you acquire a philosophy—meaning a belief in certain principles—of pronunciation if affectation is to be avoided. We begin, then, with a consideration of various standards and the possible merits of each.

Obviously, if everyone decided for himself how to pronounce every word without considering how others pronounce words, not much oral communication could occur. Hence, a *laissez faire* philosophy permitting limitless freedom of choice is certainly not desirable. But this does not imply acceptance of the alternative that everyone must pronounce every word the same way. It does mean, to say the least, that we need enough agreement on pronunciation to enable us to understand what words are meant when we speak with one another. Let us view this decision to accept at least this much agreement on pronunciation as our acceptance of a standard. Our problem then becomes, "What standard shall we choose?"

Criteria for Any Standard

It seems almost self-evident to say that any pronunciation of a word should communicate the meaning of that word as clearly as possible to as many persons as possible who may hear it and should distract attention from that meaning, toward the pronunciation itself, as little as possible for as few persons as possible. That is, good pronunciations are those with maximum intelligibility and minimum distractibility. It would seem, then, that good pronunciation is a question of fact, subject to scientific inquiry and statistical proof. All that we need to do is to discover the effects of various pronunciations on various audiences and thus derive the generally least obtrusive and most meaningful pronunciation of every word. This assumes a homogeneity in the effects of various pronunciations; but we all realize that some pronunciations that fail to offend some can produce disfavor in others. We may use a pronunciation that does not offend our superiors but does offend our peers, or vice versa. In speaking as an outsider to a group, if we use their pronunciations which are different from our usual ones, we may be praised for our acceptance of their ways or mistrusted for our pretenses. Thus, meaningfulness and unobtrusiveness are relative rather than absolute qualities, depending upon speaker status, audience status, speech situation, and many other factors, so that it is more practical to consider the matter of a pronunciation standard as a question of value rather than of fact, more akin to dress than to physics.

"Correctness" of pronunciation, then, can best be considered as a matter of taste. However, this decision does not force us to admit *laissez faire* freedom and the impossibility of accepting a standard. Consider the analogy of dress. Obviously, the cheaper the dresses, generally, the more they are bought, but that does not mean that, because they are more popular, they are best, either in the opinion of those who buy them or in our own opinion. The ones who buy them may do so because they can have no basis other than price on which to make a choice. If they do not know that better styles exist at that same price, or do not care about style, they simply buy what is available at a price they can afford. What is meant by better styles is not necessarily equivalent to higher prices; it means adherence of a person to his definition of good dress in terms of various aspects of dress design, appropriateness for him in that it emphasizes his merits and de-emphasizes his weak points in shape, complexion, and the like, and appropriateness for the formality of the occasion and the social and meteorological climate in which it is worn. Insofar as his decisions on dress are congruent with those of higher social position for whom dress is a matter of even greater concern, we can say that he is well dressed by their definition as well as his own. In fact, when we say that a person is well dressed, we either mean that his taste is compatible with our own or with the taste of persons we consider to be our social superiors. We never mean that his dress is probably acceptable to his peers, except insofar as we consider ourself to be his peer. If a person's dress meets with no disapproval from his peers, it does not follow that it meets with approval. Suppose, for example, that teen-agers consider tennis shoes *de rigueur* at their semiformal dances. One who shows up in tennis shoes is not praised by the others unless his shoes are different from the others; his footwear is simply not noticed. If he wears something other than tennis shoes, however, he runs the risk of being disapproved if the difference is noticed. However, parents who observe him would doubtless not disapprove, and probably would approve, of his choice of footwear. In matters of taste, then, we have the possibilities of being unnoticed by one's peers, of offending one's peers if they notice a departure from what they consider to be à la mode, of offending one's superiors by following the mode of one's peers, or by not offending one's superiors by being à la mode in their opinion. Ideally, we would like to avoid offending both peers and superiors. The question with respect to pronunciation then becomes, "To what extent do pronunciations which meet with approbation from one's superiors meet with no disapprobation from one's peers?" With this question in mind, and with the analogy of dress as a guide, let us consider the various standards we might employ and see how well each standard provides an answer to this question.

Possible Pronunciation Standards

1. The Majority Standard. Many persons believe that the guide to pronunciation should be pronunciations of most persons because, if most persons pronounce a word a certain way, that pronunciation must be most acceptable most of the time. Certainly linguistic historians might prefer this standard because it would make their task of discovering changes in popular pronunciations the simple one of consulting dictionaries of previous times. Philosophically, the majority standard is questionable because it is based on the fallacy of *argumentum ad populum*, i.e., if it is most popular, it is, therefore, best. However, because a standard is fallacious does not mean that it is false. Most persons prefer freedom (which we think is good) to slavery, but most persons prefer to seek medical care only when they are obviously ill (which we think is not good). The basic weakness of the majority standard, then, aside from any philosophical weakness, is that the concept of majority pronunciation is factitious. Majorities in different regions pronounce words differently, so that to make a statistical statement of what pronunciation "the" majority prefers is like saying the average weight of a piece of fruit in a basket is one-fourth pound when the basket contains apples, plums, and bananas. Obviously, the proportion of each fruit affects the statistic so that the most numerous fruit is the greatest determinant of average weight. In like manner, the speech region with the greatest proportion of the national population would statistically determine the pronunciations of the entire nation. For the United States this would mean adoption by us all of the pronunciations of the people in the East, since this is where the majority now lives, until our westward shift in population forces us statistically to adopt the pronunciations of the people in the Midwest and then, later, in the West. When a person who argues for the majority standard realizes the extent of uniqueness of pronunciations within each region, he tends to forego his adherence to such an artificial standard, preferring instead what is called the regional standard.

2. The Regional Standard. Many writers on speech, aware of regional homogeneity of pronunciation with respect to the majority in each region and the heterogeneity between the majority in one region and the majority in another, propose regional standards, suggesting that a different standard be used for each region. This standard of course does not avoid the *argumentum ad populum* fallacy; it merely redefines *populum*. However, it is practically unwise because it contravenes interregional communication, which in the United States is increasing daily in both quantity and importance. Any standard directed toward advocating regional television, films, radio, (even dictionaries) certainly vitiates our most important channels of communication. Also, consider the plight of national figures such as presidential candidates and famous speakers who would be encouraged to achieve the flexibility of at least four modes of pronunciation since we now have four predominant pronunciation regions, viz., Eastern, Southern, Western (or Southwestern), and Midwestern. Moreover, in our highly mobile society we travel to other regions and speak to many from other regions frequently. Shall we suggest teaching each child four modes or teaching each regional immigrant a new mode of pronunciation? Some writers, and these are generally from the Midwest, suggest the Midwestern standard as a national standard, terming such pronunciations General American, in the belief that such pronunciations generally encounter least opprobrium nationally. Such a belief is provincial, indicating no awareness of the effect, for example, of "Yankee" speech on Southerners or "flat 'a' [æ]" speech on Easterners. Except for such differences, the regional standard of the Midwest is, however, worthy of our consideration as a possible standard, providing no other standard seems more appropriate. We could at least learn how and when not to offend with Midwestern pronunciations.

3. The Authoritarian Standard. Another standard we might consider worthy of adoption is dictation of pronunciations by some sort of officially sanctioned council. Such a standard has been or is being established in such countries as Norway, Spain, and France. Let us examine one such policy in some detail. In France, the existence of regional homogeneities has given rise to many problems of pronunciation similar to our own in that regional pronunciations tend to offend those in other regions, yet no people in any region has earned such esteem that the peoples of other regions prefer to imitate their pronunciations. Accordingly, *L'Office du Vocabulaire Français* (The Office of French Vocabulary) was organized, under the chairmanship of the celebrated novelist Georges Duhamel, as a private, nonprofit institution with more than thirty-five hundred members entrusted with the task of writing a definitive French dictionary. Just as the majority or regional majority standards make the life of linguistic historians easier, so this standard makes the lexicographers' task extremely inexpensive. But, just as the national majority standard provokes acceptance of one region's pronunciations by all, the membership of The Office of French

Vocabulary tends to be Parisian in origin or affection, and the dictionary, if it is ever completed, will probably tend to be a Parisian one. This may provoke some dissatisfaction in the provinces. However, even if the membership were more nationally representative, the populace would probably resent dictation on a matter of taste, and perhaps especially in France, where nonpayment of income tax is popularly considered more of an assertion of independence than an infraction of the law. To revert to the analogy of dress, we may recognize the necessity for having standards in what to wear but we nevertheless resent being told that we must wear the uniform dictated by some person, committee or national survey. To construe democracy as a system that should encourage conformity in anything is but a mockery of the Anglo-American meaning of the term. It is perhaps in rebellion from such dictation that some persons and and groups have recommended what we shall call the audience standard.

4. The Audience Standard. The audience standard refers to the guide to pronunciation as the pronunciations of one's audiences, i.e., one should use the pronunciations of one's peers when speaking to one's peers, of superiors when addressing superiors, of Southerners when conversing with Southerners. The leading exponent of this standard in the United States is the National Council of Teachers of English (N.C.T.E.) which recommends that, since "all usage is relative," the teacher's "task, so far as his pupils are concerned, is not to teach any one form of speech as correct or incorrect but to develop in the pupil the same sensitivity to the appropriateness of language in each situation which he himself has developed."[1] J. Donald Adams calls this "democratic theory carried to the point of absurdity. What it implies is that, no matter what your standards of speech and usage are, you must lower or raise them to meet the situation in which you find yourself. It's all a matter of social adjustment. You mustn't be yourself, you must above everything else, conform."[2]

[1] *The English Language Arts,* Commission on the English Curriculum of the National Council of Teachers of English, Appleton-Century-Crofts (New York), 1952, pp. 277–78.

[2] J. Donald Adams, "Speaking of Books," *The New York Times Book Review,* Jan. 24, 1960, p. 2.

Again to use the analogy of dress, the standard would have us avoid having principles beyond dressing in a manner that is merely fit for various occasions. The highest goal would be mere unobtrusiveness.

The audience standard, then, is abhorrent to some because of its implicit appeal to conform, to ingratiate oneself at any cost, to have no standards other than socially determined ones. Pronounce meticulously out of a fear of being wrong; don't pronounce scrupulously out of conviction of what is right. However, this audience standard has two difficulties other than its appeal to conformism; it requires both knowledge and versatility. If we are to pronounce differently in talking to parents, friends, superiors, subordinates, or persons in other regions, we must learn what their pronunciations are and then practice saying each word until we can pronounce it each way for each situation without hesitation. Nor does such training end with pronunciation; we have grammar, dialecticisms, cants, jargons, slang, vocabulary, and idioms to be taught, for who can predict which audiences each student will address throughout the course of his life? Moreover, we cannot always address homogeneous speech groups. Suppose all that we know is that our audience is predominantly Democratic, or pro-fluoridation, or elderly? Obviously, the time spent in teaching the speech patterns of various geographic regions and social groups within the United States could very well be spent more profitably in teaching a truly foreign language such as Russian or Chinese. The audience standard carries the credo of "When in Rome do as the Romans do" to the ridiculous extent of encouraging abandonment of one's principles of aesthetics and decorum. Because it is unscrupulous and educationally wasteful, the audience standard is not to be desired. Only one other possible standard yet remains, the elite or cultured speaker standard.

5. The Elite or Cultured Speaker Standard. Those persons who have considerable prestige, engage in important oral communication frequently, and are respected for their ability to communicate effectively use what is called cultured speech. Moreover, the cultured speakers of any area differ in their pronunciations from the cultured speakers of any other area far less noticeably and far less frequently than the majorities in these areas. In fact, a strong case could be made for stating that this is true of the entire English-speaking world. The editors of the *Merriam-Webster Dictionary* state that "At present all cultivated types, when well spoken, are easily intelligible to any speaker of English, and there is a very large percentage of practical identity in the speech sounds used."[3] Remember that we are not here referring to Cockney English, Outback Australian, and Brooklynese but to the speech of cultured speakers in these regions. The philosophical basis for accepting the speech of cultured speakers as the standard is the argument that "Their speech communicates best, *ergo*, their pronunciations are best." Our dictionaries use cultured or elite speech as their standard.

It might be argued that the use of elite pronunciations will tend to make the speaker seem affected. This is true to the extent that (1) the pronunciations are obviously nonhabitual and (2) the differences between elite and other pronunciations are noticed by those with other pronunciations, and (3) if noticed, provoke disdain. Let us consider each of these in turn.

An elite pronunciation seems nonhabitual when it is inconsistent with the speaker's other pronunciations of that word or similar words or he pronounces it in such a way as to emphasize that word's importance unduly. E.g., saying [haf past tɛn] followed by the Southwestern [ðɪn ɑ læft] is almost certain to lead to some suspicion that the Texan is trying to show off his Yankee education. Many of us are familiar with the Rhodes Scholar who displays his Oxford background by dropping Oxfordisms here and there or the non-New Englander whose pronunciations advertise that he attended Harvard. Certainly any standard we adopt should be adopted to the extent that it becomes habitual, i.e., nonconscious, if we want to avoid seeming affected. The Northerner who addresses a Southerner with "Y'all" when he obviously does not include anyone other than the person addressed will almost invariably be less well received than the Northerner who does not attempt to be so folksy.

[3] *Webster's New International Dictionary*, Second Edition, "Guide to Pronunciation," p. xxvi. G. & C. Merriam Co., Springfield, Mass., 1934.

The pronunciations of the elite and the majority, whether national or regional, do not differ on most words. On words that they do pronounce differently, the differences are usually noticeable to the elite but practically never to the majority unless, of course, a difference in pronunciation is flagrantly emphasized, and such a case would be a breach of etiquette rather than a pronunciation fault. On those words which are noticeably different to those in the majority, the two groups usually have different meanings for those words (on this point, see pages 270–272).

Suppose now that a speaker's elite pronunciations are not perceived as being nonhabitual and, for the most part, any differences between his pronunciations and those of his auditors generally escape attention. The next question is to what extent those differences which do not escape their attention lead to denigration of the speaker. Obviously, these differences will rarely lead to any audience member's assuming that the speaker's pronunciations are foreign, but they will generally recognize them as being cultured pronunciations. To return to the analogy of dress, the lady who appears at a small-town formal dance, in what cultured women consider to be good taste for formal dances anywhere, would hardly be disparaged; she probably would be admired and subsequently imitated. The question is frequently raised as to who dictates women's fashions. The answer is that no one "dictates" them, but it is a matter of who initiates them and who imitates them. The dress designers of New York, Paris, and Dallas do not initiate them; many of them have gone bankrupt in that erroneous belief. They merely design clothes in the hope that the best-dressed women will buy them. Any woman realizes that she admires the dress of a certain group of women, but what she may not realize is that a truncated pyramidal hierarchy exists. At the top level of this pyramid are those with such prestige in matters of attire that they can, to a considerable extent, select from the offerings of original dress designers without being greatly influenced by what others may wear. They adhere far more to their own principles than to what others practice. To assume that because our nation is a democracy it is classless is ridiculous. It is classless in terms of distance from a royal family, but it has social, educational, economic, occupational, and other classes. To maintain that the existence of such classes is undemocratic is also ridiculous unless one believes that government should legislate on matters of taste (religion, art, architecture, politics, etc.) which is truly undemocratic. To maintain that persons should not aspire to belong to a higher social class is futile; those who wish to do so will try to do so to the extent that society permits it and their own abilities enable them to achieve it. To return to the subject of pronunciation, then, we may say that elite pronunciations which are noticed as being different are also noticed as being elite pronunciations and, rather than lowering the speaker's esteem, could enhance it.

Should the elite be enforced as a standard? Of course not. But the elite standard should be taught in such a way that:

(1) The philosophy on which it is based is clearly understood.
(2) It becomes habitual for those who choose to adopt it.
(3) Elite principles and practices are understood by those who choose another standard so that they may know in what situations they may desire to follow these principles and practices.

To use the analogy of grammar for a change, suppose Johnny says, "If I was you . . . ," "They act like they don't care," "Who did he give it to?" . . . "He didn't hardly notice it," "Me and Sally went to town," and similar forms. When he is told another grammatical form exists, he replies that, if he "was" to speak like that, his old man would clobber him for putting on airs. Perhaps he is telling the truth. If so, should he avoid learning the alternate forms and, when he subsequently leaves home to seek employment or a higher education, should he be penalized for his bad grammar? He should at least learn it in case he ever finds that he needs it. How foolish it is to try to restrict education to what every student will use, as if this were ever predictable.

One final question remains: Will the majority ever adopt the elite as its standard? Of course, but then the elite may have moved on to different pronunciations. However, the opposite could never occur; the elite would never adopt the pronunciations of the majority, except in a few instances in which the elite deems the majority pronunciation preferable. Perhaps our sound-recording devices will serve to codify pronunciation much as printing served to codify spelling. But if they do not, the majority will imitate, to the extent of its abilities and capabilities, whatever traits of any social group it admires. Eventually, the majority may consciously and openly display its admiration for good speech.

Correctness of Pronunciation

It can be seen from the foregoing discussion that, unless we state what standard we choose to follow, we cannot speak of "correctness" of pronunciation in any meaningful sense, and even then we can only say that a pronunciation is incorrect according to our chosen standard. This text will avoid any use of the term, except by implication in that it will speak of pronunciation faults; but here a fault merely refers to pronunciations which differ from elite pronunciations. These differences should be noted by all, and any change to elite pronunciations should be made at the discretion of each individual, based on his philosophy of pronunciation and his knowledge of each situation. The characteristics of elite pronunciations and, in this sense, of faulty pronunciations, will be discussed, then, not because the author advocates use of elite pronunciations by all but because he advocates that each person have clearly defined principles of pronunciation and a knowledge of elite principles and practices sufficient to enable him to adopt them if he desires. It is much the same as if this were a course in home economics pertaining to dress. It would strive to enable each student to formulate his own principles of dress, and it would also make each student aware of what is considered fashionable, as far as dress is concerned, by those in the elite. It covers the latter, not to make the students ashamed of their own dress or to emulate that of the fashionable set, but simply to offer them fashions which they may choose to make their own or avoid, as they desire. Education in matters involving answers to amoral questions of value should strive to foster knowledge without advocacy, and it is with this purpose that the following discussion is presented.

Characteristics of Elite Pronunciations

Cultured speakers seem to adhere to principles of pronunciation far more strongly than others, and these principles seem to be (1) to pronounce words so that their meanings will be least misunderstood, and (2) to be consistent. These principles are stated in this order to imply that such speakers tend to prefer being inconsistent to being misunderstood.

A few examples of elite pronunciations should help to clarify the operation of these principles. Cultured speakers tend to be inconsistent by saying ['ɒfɛns] as the opposite of ['difɛns] but an [ə'fɛns] is a breach of conduct or of law. They tend to say ['ɪmpotənt] to stress negation, ['ɔrdənɛrəlɪ] to stress "order," [dɪu] or [dju] to indicate that the word is "due" or "dew" rather than "do"; to pronounce "err" as [ɝ] to avoid confusing it with "air," "precedents" meaning examples as ['prɛsədənts] and meaning things which preceded as [prə'sidənts]; to indicate syntax by pronouncing, for example, "increase" as ['ɪnkris] when a noun and as [ɪn'kris] when a verb.

However, when no reasonable basis exists for being inconsistent, cultured speakers are exceedingly consistent. For example, they tend to say [pɪ'ænɪst] as well as [pɪ'æno], to pronounce "ph" as [f], not only in initial syllabic positions as in "telephone," "phonetics," and "symphony," but in final syllabic positions as well, as in "naphtha," 'diphtheria," and "diphthong." They tend to say ['ɒfən] and ['sɒfən], "picture ['pɪktʃʊr]" and "put your ['pʊtʃʊr]."

A comprehensive discussion of various manifestations of cultured speakers' adherence to rules is not as useful as a discussion of pronunciations such speakers tend to consider to be mispronunciations. Hence, let us examine various types of such mispronunciations, remembering, of course, that they are mispronunciations only in the sense of being looked upon unfavorably by most cultured speakers.

Common Pronunciation Faults

Several types of pronunciation indicative of nonadherence to the principles of cultured speakers are found in the pronunciations of many persons, and each of these types will now be discussed and illustrated.

1. Strong-Form Errors. Gradation of stress is an important consideration in pronunciation. A strong form of a word is the pronunciation it tends to have when, in a given context, it receives greatest stress, as the pronunciation of "poem" in "It's not a story; it's a *poem.*" A weak form of a word is the pronunciation it tends to have when it is the least stressed word in a given context, as "poem" in "Some poets portray common things uncommonly in their *poems.*"

Our language has strong and weak forms for almost all syntactical words (such as pronouns, prepositions, conjunctions and copulative verbs. For words such as "was," "am," "for," "in," "but," "have," the strong and weak forms are, respectively, [wɑz, wəz; æm, əm *or* m; fɔr, fɚ; ɪn, ən or n̩; bʌt, bət; hæv, həv *or* əv *or* v]). Many of these words have several weak forms depending on context. Thus, "and" has one strong form and four weak forms:

1. [bɪl 'ænd mɛərɪ] (not only Bill but Mary)
2. ['bɪl ənd 'mɛərɪ] (both Bill and Mary)
3. ['bɪl ən 'dɪk] ([dd] assimilated to [d])
4. ['pæt n̩d 'mɛərɪ] (preceding [t] provokes syllabic [n̩])
5. ['pæt n̩ 'dɪk] (combination of (3) and (4))

Strong forms imply something generally recognizable and different from the literal meaning of the word; for example:

Word	Strong Form	Meaning
and	[ænd]	not only the former but the latter
but	[bʌt]	and most importantly
he	[hi]	no one else but he
in	[ɪn]	not out of
is	[ɪz]	indisputably is
or	[ɔr]	but not both
some	[sʌm]	by no means all
was	[wɑz]	but no longer

Gradation of stress also occurs on nonsyntactical words such as nouns, verbs, adjectives and adverbs, in which case the prefixes, suffixes, medial, unstressed vowels, and sometimes the stressed syllables are changed; for example:

Word	Strong Form	Moderate Form	Weak Form
breeches	['brɪtʃɛz]	['brɪtʃɪz]	['brɪtʃəz]
defense	['difɛns]	[dɪ'fɛns]	[də'fɛns]
gradation	[gre'deʃən]		[grə'deʃən]
heeded	['hidɛd]	['hidɪd]	['hidəd]
illusion	[ɪ'lɪuʒən]	[ə'lɪuʒən]	[ə'luʒən]
picture	['pɪktʃʊr]		['pɪktʃɚ]
secretary	['sɛkrətɛrɪ]	['sɛkrətərɪ]	['sɛkrətrɪ]
sophomore	['sɑfomoɚ]	['sɑfəmor]	['sɑfmor]

Some words are pronounced by cultured speakers with only a weak form, but many persons erroneously use a strong form; for example, words ending in an unstressed "y" are pronounced by the elite as [ɪ] rather than [i] unless, of course, such words must be prolonged as in singing. Thus, elite pronunciations are ['prɪtɪ, 'ædmərəblɪ, 'bɪzɪ, sɪn'sɪɚlɪ, 'kævətɪ].

To imply the strong-form meaning of a word when the literal, weak form is intended obviously tends to be distracting and thus reduce comprehension and, in the process, probably introduce confusion. To illustrate this, read the following aloud and see how little communication is effected, due to this one fault of strong-form errors:

[hwɛn ðí 'sʌnlaɪt straɪks 'rendrɑps ɪn ðí 'æɚ, ðe ækt laɪk e 'prɪzm̩ ænd fɔrm e 'renbo. ðí renbo ɪz e dɪ'vɪʒən ɑv 'hwaɪt 'laɪt ɪntu mɛni 'bjutɪfʊl 'kʌlɚz. ðiz tek ðí ʃep ɑv e 'lɒŋ 'raʊnd 'ɑrtʃ, wɪð ɪts paθ haɪ e'bʌv, ænd ɪts tu ɛndz e'pæərəntli bi'jɑnd ðí ho'raɪzn̩].

W. Cabell, Greet, in the introduction to *Macmillan's Modern Dictionary*,[4] places the blame for this fault on poor English teachers who encourage their students to speak "less slovenly" or "more precisely." Even if they are not the ones solely at fault, at least it can be said that such speech is due to criticism by someone—parents or well-meaning friends.

[4] *Macmillan's Modern Dictionary*, The Macmillan Co. (New York), 1939.

To determine the extent to which you are prone to make strong-form errors, record yourself saying the following sentences so that the italicized word is the most-important-word in each sentence, and then compare your pronunciation of the words in parentheses with the proper ones—determined *after* recording.

1. (Does) he know (the) *answer?*
2. (He) *told* (them) what (would) happen.
3. (*Sally*) went (into) (her) house.
4. He paid (me) what (he) *owed.*
5. It's neither *white* (nor) *black.*
6. That (one) (is) *correct.*
7. The history (is) (a) *long* (one).
8. (We) came (upon) (them) (in) the *woods.*
9. (What) *time* is it?
10. (You) see it *now.*

If you made more than five strong-form errors in the above exercise, this can be considered one of your principal pronunciation faults. Perhaps such errors are due to your reading word by word rather than reading many words ahead of the words you are saying. Obviously, then, remedial reading exercises should prove beneficial, not only in improving your reading rate and comprehension but in improving your pronunciation as well. However, if you find that you make strong-form errors in your daily conversation because you have been convinced that such pronunciations are desirable and that weak forms are but manifestations of slurred, slovenly, or imprecise speech, you must first be convinced that your strong forms exaggerate the importance of those words and thus distract your listener's attention from words that you consider to be more important. Then, rather than try to unstress words you unintentionally stress, you should work to achieve more vocal delineation of your important words. That is, use more prolongation of continuants on important words and go from one important word to the next important word more rapidly. Strive to read by the "hurry up and hold" method, practicing on each successive reading to hurry more to the important words and to hold each longer. Check the relative duration of important and unimportant words from time to time.

2. Nonblending. Blending refers to a word which, when uttered in isolation, begins with a vowel but, when uttered in context, is initiated with the final consonant or consonantal combination borrowed from the preceding word, e.g., "Well, I" [wɛ laɪ], "said it" [sɛ dɪt], "Education occurs in each of us" [ɛdʒʊkeʃə nəkɝ zɪ 'nitʃəvəs]. A line from a song that was popular a few years ago, "Mairzy totes and dozy totes," clearly exemplified blending (Mares eat oats and does eat oats). Blending should not occur if the word beginning with a vowel is extremely important, or if a separational pause is needed, or another type of pause is indicated:

1. "She doubts it, but I believe it [bət 'aɪ]." (*emphasis*)
2. "He used some ice in the experiment (səm 'aɪs]." (*separational pause*)
3. "The heat produced, of all things, ice (θɪŋz 'aɪs]." (*parenthetical and anticipatory pause*).

Nonblending, like strong-form errors, is probably the result of someone's well-intentioned but ignorant criticism. The remark is usually "Don't slur your words" or "Pronounce your words more clearly." However, such comments fail to consider that speech is not understood word by word but in thought groups, and the avoidance of blending provokes a loss of intelligibility in much the same way that strong-form errors reduce intelligibility—by calling attention to words rather than to their meanings by the precision with which they are uttered.

Check your ability to blend by reading the following sentences aloud, preferably recording them, and then check your blends with those given on page 281.

1. Myrrh is an aromatic resin.
2. I know it is, but I believe it's otherwise.
3. His automobile is rather old.
4. Some of it is under a large awning.
5. They said it rained eleven inches in April.

3. Nonpalatalization. Palatalization refers to a change in pronunciation, when [jʊ] is preceded by [d] or [t], from [djʊ] or [dɪʊ] to a lightly stressed [dʒʊ], and from [tjʊ] or [tɪʊ] to a lightly stressed [tʃʊ], as in ['ɛdʒʊket, 'pɪktʃʊr, aɪ 'nidʒʊ, aɪ 'wɒntʃʊ, 'kʊdʒʊ, 'wʊdʒʊ, 'pʊtʃʊr]. Nonpalatalization refers to a lack of change in such situations, as in ['ɛdjʊket, 'pɪktjʊr, aɪ 'nidjʊ, aɪ wɒnt jʊ], and is again attributable to someone's bad criticism of another's speech. Such criticism is especially thoughtless in the case of nonpalatalization, since the person who consciously strives to be precise in saying ['ɛdjʊket, 'grædjʊet, 'wont jʊ], probably violates his own principle to say ['pɪktʃʊr, 'fɪkstʃʊr] and the like. Not only is palatalization permissible but, especially on individual words, nonpalatalization tends to sound affected. Notice that palatalization should not occur if the pronunciation involves [ju] or [ɪu] rather than [jʊ] or [ɪʊ]. Thus, say [wʊd 'ju] rather than [wʊ 'dʒu] if the strong form of "you" is intended. See if you can locate every instance in which palatalization should occur in the following examples, again using a recorder if possible. Indicate where you palatalized by a ligature (‿). Check your answers on page 281.

1. Naturally he paid his dues.
2. I'll meet you at your mother's house.
3. Could United Nations soldiers have been used?
4. He says that your posture is poor.
5. I met you there, but I didn't see anyone else.

4. Spelling Ignorance. Many persons pronounce words the way they spell them when their spelling is incorrect. Check your tendency to do this by underlining each nonelite pronunciation below. In referring to the elite pronunciations on page 281, check in the dictionary the spelling of any word you missed.

1. It is the [haɪtθ] of ridiculousness.
2. He put the letter in the [ɛn'vɛləp].
3. That was a [sækrə'lɪdʒəs] thing to do.
4. He was [ɛkstrə'ɔrdənɛrəlɪ] successful in curing [dɪp'θɪərɪə].
5. ['nukjʊlɚ] physics is a subject of [prɪ'mɪɚ] importance to him.
6. His [æθ'lɛtɪk] ability is known to all.
7. He is studying [ɑpθə'mɑlədʒɪ] in the ['æmfɪθɪətɚ].
8. He wanted a record of his family's [dʒinɪ'ɑlədʒɪ].
9. His [pronaʊnsɪ'eʃən] of ['pɑrləmənt] was ['grivɪəs].
10. The instruments in the ['dɪrdʒəbl̩] were cleaned with ['næpθə].

11. He raises [pɔɪn'sɛtəz].
12. She sells [læŋʒə're].
13. The coffee contains no ['kæfɪn].
14. What a ['bistʃəl] act!
15. The [mjʊ'nɪnsəpl̩] authorities are responsible for the [men'tenəns] of the streets.

5. Spelling Slavishness. When we learn words by encountering them in print without hearing them pronounced, and when we tend to use those words orally without checking their pronunciations, we tend to mispronounce, owing to what could be called spelling slavishness. However, an even larger groups of words heard by all of us almost daily are never listened to carefully and we fail to realize that others are not pronouncing them as they are spelled. The following are common words on which cultured speakers and many persons differ in pronunciation. See how many you pronounce as indicated. Check the elite pronunciations on pages 281–282.

Mispronunciations

1. almond	['ɑlmənd]	13. Monday	['mʌnde]
2. archangel	['ɑrtʃendʒəl]	14. often	['ɒftən]
3. au gratin	[ɔ 'grɑtn̩]	15. palm	[pɑlm]
4. breeches	['britʃɪz]	16. quay	[kwe]
5. brooch	[brutʃ]	17. reptile	['rɛptaɪl]
6. connoisseur	[kɑnə'suɚ]	18. schism	['ʃɪzm̩]
7. draught	[drɔt]	19. table d'hôte	[tebl de 'hot]
8. fiancé	['fɪɑns]	20. vehicle	['vihɪkl̩]
9. foyer	['fɔɪjɚ]	21. versatile	['vɝsətaɪl]
10. hiccough	['hɪkɒf]	22. vice versa	['vaɪs 'vɝsə]
11. lichen	['lɪtʃɪn]	23. Worcestershire	['wʊstɚʃaɪr]
12. maraschino	[mærə'ʃino]	24. worsted	['wɝstɪd]
		25. yesterday	['jɛstɚde]

6. Meaning Ignorance. Obviously, many words used by cultured speakers and writers are unknown to the majority. However, many words are used by both cultured speakers and the majority which have different meanings for the two groups, and these differences in meaning are frequently indicated by dif-

Elite and Majority Differences in Pronunciation and Meaning of Ten Frequently Used Words

	Elite Pronunciation	Elite Definition	Majority Pronunciation	Majority Definition
abdomen	[æb'domɪn]	intestinal area	['æbdəmɪn]	stomach or waist
au gratin	[ogrə'tæ̃]	with browned crumbs	[ɔ 'grɑtn̩]	with grilled cheese
chaise longue	[ʃez 'lɔ̃ŋ]	long chair	['tʃez laʊndʒ]	lounging chair
connoisseur	[kɑnə'sɝ]	has keen discrimination	[kɑnə'suɚ]	has great fondness
discharged	[dɪs'tʃɑrdʒd]	relieved of charge	['dɪstʃɑrdʒd]	got out of something
exponent	[ɛk'sponənt]	clearly representative	['ɛksponənt]	most representative
ordinarily	['ɔrdənɛrəlɪ]	customarily	[ɔrdə'nɛrəlɪ]	usually
primarily	['praɪmərəlɪ]	of first consideration	[praɪ'mɛrəlɪ]	of main consideration
sacrilegious	[sækrə'lidʒəs]	maltreatment of sacred objects	[sækrə'lɪdʒəs]	not very religious
short-lived	['ʃɔrt 'laɪvd]	has a short life	['ʃɔrt 'lɪvd]	lives briefly

ferences in pronunciation. Consult the list on page 271 to see which definitions, elite or majority, you would generally subscribe to.

7. Meaningless Stress. Generally, as stated previously, elite pronunciations tend to stress the root or key syllables of words. This practice is obviously not without exceptions, but the pronunciations of the elite and the majority frequently differ because of this practice. Below is a list of words accented differently by many in the two groups, with the meaning of the most important syllable indicated. The principal exception to this practice is the elite stressing of the first syllable of most four-syllable words ending in "-able" regardless of location of the most important syllable, e.g., ['ædmərəbl̩, 'kɑmpərəbl̩, 'dɛspɪkəbl̩, 'fætəgəbl̩, 'læməntəbl̩, 'rɛvəkəbl̩].

	Elite	Stressed Syllable's Meaning	Majority
acclimate	[ə'klaɪmɪt]	climate	['ækləmet]
aspirant	[ə'spaɪrənt]	aspire	['æspərənt]
cigarette	[sɪgə'rɛt]	little	['sɪgərɛt]
combatant	['kɑmbətənt]	combat (*noun*)	[kəm'bætənt]
contrary	['kɑntrɛrɪ]	contra	[kən'trɛrɪ]
discourse	[dɪs'kors]	course	['dɪskors]
domain	[do'men]	dominion	['domen]
harass	['hærəs]	harry	[hə'ræs]
hospitable	['hɑspɪtəbl̩]	hospital (*homelike*)	[hɑ'spɪtəbl̩]
impotent	['ɪmpotənt]	not	[ɪm'potənt]
inquiry	[ɪn'kwaɪrɪ]	query	['ɪnkwɪrɪ]
insurance	[ɪn'ʃurəns]	surety	['ɪnʃurəns]
mezzanine	['mɛzənin]	mess- (*middle*)	[mɛzə'nin]
mischievous	['mɪstʃəvəs]	mischief	[mɪs'tʃivɪəs]
ordinarily	['ɔrdənɛrəlɪ]	order	[ɔrdə'nɛrəlɪ]
pianist	[pɪ'ænɪst]	piano	['piənɪst]
pretense	[prɪ'tɛns]	pretend	['pritɛns]
recess (indentation)	[rɪ'sɛs]	recede	['risɛs]
resource	[rɪ'sors]	source	['risors]
traverse	['trævɚs]	travel	[trə'vɝs]

8. Nondifferentiation of Homographs. As mentioned previously, cultured speakers do not tend to be consistent on words which are spelled identically or quite similarly and have different meanings and, if they were pronounced alike, would tend to provoke confusion. Thus, to avoid confusion, such speakers alter the pronunciation of one of them. We are all familiar with this process to indicate part of speech: 'record, re'cord; 'escort, es'cort; 'insult, in'sult; but many such groups of words are not so familiar. Consider the following:

1a. absent (*adj.*)	['æbsənt]
b. absent (*vb.*)	[əb'sɛnt]
2a. annex (*n.*)	['ænɛks]
b. annex (*vb.*)	[ə'nɛks]
3a. August (*n.*)	['ɔgəst]
b. august (*adj.*)	[ɔ'gʌst]
4a. cleanly (*adj.*)	['klɛnlɪ]
b. cleanly (*adv.*)	['klinlɪ]
5a. concert (*n.*)	['kɑnsɝt]
b. concert (*vb.*)	[kən'sɝt]
6a. concrete (*n., adj.*)	['kɑnkrit]
b. concrete (*vb.*)	[kɑn'krit]
7a. consummate (*adj.*)	[kən'sʌmɪt]
b. consummate (*vb.*)	['kɑnsəmet]
8a. excess (*n.*)	['ɛksɛs]
b. excess (*adj.*)	[ɪk'sɛs]
9a. export (*n.*)	['ɛksport]
b. export (*vb.*)	[ɛks'port]
10a. frequent (*adj.*)	['frikwənt]
b. frequent (*vb.*)	[frɪ'kwɛnt]
11a. incense (*n.*)	['ɪnsɛns]
b. incense (*vb.*)	[ɪn'sɛns]
12a. lower (*to let down*)	['loɚ]
b. lower (*to frown*)	['laʊɚ]
13a. mobile (*adj.*)	['mobɪl]
b. mobile (*n.*)	['mobil]
14a. notable (*worthy of note*)	['notəbl̩]
b. notable (*efficient in housekeeping*)	['nɑtəbl̩]

15a.	precedent (*n.*)	['prɛsədənt]
b.	precedent (*adj.*)	[prɪ'sidənt]
16a.	prefix (*n.*)	['prifɪks]
b.	prefix (*vb.*)	[prɪ'fɪks]
17a.	premiere (*n.*)	[prɪ'mɪɚ]
b.	premier (*adj.*)	['primɪɚ]
18a.	presage (*n.*)	['prɛsɪdʒ]
b.	presage (*vb.*)	[prɪ'sedʒ]
19a.	produce (*n.*)	['prɑdɪus]
b.	produce (*vb.*)	[pro'dɪus]
20a.	recede (*to move back*)	[rɪ'sid]
b.	re-cede (*to cede back*)	[ri'sid]
21a.	résumé (*n.*)	[rezɪʊ'me]
b.	resume (*vb.*)	[rɪ'zɪum]
22a.	slough (*a castoff; to cast off*)	[slʌf]
b.	slough (*a swamp*)	[slu]
c.	slough (*moral degradation*)	[slaʊ]
23a.	subject (*n.*)	['sʌbdʒɪkt]
b.	subject (*vb.*)	[səb'dʒɛkt]
24a.	suspect (*n.*)	['sʌspɛkt]
b.	suspect (*vb.*)	[sə'spɛkt]
25a.	urban (*metropolitan*)	['ɝbən]
b.	urbane (*courteous*)	[ɝ'ben]

9. Differentiation of Homonyms. Words which are spelled differently but pronounced alike are termed homonyms, but many persons try to indicate spelling differences in their pronunciations of words that cultured speakers consider to be homonyms. See to what extent you pronounce the following such homonyms differently.

1. addition—edition
2. affect—effect
3. bad—bade
4. coarse—course
5. comptroller—controller
6. counsel—council
7. draught—draft
8. fiancé—fiancée
9. peek—pique
10. rheum—room

10. Nondifferentiation of Phonetic Nuances. Some phonetic distinctions are so fine that many persons fail to perceive them in the pronounciations of others and, consequently, fail to make such distinctions themselves. One such distinction is the difference between a final [z] and a final [dz] and, similarly, between a final [s] and a final [ts], pronouncing "bans" and "bands" or "guess" and "guests" alike, for example. To make such distinctions, pronounce the final [dz] or [ts] as a separate syllable, as by saying [gɛs] and then [ts] rather than [gɛs:]. Another difference is that between [hw] and [w]. Here the distinction can be effected by blowing to produce [h] prior to vocalizing [w]. See how well your can make the following distinctions:

1. Bess—bests
2. chance—chants
3. dense—dents
4. lass—lasts
5. mince—mints
6. mines—minds
7. miss—mists
8. pace—pastes
9. patience—patients
10. prince—prints
11. sense—cents
12. sex—sects
13. tense—tents
14. truss—trusts
15. weather—whether
16. wen—when
17. wile—while
18. wines—winds (*vb.*)
19. witch—which
20. y—why

11. Spelling Inconsistencies. Good speakers tend to pronounce certain letter combinations consistently, deviating from the practice usually intentionally to serve some other purpose. Knowing these consistencies should help to improve your own pronunciations of words involving these letter combinations. Some of these consistent patterns of pronunciation are the following:

a. Pronounce "ph" as [f]:

1. amphitheatre
2. diphase
3. diphtheria
4. diphthong
5. naphtha
6. ophthalmic
7. phaeton
8. phalanx
9. phlegm
10. sylph

b. Pronounce the vowel before an undoubled consonant which is followed by final "e" as a long vowel (unless the word is extremely common like "come" and "some"):

1. calcimine
2. demise
3. eglantine
4. gnome
5. leonine
6. liege
7. loathe
8. scythe
9. sinecure
10. withe

Some exceptions to this are: "carmine," "comely," "margarine" and "saccharine."

c. Pronounce silent letters when suffixes are added:

1. condemn—condemnation
2. column—columnar
3. damn—damnable
4. phlegm—phlegmatic
5. solemn—solemnity

An exception to this is in "lm" since the "l" should never be pronounced if the "l" is preceded by "a"; for example, the "l" is sounded in "film" but not in "almond," "palm," "psalm," "salmon," "qualms," etc.

d. Pronounce "ile" as [ɪl] unless it means "like a," as it does in "infantile" (like an infant), "servile" (like a servant), etc. Two exceptions to this are "juvenile" ['dʒuvənɪl] and "tactile" ['tæktɪl]. Thus, the following words should all be pronounced with [ɪl]:

1. agile
2. docile
3. domicile
4. fertile
5. hostile
6. mobile
7. puerile
8. reptile
9. versatile
10. virile

12. Contextual Influences: Assimilation, Dissimilation, Metathesis, Syncope, and Haplology. We are familiar with tongue-twisters which combine words we can easily pronounce in isolation but which, in a particular context, tend to provoke some phonetic distortion. For some persons this same difficulty is experienced in individual words as well as in context, and such difficulties may be characterized as certain types. One such type is *assimilation*, which is the effect of one sound or sound group on an adjacent, different sound or sound group which causes an alteration in one of them toward greater conformity with the other, as in ['guzbɛrɪ] for ['gusbɛrɪ], ['pʌŋkɪn] for ['pʌmpkɪn], [hɪz] for [hɪ ɪz], [stə'stɪstɪks] for [stə'tɪstɪks], ['ɪŋkʌm] for ['ɪnkʌm], ['jus tʊ] for ['juzd tʊ], [əb'sɔrbʃən] for [əb'sɔrpʃən]. *Dissimilation* is the influence of two identical, nonadjacent sounds on each other which results in changing or omitting one of them, as in ['ɑrtɪk] for ['ɑrktɪk], [klaɪ'mætɪk] for [klaɪ'mæktɪk], ['fɛbjʊɛrɪ] for ['fɛbrʊɛrɪ], ['gʌvɚmənt] for ['gʌvɚnmənt], [pə'tɪkjəlɚ] for [pɚ'tɪkjəlɚ], [θə'mɑmətɚ] for [θɚ'mɑmətɚ], [sə'praɪz] for [sɚ'praɪz]. *Metathesis* is an influence of one adjacent sound on another which produces a reversal in their order, as occurs in [prɛspə'reʃən], ['hʌnɚd], ['lærnɪks], ['æstərɪks], ['mɑdrən], pɚ'zɪum], ['kælvərɪ] (for ['kævəlrɪ]), ['ægɚvet]. *Syncope* refers to an omission of medial vowels, usually syllabic vowels, e.g., ['juʒəl], ['mjutʃəl], ['kæʒəl], [bliv], [blɔŋ], [spoz], [plis], ['daɪmənd], ['mɪnətʃɚ], ['prɑblɪ], ['tʃɑklɪt], [pom]. *Haplology* is a contraction by omission of initial syllables, e.g., 'scape, 'leven, 'bout, 'cause, 'range, 'pinion, 'magine.

Obviously, all such contextual influences should be resisted to the extent that the resultant speech is noticed by others as being lazy, slovenly, or careless. Record yourself or have some-one listen to you as you read the following paragraph to determine to what extent you are susceptible to mispronunciations because of contextual influences.

About eleven years ago I used to read about a diamond thief who casually made off with about a hundred diamonds worth several thousand dollars. The police supposed that he would try to sell them and, based on this presumption, they contacted every known "fence." As a result, he was surprised in the act of disposing of the diamonds, and he just got his parole last February. According to statistics crime doesn't pay, and this particular criminal probably wishes he had derived his income from a profession which is more governmentally approved.

Mispronunciation of Uncommon Words

Obviously, when you encounter any unfamiliar word in your reading, you should consult a dictionary. The following hundred words, however, occur in college textbooks and in literature with enough frequency that you might benefit from familiarizing yourself with their elite pronunciations. Study a few words at a time, practice pronouncing them aloud, and try to use them in your writings. We all realize that, by studying the spelling or pronunciation of new words, we may unintentionally but indubitably increase our vocabularies, and this may prove to be a bonus resulting from the study of the pronunciation of such words as below. Notice that the transcriptions provided employ a moderate degree of stress, for example the gradation of stress on the first word would be, from strongest to weakest, [ə'kjumɛn, ə'kjumɪn, ə'kjumən]. However, when medial vowels are not schwa in the strongest form of the pronunciation, they are retained in the transcriptions below, e.g., the [o] in numbers 19, 27, and 32, although these medial vowels may be reduced to schwa even in the moderately stressed form of such words.

1. acumen [ə'kjumɪn]
2. aggrandize ['ægrəndaɪz]
3. ague ['egju]
4. allusion [ə'lɪuʒən]
5. apotheosis [əpɑθɪ'osɪs]
6. appellate [ə'pɛlɪt]
7. banal ['benəl]
8. Buddhism ['bʊdɪzm̩]
9. buoy ['buɪ]
10. cache [kæʃ]
11. caffeine ['kæfɪɪn]
12. cello ['tʃɛlo]
13. carillon ['kærɪlən]
14. chimera [kaɪ'mɪərə]
15. cognomen [kɑg'nomɪn]
16. condign [kən'daɪn]
17. contumely ['kɑntjʊmilɪ]
18. coupon ['kupɑn]
19. cupola ['kjupolə]
20. dais ['deɪs]
21. debutante [dɛbjʊ'tɑnt]
22. demoniacal [dimə'naɪəkl]
23. denouement [de'numɑ̃]
24. despicable ['dɛspɪkəbl̩]
25. desuetude ['dɛswɪtɪud]

26. desultory ['dɛsəltorɪ]
27. diastole [daɪ'æstoli]
28. dishabille [dɪsə'bil]
29. dolorous ['dɑlərəs]
30. elephantine [ɛlə'fæntɪn]
31. ensemble [ɑn'sɑmbḷ]
32. epitome [ɪ'pɪtomɪ]
33. exigencies ['ɛksədʒənsɪz]
34. exude [ɛks'jud]
35. fiat ['faɪæt]
36. flaccid ['flæksɪd]
37. franchise ['fræntʃaɪz]
38. granary ['grænərɪ]
39. grimace [grɪ'mes]
40. gubernatorial [gjubɚnə'torɪəl]
41. gynecology [dʒɪnɪ'kɑlədʒɪ]
42. halfpenny ['hepənɪ]
43. hecatomb ['hɛkətɑm]
44. hegira [hɪ'dʒaɪrə]
45. heinous ['henəs]
46. hymeneal [haɪmə'niəl]
47. ignominy ['ɪgnomɪnɪ]
48. implacable [ɪm'plekəbḷ]
49. indecorous [ɪn'dɛkorəs]
50. inveigle [ɪn'vigḷ]
51. irascible [aɪ'ræsəbḷ]
52. irrefragable [ɪ'rɛfrəgəbḷ]
53. Islam ['ɪsləm]
54. jugular ['dʒʌgjʊlɚ]
55. julienne [dʒulɪ'ɛn]
56. labyrinthine [læbə'rɪnθɪn]
57. landau ['lændɔ]
58. lingerie [lɑ̃ʒə'ri]
59. maraschino [mærə'skino]
60. mezzanine ['mɛzənin]
61. minuscule [mɪ'nʌskjul]
62. misanthrope ['mɪsənθrop]
63. miscreant ['mɪskrɪənt]

64. mnemonic [nɪ'mɑnɪk]
65. nauseous ['nɔʃəs]
66. nirvana [nɪr'vɑnə]
67. obeisance [o'besəns]
68. obligatory [ə'blɪgətorɪ]
69. ouzel ['uzḷ]
70. pedagogic [pɛdə'gɑdʒɪk]
71. pekoe ['piko]
72. penchant [pɑ̃'ʃɑ̃]
73. plethora ['plɛθorə]
74. posthumous ['pɑstʃʊməs]
75. potpourri [popu'ri]
76. probity ['prɑbətɪ]
77. pseudonym ['sjudonɪm]
78. puissance ['pjuɪsəns]
79. querulous ['kwɛrjʊləs]
80. rabies ['rebɪiz]
81. regimen ['rɛdʒəmɪn]
82. repartee [rɛpɚ'ti]
83. repertoire ['rɛpɚtwɑr]
84. requiem ['rikwɪəm]
85. reservoir ['rɛzɚvwɔr]
86. sauté [so'te]
87. savant [sə'vɑ̃]
88. sinecure ['saɪnəkjur]
89. solace ['sɑlɪs]
90. subterfuge ['sʌbtɚfjudʒ]
91. sumac ['ʃumæk]
92. tableau ['tæblo]
93. tarpaulin [tɑr'pɔlɪn]
94. toucan [tʊ'kɑn]
95. vagary [və'gɛərɪ]
96. Veda ['vedə]
97. vehement ['viəmənt]
98. vignette [vɪn'jɛt]
99. virago [vɪ'rego]
100. Worcestershire ['wʊstɚʃɪr]

Permissible Blendings (Page 268)

1. ['mɜ rɪ zə næromætɪk 'rɛzɪn].
2. [aɪ 'no ɪ tɪz, bə taɪ bəli vɪ 'tsʌðɚwaɪz].
3. [hɪ 'zɔtomobi lɪz ræðə 'rold].
4. [sʌ mə vɪ tɪ zʌndə rə lɑr 'dʒɔnɪŋ].
5. [ðe sɛ dɪt ren də'lɛvə 'nɪntʃɪ zɪ 'neprəl].

Permissible Palatalizations (Page 269)

1. Naturally he paid his dues.
2. I'll meet you at your mother's house.
3. Could United Nations soldiers have been used?
4. He says that your posture is poor.
5. I met you there, but I didn't see anyone else.

Elite Pronunciations (Pages 269–270)

1. [haɪt]
2. ['ɛnvəlop]
3. [sækrə'lidʒəs]
4. [ɛk'strɔrdənɛrəlɪ], [dɪf'θɪərɪə]
5. ['nɪuklɪɚ], ['primɪɚ]
7. [ɑfθæl'mɑlədʒɪ]
8. [dʒɛnɪ'ælədʒɪ]
9. [pronʌnsɪ'eʃən], ['grivəs]
10. ['dɪrɪdʒəbl̩], ['næfθə]
11. [pɔɪn'sɛtɪəz]
12. [læ̃ʒə'ri]
13. ['kæfɪɪn]
14. ['bɛstʃəl]
15. [mjʊ'nɪsəpl̩], ['mentənəns]

Elite Pronunciation of Words on Page 270

1. ['ɑmənd]
2. ['ɑrkendʒəl]
3. [ogrə'tæ̃]
4. ['brɪtʃɪz]
5. [brotʃ]
6. [kɑnə'sɝ]

7. [draft]
8. [frɑn'se]
9. ['fɔɪe]
10. ['hɪkʌp]
11. ['laɪkən]
12. [mærə'skino]
13. ['mʌndɪ]
14. ['ɒfən]
15. [pɑm]
16. [ki]
17. ['rɛptɪl]
18. ['sɪzm̩]
19. [tablə'dot]
20. ['viəkl̩]
21. ['vɝsətɪl]
22. ['vaɪsə 'vɝsə]
23. ['wʊstɚʃɪr]
24. ['wʊstɪd]
25. ['jɛstɚdɪ]

10

Diction

The term *diction* is used by persons in the field of speech to refer either to all factors of delivery other than voice (such as pitch, loudness, and pronunciation) or to word usage. The latter definition is intended here. Specifically it refers to the quality of words employed in either oral or written communication, but for our purposes its scope will be restricted only to oral communication.

It might be thought that a chapter on diction has no rightful place in a text on delivery, but it was stated at the outset that by delivery was meant how one talks, not what one says. Delivery refers, then, to all those characteristics of a speaker not specifically related to any single act of speaking: to those speech characteristics which are present in every act of speaking. Diction is one such omnipresent characteristic. One tends to have a certain general ability to use words, no matter what the communicative situation, rather than good diction in one subject and poor diction in another. By extension we might add a chapter on reasoning, but that matter is treated at length in speech texts which are content oriented, and for that reason only it will not be covered here.

The first question that should be raised in discussing diction is the relation between diction (word usage) and vocabulary (word knowledge). Before we can discuss this relationship, however, we must define vocabulary more precisely.

One can mean one or more of many things by saying that a person knows *x* number of words. Consider the various types of tests which are administered. One test requests a student to check those words on a list with which he is familiar, another asks him to select the word that is a synonym for the given word, another requires him to indicate which word completes a sentence, etc. Examine some typical vocabulary items below:

Check the words with which you have some familiarity:
comely
clandestine
descried
spontaneity
querulous
germane

Identify the synonym:
comely 1. ugly 2. delicate 3. beautiful 4. weak
descried 1. described 2. decided 3. discerned 4. derided
querulous 1. argumentative 2. Germanic 3. pertinent 4. haughty
germane 1. noisy 2. German 3. pertinent 4. strong

Identify the antonym (word which means the opposite):
comely 1. ugly 2. delicate 3. strong 4. recent
descried 1. denied 2. overlooked 3. delayed 4. occurred
querulous 1. positive 2. noisy 3. sweet 4. agreeable
germane 1. unopposed 2. unnoticed 3. British 4. unrelated

Complete the sentence:

A girl may have to use a lot of make-up before she can be considered to be ______.
1. comely 2. acrimonious 3. effusive 4. parsimonious

He ______ the error in the bank statement.
1. exorcised 2. descried 3. ingratiated 4. laminated

His ______ manner earned him no friends.
1. specious 2. salubrious 3. querulous 4. lissome

The point he wanted to make was ______.
1. meretricious 2. nascent 3. prehensile 4. germane

We might even develop another type of test which asks the

testee to indicate which words are meaningful rather than nonsensical:

oxypodal	anctimonious
comely	querulous
mien	adjugate
descried	germane

Certain characteristics of these various kinds of tests can be observed. First, if the tests are to reveal various levels of ability, the words must be, to say the least, rather uncommon. Second, students encounter such words more often in writing than in speech, and in reading the writings of others than in their own writings. Third, a dictionary would enable one to answer any item correctly, or to indicate truthfully that one is familiar with the word, or to recognize that it is meaningful. Fourth, because one can answer an item in one form of a vocabulary test is no assurance that he can answer an item regarding that same word in every form in which it can be presented. However, each form seems to require a different degree of familiarity, so that we might guess that the degree of familiarity required, from least to most, might be: (1) check familiarity, (2) recognize meaningfulness, (3) identify synonym, (4) identify antonym, and (5) complete the sentence.

However, suppose we want to measure the diction of a person. If we examine his speaking or his writing, we would do so only under conditions in which no aids such as dictionaries were employed, for that would contaminate our measurement just as it would if we administered a vocabulary test and let him use a dictionary. Moreover, our judgment of his diction would not be based on the frequency with which he employed such uncommon words as would appear on vocabulary tests, for these would not occur often enough to permit our distinguishing between his ability and the ability of others. We are left with only one basis for judging: how *precisely* he uses the words he uses. Such characteristics as vagueness, faulty grammar, circumlocutions, and trite usages are indexes, then, of the extent of this precision.

Precision in word usage is not as dependent upon word familiarity as is vocabulary but is very dependent upon *familiarity with alternative words.* For example, on all of our vocabulary tests regarding the word *comely* we were striving to determine whether or not the testee knew what that word *generally* means. One dictionary defines it as "pleasing or agreeable to the sight." Knowing this definition or being able to define it in these or similar words would insure his giving the correct response regardless of vocabulary test format. Now, however, he would seldom say or write the word *comely*, but he would be prone to use its synonyms, e.g., pretty, attractive, pleasing, handsome, beautiful, lovely, good-looking, etc. Which of these he used in a given context might afford us some idea of his diction. He might say:

1. He is very pretty.
2. That was a lovely idea.
3. She's kind of beautiful.
4. He's sort of almost nearly good-looking.
5. I think that picture's just about the most. I mean it's too, too. It does something to me.

Or he might say:

1. It was a pretty but simple ring.
2. He had a pleasing manner.
3. His gift was lovely.
4. I think he has a handsome face.
5. He seemed more attractive when he smiled.

Obviously, the latter expressions are indicative of better diction. They show more concern for selecting the precise word from among less precise synonyms.

The ability to discriminate among synonyms, in fact, is an excellent predictor of diction, at least as good as the best vocabulary tests yet devised. Moreover, diction is probably closely related to grammar, since a person who is careful in his selection of words for meaning would probably be careful in arranging his selected words meaningfully.

The question then becomes: Can diction be improved? The answer would seem to be a qualified "Yes," provided words are studied in such a way that precision in word usage is fostered. Word study per se may tend to improve vocabulary, but an obviously better way to improve vocabulary is to learn the habit of using a dictionary when unfamiliar words are encountered in reading and listening, and to devote a considerable amount of time to reading and listening to those types of communication which occasionally present unfamiliar words. One cannot eke out much vocabulary improvement by reading comic books and by listening to soap operas. Of course, one develops a good vocabulary by being reared among great minds who discuss important things. Since very few of us are this fortunate, the next best procedure is to read the important works of great men. But few of us, unfortunately, are sufficiently motivated to do this once we have escaped the reading required in the process of formal education. The next best procedure is to study words in such a way that we learn how they function and how to discriminate among synonymous words. The remainder of this chapter attempts to provide this information.

The Relation of Words to Things

We say that words *stand for* or *represent* objects, actions, and the like. Just what do we mean? Obviously, we all have different sensory abilities, and no two persons ever have exactly the same experiences. It is not surprising, then, to conclude that no two persons have *exactly* the same mental concept of any word when we realize that we are born with no concepts at all and acquire language as a result of our experiences, no two of which are identical and none of which is identical to another's.

However, and probably more importantly, our experiences are received through our senses, which react to stimuli both within and outside our bodies; and, if there is one thing we may be sure of, it is that what we sense and what is actually there are quite different things. When we say something is pink, we tend not to realize that this is merely an opinion. After some thought we might say that the concept *pink* is a label referring to certain wavelengths of light. But does light *really* consist of waves? That is an utterly unanswerable question. More importantly, it is a useless question. We can never know what something is really. We can only define it (make inferences about it) on the basis of our observations, and our definitions (inferences) are sound only to the extent that they satisfy our goals.

Goals and Postulates

Before one defines he must have goals, and which goals one chooses determines the postulates he accepts and the kind of defining required. We in the modern Western world desire knowledge of our environment as a goal, and we measure this knowledge by our ability to control phenomena rather than to have them control us. However, other peoples have different goals. Some have serenity as their goal. Postulates are assumptions which must be made before any inferences are formed about our observations. Two such postulates of our society are that reality exists and the simplest explanation is the best. However, if our goal were serenity, we might prefer the postulates that reality is a figment of our minds and the most intellectually stimulating explanation is the best. To achieve *our* goals, then, a good definition must be simple, reliable, comprehensive, and fruitful. Let us examine each of these requirements separately.

Criteria for Definitions

A good definition is simple. This means that it explains phenomena or classifies objects in the fewest terms. Thus, we could say that the earth is the center of our solar system, but that would require highly complex formulae to describe the orbits of other planets compared with those required if the sun is assumed to be the center of our solar system. Because of simplicity, we define the sun as being at the center. However, that definition is based on the postulate that the simplest definition is the best. It may not be what God had in mind for we can never know if He prefers simple solutions. But we must formulate some postulates to enable us to come to some decision when we are confronted with several theories equally capable of explaining observations. If we then happen to believe that reality is as we define it, we are overlooking the fact that we had to accept some postulates as acts of faith. Before we can manipulate reality we must define it, and before we can define it we must accept some postulates about it. Our postulates may well be wrong, but we should protest this charge by saying that, if we keep getting the right results for the wrong reasons, who cares?

A good definition is comprehensive in that it explains more phenomena or embraces more objects than any other definition. The inability to explain certain *types* of phenomena indicates a definitional weakness. Usually progress suffers when a definition is insufficiently broad. At present our having to define light under certain conditions as being electrodynamic (waves) and under other conditions as being quanta (bundles of energy) indicates a sore need for one definition of light to apply to all conditions.

A good definition is not only simple and comprehensive but reliable. This means that someone could use our definition to classify objects or events and would place them almost invariably in the same categories as we would place them. Obviously he would not have trouble with most of the objects or events he had to classify, only with borderline cases. Hence, to be reliable a good definition must specify as clearly as possible the limits as well as the general area of applicability. On this basis we could say that all matter is solid, liquid, or gaseous, and we must specify when a solid becomes viscous enough to call it a liquid and when a liquid becomes rarefied enough to call it a gas. But a good definition must also be fruitful. That is, we can, on the basis of our definition, manipulate our environment to obtain new things. The history of science is in an important sense merely the history of changing definitions. Not too many years ago, matter was defined as consisting of earth, air, fire, and water. More recently, matter was defined as consisting of 92 elements such as hydrogen, oxygen, lead, etc. This definition gave us steel, gasoline, modern medicines, and practically all of the things our society has today which our forefathers did not have. But more recently, we discovered that we could not explain certain phenomena we could observe, such as two seemingly identical elements which behaved differently, so we redefined elements in terms of the number and proportion of protons and electrons contained. But this too soon proved inadequate and so, at last report, we have mesons, neutrons, neutrinos, positrons, and a host of other concepts. And the question "Is there really such a thing as a positron?" is beside the point; it is a concept that, at present, is fruitful. Perhaps the next year we shall change our present definition of matter drastically.

We cannot know reality as it really is, but that is not too important. What is important is the extent to which our definitions enable us to cope with reality. To ask "What is electricity really?" shows only a curiosity that should be redirected. The better question is: "How does what we call electricity behave?" As Conant has said, "A scientific fact is a policy, not a creed."

Once we realize that words are merely attempts to define on the basis of observations, and what we choose to call something is extremely important but what it really is, is an impossible and useless question, we can perceive the silliness in such seemingly profound questions as:

"If I begin to destroy a chair, when does it cease being a chair?"
"Where does the fire go when it goes out?"
"When is a person really dead?"

The answer to the first is, "It ceases to be a chair when we decide to cease calling it a chair. We merely decided to call it a chair in the first place. It isn't really a chair; it just is (we assume)."

The answer to the second is the same as the first. By a fire "going out" we mean that point at which we agree to cease calling it a fire.

The answer to the third is again dependent upon definition. We cannot know anything as it is really. Hence, we decide on a definition for "dead" and classify accordingly. Of course, if a person seems to fall on the line we draw between living and dead, we have another problem to resolve.

Myth-conceptions About Perfection

The weaknesses in the three foregoing questions all involved our confusion of words with things, our assuming that something really is because we decide to say it is. We can resolve all such problems by defining carefully and by realizing that our definitions are merely that, that something *is* means that we say it is, that something *ceases* means that we define it as ceasing, that something *is not* implies a decision to say that it is not.

However, another class of concepts, although quite useful,

has nothing to do with reality, but we confuse or trick ourselves when we think that such concepts actually do refer to reality. Consider the following questions: "How can God be omnipotent if He can't build a stone so big He can't lift it?" "How far is it from the earth to the moon?" "If everything happens in the future or the past how can there be anything happening now?"

The solution of these problems depends upon our realization that such concepts as timelessness, perfection, negation, infinity, identity, zero, absolute, and the like are pure inventions of our minds and do not and cannot possibly exist in reality. Perfect omnipotence is like a perfect vacuum, a figment of our imaginations. Consider an easy example: "If two apples are added to two apples, the result is four apples." If we were to accumulate two such sets of four apples, what would they have in common? The answer is nothing. They differ in weight, color, size, physical structure, and in every conceivable characteristic. The "fourness" we *think* they have in common is not in the apples but in our minds. Einstein has said: "So long as mathematics has no reference to reality it is perfect; insofar as it refers to reality it is imperfect." Now consider certain physical laws: "An object falling in a vacuum toward the earth will accelerate at the rate of 32 ft./sec.^{2}" "An object traveling at the speed of light will have infinite mass and its time will be zero." Since there is no such thing as a perfect vacuum, no object will accelerate at 32 ft./sec.^{2} A person traveling in space near the speed of light may return younger than his children, but he can never travel at the speed of light. We can never know if two things happen or where they are simultaneously (hence, we cannot measure the distance from the moon to the earth exactly) because it takes time to make an observation and, when it comes to slicing across a continuous event, any real slice must have real thickness (hence, the present has zero time between past and future only in our imagination). "The same instant," then, apparently means the same insofar as we are capable of measuring time. We can never prove scientifically that two things are the same; we can only estimate our confidence in saying that they are different. Consider a coin flipped 100 times. We would like to determine if it is biased. We certainly don't expect to get exactly 50 heads and 50 tails unless there is perfect flipping (impossible) and the coin is perfect (also impossible) or we obtain 50 heads by chance. Hence we have a certain number of heads or tails which could be obtained by chance so rarely that, if we obtain that many or more heads in 100 trials, we will conclude with that much confidence that the coin is biased. Suppose we obtained 100 heads and no tails. We could have flipped it on the time that such a rare sequence occurred, so under no circumstances can we be *perfectly* confident that the coin is biased. Now suppose we did obtain 50 heads. Can we now be *perfectly* confident that the coin is unbiased? Of course not. Our difficulty arises because the coin we are using is real. What constitutes proof of anything is merely probabilistic; true certitude is possible only when we are not referring to reality. Confusion occurs when we think we can refer to reality with certitude. Such expressions as "The exception which proves the rule," "She's not herself today," and "How can identical twins be so different?" illustrate thinking which, to say the least, shows little awareness of the difference between conceptual perfection and real imperfection.

This awareness of reality's imperfection can mean a difference in our actions. A person with little such awareness will flip a coin to decide the winner of a race in case of a tie; one with more awareness will strive to clock the event more precisely. A person with little awareness of the difference between words and things is distraught when events do not occur as he expects; a person more aware of this difference alters his expectations accordingly.

The Limits of Applicability of Words

What we have been saying thus far has implied certain rules to follow in definition:

1. State its general area of inclusiveness.
2. Indicate the limits of applicability contrasted with synonyms by drawing a line as precisely as possible.
3. Realize that, no matter how finely the line is drawn, some objects or events will seem to fall on the line and must arbitrarily be classified if the line cannot be drawn more finely.

4. Realize that no absolute term can be applied accurately to reality.

With these criteria in mind, we might derive such definitions as the following:

to draw a straight line: to draw a line with a straight edge whose thickness and depth are such that, by examining either side, no deviations in direction can be detected with the naked eye over the entire length.

successful: achieves or exceeds all of the goals considered to be primary and as many goals considered to be secondary as possible.

fact: statement based on observations of phenomena made by persons whom we trust, by methods of which we approve, with inferences we believe capable of describing the observations in general (although not descriptive of every single observation); and capable of predicting other phenomena, deemed similar to those observed, to the degree that no more than 1 per cent of specific exceptions will be observed in any group of phenomena and the fact will be substantiated at least 99 per cent of the times observations of phenomena are made.

Now try to define several of the following:

circle
nine
speech
full
blank verse
democracy

In all of the preceding terms, we can do little to define by contrast except with the antonym of each word which, in general, is "non———" i.e., "not a circle," "not nine," "non-speech," etc. Differentiating between a word and its antonym, however, is much easier than differentiating among synonyms. Consider defining the following examples:

theory
pretty
cost
assert
reiterate

Drawing the line between "theory" and "non-theory," or "pretty" and "not pretty" may be somewhat meaningful in helping persons to classify reliably by our definitions, but it would be more helpful if we contrasted each word with its more common synonyms:

theory, axiom, postulate, hypothesis
pretty, lovely, attractive, pleasing
cost, charge, price, expense
assert, say, state, declare
reiterate, iterate, repeat, restate

The remainder of this section will be devoted to a study of the distinctions generally made by cultured speakers and writers among 100 groups of synonyms which frequently occur in oral communications. Study each group until you can devise a sentence which uses only one word in each group meaningfully where use of the others would be confusing, meaningless, or unintentionally humorous.

Your diction will probably improve as a result of this drill, but your efforts should not terminate at the conclusion of these exercises. Remember to improve your vocabulary by using a dictionary in conjunction with your reading, by using a work such as *Merriam-Webster's Dictionary of Differentiated Synonyms* or an encyclopedia in conjunction with your speaking and writing, and by using such a work as Roget's *Thesaurus* when you cannot think of the synonym you want.

1.	*vapid:* without sparkle or zest	vapid champagne; He's vapid but not lazy.
	insipid: without taste	3 p.m. cafeteria mashed potatoes; The room was insipidly rather than poorly furnished.
	inane: figuratively, without life	bewildered pause after an inane remark
2.	*calm:* apparently undisturbed	His heart pounded, but he faced them calmly.
	tranquil: mentally undisturbed	He remained tranquil while those about him became excited.
	serene: spiritually undisturbed	serene satisfaction of certitude
	placid: bovine tranquility	his cow-like placidity
	phlegmatic: temperamentally sluggish	so phlegmatic that not even his loved ones' deaths would bother him.

3.	*sentiment:* mental expression of feeling	the sentimental salutation, "My dear sir"
	emotion: physical feeling	Humor is a salubrious emotion.
	mood: mental state due to emotion	mood of anxiety or despair
	affection: expression of liking	her pronounced affection for him
4.	*candid:* frankness due to honesty	Tell me candidly, even if it hurts.
	ingenuous: child-like inability to conceal one's emotions	her ingenuous expression of love for every living thing
	naïve: lacking ability to perceive sordidness or to cope with it effectively when necessary	a confidence racket which preys on naïve women; Most men date sophisticated women but marry naïve ones.

Note: naïveté [naiv'te] is a noun.

5.	*fussy:* inordinate attention to details	He's very fussy when he plans a party.
	meticulous: fussiness due to fear	He's so meticulous that he carries a clothes brush in his pocket.
	punctilious: fussiness about fine points	the punctilious committee member who exhausts everyone
	scrupulous: fussiness due to scruples (felt principles)	as scrupulous as any honest, active man
6.	*concise:* non-superfluous phraseology	Signs should be clear and concise.
	terse: craftsman-like conciseness	his terse style of writing
	succinct: said in fewest possible words	the sententiousness of a succinct remark
7.	*copy:* to reproduce something	Copy this letter.
	imitate: to copy loosely a non-pictorial thing or person	to imitate his style; She imitates her mother in her forgetfulness.
	mimic: to copy a person's superficial characteristics	He mimicked her coughing before she speaks.
8	*mundane:* refers to transitory and relatively unimportant affairs of humans (antonym: eternal)	His life is so filled with mundane trivia that he has no time to think.
	earthy: refers to material things of the earth (*ant.:* spiritual)	earthy humor and spiritual wit; earthy sex appeal
	earthly: refers to things on earth (*ant.:* heavenly)	Communism with its false dream of an earthly paradise.

9.	*wordy:* contains too many words	a wordy statement of the problem
	verbose: dullness, confusion, or pomposity provoked by wordiness	He concealed his paucity of thought by his verbosity.
	prolix: wordiness that pursues every detail to the extent of boredom.	His prolixity is due to his punctiliousness.
10.	*abet:* to render any service of any kind to anyone (giver is abettor; receiver is abetted)	to abet with no thought of recompense
	help: abetting achieves goal sooner or more easily (less laboriously)	Help me move this.
	aid: abetted is unable to self-abet	first aid; to aid the faint-hearted
	assist: abetted is superior in status	He hired someone to assist him.
11.	*say:* to phrase silently or aloud	he said to himself
	state: to say in detail	State your position on foreign aid.
	assert: to say positively	He asserted angrily that no one could.
	utter: to say publicly	He uttered a remark that few heard.
	declare: to assert publicly	He stood up and declared that he was divine.
	asseverate: to declare strongly	It was a passionate asseveration of previously withheld convictions.
12.	*repeat:* to say again	Please repeat what you said.
	iterate: to repeat more than once	It was mentioned twice but should be iterated.
	reiterate: to say many times	reiteration of unfulfilled promises
13.	*talkative:* prone to talk a lot	A salesman shouldn't be too talkative.
	loquacious: has ease in chatting	He enjoyed her loquacity.
	garrulous: lots of words about practically nothing ['gærjʊləs]	His garrulity prevents his having friends. [gə'rulətɪ]
14.	*vilify:* to defame directly	the shocking language used to vilify him

	Term	Example
	asperse: to defame indirectly	He meant to cast aspersions at his employer, but few knew whom he meant.
	malign: to defame unintentionally	He was maligned by their attack upon his reprehensible business partner.
	slander: to defame orally, illegally	A senator cannot win a suit for slander.
	libel: to defame in writing illegally	A senator cannot win a suit for libel.
15.	*certain:* based on evidence	certain of his guilt
	sure: based on feeling	sure that he would come
	positive: based on principles	positive in his patriotism
16.	*poignant:* emotionally moving	a poignant scene in a play
	piquant: sharp but pleasing to the taste	a piquant sauce; a piquant remark
	pungent: stings one or more senses	a pungent odor; pungency of dirty words
17.	*join:* to bring together	join hands; to join in marriage
	combine: to join until components lose separate identities	to combine the ingredients of a cake
	blend: limits of components are indistinct	The colors of the rainbow blend.
	unite: to form one thing of many	a united people; to unite in matrimony
18.	*wide:* distance side-to-side, as if two-dimensional	The paper is 8 inches wide.
	broad: relative distance side-to-side, implying third dimension	broad-shouldered; a broad valley
	deep: distance front to back or vertically	The lot is 75 feet deep; The hole is deep.
19.	*correct:* in accord with fact	Am I correct in thinking that he died?
	true: in accord with one's values or generally accepted values	He is a true scholar; a true-false exam; Science is truth based upon facts.
	right: in accord with acceptable policy or action	the right thing to wear
20.	*understand:* to know the meaning of	I didn't understand what you said.
	appreciate: to know the true worth of	Only the starving appreciate food.

	comprehend: to know the significance of	Did you comprehend what he was driving at?
21.	*deceive:* to lead one to take something for other than it is	He deceived her in saying he was at home.
	delude: to deceive so that victim appears foolish	She was deluded into spending her life's savings on his "cancer-curing" magnets.
	betray: to deceive to the extent of imperiling the victim	A spy betrays his country.
22.	*inner:* nearer the center (*ant.:* outer)	his inner nature
	interior: farther from limits (*ant.:* exterior)	travel to the interior
	internal: referring to things on the inside (*ant.:* external)	internal medicine
	inside: inner side of a barrier	Put it inside the envelope.
	inward: motion nearer the center	Move inward.
23.	*digest:* a boiling down to essentials	Prepare a digest of his report.
	survey: a looking over important features	a survey of our needs
	sketch: a tracing of the outlines	He will sketch your responsibilities.
24.	*untimely:* event not yet due	an untimely death; an untimely cue
	precocious: beyond its time	a precocious mind
	premature: process completed before its time	premature birth; a premature conviction
25.	*criticize:* to consider merits and demerits	Criticism requires knowledge and taste.
	censure: authority's adverse conclusion	He censured the play mercilessly.
	condemn: powerful authority's adverse judgment	The judge condemned him to death.
26.	*inclined:* rationally leaned	I am inclined to believe you.
	disposed: emotionally leaned	His manner disposes men to like him instantly.
	predisposed: previously disposed	She is predisposed to love someone like him.
	biased: rationally for or against	A fact revealed only in newspapers can bias a jury.
	prejudiced: emotionally for or against	prejudiced against persons of wealth

27.	*illusion:* event which mentally deceives	optical illusion
	delusion: state of mental deception	delusions of omnipotence
	hallucination: unreal event perceived as real	The ghost he saw was an hallucination.
28.	*predominant:* most noticeable or influential	the predominant thought
	preponderant: most weighty	the preponderant argument
	paramount: first in rank	point of paramount consideration
29.	*odor:* capable of being sensed with nose	to measure the odor
	scent: odor-producing substance	dog followed the scent
	smell: use of olfactory sense	smell of clover reminded him
	aroma: pleasant odor	The coffee aroma whetted his appetite.
	fragrance: aroma of vegetation	the heady fragrance of magnolias
30.	*empty:* nothing in it	empty jar; empty mind
	vacant: no human in it	vacant room
	void: absolutely none of something	Space is not entirely void of matter.
	vacuous: a figurative absence	vacuous stare
31.	*reprove:* to censure (*cf.* No. 25) kindly in hope of correction	a fatherly reproof
	chide: to reprove mildly	He chided him about his forgetfulness.
	rebuke: to reprove severely	To rebuke in anger is ineffective.
	reprimand: to censure publicly	Don't reprimand an employee before his peers.
	reproach: to find fault about something	reproached for being late
32.	*retract:* to take back	Did he retract what he said?
	retreat: to move back	The army retreated.
	recede: to move back down	The waters receded.
33.	*slant:* to turn inward or outward or away from vertical	His left eye slants inward; The tree slanted sharply.
	tilt: to lean away from horizontal	The table was tilted slightly.
	incline: (*cf.* No. 26) leaning of humans	He inclined his head to the left.

34.	*scrutinize:* to study carefully	Scrutinize his plan for any faults.
	perceive: to see into deeply	to perceive God in Nature
	discern: to make out from surroundings	discern a ship through the fog
	scan: to cover every portion	He scanned the sky for enemy planes.
	skim: to look over quickly	He skimmed through the book in an hour.
35.	*dread:* filled with fear or awe	Dread God's wrath.
	trepidation: dread plus timidity	entered haunted house with trepidation
	consternation: fear plus confusion	Consternation is the mother of neuroses.
	dismay: total loss of courage due to fear	enemy dismayed is enemy beaten
36.	*authoritative:* from an authority	an authoritative reference
	authoritarian: assumes power to exact obedience	authoritarian parent
	dogmatic: dictating principles (dogma) as indisputably true	the dogmatic way he tells us what to do
37.	*form:* general outline, figuratively	form in which the idea was presented
	shape: three-dimensional configuration	shaped like a cylinder
	figure: two-dimension configuration	her figure as seen in profile
38.	*wearied:* unwilling to continue	weary of studying algebra
	fatigued: strained to normal maximum	Ear fatigue was induced in 30 seconds.
	exhausted: strained to maximum possible	He ran until he fell exhausted.
39.	*blemish:* external disfigurement	blemish in the color of the cup
	defect: something lacking	defective cups due to missing handles
	flaw: lack of continuity	The cup's cracked rim was an irreparable flaw.
40.	*tangible:* figuratively capable of being grasped	a tangible idea
	ponderable: figuratively capable of being weighed	a ponderable influence

	palpable: figuratively capable of being touched	a palpable mist
41.	*relevant:* related in any way	unimportant but relevant question
	pertinent: related to basic points	Where he was at that time is most pertinent to his defense.
	apropos: eminently related	an apropos poem for the occasion
42.	*egoism:* excessive self-interest	Women are more egoistic than men.
	egotism: excessive striving for attention	egotism of an unloved child
	conceit: exaggerated importance or affectation	conceit of a braggart
43.	*perverse:* unnatural or abnormal behavior	the perverse child who says "No" to everything
	converse: turned around	The converse of "None but the brave deserves the fair" is "None but the fair deserves the brave."
	obverse: the right, conspicuous or important side	the portrait on the obverse side of a dollar bill
	reverse: exact opposite	The reverse is, "All but the brave deserve the fair"
44.	*devout:* believing deeply in God	a devout man and a devoted father
	religious: closely adhering to a formal religion	a religious Catholic
	pious: sincere or insincere display of devotion	Her regular attendance at church merely proves her piety.
	sanctimonious: insincere piety	sanctimonious preaching that racial segregation has Biblical sanction
45.	*portly:* fat but seemly (suitable to him)	a portly, charming gentleman
	corpulent: disfiguring excess of flesh or fat	eyes sunk behind corpulent brows
	obese: extremely fat	Obesity is a medical problem.
	rotund: round-shaped	a rotund face
	chubby: fat like a baby	chubbiness that will disappear with age
	stout: heavy-set figure (seemingly incapable of being unbalanced)	He stood stoutly in the entrance.
	plump: swelled out as if inflated	a plump tomato

	Word and meaning	Example
46.	*foolish:* not judicious or very sensible	a foolish thing to believe
	silly: having no meaning, sense or point	a silly gesture for an actor
	absurd: incompatible with common sense or reason	absurd dress for the party
	illogical: arguments (premises) do not follow logically	an illogical sequence of ideas
	fallacious: an invalid (not following rules) conclusion	a fallacious deduction
47.	*cordial:* warm and hearty	a cordial greeting
	affable: easy to talk with or confide in	an affable housemother
	genial: good cheer and sense of humor	a genial host
	gracious: kindliness and courtesy which make social inferiors feel like equals	his gracious employer
48.	*compatible:* able to be or to go together	We don't like each other, but we are compatible nevertheless.
	congruous: fit together extremely well	the congruous furnishings of a room
	congenial: giving pleasure due to harmony with one's tastes or temperament	a congenial companion
49.	*invincible:* not capable of being resisted or displaced	invincible selfishness
	indomitable: not capable of being beaten	indomitable spirit
	unassailable: not capable of being attacked	unassailable argument
50.	*era:* period of time in which idea prevails	era of religious doubt
	age: period of time in which a thing prevails	automotive age
	epoch: long period in life of person or thing	His wife's death ended that epoch.
	episode: brief and unimportant epoch	love for her was a minor episode
51.	*humane:* acting with tenderness and compassion	humane treatment of animals
	humanitarian: interested in well-being of persons and people	humanitarian philosopher

	benevolent: natural kindness	benevolent God
	charitable: acquired kindness, treating fellow men as brothers	a charitable institution
52.	*annoyed:* loss of patience due to an offense	annoyed by his constant whining
	bothered: loss of peace of mind	doubts bothered him
	exasperated: intensely irritated	an exasperating remark
53.	*disaster:* unforeseen event causing much havoc	The tornado was a major disaster.
	calamity: a great personal or public loss	The king's death was a calamity.
	catastrophe: a disastrous conclusion	the play's catastrophe in Act III
54.	*impassable:* not capable of being passed through	impassable barrier
	impenetrable: not capable of being entered into	impenetrable forest
	impervious: not capable of being permeated (affected by light, fluids, gases, etc.)	impervious to alcohol
55.	*intensified:* made more intense	the noise was intensified
	aggravated: made worse	illness aggravated by getting up too soon
	enhanced: made greater	beauty was enhanced
56.	*dispersed:* scattered in all directions from mass	troops dispersed
	dispelled: driven away	doubts dispelled
	dissipated: completely disintegrated (total loss of unifying character)	dissipation due to drink
57.	*prone:* lying face down	fire from a prone position
	supine: lying on one's back	He lay supinely on the bed and stared at the ceiling.
	prostrate: prone position of submission	He prostrated himself before the altar.
58.	*misery:* state of wretched distress	misery of their lives
	agony: unendurable suffering of body and mind	an agony of doubt
	distress: conditions causing stress or peril	ship in distress

59.	*compresses:* packs in smaller space	compresses the contents of suitcase
	contracts: shrinks to a smaller size	the heart contracts
	constricts: pinches off	sphincter muscles constrict
60.	*merit:* advantages outweigh disadvantages	the ideas have merit
	virtue: acquired moral excellence	a woman of proven virtue
	rectitude: virtue based on principles	his rectitude of purpose
61.	*continually:* unceasing succession	to provide or supply continuously
	continuously: unbroken succession	continuously increasing series of numbers
	constantly: unchanging succession	heart throbbed constantly
62.	*element:* basic part	the element of a situation
	component: basic recognizable entity	copper and zinc, the components of brass
	constituent: basis unrecognizable entity	constituents of personality
	factor: part enabling whole to operate	a factor in succeeding
63.	*harmed:* mentally hurt	harmed by what he said
	damaged: hurt producing lower value	car was damaged
	injured: hurt due to an injustice	she was injured in the accident
64.	*ability:* state of being able	his ability to work for long hours
	capacity: ability to contain	his capacity for ideas
	capability: ability to perform something	capability of the ear to distinguish tones
65.	*exterminated:* completely killed off	exterminated the rats
	eradicated: completely driven off	eradicated superstitions
	annihilated: completely wiped out	annihilated the enemy
66.	*individuals:* each considered separately	individuals of various beliefs
	persons: individuals with similar characteristics	Four persons ate dinner.

	people: a group with similar characteristics	peoples of different faiths
67.	*prize:* something striven for or won by chance	he was awarded the prize
	reward: payment for a good deed	a reward for its return
	bonus: payment in addition	Christmas bonus
68.	*baked:* cooked on inside more than outside	baked potatoes
	roasted: cooked on outside more than inside	roasted beef
	broiled: cooked on radiant heat to give juicy inside	broiled chops
	grilled: cooked over hot coals	grilled hamburgers
	barbecued: large cut of meat cooked in one piece	barbecued leg of lamb
69.	*art:* work requiring talent	glassblower's art
	trade: work requiring manual labor	carpenter's trade
	profession: work requiring formal education	doctor's profession
70.	*business:* wholesale or retail transactions	his business failed
	commerce: exchange of goods	interstate commerce
	industry: production of goods	steel industry
71.	*essential:* necessary for operation	the use of 110 volts is essential
	fundamental: figurative foundation	the fundamentals of poetry
	vital: necessary to life	His need for the drug is vital.
72.	*evaded:* escaped by cleverness	He evaded the issue.
	eluded: escaped by baffling	His true purpose eluded us.
	escaped: got away from a threatening situation	He escaped prison.
73.	*inordinate:* beyond limits of good judgement	inordinate snobbery
	extravagant: beyond limits of good taste	extravagant praise
	exorbitant: beyond customary limits	exorbitant price
74.	*thoughtless:* lack of consideration for others	a thoughtless act

	heedless: indifference or inattentiveness	heedless of the consequences
	careless: lack of care or worry	a careless mistake
75.	*sensuous:* evoking sensations rather than ideas	sensuous rhyme
	sensual: appealing to base motives	sensual eating of a glutton
	luxurious: inviting indulgence or pleasure	a luxurious meal
	voluptuous: abandoned indulgence in sensual pleasure	a voluptuous person
76.	*chaste:* avoids immoral acts	chaste because his mind is pure
	decent: due concern for what is proper	the decent thing to do
	modest: absence of boldness in chaste person	modest dress
77.	*chastise:* corporal punishment aimed at correction	Nature chastises those who violate her laws.
	castigate: severe public lashing with tongue or pen	Officers shouldn't castigate men.
	discipline: punishment to bring under control	Discipline must precede learning.
78.	*temerity:* failure to estimate chances of success	He had the temerity to propose.
	audacity: disregard of prudence	He had the audacity to wink at her.
	effrontery: derogated temerity or audacity	She was naturally shocked at his effrontery.
79.	*exquisite:* perfection or excellence perceived through study	Exquisite, but initially disliked, art
	elegant: rich but still in good taste	elegant furnishings of room
	delicate: admirable but fine or fragile	delicate fragrance
80.	*concluded:* brought to close	concluded the meeting
	terminated: brought to an end in time or space	lines terminated at a point
	completed: removed all deficiencies	completed the requirements
81.	*kindred:* likeness as if in same family	kindred minds
	allied: union by voluntary agreement	allied in a cause

	Term	Example
	affiliated: dependent alliance	colleges affiliated with the university
82.	*theories:* principles capable of being tested	theories of causation of stuttering
	axioms: self-evident, indisputable principles	axioms of conduct
	postulates: basic assumptions incapable of proof	postulate that reality exists
	hypotheses: assumptions to be tested	his experimental hypotheses
83.	*subsequently:* following in time	Let's consider that point subsequently.
	consecutively: following immediately in order	He served four years consecutively.
	successively: following in order	three successive leap years
84.	*consistent:* indisputable harmony	consistent with his views on art
	compatible: fitting without disagreement (*cf.* No. 48)	At best they are only compatible.
	congruous: capable of fitting together well (*cf.* No. 48)	congruous furnishings of a room
85.	*habit:* unconscious behavior derived from reinforced (rewarded) repetition	his habit of clearing his throat before speaking
	practice: repeated action due to choice	his practice of taking long walks
	custom: habit or practice we associate with a person or group	his customary unkemptness; the custom of addressing the chairman
86.	*contemporary:* person living at the same time	his contemporary
	contemporaneous: thing occurring at the same time	contemporaneous events
	concomitant: closely associated coincidence	Decency is a concomitant of virtue.
	concurrent: running together	concurrent terms in prison
	coincident: noncausally related contemporaneousness	Their simultaneous death was merely coincidental.
87.	*fatal:* resulting in death	To move him would be fatal.
	lethal: capable of causing death	lethal weapon
	deadly: highly probable that death will result	deadly poisons

88.	*decreased:* became less in amount	His temperature decreased.
	diminished: decreased because of something	His funds were diminished by his extravagance.
	reduced: decreased by human action	Prices were reduced.
89.	*defend:* use of means to counter threat	Soldiers defend a fort.
	protect: use of means to bar admission	The fort is protected by walls.
	guard: to stand watch over	The sentries guard the fort.
90.	*empty:* having nothing in it (*cf.* No. 30)	empty jar
	vacant: having no persons in it (*cf.* No. 30)	vacant room
	bare: having nothing on it	bare wall
91.	*fertile:* capable of giving birth to	fertile virgin
	fecund: giving birth to many	fecund mind
	fruitful: having many results	fruitful ideas
92.	*suitable:* capable of meeting requirements	suitable part for a machine
	proper: suitable on any grounds	proper thing to say
	appropriate: eminently suitable	appropriate comment at the time
93.	*phlegmatic:* emotionally aroused with difficulty and only slightly (*cf.* No. 2, placid)	His phlegmatic nature is not a mere vitamin deficiency.
	apathetic: culpable (blameworthy) indifference	the nation's apathy about its defenses
	stolid: dully apathetic	his stolid expression
	impassive: betraying no emotion (*cf.* No. 2, calm)	the impassive countenance of a good poker player
94.	*inform:* to impart necessary facts	inform him that he won
	advise: to inform about something important regarding conduct	advise him of risks involved
	notify: to inform formally	notify public of change in rules

95.	*influence:* impalpable effect of one thing on another	his influence on her belief
	authority: influence due to wisdom	respect for authority
	prestige: fame earned by excellence of performance	a stateman's prestige
96.	*big:* much bulk or mass	big mound
	large: much capacity or quantity	large box or number
	great: much importance due to size of something	great writer
97.	*flat:* no elevations or depressions	flat foot
	even: observable flatness	even hem
	level: corresponding to horizontal reference point	river runs level with its banks
	horizontal: corresponding to horizon	horizontal line
98.	*cost:* what must be paid	manufacturer's cost
	charge: cost of services	installation charge
	price: amount asked for goods	He set the price at a dollar.
99.	*medium:* near middle of scale	medium height
	moderate: not extreme on unscaled phenomenon	moderate ability to enjoy
	mediocre: far from extreme in excellence	mediocre play
100.	*think:* mental	I think that's correct.
	believe: spiritual	I believe that's true.
	feel: emotional	I feel that he's lying.

Types of Words and Their Uses

Words can be classified as either referent words or syntactical words. Referent words—nouns, pronouns, verbs, adverbs, and adjectives—refer to objects or events in reality. Syntactical words—prepositions, conjunctions, and auxiliary verbs—refer to relationships among referent words. Referent words may be classified on various continua, some of which are useful in the improvement of diction. These important continua are general-specific, connotative-denotative, and positive-negative. Let us examine each of these separately.

The General-Specific Continuum

Every referent word is an abstraction to some extent. To abstract means to take out. The word "apple" takes out or ignores all characteristics in which all individual things called apples differ. It should be remembered that they are identical in nothing. "Apple" is a definition of a class of things, the class or type being so defined that we know in general whether to assign an object to the "apple" class or to some other class.

Some words are classification of words rather than classifications of things such as "apples" or classifications of events such as "running." Such words as "fruit" or "moving" abstract differences between "apples" and "pears" or "walking" and "running." Hence, we see that a classifying system exists from more specific components to more general apexes, as illustrated in Fig. 10-1.

COMMUNICATION

I. Media
    A. Radio
        1. FM
        2. AM
            a. News programs
            b. Soap operas
                1. "Road to Life"
                2. "Stella Dallas"
                    a. Program of Feb. 12, 1938
                        1) Author
                        2) Introduction
                            a) Voice quality
                            b) Etc.
    B. TV
        1. Etc.
II. Functions
    A. Reception
        1. Listening
        2. Reading
            a. Rate
            b. Comprehension
                1. Types of testing
                2. Types of test materials
                    a. Etc.
III. Purposes
IV. Etc.

Fig. 10-1. Illustration of various levels of verbal abstraction

Your being aware of the existence of a general-specific continuum has several advantages. One important advantage of such awareness is that it enables you to cope with definitional misunderstandings adequately. Most disagreements are the result, not of different values or of values differently esteemed, but of an unawareness of different concepts for the same word. Usually, the best method for comparing concepts is to define the ambiguous word in terms of more specific (less abstract) components. Thus, if a disagreement arises over whether or not animals can reason, it might be resolved by the disputants defining the ability to reason by citing its constituents. It may then be seen by both that, if they define reasoning to include the ability to conceive of absolutes, only human animals can reason, but if reasoning excludes this ability, animals other than humans may reason. Which definition is better depends on the ability of each to satisfy the criteria of good definitions discussed previously.

Another advantage of being aware of the general-specific continuum is that it enables you to avoid confusing your listeners by being unnecessarily general (abstract). Thus, there may be an appropriate occasion for saying, "That chair is brown" and another for saying, "The term specifically applicable to the chroma of that specific article of furniture is ferruginous." Only in one sense are the two statements equivalent; disregarding abstraction level, both mean the same thing. However, an occasion in which the second might be appropriate is in a lecture on pigments. In such a case the speaker is probably discriminating among such alternatives as ochre, sepia, cupreous, and bister. How general one should be depends upon the need for generalization. It would be a dull world indeed if we always restricted ourselves to extremely specific statements, but it would be a confusing world indeed if we spoke only in superficial generalities. The best world in this respect would be one in which we unhesitatingly abstract to the extent to which we intend our words to be applicable, and to the extent to which we have confidence that our audience knows or can be led to know the locus of applicability, the limits of applicability, and the less abstract constituents of the words we employ.

Another advantage of abstraction awareness is that it provides a means of varying the relative importance of successive ideas. Neither attention nor emotion can be sustained without relief longer than about one-half minute except in certain highly unusual conditions. The use of more specific statements—examples, illustrations, definitions and, especially, less abstract phraseology—provides the relief necessary for an audience to experience increased attentiveness and emotion on subsequent statements. Study the following two paragraphs:

"As the velocity of an object approaches the speed of light, its mass approaches infinity and its time approaches zero."

"We might well ask what happens when the velocity, or speed, of an object, be it a space ship or an atomic particle, approaches roughly 186,000 miles per second, the speed of light. As it approaches this velocity, its mass or size gets larger and larger and, theoretically, becomes infinitely large as it attains the speed of light. As anything approaches the speed of light, its time slows up, since time and velocity are inversely related, and, for an object traveling at the speed of light, time theoretically would stand still. This means that a space ship traveling through space at, say, 180,000 miles per second, would be much larger than here on earth although its crew would not be able to perceive this because they too would be that much larger. Their clocks would be running slower and their bodies would therefore be aging less rapidly, so that their children on earth might even be as old as they are."

The second paragraph contains examples (space ships, atomic particles), illustrations (crew reactions), definitions (velocity of light is roughly 186,000 miles per second), and different levels of abstraction (velocity-speed, mass-size, zero time–time stands still). The first paragraph might well be inserted after the second paragraph and it would certainly be comprehended better than if no such preliminary statements were included.

As practice in determining levels of abstraction, examine the following pairs of words to see which is more specific. To test which verb, adjective, or adverb belongs as a subgroup to the other, ask yourself whether one can occur without the other necessarily occurring. If it can, it is more abstract. For example, on the first pair you can say something without stating it but you cannot state something without saying it, hence "state" is more specific. Now check the more specific term in each of the following:

1. say—state
2. know—comprehend
3. look—see
4. assist—abet
5. separate—segregate
6. noun—pronoun
7. humorous—funny
8. broad—wide
9. see—witness
10. structure—building
11. destroy—annihilate
12. pretty—personable
13. perspire—sweat
14. clear—transparent
15. vacant—empty
16. operate—manipulate
17. simple—easy
18. reduce—decrease
19. reply—refute
20. speak—converse

It is obvious from the above that many words you use frequently are more abstract than less frequently used synonyms (e.g., say, know, separate, see, clear, easy, speak). Being more abstract, they are more prone to confuse your audience, assuming that your audience is acquainted with the definition of the more specific alternative.

We can now summarize principles applicable to diction in terms of a general-specific continuum:

1. *Use more specific phraseology to increase understanding and to provide relief from more general remarks.*
2. *Use more general phraseology to increase the applicability of your remarks provided your audience knows or you can enable it to know the constituents of the more general terms.*

The Connotative-Denotative Continuum

Every referent word to some extent has connotations as well as denotations. Denotations are the objects or events to which a word refers by definition. Connotations are objects, events, or ideas suggested by the use of a word.

This connotative-denotative continuum has several subclasses which are important for our purposes. These are the *popular-technical*, *figurative-literal*, *personal-impersonal*, and *trite-fresh* continua.

Generally speaking, scientists employ a special vocabulary, and prefer neologisms to extant words, because the popular terms suggest far more than is intended by a scientist's use of them. When scientists do use popular words, they define them so that other scientists understand them but, unfortunately, laymen assume more than scientists intend them to. For example, a scientist says A causes B and means only that he gets B if and only if A occurs. He well realizes that A may cause C which in turn causes B; or, unknown to him, A and C have always been presented together and that C caused B; or some other possibility may serve to account for B. The layman thinks of no such possibilities. He thinks cause is direct and demonstrable. When he asks why something happens, he means something more than the conditions necessary for its occurrence. We have already discussed another such confusing term, "fact."

Many persons specialize to such an extent in either topic or audience, or both, that they lose the ability to communicate easily with any but their usual associates. The words they use may have more meanings or different meanings in the minds of coteries other than their own. "Ugly" to an art teacher may mean merely a violation of one or more of the elements of beauty, viz., symmetry, proportion, unity, etc., but it would be most cruel for such a teacher to label a student's design "ugly." A physician must be very careful in explaining to a patient that his illness is mental; although to a doctor a psychosomatic ill is just as real as a physical one, the patient may think that the doctor believes he is pretending to be sick. In like manner, to a physician the stomach is a digestive organ almost always situated in the chest, but to many laymen "stomach" is the genteel term for "belly." Thus, a physician who wants to avoid a waste of time says to a person complaining of a "stomach ache," "Show me where it hurts." When laymen adopt a specialist's words, they tend to become less definite in use; hence, words with which the dictionaries supply several numerically listed definitions might also be labeled "Caution; use with extreme care."

Do not be reluctant to coin a new word where a need exists and you are sure no extant word fulfills that need. For example, there is no word which says that something contains every color in the rainbow. If we need to say this frequently, we might invent the word "vibgyoric," defined as an acronym of *v*iolet, *i*ndigo, *b*lue, *g*reen, *y*ellow, *o*range, and *r*ed plus an adjectival suffix. It is not necessary to wait for lexicographers to publish the word; once defined it is a communicable term.

If we were to state a principle concerning the popular-technical continuum it would be: *To be less connotative use more technical or scientific terminology, even if such words must be defined for your listeners.*

The more figurative extreme of the figurative-literal type of connotative-denotative continuum is generally favored by poets, fictional prose writers, and persuasive speakers. This means that, given a choice between stimulating a listener both emotionally and intellectually and communicating accurately the meaning intended, such persons prefer the former when a choice must be made. More figurative words are less expected and thus have some shock effect. Poetry depends upon such phraseology for much of its effect.

Figurative speech may be employed in poetry, fiction, and persuasive speaking, but the important question is to what extent this use of figurative speech is justified. We cannot permit umlimited use of figurative speech. "Sticks and stones may break your bones, but . . . " men kill, become ill, and even die because of names. Hence, the principle we should state concerning the figurative-literal continuum is: *Use figurative language to avoid being trite and to obtain greater emotional and intellectual stimulation, but not to the extent that you distort reality for immoral purposes.*

The personal-impersonal type of connotative-denotative continuum refers to the speaker's assessment of his own refinement or importance as revealed by his choice of words. Vulgarisms are the words most persons employ; it is the speech of the common man. However, certain words of the common man, especially those referring to vegetative and reproductive processes and organs, are considered by some persons to be taboo, either because they assume some inherent naughtiness in such words (confusing words with things) or they desire to be thought of as more refined, cultured, educated, or merely better than the common man.

In the recent past the word "leg" was considered taboo by many who deemed themselves refined because the word referred to a portion of a woman's body and was, therefore, aphrodisiac in connotation. Women's legs were therefore covered and, if necessary, would be referred to as "limbs." Tables had "limbs" too, and, in more than a few refined homes, these table limbs were hidden beneath decorous skirts. The word "leg" is vulgar, but it is clearly the most denotative term we have to describe a vertebrate's lower extremity. It might be argued that legs were called limbs in an era of Puritanism, but Puritanism is a matter of degree. Today many who want us to be aware of their refinement prefer "expectorate" to "spit," "passed away" to "died," "female dog" to "bitch," "perspiration" to "sweat," "lingerie" to "women's underwear," "nude" to "naked," "bosom" to "breast."

It should be pointed out that, except perhaps for "flammable" and "inflammable," we have practically no two words which denote exactly the same thing. Hence, a genteelism denotes something different from its more vulgar equivalent. For example, "to spit" is to discharge saliva from the mouth but "to expectorate" is to discharge any mucus which drained into the throat; a "bitch" is any canine female, not merely a female dog; "sweat" is any gathering of moisture which seems to have been or was secreted through pores, but "perspiration" is the saline fluid secreted by our bodies. Hence, connotative words can also be confusing. To physicians, the stomach is situated in the chest; to many laymen it is a genteelism for belly. However, *belly* is the vulgar synonym for the technical term *abdomen*, and *gut* is the vulgar term for *stomach*.

Other kinds of personal phraseology are *sesquipedality* (a preference for long words to short ones) and *bombast* (such grandiloquence of phraseology that attention is diverted from content to style). Persons interested in impressing others with their importance rather than the importance of what they say tend to use the first word in such pairs as the following: alteration–change, assist–help, demonstrate–show, depart–leave, desire–

want, erect–build, inquire–ask, obtain–get, possess–have, repair–fix, require–need, retain–keep, etc. Principles we might apply to the personal-impersonal continuum are:

1. *The use of genteel synonyms for inoffensive, denotative words sacrifices candor to decorum.*
2. *The use of large words to express small ideas is a plea for undeserved prestige.*

The trite-fresh type of connotative-denotative continuum refers to the expected occurrence of a word in a given context. No word is inherently fresh or trite; it becomes trite only in context. A word is fresh when it is an uncommon word in a common context or a common word in an uncommon context. For example, the words "love," "fine," "nice," and "swell" may be to any extent trite or fresh depending on context. To be trite, we might say "I love spaghetti," "It's a fine day," "He's real nice," and "That's really swell." To be fresh, we might say "My bare feet and the mud were in love," "The line between a gift and a bribe is fine," "He could not make a nice distinction between those for and those not against," "I saw his chest swell with pride."

Again, we cannot say that anyone should never be trite. Freshness demands attention and perhaps thought, while triteness makes us comfortable and at ease with the expected.

Consequently, to generalize about triteness we might say: *Triteness should be used only to express ideas of little interest or importance.*

The Positive-Negative Continuum

Many referent words, especially adjectives and adverbs, lie on a continuum extending toward the highest or best at one extreme and the lowest or worst at the other. Consider the following example:

superior–outstanding–excellent–good–acceptable–fair–poor

Use of the most descriptive term in any such scale of terms requires a familiarity not only with the various terms on each scale but an awareness of their relative scalar positions. See how well you can arrange the following groups in order by placing a 3 at each extreme, a 0 in the middle, and assigning a 1 or 2 to those words between these limits. Check your answers with those on the opposite page.

Positive and Negative Terms To Be Assigned to a Continuum

1. usual rare unique random frequent invariable unusual
2. fair presentable beautiful ugly unsightly unpresentable pretty
3. able strong tired exhausted fatigued powerful energetic
4. feasible impossible formidable easy facile difficult possible
5. great moderate large enormous small fractional infinitesimal
6. unfit improper proper fit appropriate apropos inappropriate
7. vapid phlegmatic excitable spirited vivacious lethargic even-tempered
8. low-priced exorbitant dear expensive inexpensive cheap reasonable
9. taciturn close laconic talkative fluent garrulous voluble
10. liking fondness detestation loathing coolness love antipathy
11. randomness invariance regularity order irregularity disorder uniformity
12. servile dictatorial dependent dominant submissive independent domineering
13. harmful salubrious detrimental innocuous healthful beneficial pernicious
14. weariness interest ennui excitement boredom ecstasy inattention
15. aged mature youthful young immature old elderly
16. useful relevant insignificant necessary indispensable unnecessary worthless
17. liberal munificent niggardly close generous stingy penurious
18. unclear abstruse intelligible clear understandable comprehensible obscure
19. observed overlooked scrutinized ignored noticed disregarded studied
20. likely impossible uncertain probable certain possible doubtful

Answers

1. unique–rare–unusual–random–usual–frequent–invariable
2. beautiful–pretty–fair–presentable–unpresentable–unsightly–ugly
3. powerful–strong–energetic–able–tired–fatigued–exhausted
4. facile–easy–feasible–possible–difficult–formidable–impossible
5. enormous–great–large–moderate–small–fractional–infinitesimal
6. apropos–appropriate–proper–fit–inappropriate–improper–unfit
7. vivacious–spirited–excitable–even-tempered–vapid–lethargic–phlegmatic
8. dear–exorbitant–expensive–resonable–inexpensive–low-priced–cheap
9. garrulous–voluble–talkative–fluent–close–taciturn–laconic
10. loathing–detestation–antipathy–coolness–liking–fondness–love
11. invariance–uniformity–regularity–order–disorder–irregularity–randomness
12. dictatorial–domineering–dominant–independent–dependent–submissive–servile
13. healthful–salubrious–beneficial–innocuous–detrimental–harmful–pernicious
14. ecstasy–excitement–interest–inattention–weariness–boredom–ennui
15. old–aged–elderly–mature–immature–youthful–young
16. indispensable–useful–necessary–relevant–unnecessary–insignificant–worthless
17. munificent–generous–liberal–close–stingy–niggardly–penurious
18. comprehensible–understandable–clear–intelligible–unclear–obscure–abstruse
19. scrutinized–studied–observed–noticed–overlooked–disregarded–ignored
20. certain–likely–probable–possible–uncertain–doubtful–impossible

When the word employed is obviously more extreme on the positive-negative continuum than is deserved, the effect is hyperbolic—an exaggeration. When a word is employed that is lower than is obviously deserved, the effect is litotic—an understatement. Generally, a little exaggeration is permissible; frequent exaggeration provokes mistrust. We tend to exaggerate to impress others with the importance of what we say. "It was the funniest story I ever heard" will probably arrest our attention if spoken by one who almost never exaggerates; coming from one who frequently speaks hyperbolically, it is interpreted, if noticed at all, as "The story was somewhat humorous." However, we do not become so innured to understatement. Litotes arrest our attention in spite of their frequency: "It wasn't the least humorous story I every heard"; "She isn't the least beautiful girl I've ever seen"; "I'd say he was rather good-looking" (said of an extremely handsome man) "I'm not in a mood for dancing" (when obviously tired).

An oxymoron is another effective method of using words on the positive-negative continuum and, like litotes, is a frequently employed poetic device (see page 231).

Lack of knowledge of a wide range of terms on the positive-negative continuum results in the excessive employment of adjectival modifiers such as very, rather, sort of, kind of, quite, very-very, kind of like, etc. and even the implicit admission of inadequate diction, "Oh, you know what I mean."

Principles concerning the positive-negative continuum would be:

1. *Prefer understatement to exaggeration.*
2. *Use modifiers as infrequently as possible by being aware of the scalar positions of synonyms and antonyms.*

Some psychologists have claimed that a person cannot think unless he has a word; so that the remark, "I know what I want to say, but I just can't find the right words," is untrue, they maintain, because he does not know what he wants to say until he finds the words he wants. This may be true to some extent, but anyone can conceive of a position on any scale for which no word exists, or for which the word is unknown to him, or cannot be recalled. Good diction requires quick recall and considerable knowledge of the scalar positions of words. The latter has been termed until now the limits of applicability of words. We now realize that there are many dimensions of words, and some day most of these important dimensions will be identified. This means that some day we may have a geometric statement of the location of referent words, just as we locate a point in three dimensions by citing its x, y, and z coordinates. If 7-point scales were accepted as the standard, a dictionary of the future might define a word by saying it was $2.1P$ on the P-N (positive-negative) scale, $0.4L$ on the F-L (figurative-literal) scale, $1.8S$ on the

G-S (general-specific) scale, etc. The scale values would be obtained by having cultured speakers rate words thus:

GREAT

Positive							Negative
Figurative							Literal
General							Specific
Technical							Popular
	3	2	1	0	1	2	3

Dictionaries would report the means of the scale values assigned. Until that day, however, each of us must strive to compile such data for himself.

Style

The quality of one's diction is probably not entirely dependent on the words employed; in part, it is almost certainly dependent upon the manner in which words are arranged. Arrangement is partly a matter of grammatical correctness, but at the beginning of this chapter it was explained that grammar, although important, would not be discussed here.

Most speaking lacks sufficient rhythm because it is invariant in that it consists almost entirely of a series of positive statements, all of approximately the same length. Some devices for varying such a sequence are double negations, litotes, parentheses, parallel constructions, rhetorical questions, impersonal constructions, shifts in conjugation, word omissions, word additions, word rearrangements; and, since the preceding discussion about words is applicable to statements as well, we can vary the level of statements on all the continua which have just been discussed.

Notice in the following examples how each statement employs one of the above devices:

All men deserve adequate food.
No man deserves to starve. (*double negation*)
What man deserves to starve? (*rhetorical question*)
Some men are well-fed while others starve. (*parallel construction*)
Some men are well-fed; others starve. (*verbal elision*)
Few men deserve to starve. (*litotes*)
Few men deserve starvation. (*shift in conjugation*)

Few men are deserving of starvation. (*shift in conjugation*)
Starvation is deserved by few. (*word rearrangement*)
Few are deserving of starvation. (*verbal omission*)
There are few who are deserving of starvation. (*verbal addition*)

Obviously, dozens of other constructions, as well as many combinations of the above devices, are possible. Let us see how rhythm influences our choice of these devices.

As we have seen in the chapter on rate, rhythm is a modulation of (pulling away from and a returning to) meter in poetry; in prose it is a modulation of whatever regularity is being employed. What we must determine, then, is the kind of regularity we have been employing before we can decide how to vary it.

Suppose our regularity has been metrical; in English, this probably means iambic meter. We have just said, "Few of us deserve to starve" or, with the feminine ending, "Few of us deserve starvation." To introduce rhythm on the following statement we should alter the pattern we have set up. For example:

Few of us deserve to starve.
  But most men on earth still have to.
Few of us deserve starvation,
  but, then, most men on earth still have to.

Hence, in the very abbreviated table shown on page 323, if the regularity is one of the patterns given, rhythm is created by employing the device indicated.

One develops an unpedestrian style of speaking when his speech has a rhythm. Rhythm implies a modulation of regularity. Even a total absence of any kind or kinds of regularity is a rhythm, but even that extreme requires conscious awareness of that purpose in arranging words. Until you analyze your typical patterns of word arrangement, you cannot introduce rhythm except accidentally. Some art may be accidental in that, given a million monkeys with millions of paint brushes and millions of years, some accidental works of art will surely be produced. But an artist is one who produces more than one work of art, and we have no assurance that any one monkey will ever produce two works of art. Every art is to some extent a craft, and a craft must be studied. It is more efficient to study intelligently rather than by trial and error. Talent alone may produce an artistic skyrocket, the author of one play, or one good poem, or the painter of one good painting, or the actor of one good role, or the speaker of one good speech, but years of training produce craftsmanship, and talent plus craftsmanship produces many works of art. The purpose of this text has been to attempt to reduce the number of years required to become a

Pattern Discerned	Rhythm Introduced by
Metrically identical feet	Alteration of meter
Unmetrical words	Metrical words
Series of short statements	Long statement
Series of long statements	Short statement
Series of general statements	Specific statement
Series of specific statements	General statement
Series of positive statements	Negative statement
Series of statements	Question
Series of descriptive statements	Interpretative statement
Series of literal statements	Figurative statement
Series of concise statements	Wordy statement
Series of wordy statements	Concise statement
Series of intellectual statements	Emotional or sensory statement
Series of emotional or sensory statements	Intellectual statement
Series of important statements	Unimportant statement
Series of unimportant statements	Important statement
Statements in passive voice[1]	Statement in active voice
Statements in active voice	Statement in passive voice

craftsman in matters of oral delivery by presenting the elements of that craft factually and systematically.

The greater the mastery of a craft one acquires, the more freely he can choose among alternatives. The talent with but one voice is by no means free; the best he can hope for without training is to find that situation for which his voice is appropriate. It is the hope of the author that this text efficiently enables some to achieve greater vocal freedom.

[1] For example: You told him (*active voice*); He was told by you (*passive voice*).

Appendix

Pronunciations of Words Frequently Employed in the Text

1.	abdomen	[æb'domɪn]
2.	affricate	['æfrɪkɪt]
3.	agonists	['ægənɪsts]
4.	ala	['elə]
5.	alae	['eli]
6.	alar	['elɚ]
7.	alveolar	[æl'violɚ]
8.	anapest	['ænəpɛst]
9.	anapestic	[ænə'pɛstɪk]
10.	anterolateral	['æntəro'lætərəl]
11.	aponeurosis	[æponjʊ'rosɪs]
12.	aposiopesis	[æposaɪo'pisɪs]
13.	*argumentum ad populum*	[ɑrgjʊmɛntəmæd 'pɑpjʊləm]
14.	aryepiglottic	[ærɪɛpɪ'glɑtɪk]
15.	aryvocalic	[ærɪvo'kelɪk]
16.	arytenoid	[ærɪ'tinɔɪd]
17.	assonance	['æsənəns]
18.	atavistic	[ætə'vɪstɪk]
19.	Bernoulli	[bɚ'nujɪ]
20.	buccal	['bʌkl̩]
21.	buccinator	['bʌkənetɚ]
22.	caninus	['kenɪnəs]

23. choana [ko'ænə]
24. choanae [ko'æni]
25. clavicular [klə'vɪkjʊlɚ]
26. coccyx ['kɑksɪks]
27. concha ['kɑŋkə]
28. conchae ['kɑŋki]
29. condyle ['kɑndɪl]
30. condyloid ['kɑndəlɔɪd]
31. consonance ['kɑnsənəns]
32. corniculate [kɔr'nɪkjʊlɪt]
33. cornu ['kɔrnju]
34. cornua ['kɔrnjʊə]
35. coronoid ['kɔrənɔɪd]
36. costa ['kɑstə]
37. costae ['kɑsti]
38. costal ['kɑstəl]
39. cricoid ['kraɪkɔɪd]
40. cuneiform [kju'niəfɔrm]
41. dactyl ['dæktɪl
42. dactylic [dæk'tɪlɪk]
43. *de rigueur* [də ri'gɝ]
44. dimeter ['dɪmɪtɚ]
45. diverticulum [daɪvɚ'tɪkjʊləm]
46. dorsal ['dɔrsəl]
47. *double entendre* ['dublə ɑ̃'tɑ̃drə]
48. enjambment [ɛn'dʒæm:ənt]
49. enthymeme ['ɛnθɪmim]
50. esophagus [ɪ'sɑfəgəs]
51. esophageal [iso'fædʒɪəl]
52. ethmoid ['ɛθmɔɪd]
53. extempore [ɛk'stɛmporɪ]
54. facet ['fæsɪt]
55. factitious [fæk'tɪʃəs]
56. fauces ['fɔsiz]
57. faucial pillar ['fɔʃəl 'pɪlɚz]
58. genioglossus [dʒinɪo'glɑsəs]
59. geniohyoid [dʒinɪo'haɪɔɪd]
60. glottal ['glɑtl̩]

61. glottis	['glɑtɪs]
62. hamulus	['hæmjuləs]
63. Helmholtz	['hɛlmholts]
64. homophony	['hɑməfonɪ]
65. humerus	['hjumərəs]
66. iamb	['aɪæm]
67. iambic	[aɪ'æmbɪk]
68. ictus	['ɪktəs]
69. intercostals	[ɪntɚ'kɑstəlz]
70. labis	['lebɪs]
71. lamina	['læmɪnə]
72. laminae	['læməni]
73. laryngopharynx	[lə'rɪŋgo'færɪŋks]
74. larynx	['lærɪŋks]
75. latissimus dorsi	[lə'tɪsɪməs 'dɔrsɪ]
76. levator	[lɪ'vetɚ]
77. litotes	['laɪtotiz]
78. lumbar	['lʌmbɚ]
79. Mach	[mɑk]
80. manubrium	[mə'nɪubrɪəm]
81. masseter	[mə'sitɚ]
82. meati	[mɪ'eti]
83. meatus	[mɪ'etəs]
84. metathesis	[mɪ'tæθɪsɪs]
85. metonymy	[mɪ'tɑnəmɪ]
86. nares	['neriz]
87. naris	['nerɪs]
88. nasopharynx	['næzo'færɪŋks]
89. neologism	[nɪ'ɑlodʒɪzm̩]
90. nodule	['nɑdjul]
91. occipital	[ɑk'sɪpətəl]
92. onomatopoeia	[ɑnəmɑtə'pijə]
93. orbiscularis oris	[ɔrbɪskjʊlærɪs 'ɔrɪs]
94. oropharynx	['oro'færɪŋks]
95. oxymoron	[ɑksɪ'morɑn]
96. pectoralis	[pɛkto'rælɪs]
97. pentameter	[pɛn'tæmətɚ]
98. petrous	['pɛtrəs]

99. pharynx ['færɪŋks]
100. phoneme ['fonim]
101. phonemic [fo'nimɪk]
102. platysma ['p'ætɪzmə]
103. posterolateral ['pɑstəro'lætərəl]
104. pterygoid ['tɛrɪgɔɪd]
105. pyriform ['pɪrɪfərm]
106. quadratus lumborum [kwɑ'dretəs lʌm'borəm]
107. rami ['remaɪ]
108. ramus ['reməs]
109. raphe ['refi]
110. rectus abdominis [rɛktəs æb'dɑmɪnɪs]
111. risorius [rɪ'sorɪəs]
112. sacrospinalis [sekrospaɪ'nælɪs]
113. sagittal ['sædʒɪtəl]
114. scaleni]ske'lini]
115. scalenus]ske'linəs]
116. scapula ['skæpjʊlə]
117. serratus [sə'retəs]
118. sinusoid ['saɪnəsɔɪd]
119. sphenoid ['sfinɔɪd]
120. squamous epithelium ['skweməs ɛpɪ'θilɪəm]
121. sternocleidomastoid [stɝnoklaɪdo'mæstɔɪd]
122. sternum ['stɝnəm]
123. stroboscope ['strɑbəskop]
124. stylopharyngeus [staɪlofə'rɪndʒɪəs]
125. subclavius [sʌb'klævɪəs]
126. symphysis ['sɪmfɪsɪs]
127. syncope ['sɪŋkopi]
128. synecdoche [sɪ'nɛkdokɪ]
129. tempi ['tempi]
130. temporal ['tɛmporəl
131. temporalis [tɛmpo'rælɪs]
132. tetrameter [tɛ'træmɪtɚ]
133. thoracis [θo'ræsɪs]
134. thorax ['θoræks]
135. tremolo ['trɛmolo]
136. trimeter ['trɪmɪtɚ]

137.	trochaic	[tro'keɪk]
138.	trochee	['troki]
139.	tropes	[trop]
140.	tubercle	['tjubɚkl̩]
141.	uvula	['juvjʊlə]
142.	velopharyngeal	[vilofə'rɪndʒɪəl]
143.	veli palatini	[vilɪ pælə'tinɪ]
144.	velum	['viləm]
145.	ventral	['vɛntrəl]
146.	ventricularis	[vɛntrɪkjʊ'lærɪs]
147.	*vers libre*	[vɛɚ 'librə]
148.	vertebra	['vɝtɪbrə]
149.	vertebrae	['vɝtɪbri]
150.	vibrato	[vɪ'brɑto]
151.	viscera	['vɪsərə]
152.	vitiates	['vɪʃɪets]
153.	vocalis	[vo'kelɪs]
154.	vomerine	['vomərin]
155.	zygomaticus	[zaɪgo'mætɪkəs]

Answers to Crossword Puzzles

Pages 34–35

1 p	2 r	3 ɪ	t	4 ɪ		5 m	6 ɪ	d	7 r	8 ɪ	9 f
10 l	e	d		11 t	12 r	i	t		13 ɑ	v	e
14 i	l		15 æ	s	ɛ	t		16 s	t	e	l
17 t	r	18 e	s		s		19 b	ɑ	n	d	z
20 s	ɑ	d		21 s	t	22 ɑ	r	k			
	23 d	ɪ	24 l	ɪ		25 g	ɛ	t		26 s	27 e
28 s		29 d	æ	ŋ	30 g	l	d		31 l	ɛ	d
32 ɪ	33 t		s		34 e	z		35 d	ɛ	m	ɪ
36 k	i	p	ɪ	ŋ			37 p	e	s	ɪ	ŋ

Page 53

1 m	2 æ	3 l		4 ɪ	t	5 ə
8 ɑ	d	ɪ	9 s	t		10 r
11 p	ɚ	s	u		12 b	ɛ
		t		13 m	ɒ	s
14 ʃ	15 ɪ		16 b	ɛ	s	t
18 ɔ	l		19 a	n	t	
r		21 k	ɪ	t	ə	22 n
23 t	r	i			24 n	i

Bibliography

General References

BEIGHLEY, K. "An experimental study of the effect of four speech variables on listener comprehension," *Speech Monog.*, **19** (1952), 249–58.

———. "An experimental study of the effect of three speech variables on listener comprehension," *Speech Monog.*, **21** (1954), 248–53.

BIRD, D. "Bibliography of selected materials about listening," *Education*, **75** (1955), 327–33.

BORING, E. *Sensation and Perception in the History of Experimental Psychology*. Appleton-Century-Crofts (New York), 1942.

CHANDLER, A., and BARNHART, E. *A Bibliography of Psychological and Experimental Aesthetics*, 1864–1937, University of California Press (Berkeley), 1938.

CHERRY, C. *On Human Communication*. John Wiley & Sons (New York), 1957.

DUSENBERRY, D., and KNOWER, F. "Experimental studies of the symbolism of action and voice: II. A study of the specificity of meaning in abstract tonal symbols," *Quarterly Jour. Speech*, **25** (1939), 67–75.

EHRENSBERGER, R. "An experimental study of the relative effectiveness of certain forms of emphasis in public speaking," *Speech Monog.*, **12** (1945), 94–111.

GABOR, D. "Theory of communication," *Jour. Instit. Elec. Eng.*, **93** (1946), 429–57.

GILKINSON, H. *Outlines of Research in General Speech*. Burgess Publishing Co. (Minneapolis), 1943.

———. "Experimental and statistical research in general speech:

effects of training and correlates of speech skill," *Quarterly Jour. Speech,* 30 (1944), 95–101, 180–86.

GRAY, G., and WISE, C. *The Bases of Speech,* 3d ed. Harper & Row (New York), 1959.

HEINBERG, P. "Relationships of content and delivery to general effectiveness," *Speech Monog.*, 30 (1963), 105–107.

HOWELL, W., and BREMBECK, W. "Experimental studies in debate, discussion, and general public speaking," *Bull. of Nat'l. Assn. of Secondary Sch. Principals,* 36 (May, 1952), 175–92.

JUDSON, L., and WEAVER, A. *Voice Science,* Appleton-Century-Crofts (New York), 1942.

LANDES, B. "Selected bibliography on voice disorders," *Jour. of Speech and Hearing Disorders,* 24 (1959), 285–99.

LEWIS, D., and TIFFIN, J. "A psychophysical study of individual differences in speaking ability," *Arch. Speech,* 1 (1934), 43–60.

LYNCH, G. "A phonophotographic study of trained and untrained voices," *Arch. Speech* 1 (1934), 9–25.

MILLER, G. *Language and Communication.* McGraw-Hill Book Co., Inc. (New York), 1951.

MURRAY, E., and TIFFIN, J. "An analysis of the basic aspects of effective speech," *Arch. Speech,* 1 (1934), 61–83.

PAGET, R. *Human Speech.* Harcourt, Brace & World (New York), 1930.

POTTER, R., *et al. Visible Speech.* D. Van Nostrand Co., Inc. (New York), 1947.

ROBSON, E. *The Orchestra of the Language.* Thomas Yoseloff, Inc. (New York), 1959.

ROSS, R. "Studies in the psychology of the theatre," *Psych. Record,* 2 (1938), 127–90.

RUBENSTEIN, H., and ABORN, M. "Psycholinguistics," *Ann. Rev. Psychol.*, 11 (1960), 291–322.

STEVENS, S. *Handbook of Experimental Psychology.* John Wiley & Sons (New York), 1951.

TRAVIS, L., ed. *Handbook of Speech Pathology.* Appleton-Century-Crofts (New York), 1957.

VAN RIPER, C., and IRWIN, J. *Voice and Articulation.* Prentice-Hall, Inc. (Englewood Cliffs, N.J.), 1958.

Chapter 1: Speech Training and Personality

ADDINGTON, D. "An experimental study of vocal stereotypes," Ph.D. dissertation, State University of Iowa, 1963.

BALL, J. "An experimental study of the relation between the ability to impart information orally and the primary mental abilities, verbal comprehension and general reasoning," *Speech Monog.*, 19 (1952), 112–16.

BARNES, T. "An experimental study of the relationship between personality traits and speaking effectiveness," Ph. D. dissertation, State University of Iowa, 1960.

BONAVENTURA, M. "Ausdruck der Persönlichkeit in der Sprechstimme und im Photogramm, *Arch. ges. Psychol.*, **94** (1935) 501–70.

BRYNGELSON, B. "Personality changes as a result of speech training," *Quarterly Jour. Speech*, **14** (1928), 207–18.

CANTRIL, H., and ALLPORT, G. "Voice and personality," *The Psychology of Radio*. Harper & Row (New York), Rev. 1941, 181–98.

DANWITZ, H. "An experimental study of the correlation between the degree of speech ability and personality traints," M.A. thesis, Brooklyn College, 1941.

DOW, C. "Intelligence and ability in public performance," *Quarterly Jour. Speech*, **27** (1941), 110–15.

———. "The personality traits of effective public speakers," *Quarterly Jour. Speech*, **27** (1941), 525–32.

DREWS, C. "An experimental study of some of the relationships between specific speech characteristics and aspects of personality as measured by the Minnesota Personality Scale," M.A. thesis, University of Syracuse, 1951.

DUNCAN, M. "An experimental study of some of the relationships between voice and personality among students of speech," *Speech Monog.*, **12** (1945), 47–60.

DUSENBURY, D., and KNOWER, F. "Experimental studies of the symbolism of action and voice," *Quarterly Jour. Speech*, **24** (1938), 424–35.

ECKERT, R., and KEYS, N. "Public speaking as a cue to personality adjustment," *Jour. Appl. Psychol.*, **24** (1940), 144–53.

EISENBERG, P., and ZALOWITZ, E. "Judging expressive movement: III. Judgments of dominance-feeling from phonograph records of voice," *Jour. Appl. Psychol.*, **22** (1938), 620–31.

FAY, P., and MIDDLETON, W. "Judgment of Spranger personality types from the voice as transmitted over a public address system," *Character and Pers.*, **8** (1939), 144–55.

———. "Judgment of occupation from the voice as transmitted over a public address system and over a radio," *Jour. Appl. Psychol.*, **23** (1939), 586–601.

———. "The ability to judge the rested or tired condition of a speaker from his voice as transmitted over a public address system," *Jour. Appl. Psychol.*, **24** (1940), 645–50.

———. "Judgment of Kretschmerian body types from the voice as transmitted over a public address system," *Jour. Soc. Psychol.*, **12** (1940), 151–62.

———. "Judgment of intelligence from the voice transmitted over a public address system," *Sociometry*, **3** (1940), 186–91.

———. "Rating a speaker's natural voice when heard over a public address system," *Quarterly Jour. Speech*, **27** (1941), 120–24.

———. "The ability to judge sociability from the voice as transmitted over a public address system," *Jour. Soc. Psychol.*, 13 (1941), 303-9.

———. "The ability to judge truth-telling, or lying, from the voice as transmitted over a public address system," *Jour. Gen. Psychol.*, 24 (1941), 211–15.

———. "Judgment of emotional balance from the voice as transmitted over a public address system," *Character and Pers.*, 10 (1941), 109–13.

———. "Measurement of persuasiveness of the transcribed voice," *Jour. Psychol.*, 14 (1942), 259–67.

———. "Relationship between sales ability and ratings of the transcribed voices of salesmen," *Jour. Appl. Psychol.*, 26 (1942), 499–510.

———. "Judgment of introversion from the transcribed voice," *Quarterly Jour. Speech*, 28 (1942), 226–28.

———. "Judgment of leadership from the transmitted voice," *Jour. Soc. Psychol.*, 17 (1943), 99–102.

———. "Judgment of confidence from voice," *Jour. Gen. Psychol.*, 30 (1944), 93–97.

FLEMMING, E. "Expression and personality," *Quarterly Jour. Speech*, 18 (1932), 270–76.

GAYLORD, J. "Teaching reading and spelling [title error which should read, " . . . reading and speech"] as functions of personality," *Quarterly Jour. Speech*, 3 (1917), 265–72.

GILKINSON, H. "Indexes of change in attitudes and behavior among students enrolled in general speech courses," *Speech Monog.*, 8 (1941), 23–33.

GILKINSON, H., and KNOWER, F. "Individual differences among students of speech as revealed by psychological tests," *Quarterly Jour. Speech*, 26 (1940), 243–56.

———. "A study of standardized personality tests and skill in speech," *Jour. Ed. Psychol.*, 26 (1941), 161–75.

GILLIS, H. "A study of some characteristics of superior speech majors," *Speech Monog.*, 14 (1947), 165–75.

GOODSTEIN, L. "Functional speech disorders and personality: a survey of the research," *Jour. Speech & Hear. Res.*, 1 (1958), 359–76.

———. "Functional speech disorders and personality: methodological and theoretical considerations," *Jour. Speech & Hear. Res.*, 1 (1958), 377-82.

HEINBERG, P. "Factors related to an individual's ability to perceive implications of dialogues," *Speech Monog.*, 28 (1961), 274–81.

HENRIKSON, E. "An analysis of the characteristics of some 'good' and 'poor' speakers," *Speech Monog.*, 20 (1944), 120–24.

HERZOG, H. "Stimme und Persönlichkeit," *Z. Psychol.*, 130 (1933), 300–79.

HILDRETH, R. "An experimental study of audiences' ability to distinguish between sincere and insincere speeches," Ph.D. dissertation, University of Southern California, 1954.

HUNTER, A. "A comparison of introverted and extroverted high school speakers," *Speech Monog.*, **2** (1935), 50–53.

MALLORY, E., and Miller, V. "A possible basis for the association of voice characteristics and personality traits," *Speech Monog.*, **25** (1958), 255–60.

McDONALD, E. "A study of some factors related to conversational ability," *Speech Monog.*, **12** (1945), 88–93.

MOORE, G. "Personality changes resulting from training in speech fundamentals," *Speech Monog.*, **2** (1935), 56–59.

MOORE, P. "Personality traits and voice quality deficiencies," *Jour. Speech & Hear. Dis.*, **4** (1939), 33–36.

MOORE, W. "Factors related to achievement and improvement in public speaking," *Quarterly Jour. Speech*, **29** (1943), 213–17.

MURRAY, E. "Personality studies in speech," *Speech Monog.*, **2** (1935), 50–89.

PAULSON, S. "Changes in confidence during a period of speech training: transfer of training and comparison of improved and non-improved groups on the Bell Adjustment Inventory," *Speech Monog.*, **18** (1951), 260–65.

PEAR, T. *Voice and Personality.* Chapman & Hall, Ltd. (London), 1931.

———. *Personality, Appearance and Speech.* George Allen & Unwin (London), 1957.

PFAFF, P. "An experimental study of the communication of feeling without contextual material," Ph.D. dissertation, University of Southern California, 1953.

ROSE, F. "Training in speech and changes in personality," *Quarterly Jour. Speech*, **26** (1940), 243–55.

SANFORD, F. "Speech and personality," *Psychol. Bull.*, **39** (1942), 811–45.

———. "Speech and personality: a comparative case study," *Character and Pers.*, **10** (1942), 169–98.

SAPIR, E. "Speech as a personality trait," *Amer. Jour. Sociol.* **32**, (1927), 892–905.

SCHIEDEL, T., *et al.* "Personality and discussion behavior: a study of possible relationships," *Speech Monog.*, **25** (1958), 261–67.

SHEPHERD, J., and SCHIEDEL, T. "A study of the personality configuration of effective oral readers," *Speech Monog.*, **23** (1956), 298–304.

STAGNER, R. "Judgments of voice and personality," *Jour. Ed. Psychol.*, **27** (1936), 272–77.

STARKWEATHER, J. "Content-free speech as a source of information about the speaker," *Jour. Abnorm. Psychol.*, **52** (1956), 394–402.

TAFT, R. "The ability to judge people," *Psychol. Bull.*, **52** (1955), 1–23.

TAYLOR, A. "Social agreement on personality traits as judged from speech," *Jour. Soc. Psychol.*, 5 (1934), 244–48.

TRACY, J. "A study of the personality traits of mature actors and mature public speakers," *Speech Monog.*, 2 (1935), 53–56.

WAGONER, L. "Speech as an indication of temperamental traits," *Quarterly Jour. Speech*, 11 (1925), 237–42.

WEAVER, A. "Experimental studies in vocal expression," *Quarterly Jour. Speech*, 10 (1924), 199–204.

WILKE, W., and SNYDER, J. "Attitudes towards American dialects," *Jour. Soc. Psychol.*, 14 (1941), 349–62.

Chapter 2: Phonetics

BLOCH, B., and TRAGER, G. *Outline of Linguistic Analysis.* Linguistic Society of America (Baltimore), 1942.

FLETCHER, H., and GALT, R. "The perception of speech and its relation to telephony," *Jour. Acoust. Soc. Amer.*, 22 (1950), 89–151.

HOUSE, A. "Formant band widths and vowel preference," *Jour. Speech. & Hear. Res.*, 3 (1960), 3–8.

JONES, D. *An Outline of English Phonetics*, 6th ed. Teubner Verlag (Stuttgart), 1939.

KAISER, L. ed. *Manual of Phonetics.* North-Holland Pub. Co. (Amsterdam), 1957.

KENYON, J. *American Pronunciation: A Textbook of Phonetics for Students of English.* George Wahr, Publisher, (Ann Arbor, Mich.), 1932.

LADEFOGED, P., and BROADBENT, D. "Information conveyed by vowels," *Jour. Acoust. Soc. Amer.*, 29 (1957), 98–103.

PRONKO, N. "Language and psycholinguistics: a review," *Psych. Bull.*, 43 (1946), 189–239.

SOLOMON, L., *et al.* "A factorial study of speech perception," *Jour. Speech & Hear. Res.*, 3 (1960), 101–7.

STREVENS, P. "Spectra of fricative noise in human speech," *Lang. Speech* (London), 3 (1960), 32–49.

VAN RIPER, C., and SMITH, D. *An Introduction to General American Phonetics.* Harper & Row (New York), 1962.

Chapter 3: Anatomy and Physiology of Speech

BARNES, J. "Vital capacity and ability in oral reading," *Quart. Jour. Speech*, 12 (1926), 176–82.

BLOOMER, H. "A roentgenographic study of the mechanism of respiration," *Speech Monog.*, 3 (1936), 118–24.

BLOOMER, H., and SHOHARA, H. "The study of respiratory movements by Roentgen kymography," *Speech Monog.*, 8 (1941), 91–101.

BOIES, L. *Fundamentals of Otolaryngology*, 2d ed. W. B. Saunders Co. (Philadelphia), 1955.

CARHART, R. "Some aspects of model larynx function," *Jour. Acoust. Soc. Amer.*, 14 (1942), 36–40.

CURRY, E. "An objective study of the pitch characteristics of the adolescent male voice," *Speech Monog.*, 7 (1940), 48–62.

CURRY, R. *Mechanism of the Human Voice.* Longmans Green & Co., Inc. (New York), 1940.

CURTIS, J. "Systematic research in experimental phonetics: the case for dynamic analysis in acoustic phonetics," *Jour. Speech Hearing Dis.*, 19 (1954), 147–57.

DELATTRE, P. "The physiological interpretation of sound spectrograms," *Publ. Mod. Lang. Assn.*, 66 (1951), 864.

DRAPER, M., *et al.* "Respiratory muscles in speech," *Jour. Speech & Hearing Res.*, 2 (1959), 16–27.

DUFFY, R. "The vocal pitch characteristics of eleven, thirteen, and fifteen-year-old female speakers," Ph.D. diss., State University of Iowa, 1958.

ERICKSON, C. "The basic factors in the human voice," *Psychol. Monog.*, 36 (1926), 82–112.

FAABORG-ANDERSEN, K. "Electromyographic investigation of intrinsic laryngeal muscles in humans," *Acta physiol. scandinav.*, 41 Suppl. (1957), 1–149.

FAABORG-ANDERSEN, K., and SONNINEN, A. "The function of the extrinsic laryngeal muscles at different pitch," *Acta Oto-Laryngol.*, 51 (1960), 89–93.

FAIRBANKS, G., *et al.* "An acoustical study of vocal pitch in seven and eight-year old boys," *Child Develop.*, 20 (1949), 63–69.

———. "An acoustical study of vocal pitch in seven and eight-year old girls," *Child Develop.*, 20 (1949), 71–78.

FARNSWORTH, D. "High speed motion pictures of the vocal cords," *Bell Labs. Record,* 18 (1940), 203–8.

FLETCHER, H. *Speech and Hearing.* D. Van Nostrand Co., Inc. (New York), 1929, p. 50.

FREUD, E. "Voice and breathing," *Arch. Otolaryngol.*, 67 (1958), 1–7.

GARDE, E. *La Voix.* Les Presses Universitaires de France (Paris), 1954.

GRANT, J. *A Method for Anatomy.* The Williams & Wilkins Co. (Baltimore), 1944.

GRAY, G., *et al.* *Studies in Experimental Phonetics,* Louisiana State University Studies, No. 27, 1936.

HAGERTY, R., *et al.* "Posterior pharyngeal wall movement in normals," *Jour. Speech & Hear. Res.*, 1 (1958), 203–10.

HARRINGTON, R. "A study of the mechanism of velopharyngeal closure," *Jour. Speech & Hear. Dis.*, 9 (1944), 325–45.

HIXON, E. "An X-ray study comparing oral and pharyngeal structures of individuals with nasal voices and individuals with superior voices," M.S. thesis, State University of Iowa, 1949.

HOLBROOK, R., and CARMODY, F. "X-ray studies of speech articulation," *Univ. of Calif. Publ. in Mod. Philol.*, 20, No. 4, 1937.

HOLLEIN, H. "Some basic measurements of the laryngeal tract obtained by laminagraphic radiographic techniques," Ph.D. dissertation, State University of Iowa, 1955.

———. "Some laryngeal correlates of vocal pitch," *Jour. Speech & Hearing Res.*, **3** (1960), 52–58.

———. "Vocal pitch variation related to changes in vocal fold length," *Jour. Speech & Hearing Res.*, **3** (1960), 150–56.

HOLLEIN, H., and MOORE, G. "Measurements of the vocal folds during changes in pitch," *Jour. Speech & Hearing Res.*, **3** (1960), 157–65.

HOSHIKO, M. "Sequence of action of breathing muscles during speech," *Jour. Speech & Hearing Res.*, **3** (1960), 291–97.

HUSSON, R. "Physiology of the vibration of the vocal cords," *C. R. Acal. Sci. Paris* (in French), **241** (1955), 242–44.

———. "The present state of physiological phonetics," *Phonetica* (Basel), **4** (1959), 1–32.

HUYCK, E., and ALLEN, K. "Diaphragmatic action of good and poor speaking voices," *Speech Monog.*, **4** (1937), 101–9.

KAISER, L. *Biological and Statistical Research Concerning the Speech of 216 Dutch Students.* Noord-Hollandsche Vitgevers Maatschappij (Amsterdam), 1943.

KAPLAN, H. *Anatomy and Physiology of Speech.* McGraw-Hill Book Co., Inc. (New York), 1960.

KELLY, J., and HIGLEY, L. "Contributions to the X-ray study of tongue positions in certain vowels," *Arch. of Speech*, **1** (1934), 84–95.

LUCHSINGER, R., and PFISTER, K. "Ergebnisse von Kehlkopfaufnahmen mit einer Zeitdehnerapparatur," *Bull. Schweiz. Akad. Med. Wiss.*, **15** (1959), 164–77.

METFESSEL, M. "Experimental phonetics," *Psych. Bull.*, **26** (1929), 305–23.

METZGER, W. "How do the vocal cords vibrate?" *Quarterly Jour. Speech*, **14** (1928), 29–39.

MOORE, P. "A short history of laryngeal investigation," *Quarterly Jour. Speech*, **23** (1937), 531–64.

———. "Vocal fold movement during vocalization," *Speech Monog.*, **4** (1937), 44–45.

———. "Motion picture studies of the vocal folds and vocal attack," *Jour. Speech Dis.*, **3** (1938), 235–38.

NEGUS, V. *The Mechanism of the Larynx.* The C. V. Mosby Co. (St. Louis), 1929.

———. "The mechanism of the larynx," *Laryngoscope*, **67** (1957), 961–86.

NEGUS, V., NEIL, E., and FLOYD, W. "The mechanism of phonation." *Ann. Otol. Rhin. & Laryng.*, **66** (1957), 817–29.

PAGET, SIR R. "Nature and reproduction of speech sounds," *Nature*, **111** (1923), 21–23.

PANCONCELLI-CALZIA, G. "Husson's theory of cerebral production of vocal cord vibrations; its experimental confirmation by Laget and Moulonguet," *Rev. Laryngol. Bord.* (in German), **76** Suppl. (1955), 659–65.

PETERSON, G. "Systematic research in experimental phonetics: 4. The evaluation of speech signals," *Jour. Speech & Hearing Dis.*, **19** (1954), 159–68.

PORTMANN, G. "The physiology of phonation," *Jour. Laryng. & Otol.*, **71** (1957), 1–15.

PORTMANN, G., *et al.* "Physiology of voice," *Rev. Laryngol. Otol. Rhinol.* (in French), **80** (1959), 1–20.

PRESSMAN, J. "Physiology of the vocal cords in phonation and respiration," *Arch. Otolaryng.*, **35** (1942), 355–98.

RUSSELL, G. *The Vowel.* Ohio State University Press (Columbus), 1928.

———. "Mechanism of speech," *Jour. Acoust. Soc. Amer.*, **1** (1929), 83–109.

———. *Speech and Voice.* The Macmillan Co. (New York), 1931.

SCHAEFFER, J., ed. *Human Anatomy.* McGraw-Hill Book Co., Inc. (New York), 1953.

SCRIPTURE, E. *The Elements of Experimental Phonetics.* Charles Scribner's Sons (New York), 1902.

———. *Researches in experimental phonetics.* Carnegie Institution (Washington, D.C.), 1906.

———. *Anwendung der graphischen Methode auf Sprache und Gesang*, Barth Verlag (Munich), 1927.

———. *Grundzüge der englischen Verswissenschaft*, N. G. Elevert (Marburg), 1929.

SICHER, H. *Oral Anatomy.* 2d ed. The C. V. Mosby Co. (St. Louis), 1952.

STETSON, R. "Motor phonetics," *Arch. Néerlandaises de Phonétique Expérimentale*, **3** (1928), 1–216.

———. "Speech movements in action," *Trans. Amer. Laryng. Assn.*, **55** (1933), 29–41.

STETSON, R., *et al.* "Palatograms change with rate of articulation," *Arch. Néerlandaises de Phonétique Expérimentale*, **11** (1935), 1–28.

STETSON, R. *Motor Phonetics: A Study of Speech Movements in Action.* North-Holland Pub. Co. (Amsterdam), 1951.

STETSON, R., and HUDGINS, C. "Functions of the breathing movements in the mechanism of speech," *Arch. Néerlandaises de Phonétique Expérimentale*, **5** (1930), 1–30.

TARNÒCZY, T. "Opening time and opening-quotient of the vocal cords during phonation," *Jour. Acoust. Soc. Amer.*, **23** (1951), 42–44.

TIFFEN, J., SAETVEIDT, J., and SNIDECOR, J. "An approach to the analysis of the vibration of the vocal cords," *Quarterly Jour. Speech*, **24** (1938), 1–11.

TREVINO, S., and PARMENTER, C. "Vowel positions as shown by X-ray," *Quarterly Jour. of Speech*, **18** (1932), 351–69.

VAN DEN BERG, J. "Physiology and physics of voice production," *Acta Physiol. Neerl.*, **5** (1956), 40–55.

VAN DEN BERG, J., and TAN, T. "Recent findings on the laryngeal function," *Jour. Fr. Oto-Rhino-Laryng.* (in French), **3** (1959), 103–11.

VON LEDEN, H. "Laryngeal physiology," *Jour. Laryngol. & Otol.*, **74** (1960), 705–12.

WEISS, D. "Vibration of the vocal cords," *An. Fonol. Audiol.* (in Spanish), **1** (1956), 205–11.

WEST, R. "The nature of vocal sounds," *Quarterly Jour. Speech*, **12** (1926), 244–95.

WOODBURNE, R. *Essentials of Human Anatomy.* Oxford University Press (New York), 1957.

WUSTROW, F. "On the anatomy of the vocalis muscle," *Z. Laryngol.* (in German), **35** (1956), 126–30.

ZENKER, V., and ZENKER, A. "Concerning the action of extrinsic mechanisms and vocal fold tension," *Fol. Phoniat.* (in German), **12** (1960), 1–36.

ZERFFI, W. "Male and female voices," *Arch. Otolaryngol.*, **65** (1957), 7–10.

Chapter 4: Acoustics of Speech

BERANEK, L. *Acoustics.* McGraw-Hill Book Co., Inc. (New York), 1954.

BLACK, J. "The quality of a spoken vowel," *Arch. Speech*, **2** (1937), 7–27.

———. "The effect of the consonant on the vowel," *Jour. Acoust. Soc. Amer.*, **10** (1939), 203–5.

BOYS, C. "Quartz fibres," *Nature*, **42** (1890), 604–8.

CARHART, R. "Infra-glottal resonance and a cushion pipe," *Speech Monog.*, **5** (1938), 65–97.

CHIBA, T., and KAJIYAMA, M. *The Vowel—Its Nature and Structure*, Kaiseidan Pub. Co. (Tokyo), 1941.

COTTON, J. "A study of certain phoniatric resonance phenomena, *Jour. Speech & Hear. Dis.*, **5** (1940), 289–93.

CRANDALL, I. "The sounds of speech," *Bell Syst. Tech. Jour.*, **4** (1925), 586–626.

DAVIS, H., ed. *Hearing and Deafness.* Murray Hill Books (New York), 1947.

DELATTRE, P., *et al.* "An experimental study of the acoustic determinants of vowel color," *Word*, **8** (1952), 195–210.

DUNN, H., and WHITE, S. "Statistical measurements of conversational speech," *Jour. Acoust. Soc. Amer.*, **11** (1940), 278–88.

DUNN, H. "The calculation of vowel resonances, and an electrical vocal tract," *Jour. Acoust. Soc. Amer.*, **22** (1950), 740–53.

FAIRBANKS, G. "Systematic research in experimental phonetics: theory of the speech mechanism as a servomechanism," *Jour. Speech & Hear. Dis.*, **19** (1954), 133–39.

FAIRBANKS, G., and GRUBB, P. "A psychophysical investigation of vowel formants," *Jour. Speech & Hear. Res.*, **4** (1961), 203–19.

FANT, G. *Acoustic Theory of Speech Production.* Humanities Press (New York), 1960.

FERRERI, G., and CERQUIGLINI, S. "Photoelectro-laryngography and function of vocal cords," *Acta Otolaryngol.*, **50** (1959), 344–47.

GRUBB, P. "A psychophysical study of vowel formants," *Diss. Abstr.*, **16** (1956), 1736.

HARVARD UNIVERSITY PSYCHO-ACOUSTICS LABORATORY. *A Bibliography in Audition; A Project.* 2 vols. Harvard University Press (Cambridge), 1950.

HOOPS, R. *Speech Science: Acoustics in Speech,* Charles Thomas (Springfield, Ill.), 1960.

HOUSE, A. "Formant band widths and vowel preference," *Jour. Speech & Hear. Res.*, **3** (1960), 1–8.

JOOS, M. *Acoustic Phonetics,* Linguistic Society of America (Baltimore), 1948.

KEENAN, J., and BARRETT, G. "Intralaryngeal relationships during pitch and intensity changes," *Jour. Speech & Hear. Res.*, **5** (1962), 173–78.

LAASE, L. "The effect of pitch and intensity on the quality of vowels in speech," *Arch. of Speech,* **2** (1937), 41–60.

LEWIS, D. "Vocal resonance," *Jour. Acoust. Soc. Amer.*, **8** (1936), 91–99.

LIEBERMAN , P. "Some acoustic correlates of word stress inAmerican English," *Jour. Acoust. Soc. Amer.*, **32** (1960), 451–54.

MAYER, A. "Researches in acoustics," *Philol. Mag.*, **37** (1894) 259–88.

MILLER, D. *The Science of Musical Sounds.* The Macmillan Co. (New York), 1926.

MILLER, R. "Nature of the vocal cord wave," *Jour. Acoust. Soc. Amer.*, **31** (1959), 667–77.

MOORE, P., and VON LEDEN, H. "Dynamic variations of the vibratory pattern in the normal larynx," *Folia Phoniat.*, **10** (1958), 205–38.

MORSE, P. *Vibration and Sound.* McGraw-Hill Book Co., Inc. (New York), 1948.

NEGUS, V. "The mechanism of phonation," *Ann. Otol. Rhinol. & Laryngol.*, **66** (1957), 817–29.

PETERSON, G. "The information-bearing elements of speech," *Jour. Acoust. Soc. Amer.*, **24** (1952), 629–37.

———. "Some observations on speech," *Quart. Jour. Speech*, **44** (1958), 402–12.

PETERSON, G., and BARNEY, H. "Control methods used in a study of the vowels," *Jour. Acoust. Soc. Amer.*, **24** (1952), 175–84.

PIERCE, J., and DAVID, E. *Man's World of Sound.* Doubleday & Co., Inc. (New York), 1958.

POTTER, R., *et al. Visible Speech.* D. Van Nostrand Co., Inc. (New York), 1947.

POTTER, R., and PETERSON, G. "Representation of vowels and their movements," *Jour. Acoust. Soc. Amer.*, **20** (1948), 528–35.

POTTER, R., and STEINBERG, J. "Toward the specification of speech," *Jour. Acoust. Soc. Amer.*, **22** (1950), 807–20.

RICHARDSON, E. "Recent developments in vocal acoustics," *Discovery*, **8** (1958), 333–38.

RUBIN, H. "The neurochronaxic theory of voice production—a refutation," *Arch. Otolaryngol.*, **71** (1960), 913–20.

SIVIAN, L., and WHITE, S. "On minimum audible sound fields," *Jour. Acoust. Soc. Amer.*, **4** (1933), 288–321.

STEVENS, K., *et al.* "An electrical analog of the vocal tract," *Jour. Acoust. Soc. Amer.*, **25** (1953), 734–42.

STEVENS, K., and HOUSE, A. "Development of a quantitative description of vowel articulation," *Jour. Acoust. Soc. Amer.*, **27** (1955), 484–93.

———. "An acoustical theory of vowel production and some of its implications," *Jour. Speech and Hear. Res.*, **4** (1961) 303–20.

STEVENS, S., *et al. Bibliography on Hearing.* Harvard University Press (Cambridge), 1955.

STEVENS, S., and DAVIS, H. *Hearing, its Psychology and Physiology.* John Wiley & Sons (New York), 1938.

STEWART, G. *Acoustics.* D. Van Nostrand Co., Inc. (New York), 1932.

STEWART, J. "An electrical analogue of the vocal organs," *Nature*, **110** (1922), 311–12.

TARNÒCZY, T. "Opening time and opening-quotient of the vocal cords during phonation," *Jour. Acoust. Soc. Amer.*, **23** (1951), 42–44.

TIFFIN, J., *et al.* "An approach to the analysis of the vibration of the vocal cords," *Quarterly Jour. Speech*, **24** (1938), 1–11.

TIMCKE, R., VON LEDEN, H., and MOORE, P. "Laryngeal vibrations: measurements of the glottic wave," *Arch. Otolaryng.*, **68** (1958), 1–19.

UNGEHEUER, G., *Elemente einer akustischen Theorie der Vokalartikulation* (Elements of an acoustic theory of vowel articulation), Springer-Verlag (Berlin), 1960.

VAN DEN BERG, J. "Transmission of the vocal cavities," *Jour. Acoust. Soc. Amer.*, **27** (1955), 161–68.

———. "On the air resistance and the Bernoulli effect of the human larynx," *Jour. Acoust. Soc. Amer.*, **29** (1957), 626–31.

———. "Myoelastic-aerodynamic theory of voice production," *Jour. Speech & Hear. Res.*, **1** (1958), 227–44.

Wendahl, R. "Fundamental frequency and absolute vowel identification," *Jour. Acoust. Soc. Amer.*, **31** (1959), 109.

West, R. "The nature of vocal sounds," *Quarterly Jour. Speech*, **12** (1926), 244–95.

Wood, A. *Acoustics*. Interscience Publishers, Inc. (New York), 1941.

Chapter 5: Voice Quality

Black, J. "A study of voice merit," *Quarterly Jour. Speech*, **28** (1942), 67–74.

Bloomer, H., and Peterson, G. "A spectrographic study of hypernasality," *Cleft Palate Bull.*, **5** (1955), 5–6.

Curtis, J. "An experimental study of the wave-composition of nasal voice quality," Ph.D. dissertation, State University of Iowa, 1942.

Dickson, D. "An acoustic study of nasality," *Jour. Speech & Hear. Res.*, **5** (1962), 103–11.

Diehl, C. "Voice quality and anxiety," *Jour. Speech & Hear. Res.*, **2** (1959), 282–85.

Diehl, C., and McDonald, E. "Effect of voice quality on communication," *Jour. Speech & Hear. Dis.*, **21** (1956), 233–37.

Ernst, R. "Stroboskopische Untersuchungen bei Berufssprechern," *H. N. O.*, Berlin, **8** (1960), 170–74.

Froeschels, E. "Nose and nasality," *Arch. Otolaryngol.*, **66** (1957), 629–33.

Hadwiger, K. "The relative effectiveness of four voice qualities in imparting factual information via audio-visual and audio-only media," M.A. thesis, State University of Iowa, 1959.

Harrington, R. "A note on a lingua-velar relationship," *Jour. Speech Dis.*, **11** (1946), 25.

Hattori, S., *et al.* "Nasalization of vowels," *Jour. Acoust. Soc. Japan* (in Japanese), **12** (1956), 189–96.

Holmes, F. "An experimental study of individual vocal quality," *Quarterly Jour. Speech*, 16 (1930), 344–51.

House, A., and Stevens, K. "Analog studies of the nasalization of vowels," *Jour. Speech & Hear. Dis.*, **21** (1956), 218–32.

Kelly, J. "Studies in nasality," *Arch. Speech*, **1** (1934), 26–42.

Lafon, J., *et al.* "The acoustic part of the nasal fossae in phonation," *Oto-Rhino-Laryngol.* (in French), **9** (1960), 307–16.

Lindsley, C. "Psycho-physical determinants of voice quality," *Speech Monog.*, 1 (1934), 79–116.

Lintz, L., and Sherman, D. "Phonetic elements and perception of nasality," *Jour. Speech & Hear. Res.*, **4** (1961), 381–98.

McIntosh, C. "An auditory study of nasality," M.A. thesis, State University of Iowa, 1937.

MOLL, K. "Velopharyngeal closure on vowels," *Jour. Speech & Hear. Res.*, **5** (1962), 30–37.

MOSER, H., *et al.* "Comparison of hyponasality, hypernasality, and normal voice quality on the intelligibility of two-digit numbers," *Jour. Acoust. Soc. Amer.*, **27** (1955), 872–73.

MOSER, H., and OYER, H. "Relative intensities of sounds at various anatomical locations of the head and neck during phonation of the vowels," *Jour. Acoust. Soc. Amer.*, **30** (1958), 275–77.

OCHIAI, Y., and FUKUMURA, T. "Preliminaries to analysis of quality in speech, "*Mem. Fac. Eng. Nagoya Univ.*, **9** (1957), 306–15.

———. "On the essential qualities of voice," *Annales Telecomm* (in French), **15** (1960), 277–91.

SHAMES, G., *et al.* "The relationships among nasal voice quality, speech intelligibility, and articulation," *Cleft Palate Bull.*, **10** (1960), 62–63.

SHERMAN, D., and GOODWIN, F. "Pitch level and nasality," *Jour. Speech & Hear. Dis.*, **19** (1954), 423–28.

SUGAWARA, A. "Experimental study on the nasal resonance," *Jour. Otorhinolaryngol. Soc.*, **57** (1954), 7–33.

TIFFANY, W. "Nonrandom sources of variation in vowel quality," *Jour. Speech & Hear. Res.*, **2** (1959), 305–17.

VAN DEN BERG, J. "Calculations on a model of the vocal tract for vowel [i] (meat) and on the larynx," *Jour. Acoust. Soc. Amer.*, **27** (1955), 332–37.

WILLIAMS, R. "A serial radiographic study of velopharyngeal closure and tongue positions in certain vowel sounds," *Northwestern Univ. Bull.*, **52** (1952), 9-12.

WINCKEL, V. "The psychoacoustic evaluation of the vocal spectrum," *Folia Phoniat.*, **12** (1960), 129–36.

WOLFE, W. "X-ray study of certain structures and movements involved in nasopharyngeal closure," M.A. thesis, State University of Iowa, 1942.

Chapter 6: Pitch and Intonation

BECK, J., and SHAW, W. "Magnitude estimations of pitch," *Jour. Acoust. Soc. Amer.*, **34** (1962), 92–98.

COHEN, A. "Further investigation of the effects of intensity upon the pitch of pure tones," *Jour. Acoust. Soc. Amer.*, **33** (1961), 1363–75.

COWAN, J. "Pitch and intensity characteristics of stage speech," *Arch. Speech*, **1** Suppl. (1936), 7–85.

DIEHL, C., *et al.* "Pitch change and comprehension," *Speech Monog.*, **28** (1961), 65–68.

DOUGHTY, J., and GARNER, W. "Pitch characteristics of short tones. I. Two kinds of pitch threshold," *Jour. Exper. Psychol.*, **37** (1947), 351–65.

DREHER, J. "Judgment of pitch contours in context," *Speech Monog.*, 19 (1952), 60–63.

FAIRBANKS, G. "Recent experimental investigations of vocal pitch in speech," *Jour. Acoust. Soc. Amer.*, 11 (1940), 457–66.

FAIRBANKS, G., and PRONOVOST, W. "An experimental study of the pitch characteristics of the voice during the expression of emotion," *Speech Monog.*, 6 (1939), 87–104.

FRY, D. "Experiments in the perception of stress," *Lang. & Speech*, 1 (1958), 126–52.

GLASGOW, G. "A semantic index of vocal pitch," *Speech Monog.*, 19 (1952), 64–68.

HOLLEIN, H., and CURTIS, J. "A laminagraphic study of vocal pitch," *Jour. Speech & Hear. Res.*, 3 (1960), 361–71.

HOLLEIN, H., and MOORE, G. "Measurements of the vocal folds during changes in pitch," *Jour. Speech & Hear. Res.*, 3 (1960), 157–65.

LAASE, L. "Effect of pitch and intensity on the quality of vowels in speech," *Arch. Speech*, 2 (1937), 41–60.

LEHISTE, I., and PETERSON, G. "Some basic considerations in the analysis of intonation," *Jour. Acoust. Soc. Amer.*, 33 (1961), 419–25.

LIEBERMAN, P. "Perturbations in vocal pitch," *Jour. Acoust. Soc. Amer.*, 33 (1961), 597–603.

LIEBERMAN, P., and MICHAELS, S. "Some aspects of fundamental frequency and envelope amplitude as related to the emotional content of speech," *Jour. Acoust. Soc. Amer.*, 34 (1962), 922–27.

LINKE, C. "A study of pitch characteristics of female voices and their relationships to vocal effectiveness," Ph.D. diss., State University of Iowa, 1953.

McINTOSH, C. "A study of the relationship between pitch level and variability in the voices of superior speakers," Ph.D. dissertation, State University of Iowa, 1939.

ORTLEB, R., and TIFFIN, J. "An objective study of emphasis in oral reading of emotional and unemotional material," *Speech Monog.*, 4 (1937), 56–68.

PIKE, K. *The Intonation of American English.* University of Michigan Press (Ann Arbor), 1945.

PRONOVOST, W. "An experimental study of methods for determining natural and habitual pitch levels," *Speech Monog.*, 9 (1942), 111–23.

SCHOUTEN, J. "The perception of pitch," *Philips Tech. Rev.*, 5 (1940), 286–94.

SNIDECOR, J. "Studies in the pitch and duration characteristics of superior speakers," Ph.D. dissertation, State University of Iowa, 1940.

STEVENS, S., and VOLKMANN, J. "The relation of pitch to frequency," *Amer. Jour. Psychol.*, 53 (1940), 329–53.

TIFFIN, J., and STEER, M. "An experimental analysis of emphasis," *Speech Monog.*, 4 (1937), 69–74.

WODARZ, V. "Über vergleichende satzmelodische Untersuchungen," *Phonetica*, Basel, 5 (1960), 75–98.

Chapter 7: Loudness

BARCZINSKI, L., and THIENHAUS, E. "Klangspektren und Lautstärke deutscher Sprachlaute," *Arch. Néerlandaises de Phonétique Expérimentale*, 11 (1935), 47–68.

BLACK, J. "Natural frequency, duration, and intensity of vowels in reading," *Jour. Speech & Hear. Dis.*, 14 (1949), 216–21.

BLACK, J., and MASON, H. "Training for voice communication," *Jour. Acoust. Soc. Amer.*, 18 (1946), 441–45.

BLACK, J., and TOMLINSON, W. "Loud voice: immediate effects upon the listener," *Speech Monog.*, 19 (1952), 299–302.

DUNN, H., and FARNSWORTH, D. "Exploration of pressure field around the human head during speech," *Jour. Acoust. Soc. Amer.*, 10 (1939), 184–99.

DUNN, H., and WHITE, S. "Statistical measurements on conversational speech," *Jour. Acoust. Soc. Amer.*, 11 (1940), 278–88.

EGAN, J., and WIENER, F. "On the intelligibility of bands of speech in noise," *Jour. Acoust. Soc. Amer.*, 18 (1946), 435–41.

FAIRBANKS, G. "A physiological correlative of vowel intensity," *Speech Monog.*, 17 (1950), 390–95.

FLETCHER, H. "Newer concepts of the pitch, the loudness and the timbre of muscial tones," *Jour. Franklin Instit.*, 220 (1935), 405–29.

———. "The pitch, loudness, and quality of muscial tones," *Amer. Jour. Physics*, 14 (1946), 215–23.

FLETCHER, H., and MUNSON, W. "Loudness, its definition, measurement, and calculation," *Jour. Acoust. Soc. Amer.*, 5 (1933), 82–108.

FLETCHER, W. "Vocal fold activity and sub-glottic air pressure in relation to vocal intensity: a brief historical review," *Speech Monog.*, 21 (1954), 73–78.

FRENCH, N., and STEINBERG, J. "Factors governing the intelligibility of speech sounds," *Jour. Acoust. Soc. Amer.*, 19 (1947), 90–119.

HAM, L., and PARKINSON, J. "Loudness and intensity relations," *Jour. Acoust. Soc. Amer.*, 3 (1932), 511–34.

HAWKINS, J., and STEVENS, S. "The masking of pure tones and of speech by white noise," *Jour. Acoust. Soc. Amer.*, 22 (1950), 6–13.

HELLMAN, R., and ZUISLOCKI, J. "Some factors affecting the estimation of loudness," *Jour. Acoust. Soc. Amer.*, 33 (1961), 687–94.

HOLLEIN, H., and CURTIS, J. "Laminagraphic study of vocal intensity," *Jour. Acoust. Soc. Amer.*, 33 (1961), 843.

HOWES, D. "The loudness of multicomponent tones," *Amer. Jour. Psychol.*, 63 (1950), 1–30.

HUSSON, R. "On the physiological conditioning of vocal intensity," *Jour. Physiol. Path. Gen.* (in French), 47 (1955), 197–200.

KARLIN, J., *et al.* "Auditory tests of the ability to hear speech in noise," OSRD Report 3516, Psychoacoustics Laboratory, Harvard University, 1944.

KNUDSEN, V. "The hearing of speech in auditoriums," *Jour. Acoust. Soc. Amer.*, 1 (1929), 56–82.

LIEBERMAN, P. "Some acoustic correlates of word stress in American English," *Jour. Acoust. Soc. Amer.*, 32 (1960), 451–53.

LAIRD, D., and Coye, K. "Psychological measurement of annoyance as related to pitch and loudness," *Jour. Acoust. Soc. Amer.*, 1 (1929), 158–63.

MILLER, G., and LICKLIDER, J. "The intelligibility of interrupted speech," *Jour. Acoust. Soc. Amer.*, 22 (1950), 167–73.

MORGAN, C., and GARNER, W. "Further measurements of the relation of pitch to intensity," *Amer. Psychologist*, 2 (1947), 433.

PICKETT, J. "Effects of vocal force on the intelligibility of speech sounds," *Jour. Acoust. Soc. Amer.*, 28 (1956), 902–5.

POLLACK, I. "Effects of high pass and low pass filtering on the intelligibility of speech in noise," *Jour. Acoust. Soc. Amer.*, 20 (1948), 259–66.

———. "Studies in the loudness of complex sounds," Ph.D. dissertation, Harvard University, 1948.

ROBINSON, D., and DADSON, R. "Threshold of hearing and equal-loudness relations for pure tones, and the loudness function," *Jour. Acoust. Soc. Amer.*, 29 (1957), 1284–88.

SACIA, C. "Speech power and energy," *Bell System Tech. Jour.*, 4 (1925), 627–41.

SACIA, C., and BECK, C. "The power of fundamental speech sounds," *Bell System Tech., Jour.* 5 (1926), 393–403.

SIVIAN, L. "Speech power and its measurement," *Bell System Tech. Jour.*, 8 (1929), 646–61.

SOLOMON, L. "Search for physical correlates to psychological dimensions of sounds," *Jour. Acoust. Soc. Amer.*, 31 (1959), 492–97.

STEVENS, S. "The relation of pitch to intensity," *Jour. Acoust. Soc. Amer.*, 6 (1935), 150–54.

———. "The measurement of loudness," *Jour. Acoust. Soc. Amer.*, 27 (1955), 815–29.

VON ZUBERBIER, E., and GRÜNEWALD, G. "Studien zur Psychomotorik der Sprechintensität" (Studies of the psychomotorics of speech intensity), *Phonetica*, 5 (1960), 99–115.

ZOLL, P. "The relation of tonal volume, intensity, and pitch," *Amer. Jour. Psychol.*, 46 (1934), 99–106.

Chapter 8: Rate

BLACK, J. "The relation between message-type and vocal rate and intensity," *Speech Monog.*, 16 (1949), 217–20.

———. "Relations among fundamental frequency, vocal sound pressure, and rate of speaking," Ohio State University Research Foundation Press (Columbus), 1958.

DESRETS, M. "Determination of the average speed of speech and its extremes," *Fono Audiologica* (in Spanish), 6 (1960), 113–14.

FAIRBANKS, G. "An experimental study of the durational characteristics of the voice during the expression of emotion," *Speech Monog.*, 8 (1941), 85–90.

GIBBONS, E., *et al.* "The variability of oral reading rate," *Jour. Speech & Hear. Dis.*, 23 (1958), 591–93.

GOODMAN-MALOMUTH, L. "An experimental study of the effects of speaking rate upon listenability," *Speech Monog.*, 24 (1957), 89–90.

HARWOOD, K. "Listenability and rate of presentation," *Speech Monog.*, 22 (1955), 57–59.

HUTTON, C. "A psychophysical study of speech rate," *Diss. Abstr.*, 15 (1955), 168.

SCHWARTZ, M. "Differential effect of instructions upon the rate of oral reading," *Jour. Acoust. Soc. Amer.*, 33 (1961), 1801.

SNIDECOR, J. "A comparative study of the pitch and duration characteristics of impromptu speaking and oral reading," *Speech Monog.*, 10 (1943), 50–56.

Chapter 9: Pronunciation

KNOTT, T. "How the dictionary determines what pronunciations to use," *Quarterly Jour. Speech*, 21 (1935), 1–10.

LANGE, P. "Pronunciation and the dictionaries," *Quarterly Jour. Speech*, 32 (1946), 190–93.

ORTLEB, R. "An objective study of emphasis in oral reading," *Speech Monog.*, 4 (1937), 56–68.

SCHRAMM, W. "The acoustical nature of accent in American speech," *Amer. Speech*, 12 (1937), 39–56.

SHOHARA, H. "An experimental study of the control of pronunciation," *Speech Monog.*, 6 (1939), 105–7.

TIFFIN, J., and STEER, M. "An experimental analysis of emphasis," *Speech Monog.*, 4 (1937), 69–74.

WILSON, G. "Standards of correct pronunciation," *Quarterly Jour. Speech*, 23 (1937), 568–76.

Chapter 10: Diction

CONDON, E. "Statistics of vocabulary," *Science*, 67 (1928), 300.

DALE, E., and REICHERT, D. *Bibliography of Vocabulary Studies*, Rev. ed. Bureau of Educational Research, Ohio State University (Columbus), 1957.

HEINBERG, P. "An experimental investigation of measuring diction," *Jour. Ed. Res.*, 52 (1959), 303–6.

HOWES, D. "The definition and measurement of word probability," Ph.D. dissertation, Harvard University, 1950.

KRASNER, L. "Studies of the conditioning of verbal behavior," *Psych. Bull.*, 55 (1958), 148–70.

MILLER, G., and SELFRIDGE, J. "Verbal context and the recall of meaningful material," *Amer. Jour. Psychol.*, 63 (1950), 176–85.

SEASHORE, R., and ECKERSON, L. "The measurement of individual differences in general English vocabularies," *Jour. Ed. Psychol.*, 31 (1940), 14–38.

Index